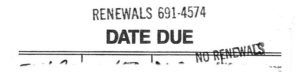

Moral Vision in
The Histories of Polybius

Hellenistic Culture and Society
General Editors: Anthony W. Bulloch, Erich S. Gruen, A. A. Long,
and Andrew F. Stewart

Moral Vision in
The Histories
of Polybius

Arthur M. Eckstein

UNIVERSITY OF CALIFORNIA PRESS
Berkeley   Los Angeles   London

The publisher gratefully acknowledges the contribution provided by the General Endow-
ment Fund of the Associates of the University of California Press.
University of California Press
Berkeley and Los Angeles, California
University of California Press, Ltd.
London, England
© 1995 by
The Regents of the University of California

Library of Congress Cataloging-in-Publication Data
Eckstein, Arthur M.
    Moral vision in the Histories of Polybius / Arthur M. Eckstein.
    p.   cm.—(Hellenistic culture and society ; 16)
    Includes bibliographical references (p.) and index.
    ISBN 0-520-08520-5 (alk. paper)
    1. Polybius. Historiae.   2. Polybius—Ethics.   3. Ethics,
Ancient.   I. Title.   II. Series.
D58.E35   1994
930—dc20   94-10638
                                                                    CIP

Printed in the United States of America
9 8 7 6 5 4 3 2 1
The paper used in this publication meets the minimum requirements of American National Standard for Information Sciences—Permanence of Paper for Printed Library Materials, ANSI Z39.48-1984.

For Jeannie

The language of ethics . . . is entirely a matter of epithets.
—P. N. FURBANK

CONTENTS

ACKNOWLEDGMENTS

My colleagues Gabrielle Spiegel and Brigitte Bedos-Rezak were very helpful in reading and commenting on various portions of the present study. Jeanne Rutenburg, as usual, provided much historical insight and careful discussion throughout. The completed manuscript benefited greatly from the criticisms and suggestions of Philip A. Stadter. And its writing was facilitated by a generous Research Board grant from the University of Maryland in 1990.

It will be apparent that my interpretation of the world view of the Hellenistic historian Polybius differs sharply from the interpretations offered by F. W. Walbank and K. S. Sacks. Sacks's work is always highly stimulating; Walbank is the greatest student of Polybius since the Renaissance, and the present study probably could not have been written without his three-volume *Historical Commentary* (which is the single most cited secondary work here); and I count both these scholars—who have always been unfailingly kind to me—as personal friends.

ONE

Introduction:
Polybius and "Machiavellianism"

One doesn't expect to find philosophers in Arcadia.
—LUCIAN

Polybius of Megalopolis eventually became the great historian of the rise of Rome to world power; it had not been his original intention in life. The purpose of this introductory chapter is twofold. First, the reader will be presented with a brief conspectus of what is known about Polybius's career and the writing of his *Histories*. Here the idea is to place Polybius firmly within the aristocratic setting in which he lived his entire life; but in addition, certain crucial actions of the historian will be underlined as indicators of the type of concerns that were, I think, central not only to his life but to his writing. The second purpose of the chapter is to set forth the controversy over the extent to which Polybius as a historian should be viewed as a "Machiavellian"—that is, as someone who rendered judgment on human conduct by employing the utterly practical and even amoral standard of success or failure. The controversy over this aspect of Polybius's thought and writing is the focus of this study.[1]

POLYBIUS OF MEGALOPOLIS

Polybius was born into one of the leading families of the Arcadian city of Megalopolis.[2] Megalopolis was one of the constituent members of the Achaean League, a federation of city-states in the northern and central Peloponnese. The League had existed in one form or another for centu-

1. The connection between the term "Machiavellian" and the actual political philosophy of Niccolò Machiavelli (1469–1527) is highly controversial; see, most recently, de Grazia, *Machiavelli in Hell*, chap. 9. In using the term "Machiavellian" to denote a cold ruthlessness of historical approach, I merely employ the same convention used by other scholars in Polybian studies.
2. On Megalopolis as Polybius's home town, see *Suda* s.v. Πολύβιος (and cf. Paus. 8.30.8), with Walbank, *Commentary* I: 12.

1

ries; but after 250 B.C. it had undergone a process of expansion that had made it into one of the major powers of the Greek peninsula. The architect of that expansion was Aratus of Sicyon—whom Polybius, naturally enough, views primarily in a heroic light.[3]

In Polybius's time, the constitution of the League was a three-tiered system that in its basics was typical of ancient Mediterranean republics. There was a federal general (*stratēgos*), assisted by a federal cavalry commander (*hipparchos*), both of whom were elected by a federal assembly of male citizens. This assembly also decided on peace and war, and on alliances. The federal executives and the federal assembly were, in turn, advised by a federal council (the *damiurgoi*)—to which each member city sent the same number of representatives.[4] It is this equality of representation (along, perhaps, with the full local autonomy enjoyed by the member cities) that led Polybius to emphasize the democratic and freedom-loving character of the League.[5]

It is sometimes held that the region of Megalopolis and its environs was harsh and mountainous, and that Polybius somehow exemplifies the inner hardness and stubbornness of the mountain-born man.[6] But while Arcadia was in general an area famed for the harshness both of its climate and its people—as Polybius himself says (4.20)[7]—Megalopolis itself, although it confronted high mountains to its south and west, lay in the wide and fertile valley of the Alpheus River. The Megalopolitan region in fact produced abundant harvests both of wheat and wine (cf. Plut. *Cleom.* 6.2), and was famous in antiquity for its rich pasturages, which supported a particularly fine strain of horses (Strabo 8.8.1).[8] Megalopolis itself (founded in 368) was a planned city, and intellectuals had presided at its founding (cf. Paus. 8.27.2). And when the city was destroyed by the Spartan king Cleomenes III in 223, philosophers presided again over its refounding (Prytanis the Peripatetic; cf. Polyb. 5.93.8). The city council met in a very large and impressive building (to judge by what remains); and right next to the impressive council house there was (and still is) one of the largest amphitheaters in Greece. All this bespeaks a town that, though somewhat out of the way in the central Peloponnese, was a prosperous place strongly influenced by traditional Greek high culture.

In 235, under pressure from Aratus, the Megalopolitan tyrant Lydia-

---

3. On the career of Aratus of Sicyon, see Urban, *Wachstum und Krise;* also still useful is Walbank, *Aratos.*

4. On the organization of the Achaean League, see Aymard, *Assemblées,* with the comments of Larsen, *Representative Government,* 75–84.

5. Cf. Welwei, "Demokratie und Masse bei Polybios," 284–88.

6. So von Scala, *Studien,* 36–37; Mioni, *Polibio,* 12.

7. Cf. also Lucian, *Iupp. Trag.* 11; *Astrol.* 26.

8. See, rightly, Pédech, "Biographie de Polybe," 145 and n. 1.

das stepped down from power, and the city joined the expanding Achaean League. Megalopolis was a major acquisition—and it transformed the focus of League policy. With Megalopolis came several other Arcadian towns, and with the adherence of Arcadia came the long-standing Arcadian tension with Sparta. The attention of the League now became permanently divided between the region around the Isthmus of Corinth (the traditional focus of League concern) and the problems of the central and southern Peloponnese.[9] The direct influence of Megalopolis within League affairs was also immediately felt—as is shown by the election of Lydiadas himself as League *stratēgos* three times between 234 and 230. Indeed, from the 230s onward, men from Megalopolis are continually found in positions of power and influence within the League. Most noticeable here is Philopoemen, *stratēgos* eight times between 208 and 183. But Polybius's own father, Lycortas, was *stratēgos* of the League at least twice in the 180s (and perhaps three times).[10]

Involvement in politics on a League-wide scale by Polybius's father is an indication of substantial family wealth. Indeed, it is likely that the family was already prominent at Megalopolis in the generation of Polybius's grandfather.[11] The wealth to which Polybius was heir is symbolized by his lifelong love of horses and horse raising (a very expensive proposition in the second-century Peloponnese)—or by the fact that he unselfconsciously calls slaves "one of the necessities of life" (4.38.4).[12] But in addition, inscriptions reveal that Polybius's family contributed large sums of money to public building projects at Megalopolis (*IG* V.2, 442 and 535), and that his brother Thearidas was honored for benefactions as far away as Epidaurus (*IG* IV 1442). Not surprisingly, the great Philopoemen was a family friend.[13]

9. On the paradoxical increase in both strength and problems caused by the Achaean acquisition of Megalopolis and Arcadia, see esp. Gruen, "Aratus and the Achaean Alliance with Macedon," 612–15.

10. Note also Diophanes of Megalopolis, son of Diaeus, *stratēgos* in 192/191, and Diaeus of Megalopolis, *stratēgos* in 150/149 (Diophanes' son?); cf. Errington, *Philopoemen*, 7–8. The Achaean envoy to Rome in 179 was Lydiadas—clearly a descendent of the old Megalopolitan tyrant (ibid.).

11. It is likely that the Thearidas who played an important part in Megalopolitan politics in 223 (Plut. *Cleom.* 24–25) came from the family into which Polybius was born, for Thearidas was a family name: see Gabba, "Studi su Filarco," 12 n. 1; Urban, *Wachstum und Krise*, 194. More cautious: Walbank, *Commentary* I: 259.

12. Horses and horse raising: see 3.117.4–5; 10.26.8; 21.15.9; 36.8.1; cf. Pseudo-Lucian, *Macrob.* 22; and Plut. *Phil.* 12.1. Polybius was a cavalryman in his youth, and Plutarch emphasizes that the Achaean cavalry came from the most prominent citizens (*Phil.* 18.7); cf. von Scala, *Studien*, 14. Polybius's attitude toward slaves: see Africa, *Phylarchus and the Spartan Revolution*, 9.

13. It is even possible that Philopoemen was related by marriage to Polybius's father: see Ziegler, col. 1445; Errington, *Philopoemen*, 7.

Polybius the son of Lycortas was born into this wealthy and influential family probably around the year 200 B.C.[14] The scion of such a family, in such a prosperous place as Megalopolis, could expect to receive a good formal education (perhaps partly through private tutors). Polybius in fact remembered his formal education with pleasure and pride, in addition to being deeply interested in educational technique *per se*. He has great confidence in his own formal literary skill (36.1.4–5), and, conversely, he chastises the historian Timaeus for a rhetoric that never rises above grammar-school clichés (12.26.9)—and the polymath Dicaearchus for having only an elementary knowledge of geometry (34.6.8). He can discuss in minute detail the stages of how one learns to read (10.47), and he criticizes the Romans for their failure to provide their children with formal educations (Cic. *de Rep.* 4.3.3). Not that Polybius was a personage particularly enamored of abstract philosophical problems: for instance, he was contemptuous of epistemological debate, laughing at "those philosophers who wonder whether they are at the Academy or at home in bed" (12.26c.2).[15] And his education was probably old-fashioned as far as literature went; while *The Histories* are replete with quotations from Homer and the Classical authors, there is a complete absence of references to contemporary Hellenistic literature.[16] Still, Polybius was also a man capable of holding his own in discussions of political theory with the Stoic Panaetius (Cic. *de Rep.* 1.34; cf. Vell. Pat. 1.13.3).

As the son of an important politician, it was natural as well that Polybius should receive an education in practical politics. Even as an adolescent he was present at debates within the Achaean faction headed by Philopoemen and Lycortas (cf. Polyb. 22.19). He was, of course, groomed for high political office. Early on he received the signal honor of carrying the ashes of Philopoemen in the great man's state funeral (Plut. *Phil.* 21.5). A few years later (181/180), he was chosen by the Achaeans for membership on an embassy to Ptolemaic Egypt, although (as he proudly says) he was still under the legal age (24.6.5). An inscription also reveals his presence about this time (along with his brother Thearidas) on a commission establishing the frontier between Megalopolis and Messene; in the aftermath of the war with Messene in 183/182, this was an important task.[17] Finally, Polybius was elected League *hipparchos* in autumn 170—probably when he was at the minimum legal age of 30. An outstanding political career seemed assured. But it was not to be.

14. For detailed discussion of the chronology, see now Eckstein, "Birth and Death of Polybius," 387–406.

15. Cf. von Scala, *Studien*, 19–20.

16. See esp. the comments of Wunderer, *Citate*, 92–93.

17. On this inscription, see Dittenberger and Purgold, no. 46, line 6 (Thearidas) and line 7 (Polybius), with Walbank, *Commentary* III: 249–50.

Polybius entered office at a time of war between Rome and the Macedonian monarchy, under King Perseus (the Third Macedonian War). Since 198 the policy of the Achaean League had always been to support the Romans in war, while simultaneously seeking to maintain its own independence. This policy had stood the League in good stead, for in the 190s and 180s the Achaeans gradually seized control of the entire Peloponnese (including Messene and Sparta), and at some point the League had even sworn a formal treaty of alliance with Rome.[18] Yet Roman assumptions of overlordship grated, and one of the most outspoken opponents of such Roman presumption was Polybius's father, Lycortas.[19] As hipparch in 170/169, however, Polybius followed the course set by his father's associate Archon (now League *stratēgos* for the second time), who advocated full cooperation with Rome. Archon argued that both for the general good of the Achaean people, and also to protect the specific group of men around Lycortas and himself—under particular Roman suspicion precisely because of previous advocacy of independence—the policy of cooperation was a necessity.[20] Polybius evidently found these arguments of Archon convincing, perhaps especially because of his sense of political responsibility as someone who was now running for high public office.[21]

As hipparch for 170/169, Polybius seems to have attempted a quite careful balancing act between such political necessity and his own sense of honor. Thus his first act as hipparch was to carry a proposal in the assembly restoring certain Achaean honors to the pro-Roman Eumenes of Pergamum—but not those he considered too extravagant (28.7). Later,

18. The Achaean policy toward Rome, and Polybius's attitude toward it, is discussed in detail in Chap. VII, below. On the treaty of alliance, see Badian, "Treaty between Rome and the Achaean League," 76–80.

19. See esp. Lycortas's strong words to the Roman Senate in winter 189/188 (Livy 38.32.6–8), and his bluntly anti-Roman speech to the Achaean assembly in 184 (Livy 39.36–37). Both of these passages obviously derive from Polybian material: cf. Nissen, *Kritische Untersuchungen*, 204 and 224.

20. On the political difficulties with the Romans experienced by the Archon-Lycortas group, see Errington, *Philopoemen*, 207–8. Lycortas actually advocated Achaean neutrality in autumn 170, and other members of Polybius's faction were even more anti-Roman (Polyb. 28.6.3–6). That the policy advocated by Archon at this time was one of cooperation with the Romans—and not merely one of "waiting upon events"—and that Polybius agreed with Archon (thus breaking momentarily with his own father), is proven by 28.7.1, where Polybius is explicit that the policy of Archon and himself was "to work with the Romans" and their friends (συμπράττειν Ῥωμαίοις). Cooperation with Rome in the new war against Macedon had indeed already been Archon's policy as *stratēgos* in 172/171 (Livy [P] 42.55.10). See, further, Eckstein, "Polybius, Syracuse, and the Politics of Accommodation," 278–79, against the reconstructions of Pédech, "Polybe hipparque," 254–55, and Gruen, *Hellenistic World and the Coming of Rome* II: 508.

21. See esp. Walbank, *Polybius*, 167.

Archon persuaded the federal assembly to offer the full Achaean military levy voluntarily to the consul Q. Marcius Philippus, the new Roman commander in Greece; and Polybius was sent as the head of a delegation to make this offer (28.12.1–13.7). Yet Polybius also says that he delayed the offer until the Achaean troops were actually no longer needed—although, conversely, he himself partook in the dangers of Marcius's campaign (28.13.1–7). After returning to Achaea, Polybius argued against Achaean compliance with a request for troops from Ap. Claudius Centho, the Roman commander in Illyria—and won the day (13.7–14). The historian says that he acted here at the behest of Q. Marcius (13.7). But it still must have given Polybius some satisfaction to be able to argue publicly that the Achaeans should comply only with official Roman requests backed by the Senate, rather than with any request from a Roman that happened to come along (13.12–13); for this had been the position of Philopoemen and Lycortas.[22] Shortly after leaving office, Polybius also joined with Archon and Lycortas in proposing that Achaea send a small military force to aid Ptolemaic Egypt, now threatened by Antiochus IV (winter 169/168); this would have been in accordance with a treaty with Egypt that Lycortas himself had helped engineer.[23] But when Q. Marcius Philippus urged the League to support instead the Roman policy of mediation of the conflict, the proponents of military aid to Egypt immediately withdrew their idea (29.25.5–6).

Polybius and many other Achaeans nevertheless found themselves deported to Italy after the war because of accusations of anti-Roman conduct put forth by Callicrates of Leontium—a man who had always advocated total Achaean cooperation with Rome in all things.[24] Polybius denies all Callicrates' allegations of anti-Roman conduct (30.13.9–11). His account of 170–168 seems to bear him out—and it should probably be trusted. First, Polybius's public behavior makes good sense given the Roman pressures on the men around Lycortas and Archon. Indeed, Archon's concern to turn aside Roman suspicion is presented not only as the reason behind the general policy of Archon's group in this period (28.6.7), but as the reason behind advocacy by the group of the specific policy of Achaean military aid to Rome (28.12.1). Second, it is clear that Polybius here is not simply engaged in propaganda aimed at endearing himself and his friends to the Romans. He makes no secret of the hostility to Rome of some of his closest associates, not least his own father (cf. 28.6.3–6); he also indicates that he personally delayed making the offer

22. Cf. Eckstein, "Polybius, Syracuse, and the Politics of Accommodation," 280 n. 56.

23. The proposal: Polyb. 29.23–25. Lycortas's treaty: see Walbank, *Commentary* III: 398, with 178–79.

24. On Callicrates' policy (dating from 180), and Polybius's view of it as both dangerous and dishonorable, see Chap. VII, below.

of Achaean troops to Q. Marcius Philippus until the time was most suit-able to *Achaean* interests—not those of Rome (28.13.1–4).[25] On the other hand, Polybius does not appear to be pandering to any residual anti-Roman feelings among his (primarily Greek) audience, either. He does not hide the fact that he participated voluntarily in the Roman campaign against Macedon in 169 (28.13.2); he says that a crucial factor in his advo-cacy of the Achaean refusal of Ap. Claudius Centho was the fact that he was acting in the interests not just of Achaean independence but in the interests of Q. Marcius (28.13.7); he does not deny that he immediately withdrew from public discussion when Marcius desired Achaea to follow a policy toward Egypt different from the one he himself had been advo-cating—although he did not overtly support Marcius here, either (29.25.5).[26] This is the complicated depiction of a complex political situa-tion—not a whitewash. In the absence of contrary evidence, we should assume that Polybius is telling the truth about his own public acts.[27]

Despite his careful balancing act between necessity and honor, Polybi-us's bright political career was shattered by the war, and he ended up a political detainee in Italy. He thought this a totally unjust catastrophe (cf. 30.13.9–11). It was, in fact, a catastrophe that struck politicians all over Greece (30.13 *passim*): Pausanias says that a thousand men were deported on charges of anti-Roman conduct from Achaea alone (7.10.11); and there were similar purges in Acarnania, Aetolia, Boeotia, Epirus, Perrhae-bia, and Thessaly.[28] Originally a formal investigation was planned of the various accusations made against all the detainees, but this never oc-curred. Instead they were simply left to languish in Italy at the pleasure of the Senate (Polyb. 30.32).

Polybius nevertheless soon won for himself a favored position. He was allowed to reside in Rome itself—now the center of the world—while most other detainees were scattered by the Senate to live in what must have been the intellectually stultifying atmosphere of the small towns of Italy (Polyb. 31.23.5). And in Rome he lived a comfortable life, with his own slaves (31.13.9), and, for instance, the freedom to indulge his passion for hunting (cf. 31.14.3 and 29.8). Most of all, Polybius retained the wealth and leisure to begin writing his great history of the rise of Rome—a project that he probably began contemplating almost immediately upon his arrival in Italy in autumn 167 (cf. 31.23.4). The beginning of work on

25. On these points, see the comments of Lehmann, *Glaubwürdigkeit des Polybios*, 201 and 203.

26. Archon himself, on the other hand, actually headed the Achaean embassy of media-tion to Egypt sent out in response to Philippus's letter (Polyb. 29.25.6).

27. See the persuasive general discussion of Lehmann, *Glaubwürdigkeit des Polybios*, 200–205; and the remarks of Walbank, *Commentary* III: 346–47.

28. For discussion, see Gruen, *Hellenistic World and the Coming of Rome* II: 516.

The Histories is an indication that, vigorous person that he was, Polybius had not been broken psychologically by political catastrophe (cf. 1.1.2). Continued residence in Rome offered the additional advantages of direct access to much crucial written information (including Roman archives, and the confiscated library of the Antigonid kings), and direct access to many important oral informants, both Greek and Roman.[29]

Polybius owed his privileged position primarily to the intervention of L. Aemilius Paullus, the conqueror of Perseus, who was acting here at the behest of his two sons, Q. Fabius Maximus Aemilianus and P. Cornelius Scipio Aemilianus (cf. Polyb. 31.23.5). The relationship between Polybius and these two sons of Paullus was already a close one in autumn 167;[30] and, of course, the friendship between Polybius and Scipio Aemilianus is one of the most famous in antiquity.[31] It is clear that Scipio, attracted by the high quality of Polybius's political discourse with Fabius Aemilianus, took the initiative (Polyb. 31.23.2–25.1), and that the result was that Polybius became one of Scipio's mentors and political advisers (25.1). It is sometimes said that Polybius became Scipio's tutor, which has an unfortunate implication of semi-servile status; and indeed, some scholars present Polybius as henceforth almost a servant in the house of the Aemilii.[32] It is often further suggested that because of his ties of obligation to the Aemilii Paulli (and the specially close ties with Scipio Aemilianus) Polybius has consciously distorted *The Histories* in order to show the members of the Aemilii Paulli and Cornelii Scipiones in as positive a light as possible.[33]

No doubt Polybius felt that he owed the Aemilii a special debt of gratitude; and he was certainly well aware of the contemporary status and power of the family (cf. 31.24.11). But the historian also says that his relationship with young Scipio Aemilianus became like that of the affection between father and son, or between close blood relatives (31.25.1). In other words, as is typical of formal ancient friendships, the courtesy and feelings that were displayed were those belonging to kinsmen—not those between a Roman patron and a Greek client.[34] Moreover, though

---

29. Polybius's access to Roman archives: see 3.26.1; cf. 22.3. His access to the Antigonid library: this had been brought to Rome as L. Aemilius Paullus's share of the loot from Macedon (Plut. *Aem.* 26.8; cf. Walbank, *Commentary* III: 495). Polybius's access both to Roman senators and to visiting Greek diplomats during this period: see Pédech, *Méthode*, 360–67.

30. See Walbank, *Commentary* III: 497.

31. See now Herman, *Ritualised Friendship*, 18.

32. See Edlund, "Invisible Bonds," 129–36; Reiter, *Aemilius Paullus*, 32 (cf. 20–21); and Green, *Alexander to Actium*, 277–78.

33. See Walbank, "Polybius between Greece and Rome," 10–11 and 20; so, too, now Reiter, *Aemilius Paullus*, 20–21, 33, 137; and Green, *Alexander to Actium*, 277–78, expanding the ideas of Usher, *Historians of Greece and Rome*, 121.

34. See the remarks of Herman, *Ritualised Friendship*, 18.

Polybius's relations with the Aemilii were close, he had established other close associations at Rome as well—both among Romans and among resident Greeks.[35] Thus Polybius also acted as a mentor and adviser to Demetrius of Syria, a young man who had a legitimate claim to the Seleucid throne, and who eventually seized it (cf. Polyb. 31.11 and 13–15); this gives an indication of the kind of circles in which Polybius moved at Rome. One must assume that Polybius's intellectual brilliance—*The Histories* themselves, of course, mark him out as a prodigy—stood him in good stead in his new situation, as it had previously stood him in good stead in fostering a prominent political career in Achaea despite his relative youth.

As for the pro-Aemilian and pro-Scipionic *Tendenz* in Polybius's work, this should not be exaggerated. Certainly Polybius praises L. Aemilius Paullus who fell at Cannae in 216 (see 3.116.9), and L. Aemilius Paullus the victor of Pydna in 168 (see 18.35 and 31.22), and Scipio Aemilianus (see 31.25.10 and 38.21–22). In addition, he certainly viewed P. Cornelius Scipio Africanus as a great man (see esp. 10.40). But the fact is that Polybius was also not in the least averse to criticizing the relatives of L. Aemilius Paullus of Pydna, or of Scipio Aemilianus.

Thus Polybius reports that Cn. Cornelius Scipio Asina, the consul of 260 (and grandfather of Scipio Africanus), panicked and surrendered to the Carthaginians while in command of part of the Roman fleet (1.21.7); yet other traditions on this incident were much kinder to Scipio.[36] Again, Polybius is harshly negative—by name—toward M. Aemilius Paullus the consul of 255 (father of the Paullus of Cannae, grandfather of the Paullus of Pydna), because he arrogantly led the Roman fleet to total destruction in storms off the coast of Sicily (1.36.10–37.10).[37] The historian also totally ignores an important victory won by P. and Cn. Cornelius Scipio (father and uncle of Africanus) in Spain in 216—in order, for his own dramatic purposes, to make the situation for Rome after Cannae look truly hopeless;[38] and later he criticizes the generalship of these men in 211 (cf. 10.6.2: rashness and naiveté). Equally striking is Polybius's attitude toward Ti. Sempronius Gracchus, the consul of 177. As tribune, Gracchus had protected either Scipio Africanus or Africanus's brother Lucius dur-

35. Cf. Walbank, *Polybius*, 8–9.

36. The alternative tradition asserted that Scipio had been captured by Punic treachery during a conference: see Broughton, *Magistrates* I: 205 and n. 1.

37. Despite some scholars, there is no reason to believe that in this criticism Polybius was merely copying out the remarks of the anti-Roman historian Philinus; the discussion is much too close to Polybius's own philosophical theme of arrogance followed by disaster. See, rightly, Walbank, *Commentary* I: 97. In any case, the material appearing in *The Histories* is there as a result of Polybius's independent volition; he was a sophisticated intellectual, not a copying machine. See, rightly, Badian, "Review of La Bua," 208.

38. For detailed discussion, see Chap. III, below.

ing the famous scandals of the 180s; and he became Africanus's son-in-law as well as Scipio Aemilianus's father-in-law. Yet Polybius held this man in overt contempt: naive (30.27), incompetent (30.30.7–8), deceitful (31.1.1), stingy (31.27.16). Finally, although Polybius presents him as a man of many virtues, not even L. Aemilius Paullus the victor of Pydna escapes criticism from the historian. This is shown by Livy 45.31, a passage clearly based on Polybius, which passes a highly negative judgment on Aemilius for his unfair investigation of conditions in Aetolia in 167.[39]

Given the fact that Polybius wrote a great deal of *The Histories* (though not all of the work) while a detainee in Rome, it makes sense that there would be various pressures on him. But he was much more at liberty to say what he liked than many scholars have assumed; certainly, an independence of judgment is quite in evidence in the above instances.[40]

It is clear that Polybius worked diligently on *The Histories* while residing in Rome between 167 and 150. His original intention was to trace the rise of Roman power between 220 and 168/167, and the reasons for it, with an introductory section taking the story back to 264 (cf. 1.1.5, 3.4.1–2). His stage was the entire Mediterranean world from Spain to Syria (and sometimes much farther east), and the intended original length of the work was thirty volumes—a very ambitious project.[41] Judging from the references to Carthage as an existing polity in Books 1–15, it seems that at least this section of *The Histories,* down to the end of the Second Punic War, had been completed—and probably published—before 150. This would mean that Polybius was producing about a volume a year, and that by 150 the work was already longer than Herodotus or Thucydides. Polybius may even have gotten much farther than Book 15 by 150; there is simply no way of knowing.[42]

What Polybius does say, however, is that the cataclysmic events of 152–146—the great new wars in Spain, combined with the destruction of Car-

39. The criticism here is that Paullus had been much more concerned with politics than with justice—with which Aetolian faction had backed Rome in the war, rather than with which one had inflicted violence and massacre upon the other (Livy 45.31.1–2). For the Polybian derivation of Livy 45.31, see Nissen, *Kritische Untersuchungen,* 276–77.

40. For other Polybian criticisms of Rome and Romans in *The Histories,* see Chaps. IV, VII, and VIII below.

41. For discussion of the intended original length, see Walbank, "Polybius' Last Ten Books," 139 (definitive).

42. For discussion of the date of writing and publication of Books 1–15, see Walbank, *Polybius,* 18–19, definitive against the thesis of Erbse that the entire text of *The Histories* dates from after 146 ("Zur Enstehung des polybianischen Geschichtswerkes," 157–79, and "Polybios-Interpretationen," 269–97). Walbank's arguments here and in "Polybius' Last Ten Books," 139 (see n. 41, above), also form a useful corrective to the recent thesis of Weil, "Composition de l'*Histoire* de Polybe," 185–206, that almost nothing can be known about when Polybius's work was written, or under what circumstances. This seems overly pessimistic.

thage, Macedon, and Achaea—caused him to rethink the entire structure and purpose of his work (3.4). He decided to add a further ten volumes, bringing his history of the Mediterranean down to 146/145. In this extension, the focus would be radically different: not on the reasons for the rise of Rome (cf. 1.1.5), but on the consequences of the new Roman dominion, positive or negative, for both the conquered peoples and for the Romans themselves (3.4.6–7). The writing of this large extension of *The Histories* began at the earliest shortly after Polybius retired to Megalopolis in 145/144—and perhaps substantially later, if (as seems likely) the original thirty volumes were still not complete by that time.[43]

Yet while Polybius was producing volume after volume of his *Histories* during the 160s and 150s, he also had the time—and inclination—to delve into practical politics. More was involved than acting as a political mentor to Scipio Aemilianus or Demetrius of Syria. When in the mid-150s the people of Italiote Locri sought to avoid the naval service they owed Rome by treaty of alliance, they twice went to none other than Polybius for help—and both times he was successful in helping them (12.5.2–3). Presumably this was accomplished via his contacts within the senatorial aristocracy. Even so, one should emphasize the fact that the Locrians directly and publicly honored him for the favors he had done them (12.5.1). This is again suggestive of the position of prominence that Polybius had—somehow—won for himself at Rome, though technically he was still a political detainee.

Even more striking is the fact that a decade earlier, in the late 160s, Polybius—convinced of senatorial injustice toward Demetrius of Syria (31.2.1 and 11.11)—helped organize Demetrius's successful escape from Rome. In his detailed account of this incident (31.11–15), Polybius depicts himself as a central figure, acting in concert with a few of Demetrius's Greek friends and without the knowledge of any Roman.[44] Modern scholars usually argue, however, that Polybius in fact acted here as an agent of powerful forces within the Senate. Thus Pédech suggests that he was working for the prominent Ti. Sempronius Gracchus (consul 177, consul II 163)—who later played a role in obtaining senatorial acquiescence in Demetrius's coup in Syria (cf. Polyb. 31.33.4).[45] But Polybius despised Gracchus.[46] More popular has therefore been the hypothesis

---

43. Books 31–39 of *The Histories*, even in their highly fragmentary condition, provide enough evidence to show that Polybius did indeed attempt to answer the questions he posed in 3.4.6–7—though his answers were complex and equivocal. See now Ferrary, *Philhellénisme et impérialisme*, 289–316, against Walbank, "Polybius' Last Ten Books," 145–50 and 159–62.

44. It is likely that this account is based upon detailed notes of the incident that Polybius made at the time: cf. Walbank, *Commentary* III: 478.

45. *Méthode*, 525 n. 59.

46. Cf., rightly, Walbank, *Commentary* III: 478, against Pédech (and see above, p. 10).

that Polybius enjoyed the backing of L. Aemilius Paullus himself, and his senatorial supporters.[47] But that would imply a very serious division of opinion among the *Patres* concerning Demetrius (or concerning the justice of his case), and Polybius leaves the opposite impression (cf. 31.2.6–7 and 11.10). The hypothesis of some sort of senatorial backing for Polybius's act thus remains highly speculative. As Gruen suggests, a conspiracy among Demetrius's Greek friends—the story Polybius tells—is equally plausible.[48]

In any case, in 31.11–15 Polybius's image is that of a man willing to take dangerous action out of a sense of justice—for given his own precarious position as a detainee, it was a highly dangerous act that he had undertaken. And this is more than just an image. Involvement in the escape of Demetrius *was* a highly dangerous act—whether he had Roman backing or not.[49]

After a long period of essentially sedentary life in Rome, from the late 150s Polybius suddenly entered upon a period of continuous activity and travel (cf. 3.4.13). In 151/150 he accompanied Scipio Aemilianus across the Alps to Spain, where he witnessed Scipio's heroics as a military tribune during the siege of Intercatia.[50] Polybius also went with Scipio to North Africa, where he met and interviewed the great Massinissa of Numidia, who had been put on his throne by Africanus himself, and who could remember fighting the Carthaginians and Hannibal during the Second Punic War (cf. 9.25.4).[51] Back in Rome in 150, Polybius finally managed to obtain approval from the Senate for the return of the Achaean detainees, himself among them, to their homeland (35.6.1).

Thus Polybius finally returned to Megalopolis, after seventeen years of exile (late 150). But he did not stay long. In 149 a new war threatened between Rome and Carthage, and the consul M'. Manilius requested the Achaean authorities to send Polybius to him as a military adviser in the war (36.11.1).[52] Polybius had reached Corcyra when news of Punic diplo-

47. So Ziegler, col. 1452; Briscoe, "Eastern Policy and Senatorial Politics," 60–61; Doria, "Diodoro e Ariarate V," 127; Walbank, *Commentary* III: 478; and now Reiter, *Aemilius Paullus*, 144–45.

48. *Hellenistic World and the Coming of Rome* II: 664–65.

49. Even if Polybius had the backing of certain senatorial circles—which is highly speculative—it is difficult to believe that they could have protected him if his role in Demetrius's escape had come to light.

50. For 151/150 (rather than any later time) as the probable date for Polybius's personal crossing of the Alps, see the convincing discussion in Walbank, *Polybius*, 11 and n. 53. On Scipio Aemilianus's heroics, see Polyb. 35.5.1–2, and frgs. 6 and 18 B-W.

51. For detailed discussion of Scipio's diplomatic mission in North Africa, see Astin, *Scipio Aemilianus*, 47.

52. Manilius's request for Polybius as a military adviser is another indication of the powerful impression the historian had made on certain circles of the Roman senatorial aristocracy. Manilius later had some sort of tie with Scipio Aemilianus (attested only in a brief

matic concessions convinced him that the crisis was over; so he returned home (36.11.1). But war did occur, and later he joined Scipio Aemilianus when the latter, now consul for 147, was conducting the siege of Carthage. Despite some scholars,[53] there need not be any implication here that Polybius wholeheartedly approved of the aggressive policy of Rome toward Carthage in this period, or that he went on to write approvingly of it in *The Histories*. In Manilius's case, Polybius was acting at the behest of his government; in the case of Aemilianus, either Scipio repeated the official request for Polybius's aid, or else the historian joined him because of the specially close bonds between them. And Polybius speaks approvingly of Scipio's sentiment that what was happening to Carthage could just as well happen to Rome (38.21–22).[54]

At Carthage, Polybius was engaged primarily in giving technical military advice (38.19; cf. Paus. 8.30.9). But in terms of understanding Polybius's character, a story in Ammianus Marcellinus (24.2.16–17) is more intriguing: Polybius accompanied Scipio Aemilianus and a select squad of some thirty Roman soldiers when they attempted, in *testudo* formation, a dangerous *coup de main* against one of the gates of the city.[55] Walbank must be right that this story ultimately derives from an account of the incident in *The Histories*.[56] But what we have, then, is Polybius in his mid-fifties voluntarily engaged in a dangerous small-unit action.

The incident at the gate of Carthage in fact suggests that the historian himself was not averse to performing "shining deeds" of physical courage (λαμπρόν τι, καὶ μνήμης ἄξιον: cf. 31.29.9). This is a significant aspect of Polybius's personality, though one that tends to be overshadowed by the more familiar image of the severe intellectual.[57] But after all, this is a man who states that to be a worthwhile historian one must not only have

---

remark at Cic. *de Rep.* 1.18). But in this period Scipio was still a relatively junior personage within the Senate, and the consul Manilius was definitely an independent figure in politics (see Astin, *Scipio Aemilianus*, 55).

53. Most recently Green, *Alexander to Actium*, 279 and 281.

54. Walbank, *Polybius*, 10 n. 49, rightly, points out the special circumstances that first led Polybius to agree to join Manilius in 149 and then to be present at Carthage. On Scipio Aemilianus's hardly triumphant sentiments as Carthage burned, and Polybius's approval of those hardly triumphant sentiments, see Chaps. VII and (in more detail) VIII, below.

55. "Aemilianum Scipionem, cum historiarum conditore Polybio, Megalopolitano Arcade, et triginta militibus, portam Carthaginis impetu simili subfodisse. . . . Aemilianus enim testudine lapidea tectam successerat portam, sub qua tutus et latens, dum moles saxeas detegunt hostes, urbem nudatam irrupit."

56. *Commentary* III: 718.

57. Von Scala, *Studien*, 5, accepts that Polybius personally fought in the battle line. By contrast Walbank, *Polybius*, chap. 1 ("The Man and His Work"), does not mention this incident at all. On the dangers involved in such an operation, see esp. Amm. Marc. 24.2.15—the emperor Julian's deep peril when he attempted to imitate at Pirisabora in 363 A.D. the *coup de main* of Scipio described by Polybius.

served in an army but must actually have risked one's life in battle
(12.25h.5). In a society much given to ridicule and polemic, Polybius is
not likely to have risked making such a statement unless he himself had
actually done this (cf. 28.13.1–2). Indeed, this vigorous aspect of Polybius's personality is borne out by his attested love of boar hunting
(31.14.2–3 and 29.8; cf. 34.3.8), for hunting wild boar was an extremely
dangerous endeavor—"as dangerous as it had been in the Age of the
Heroes."[58] And that was precisely one of its great attractions to Polybius:
hunting offered opportunities for valorous deeds (31.29.9 and 11), and
was thus good training for courage in struggle and war (cf. 29.5).[59] It may
not be mere polite symbolism that the statue of Polybius honoring him at
Cleitor in the Peloponnese shows him spear—not scroll—in hand.[60]

At some point in 147/146 Polybius also personally explored the Atlantic coasts of Africa and Spain, using a ship lent him by Scipio (34.15.7).
The historian's energetic scientific interest in geographical questions is
also shown by the many interviews he conducted on these subjects
(34.10.7), by the long geographical excursus of Book 34 as a whole—and
by an entire separate monograph on the habitability of the equatorial
regions, now lost.[61]

While Polybius was busily engaged at Carthage and along the Atlantic
coasts, relations between Rome and the Achaean League had deterio-
rated; the main issue was Roman support for the desire of Sparta to se-
cede from the League. The ultimate result was a war between the
Achaeans and Rome (146)—a war quickly won by the Romans.[62] Polybius
arrived back in Achaea shortly after the fall of Corinth to the troops of L.
Mummius (cf. Polyb. 39.2). The senatorial commission for settling the
aftermath of the war later appointed Polybius to establish the laws in certain cities, and to regulate certain aspects of the new legal relations between cities (39.5; cf. Paus. 8.30.9).

Polybius's role in the postwar regulation of Achaean affairs has led
some scholars to call him a "collaborator," a "quisling"—even a traitor.[63]

58. Anderson, *Hunting in the Ancient World,* 51.
59. The sentiment at Polyb. 31.29.5 is actually attributed by Polybius to L. Aemilius Paullus, but it is clear that Polybius heartily agreed with it.
60. On this statue, see Walbank, *Commentary* I: 5 n. 8 (and frontispiece). Polybius even
seems to have favored gladiatorial combat as a training for young men (in this case, Greeks):
see Livy 41.20.11–12, on Antiochus IV's importation of gladiatorial combat into the Greek
East. Polybian derivation of the passage: see Nissen, *Kritische Untersuchungen,* 240–41; Welwei, *Könige und Königtum,* 73 (cf. 68–69).
61. On this work, see Geminus 16.32–38 ed. Manitius, with Walbank, *Polybius,* 15 and
122.
62. On the tensions and very complicated politics that led up to the catastrophe of 147/
146, see esp. Gruen, "Origins of the Achaean War," 46–69.
63. See most recently Green, *Alexander to Actium,* 279–81.

The question of Polybius's attitude toward Roman power and Roman rule will be dealt with in detail in Chapter VII below, but this accusation seems to me quite unfair. Polybius believed the war was an act of criminal stupidity and irrationality, an unnecessary conflict provoked by demagogic and self-serving Achaean politicians—who thereby destroyed the prosperity and local power that Achaea had previously enjoyed (cf. 38.1–3 and 9–18). He now did his best, in what he obviously viewed as a tragic situation, to ameliorate the terrible effects of others' political mistakes. His general attitude in this difficult period was summed up by his refusal to accept from the Romans any gift of confiscated Achaean property: it must have required careful diplomacy on his part to prevent this from being seen as an insult (39.4.1–3). But, Polybius says, a reputation for "shining honor" (καλλίστη δόξα) was more important than any financial gain (39.4.4)—and he chastises friends of his who did not follow his policy (ibid.). He also managed to prevent the Romans from looting the statues of Aratus, Philopoemen, and other Achaean heroes—although these were already halfway to Italy when Polybius intervened to get them back (39.3). He journeyed to Rome again (winter 145/144), in order to obtain from the Senate better conditions of peace for the Achaeans than they would otherwise have received (39.8.1). He may even have played a role in preventing the entire dissolution of the Achaean League by Rome.[64]

These salutary and patriotic actions by the historian explain the claim of the inscription honoring Polybius at Acacesium in Arcadia: "When Greece met disaster, through him alone did help come" (Paus. 8.37.2). An honorific inscription at Megalopolis was similar: "He stayed the wrath of the Romans against the Hellenes" (Paus. 8.30.8). In sum: it is true enough that Polybius believed the terrible imbalance of power between Rome and Achaea mandated that Roman hegemony be acknowledged, in 146 as in 170; but Polybius still did what he could to preserve Achaean interests—and his own dignity.[65]

After winter 145/144 the historian is lost to view. At some point after

64. It is likely that the Achaean League, after its collapse in 146, was immediately reconstituted in some form by L. Mummius and the senatorial commission of 146/145: see Schwertfeger, *Der achaiische Bund von 146 bis 26 v. Chr.*, 19–26. Schwertfeger's case is now greatly strengthened by the redating of the Dyme Inscription (*Syll.*[3] 684), with its reference to "the *politeia* restored to the Achaeans by the Romans" (line 10), from 115 B.C. back to 144/143: see Kallet-Marx, "Quintus Fabius Maximus and the Dyme Affair" (forthcoming). And the period immediately after the war was just the period when Polybius was exercising some influence on the character of the Roman diplomatic settlement (see 39.4–5 and 39.8.1).

65. Nothing survives of Polybius's account of the Achaean War, but his outraged remarks on the brutal Roman looting of art work at Corinth (39.2) are hardly intended to be complimentary; and he does not hide the existence of other Roman atrocities (39.6.4–5).

145 he visited Egypt when it was under the harsh regime of Ptolemy VIII (Polyb. 34.14).[66] Perhaps Polybius acted as a military adviser again to Scipio Aemilianus when the latter, now consul for the second time, was conducting the siege of Numantia in Spain in 134/133.[67] In all probability, however, Polybius spent most of his time at Megalopolis, working on his massive *Histories*. In the end they were four times the length of either Thucydides or Herodotus, and in one sense he was never quite satisfied or finished with them, for he continued to add passages into them right up until his death.[68]

It does not seem too much to say, then, that the author of *The Histories* strove to lead a life of honorable conduct, under complex, sometimes difficult (and even dangerous) circumstances. Certainly it was a consistently energetic and hard-working life—one characterized by early brilliant political success, then sudden catastrophe and rupture, followed by long-term recovery and accomplishment. Indeed, it is typical of Polybius that he is supposed to have died, a vigorous old man of eighty-two, from injuries sustained in a fall from his horse while out riding in the countryside around Megalopolis.[69]

POLYBIUS AND "MACHIAVELLIANISM"

The Histories had both a technical purpose and two broader purposes. The technical purpose (in itself a large enough task) was to discover the origins and chronicle the means by which the Roman conquest of the Mediterranean was accomplished (cf. 1.1.5), to which Polybius later added an evaluation of the dominion that the Romans had established (cf. 3.4.6–7). Beyond this, Polybius intended *The Histories* as a handbook for political men, an exploration of good and bad statecraft (see below). And even more broadly, *The Histories* were intended as a discussion of the problems

66. Cf. Walbank, *Commentary* III: 629–30.

67. See Walbank, *Polybius,* 12 and n. 60, who notes that Polybius, nearing 70 in 134/133, would have been quite elderly for such a long and strenuous journey. Polybius did, however, write a special monograph on the Numantine War (cf. Cic. *Fam.* 5.12.2—the only surviving reference to this work).

68. Late additions: see 3.39.8 (now with the comments of Eckstein, "Birth and Death of Polybius," 393–97); cf. also 3.36–38 (with Pédech, *Méthode,* 565 and 572), and 3.59.4 (with Walbank, *Commentary* I: 393–94). In addition to *The Histories,* the monograph on the Numantine War (above, n. 67), and the monograph on the equatorial regions (above, n. 61), we know that Polybius also wrote an important treatise on military tactics (Polyb. 9.20.4; with Walbank, *Polybius,* 15), and an encomiastic biography of the Achaean statesman Philopomen (see Pédech "Polybe et l'éloge," *passim*). The latter two works may have preceded the writing of *The Histories* themselves; and all in all, it is a very substantial literary production.

69. The story appears in Pseudo-Lucian, *Macrob.* 22—a source of uncertain reliability, however.

of human life in general. Indeed, among the ancient historical writers now extant, no one more frequently breaks his narrative in order to comment in moralizing terms on human character and the lessons of life.[70] Yet from the time of his rediscovery by the West during the Renaissance, Polybius has rarely been accepted on his own terms as a man who felt he had something important to say on human character and affairs. In the sixteenth and seventeenth centuries, he was used primarily as an authority on technical military matters.[71] In the eighteenth century, as interest in Polybius's technical military observations waned, he was employed primarily as a force in the political debates over republican theory and the "mixed" constitution.[72] In the nineteenth century, *The Histories* were mined merely as an excellent source of information on the rise of Rome—to be put to use, it was sometimes suggested, by minds more subtle than their author's. This latter attitude, of course, remains powerful in Polybian studies today.[73]

All along, however, some thinkers have taken Polybius's widest claims seriously. In the sixteenth century, Jean Bodin thought that Polybius was as much a philosopher as a historian, and Christopher Watson praised his "holesome counsels."[74] In the seventeenth century, Isaac Casaubon emphasized how often Polybius spoke out for virtuous behavior, while John Dryden remarked that Polybius "reproaches all faithless practices . . . [and] commends nothing but plainness, sincerity and the common good."[75] For this very reason, Dryden agreed with Casaubon that "Youth . . . should read him carefully, and imbibe him thoroughly, detesting the Maxims that are given by Machiavel and others."[76] In the eighteenth century, John Adams's view was similar: he was influenced by Polybius's theory of the virtue of the "mixed" constitution (in Book 6) in good part because he found Polybius to have been a man who had thought deeply about life, with a character deserving of reverence.[77]

---

70. This aspect of *The Histories* is discussed in detail in Chap. VIII, below.

71. See Momigliano, "Polybius' Reappearance," 88–93.

72. See Chinard, "Polybius and the American Constitution," 38–58.

73. Thus Ziegler, col. 1552 (cf. 1466), expresses irritation at how often Polybius's reflections on life interrupt the flow of useful historical information in the text. Cf. also Green, *Alexander to Actium*, 281, 283, 285.

74. On Bodin, see Momigliano, "Polybius between the English and the Turks," 132; cf. *id.,* "Historian's Skin," 76. On Watson, see Walbank, "Introduction to *Polybius* (tr. Scott-Kilvert)," 19.

75. J. Dryden, "The Character of Polybius and His Writings," in *The History of Polybius . . . translated by Sir Henry Sheeres* (London, 1698).

76. Ibid. Dryden had read the introduction to I. Casaubon's crucial edition and Latin translation of Polybius (Paris, 1609)—which emphasized Polybius's moral virtue. On Casaubon, see Momigliano, "Polybius's Reappearance," 93.

77. For discussion, see Chinard, "Polybius and the American Constitution," 43–44.

Again, in the nineteenth century Friedrich Nietzsche saw Polybius as one of the primary exponents of teaching by use of moralizing exemplars.[78] And this way of reading Polybius's text was characteristic of some scholars even at the beginning of the twentieth century. Thus Rudolf von Scala and Carl Wunderer, each of whom produced major studies of Polybian thought, asserted confidently that Polybius viewed traditional morality as a crucial component of political behavior.[79]

Yet this is no longer the established view. On the contrary: the current scholarly *communis opinio* on Polybius is that he believed success in the real world was the sole standard by which every human action should be measured and judged.

This is an understanding of Polybius's work that has grown up since mid-century. It appears to have originated with André Aymard, the great modern expert on the Achaean League, who argued in 1940 that Polybius's basic intellectual stance was one of brutal realism—and thereupon called into serious question Polybius's standards of historical judgment.[80] The new tradition also found expression in Paul Pédech's magisterial study of Polybius's historical method (1964), where Pédech emphasized what seemed to him Polybius's total lack of sentiment—or even scruple.[81] But it is F. W. Walbank—the greatest Polybian scholar of modern times— who has become the primary exponent of the new view of Polybius. In several important articles starting in the 1960s, and in his book on Polybius based on his Sather Lectures (1972), Walbank has underlined Polybius's sternly "utilitarian" and "ruthless" standard of judgment regarding the actions of individuals and states. Success was the main criterion: Polybius was not interested in ethics *per se;* he did not condemn the absence of ethics in an individual or polity on purely moral grounds; he did not regard "Machiavellian" policies as evidence of moral decline. What counted was whether actions led to the maintenance or expansion of power—and he had very little sympathy for failure.[82] This view is also woven into Walbank's three-volume *Historical Commentary on Polybius* (1957–1979). The *Commentary* is one of the magnificent accomplishments of twentieth-century Classical scholarship; but in it, moralizing passages in Polybius's *Histories* receive little scrutiny, and what is emphasized in-

---

78. Nietzsche, *Advantage and Disadvantage of History for Life,* 15.

79. Von Scala, *Studien,* emphasizes—and, it seems, overemphasizes—the influence of Stoic philosophy upon the historian; Wunderer, *Psychologische Anschauungen,* esp. 30; *id., Polybios,* esp. 15–18.

80. Aymard, "Fragment de Polybe 'Sur les traîtres,'" 19 and n. 3.

81. *Méthode,* 219.

82. Polybius's utilitarianism and lack of interest in ethics per se: Walbank, "Political Morality," 8; cf. *Polybius,* 173. Polybius's ruthlessness and lack of sympathy for failure: "Political Morality," 11; "Polybius and Macedonia," 304; *Polybius,* 178–81; "Polybius between Greece and Rome," 9–13, 23, 27–28.

stead is Polybius's "Machiavellian" worldview. This is a far cry from the opinion of Casaubon, Dryden, or Adams.[83]

A few voices have been raised against this interpretation of Polybius, but they have been ineffectual. In 1969, K.-E. Petzold argued that Polybius had perhaps taken a "Machiavellian" stance in the early volumes of *The Histories*, but as the years and the work progressed, issues of ethics became of great concern to him; this is evident, according to Petzold, in the tone of the later volumes. But Petzold's thesis was rejected in 1974 by Walbank, who insisted that Polybius remained a ruthless personality throughout.[84] The image of an amoral and utterly pragmatic Polybius was again reasserted in the important study of Polybian historiographical method by Kenneth Sacks (1980).[85] True, Petzold's student Burkhard Meissner once more protested against the prevailing view in a 1986 article: Polybius aimed at both the practical but also the moral instruction of his readers. But Meissner has either been modified to the point of dismissal, or (more often) simply ignored.[86] Thus the Walbank-influenced image of Polybius the cynical and ruthless thinker appears in David Ladouceur's recent study of ancient attitudes toward suicide (1987), in William Reiter's monograph on L. Aemilius Paullus the conqueror of Macedon (1988), in Peter Green's chapter on Polybius in his major work on the Hellenistic age (1990), and in Andrew Erskine's new examination of Hellenistic political thought (1990).[87] And Walbank himself has re-

83. Moralizing passages in *The Histories* receive little scrutiny in the *Commentary:* cf. II: 132 (on Polyb. 9.9.9–10); II: 264 (on Polyb. 10.49); III: 320 (on Polyb. 27.20); III: 403 (on Polyb. 29.26). Emphasis on Polybius's amoral world view and amoral criterion for judging behavior, and on his "Machiavellianism": cf. *Commentary* II: 480 (on Polyb. 15.24.4–6); III: 454 (on Polyb. 30.27).

84. Petzold, *Methode des Polybios,* 43–45, 49 and n. 1, 53–64; denied by Walbank, "Polybius between Greece and Rome," 6–7 and 23; cf. also Gabba, "Aspetti culturali dell'imperialismo romano," 71. Petzold's thesis is also rejected by Musti, "Polibio negli studi dell'ultimo ventennio (1950–1970)," 1120–21; but in *Polibio e l'imperialismo romano,* 74 (cf. 81 and 83), Musti is more sympathetic to the idea that Polybius's evaluation of Roman rule in the last ten volumes contains a moralizing component. Musti's new position is, in turn, rejected by Gruen, *Hellenistic World and the Coming of Rome* I: 247 and n. 162. Cf. also van Hooff, "Polybios als Machiavellist," 56–67.

85. *Polybius on the Writing of History,* esp. 132–35, and 136 with n. 30.

86. Meissner, "Polybios," esp. 331–33 and 337–38. Meissner's thesis emphasizing that Polybius had not only pragmatic but also strong ethical concerns is accepted, but only with severe reservations and modifications, by Podes, "Handelserklärung bei Polybios," 225–26. Meissner's study goes unnoticed by the rest of the scholars cited below.

87. Ladouceur, "Josephus and Masada," 108–9 (on Polybius and ancient suicide, heavily influenced by Walbank, "Political Morality"); Reiter, *Aemilius Paullus,* 30–31 and 33 (citing Walbank, *op. cit.*); Green, *Alexander to Actium,* 278–82; Erskine, *Hellenistic Stoa,* 185–86. Cf. also A. J. Pomeroy, "Polybius's Death Notices," esp. 422–23, who—while acknowledging a moralizing element in the Polybian obituaries of famous men—ends by emphasizing his pragmatic and political goals instead.

cently (1990) reasserted his position, arguing that Polybius is in fact the sole exception to the emphasis of the Hellenistic historians on the moral lessons to be derived from the study of the past—for in contrast to his fellow writers, Polybius's purpose is (by and large) not moralizing but practical.[88]

Now, it is certainly the case that Polybius in writing *The Histories* intended that a close reading of his work would produce better and more effective statesmanship in his (primarily Greek) audience. Indeed, Polybius repeatedly asserts that his *Histories* are in good part an extended meditation on what constitutes effective as opposed to ineffective or counter-productive political decision making. In such passages the pragmatic aspect of his work is patient—and Polybius's conception of the struggle for rational decision making is in fact one of the major sub-themes of the present study.[89] Nevertheless, the conclusion drawn here is that Polybius was not at all an exception to the tradition of Greek historical writing that emphasized the moral lessons to be drawn from contemplation of the past. His work is much more traditionally moralistic than has recently been thought.

It is worthwhile at this point to establish some *prima facie* evidence for Polybius's approval in *The Histories* of conduct he considers honorable and "manly," and his disapproval of conduct he considers "shameful" and "base"—regardless of whether or not such conduct leads to pragmatic success in the real world. A few examples of the very powerful expression these attitudes find in his work will set the stage for the far more detailed investigation of Polybius's moral vision that follows.

A classic example of Polybius's approbation of noble and energetic conduct, regardless of its success or failure, can be found in Polyb. 9.8–9, at the end of his detailed narrative of Hannibal's generalship in the hard-fought campaign of 211 (including his famous—but abortive—march on Rome). Polybius emphasizes that no one can refuse to admire Hannibal, or to marvel at him, despite his failure (9.9.1–5); these remarks are closely linked to Polybius's previous and equally admiring discussion of the campaign of the Theban general Epaminondas against Mantineia in 326—which also failed (9.8, *passim*). And shortly thereafter, Polybius explains why he praises both the winning and the losing sides in 211, both the Romans and the Carthaginians. By doing so, he asserts, he is seeking to

---

88. "Motives of Hellenistic Historians," esp. 263–66.

89. For Polybius's work as a handbook of decision making primarily intended for statesmen, see 3.7.5; 6.53.6–54.3 and 55.4; 10.21.3–22.4; 11.10.1; 16.28.9; 38.2. But despite Mohm, *Anschauungen des Polybios,* 174–81, Polybius also casts his net somewhat wider than this, to include "lovers of knowledge" (φιλομαθοῦντες) in general. See Walbank, *Commentary* I: 7, based on 3.1.6 and 21.9, to which add 2.40.5 and 32.11.7. Walbank's position is rightly supported by Sacks, *Polybius on the Writing of History,* 134 n. 29.

hold up a model of outstanding conduct to the leaders of all states, and to anyone who shall ever be entrusted with public affairs (9.9.9–10):

> By recalling or picturing to themselves this conduct, let statesmen emulate it, and not shrink from projects that may seem fraught with risk and peril but that on the contrary are bold without being hazardous, are admirable in conception, *and whose excellence—whether the result be success or failure—will deserve to live in men's memories forever,*[90] always provided that the actions taken are based on sound reasoning.

The fundamental idea in this long and personal interjection by Polybius into his narrative is that the point of all human endeavor is "excellence" or "brilliance." It is this quality (which Polybius generally calls the καλόν) that makes human conduct worthy of eternal memory—not whether the conduct actually leads to success or (unfortunately) to failure.[91] The sentiment here is hardly ruthless, cynical, or "Machiavellian"; rather, it has an archaic, almost Homeric quality to it. Indeed, the passage bears a resemblance to the historiographic purpose of Herodotus (itself powerfully influenced by Homer) as set forth at the beginning of Herodotus's own historical work: to preserve the memory of the great and wonderful deeds of Greeks and non-Greeks (1.1.1).[92]

Similarly, Polybius praises the courage of both the Roman besiegers and the Punic defenders of Lilybaeum in Sicily in 250, although the ferocious fighting merely ended in bloody stalemate (1.45.11–12); and he praises the energy and courage of both Hamilcar Barca and his Roman opponents during the terrible fighting for Mount Eryx a little later—although nothing came of this struggle, either (1.58.1–8). These are incidents (and moralizing judgments) from Book 1; but the very same ideas can be found thirty volumes later, in the post-146 extension. They emerge from Polybius's account of how he encouraged Demetrius of Syria to attempt his escape from Rome. Though sick in bed himself (31.13.7), he sent Demetrius a copy of one of his favorite poems, by Epicharmus. It must come as a shock to the advocates of the ruthless Polybius, whose sole standard of human judgment is practical success in the

---

90. ἀείμνηστον δὲ καὶ καλὴν ἔχει τὴν προαίρεσιν καὶ κατορθωθέντα καὶ διαψευσθέντα παραπλησίως. There is some corruption of the manuscript at 9.9.10, but it does not affect this crucial phrase: see Walbank, *Commentary* II: 132–33.

91. Walbank (ibid.) takes no notice of the "anti-Machiavellianism" of 9.9.10; and the passage goes completely undiscussed in Pédech, *Méthode*. Sacks, *Polybius on the Writing of History*, 136 n. 30, finds the moral meaning in 9.9.10 "not easily determined." Even Petzold (*Methode des Polybios*, 36 n. 10) mentions 9.9.9–10 only in the context of Polybius's habit of comparing nationalities (in this case, Carthaginians and Romans: cf. 9.9.9).

92. On the enduring and "Homeric" impact of Herodotus on the purposes of Greek historiography, see Fornara, *Nature of History in Greece and Rome*, 96–98; cf. 63–64. On the direct influence of Homer himself, see esp. Havelock, "Heroism and History," 19–55.

real world, to discover that this poem emphasized the simple virtue of action, whether that action succeeded or failed (31.13.13):

> Be courageous, take a risk, act, to lose
> or win [ἀποτύγχανε, ἐπίτυχε]—
> anything,
> rather than betray oneself.

This reads like something out of Edmond Rostand.[93]

Similar in sentiment, too, is Polybius's earlier remark that the purpose of historical writing is not so much to record the misdeeds and crimes of the past as "to call attention to right and honorable actions" (τὰ καλὰ καὶ δίκαια), for attention to these, and emulation of these, will especially improve the reader (2.61.3). The idea that the special virtue of historical writing is the commendation and honoring of noble conduct is repeated at 2.61.6, and again at 12.15.9. It is true enough that all three of these passages occur in highly polemical contexts, elements in separate Polybian attacks on the historians Phylarchus and Timaeus. As a result, scholars tend to dismiss the sentiments here as mere momentary rhetoric.[94] Yet the very repetition of Polybius's assertion might suggest that this was an idea about which he felt strongly, and the fact is that the maxim appears in two other passages where politics and polemic are not involved.

First, 16.22a, where the historian discusses the siege of Gaza by Antiochus III in 202/201. To his account of the siege (now lost), Polybius appends an essay in praise of the character of the Gazan people. He feels that this is "just and proper" (δίκαιον, πρέπον, 22a.2), for the Gazans have a fine tradition of manliness and bravery (ἀνδρεία, 22a.3), which they now demonstrated once again. He further explains that just as it is necessary to make special mention of brave and virtuous individuals when writing history (22a.7), so too it is necessary to mention favorably those whole cities that, by tradition, act nobly (τῶν καλῶν . . . πράττειν, ibid.). Second, in 16.30.2–3 Polybius explains why he has included in his narrative a detailed account of the siege of Abydus. It is not the strategic importance of this action that recommends it for study, he says, but rather "the nobility and extraordinary courage" of the besieged that makes it "worthy of remembrance."[95]

93. Having mandated the taking of action—whether successful or not—as noble, the rest of the poem advocates carefulness (31.13.14); the parallel with the sentiment in Polyb. 9.9.9–10 (see above) is obvious. Polybius quotes the same Epicharmus poem in 18.40 (in a context where, as in 31.13, he is quite agitated). Wunderer, *Polybios,* 13, long ago emphasized the ethical content of the message to Demetrius as central to Polybius's worldview. But this aspect of the story in 31.13 is ignored in modern discussion.

94. See Meister, *Historische Kritik bei Polybios,* 104–6, and 107; Sacks, *Polybius on the Writing of History,* 143; cf. the general comments of Urban, *Wachstum und Krise,* 193–200.

95. ἣν γενναιότητα . . . καὶ τὴν ὑπερβολὴν τῆς εὐψυχίας . . . μνήμης ἀξία.

Obviously, there is a close intellectual connection between Polybius's remarks here in Book 16 on the necessity for historians to emphasize noble conduct and his earlier remarks in Books 2 and 12.[96] This strongly suggests that the historiographical-moral advice in those latter passages was not simply trotted out for a momentary polemical purpose. It was seriously meant: for across fourteen volumes of *The Histories*, and years of work, Polybius's comments on the morally edifying purpose of historical writing turn out to be completely consistent.[97]

Moreover, Polybius vividly praises the courageous and noble behavior of the people of Gaza and of Abydus despite the fact that their conduct was to no avail; both cities eventually fell to their besiegers (16.22a.1, 33–34). That is, Polybius does not at all apply a utilitarian standard of judgment here. It is the losers, not the winners, who are praised—because of the nobility, not the ultimate effectiveness, of their conduct.

Yet if failure can thus be shown actually irrelevant to Polybius's decision to praise certain actions in *The Histories*, a *prima facie* case can also easily be made for the reverse: that mere pragmatic success was *not* enough, in itself, to win Polybius's praise. A few examples should serve to demonstrate this.

First, Polybius's criticism of the conduct of the Aetolian statesman Alexander of Isus. In 189 Alexander and other Aetolian envoys to Rome were captured by Epirote privateers. The Epirotes at first demanded five talents per man as ransom; the other envoys were willing to pay, but not Alexander—though, Polybius says, he was the richest man in Greece (21.26.9–10). The privateers eventually reduced their demand to three talents per man, and the other envoys arranged payment and left. But Alexander preferred to remain a captive rather than pay more than one talent (26.12–14). And in fact, events worked out completely to his financial advantage; for orders soon arrived from the Romans demanding the release of the envoys, and the Epirotes complied by releasing Alexander (the only captive left). Thus Alexander, of all the envoys, never had to pay any ransom (26.17).

Polybius says that Alexander's behavior met with universal praise and approval among the Greeks (26.16). And if Polybius's fundamental criterion for judging conduct was success versus failure (or in this case, profit versus loss), then he should have joined the chorus. But instead his com-

96. Cf. Walbank, *Commentary* II: 528.
97. This must be one of the reasons why Polyb. 2.61 is one of the few moralizing statements by Polybius that Walbank takes seriously: cf. *Commentary* I: 297 (which stands in stark contrast to the scholars cited in n. 94, above). Yet such an interpretation fits very uncomfortably with the ruthless and amoral Polybius emphasized by Walbank more recently. Meissner, "Polybios" (322 and n. 88; 340 and n. 288; 343 and n. 317), simply assumes—without offering any argument—that Polyb. 2.61.2–3 is sincere.

ments are bitter: Alexander, gripped by uncontrollable avarice and lust to accumulate wealth, would have preferred even to give up his life rather than pay a relatively minor ransom (26.14–16).

The historian obviously did not have to interpret the incident in this way; most people interpreted it in precisely the opposite way—as evidence of Alexander's sagacity (cf. 21.26.16). But Polybius criticizes Alexander's behavior because he considers it disgraceful for a person to be at the mercy of lust for money (cf. his reference to Alexander's helpless ἀλογιστία, ibid.). And it makes no difference to his assessment of Alexander that, as it happened, Alexander came out ahead in this episode.

But Alexander of Isus was an Aetolian, and perhaps one might argue that for Polybius nothing an Aetolian does can be morally correct.[98] Yet Polybius praises Alexander elsewhere in *The Histories*—and indeed, precisely for his advocacy of sound financial policy (13.1a, *passim*). Alexander was thus no cartoon Aetolian, and this reinforces the idea that Polybius's upset with his behavior in 189 was genuine.[99]

That hypothesis is strengthened by three other examples where mere pragmatic success fails to win Polybius's praise for what he considers poor-quality behavior. In 171/170, the people of Cydonia in Crete seized the town of Apollonia in a surprise attack, despite the fact that the Apollonians enjoyed joint citizenship with them by solemnly sworn treaty (Polyb. 28.14.5). The Cydonians killed all the men of Apollonia, divided the property, and kept for themselves the women and children (14.4). They retained the city for at least some time (though they came under threat from Gortyn: 28.15), and certainly never had to give up their other loot. Yet Polybius's comments are harshly condemnatory, on moral grounds. The people of Cydonia had committed "an act universally agreed to have been terrible and treacherous" (14.1; cf. 14.4), surpassing even the habitual treachery of Crete (14.2).[100]

Von Scala sees Polybius's angry criticism of the Cydonians as part of the historian's general advocacy of ethical conduct and self-restraint in international relations.[101] By contrast, Walbank tends to take the passage as merely another indication of Polybius's inveterate political hostility toward Cretans.[102] This is an excellent case of the contrast between the

---

98. On Polybius's general prejudice against the Aetolians, see esp. Mendels, "Did Polybius Have 'Another' View of the Aetolian League?" 63–72.

99. For the Aetolian statesman Alexander in Polyb. 13.1a as identical to Alexander of Isus, see the argument in Walbank, *Commentary* II: 413.

100. On the possible political consequences of the Cydonian seizure of Apollonia, see Walbank, *Commentary* III: 348 and 349. It is not clear which Apollonia in Crete this is (III: 348).

101. *Studien*, 309 and n. 4.

102. *Commentary* III: 348.

old and the new ways of interpreting *The Histories*. But in von Scala's favor is, for instance, Polybius's violent condemnation of the Mamertines for betraying the trust of Messana in Sicily, and seizing the city (1.7.2–3)—though the Mamertines remained in successful possession of Messana ever after; or his criticism of Philip V of Macedon for even considering seizing Messene in Greece contrary to treaty (7.12); or his condemnation of the attempted seizure of Messene, contrary to treaty, by Nabis of Sparta (16.13.3); or his criticism of the Romans themselves for seizing Sardinia from Carthage, in his opinion contrary to treaty (3.30.4; cf. 1.88.8–12, with 83.5). Polybius's position concerning this sort of behavior seems consistent, no matter who is involved.

Two final examples, involving Polybian moral criticism of policies associated with his own known friends, serve to demonstrate that latter point. First, although Polybius had done important favors for the people of Italiote Locri, and the Locrians had in turn honored him publicly,[103] he apparently criticized them for failing to maintain the legal compacts into which they entered (cf. 12.12a, with 12.5.4)—although, of course, the Locrians only broke such compacts when it was to their direct pragmatic advantage to do so.[104] Second, although Demetrius of Syria was Polybius's close friend, the historian not only criticizes him for drunkenness and a dissolute life (33.19; cf. 31.13.8), but also criticizes Miltiades, Demetrius's envoy to Rome in 158/157, for using falsehoods to attack Ariarathes, the deposed king of Cappadocia, and to support Oropherenes, the pretender to the Cappadocian throne (32.10.7–8). Yet Miltiades was not only the agent here of the policy of Polybius's friend, but Miltiades' lies were in good part successful (32.10.8, explicit).[105]

If Polybius's stance in *The Histories* had been one of utter pragmatism and ruthless Machiavellianism, none of the above judgments would ever

103. Polyb. 12.5.1–3; see above, p. 11.

104. Polybius here is attempting to explain the origins of the insulting proverbial phrase "the Locrians and the pact" (i.e., betrayal of a sworn oath), and is intent on arguing that the Locrians of the proverb are the Italiote Locrians, not the Locrians of Greece; for discussion, see Walbank, *Commentary* II: 351–52; cf. Pédech, *Polybe: Histoires XII*, xxi–xxii. Note also that despite the mutual interaction of favors and honors between Polybius and the Italiote Locrians, the historian also does not hesitate to argue that the latter were descended from slaves (12.5–6b). This is another example of Polybius's historical objectivity—as he himself says (12.5.3–4).

105. Walbank suggests that Polybius's attitude here in 32.10 is merely "cynical and detached" (*Polybius*, 169; cf. *Commentary* III: 530)—i.e., not condemnatory of the conduct of the envoys of Demetrius and Oropherenes. But the tone of outrage is patent in Polybius's blunt choice of description (the envoys "dared to say anything, with a total disregard for the truth, and took no responsibility," 10.7; "lies had no trouble winning the day," 10.8). Note that Polybius intensely disliked Oropherenes' character, viewing him as greedy and corrupt (cf. 32.11.1 and 10).

have been delivered. Those judgments are deeply expressive of a concern for the maintenance of ethical behavior in a difficult and complex world. They suggest that Polybius's desire for the "improvement" of his audience (1.1.1, διόρθωσις) was not limited to the creation of more pragmatically efficient decision makers—although of course he had much to say in that direction. Rather, Polybius also hoped that those who studied his *Histories* would emerge with a firm determination to live their lives nobly (cf. 1.1.2, γενναίως)—according to the καλόν. And this was an important constant in *The Histories* from the earliest stages of their composition right through to the very last volume.[106]

The insights into *The Histories* and their author offered by older scholars from Bodin to Wunderer should therefore not be ignored, as has come increasingly to be the case. The main purpose of the present study is in fact to reemphasize the moral dimension in Polybius's work—to rescue his moral seriousness from the oblivion into which the past half-century of scholarship has consigned it.

This book, however, seeks to go beyond an extended and detailed argument in favor of Polybius's moralizing tendency as opposed to the current image of Polybius the utterly pragmatic writer. It is also a study of the specific elements within that moralizing tendency itself: in other words, it is a description of Polybius's moral world. Hence the topics discussed below include Polybius's attitudes toward courage (both physical and moral), conduct undertaken for reasons of honor rather than for pragmatic gain, the use (or avoidance) of deceit in human interactions, the nature of duty, the necessity for self-control. Moreover, Polybius's extensive thinking on such subjects—and in particular, his considered conclusions about the weaknesses of the human personality and the temptations to which it was heir (i.e., the gap Polybius observed between ideal behavior and humans' real conduct)—in turn had a profound impact upon his view of the possibility of human achievement in history, as well as upon the threats of anarchy that he believed faced his own society. Indeed, such

106. Most of the material after Book 18 of *The Histories* survives only in the tenth-century-A.D. Byzantine epitomes put together by order of the emperor Constantine VII Porphyrogenitus; and one of those epitomes is entitled *Virtues and Vices*. This might suggest that the surviving fragments of *The Histories* as we have them are somewhat skewed toward passages with a moralizing content. But much of the material after Book 18 also comes from the Constantinian epitome *On Embassies*—which has no moralizing bias. In addition, the first five volumes of *The Histories* survive entire, and there is no apparent divergence in frequency of moralizing language between these five volumes and the later, highly fragmentary ones. See, e.g., the distribution of usage in Mauersberger *Polybios-Lexikon* I:3, s.v. τὸ καθῆκον ("duty"), cols. 1199–2000; or s.v. κακία ("evil"), cols. 1241–42; or s.v. καλόν ("good, noble"), cols. 1255–56; or I:4, s.v. μεγαλοψυχία ("greatness or nobility of spirit"), cols. 1521–22.

thinking had powerful implications for the moral meaning of his own enormous effort in composing *The Histories* in the first place. These topics, too, will deserve their own discussion.

The rest of this book is concerned with delineating the various aspects of Polybius's moral vision that deeply inform his *Histories*—and that deeply informed his own life.

TWO

Polybius's Aristocratic Ethos: Deeds of Personal Courage

Glaucus, we are held in godlike honor in Lycia, and possess great lands. . . .
Therefore, we must take our stand in the foremost rank, and confront
the blazing battle.
—*ILIAD* 12.310–16
(SPEECH OF SARPEDON)

INTRODUCTION

The purpose of the present chapter is to begin a detailed investigation of Polybius's traditional aristocratic ethos, an ethos that stressed achievement of "the honorable" and "the brilliant"—τὸ καλόν. In traditional Greek culture, no activity was more important in achieving the καλόν than the demonstration of physical courage. Here the standards of conduct had been established by the poems of Homer—poems that came to form the core of Greek education.[1] Two specific areas are of particular interest, for in both, Polybius's attitude—insofar as it has been studied at all—has been taken to be not traditional but strictly pragmatic. First is Polybius's attitude toward commanding generals who actually fought in the battle line; second is his attitude toward those who commit suicide when confronted with total defeat. Yet in both areas it can be shown that Polybius in fact fully participated in the aristocratic ethos of physical combat, heroism, and glorious acceptance of death.

GENERALS IN THE BATTLE LINE

In 208, the consul M. Claudius Marcellus lost his life in an accidental skirmish while engaged in a personal reconnaissance on horseback of the ground surrounding the camp of Hannibal (Polyb. 10.32.1–6).[2] Polybius appends to his account of this incident a lengthy and contemptuous com-

---

1. On the influence of the Homeric poems on the Greek attitude toward violence, heroism, and death, see esp. Havelock, "Heroism and History," 19–55. On the impact of Homer upon Polybius, see esp. von Scala, *Studien*, 63–72. The historian's attitude toward Homer is always positive, but note esp. 34.4.4.
2. Other sources on the death of Marcellus: see Broughton, *Magistrates* I: 200.

ment. Marcellus had behaved more like a simpleton than a general (10.32.7), for a general must take the greatest care to keep himself safe, especially when the fate of the whole army is not involved (32.9). Thus Hannibal is very rightly to be praised for the great care he took for his own safety in the many fierce battles he directed, for as long as the general is alive, defeat can be retrieved, but if the general falls, then even victory will be useless to the leaderless mass of the soldiery (33.1–5). So one should never commit Marcellus's error—which can derive from ostentation, childish love of excitement, inexperience, or contempt for the enemy (33.6).

Polybius's praise of Scipio Africanus is similar. Scipio established a reputation for courage by rescuing his father at the battle of the Ticenum, but thereafter he rarely risked his life in battle, since his country reposed all her hopes in him; in this, Polybius says, he acted intelligently (νοῦν ἔχοντος, 10.3.7).[3] And a book later, in praising the behavior of Hasdrubal at the battle of the Metaurus, Polybius again underlines that a general should not expose himself recklessly to the dangers of combat (11.2.11).

These passages have led modern scholars to stress that Polybius's approach to a commander's conduct was highly unsentimental—an approach at odds with the usual ancient focus on the glories of personal bravery.[4] Further, this "unsentimental" attitude is then made to seem part of a wider Polybian framework of cold calculation and even ruthlessness.[5]

The usual scholarly interpretation of the above passages, however, is too simplistic. First of all, Polybius's point about Marcellus is not that generals should *never* risk their lives in battle, but that he threw his life away in a minor skirmish, in the type of action where to risk one's life when a commanding general was an act of irresponsibility (cf. 10.32.10). Polybius's point about Hasdrubal is similar: a commander should not risk his life recklessly (προπετῶς, 11.2.11). The implication is that there might well be situations when a commander would be justified in risking his life—perhaps when the fate of the entire army hangs in the balance (see

3. For Scipio's behavior in battle, see also Polyb. 10.13.1 (a remark missing from the parallel passage in Livy, perhaps because Livy considered it discreditable: Walbank, *Commentary* II: 244).

4. See Pédech, *Méthode*, 219; Walbank, *Commentary* II: 199 and 244; A. J. Pomeroy, "Polybius' Death Notices," 413. Walbank also adduces Polyb. 10.24.4 in this context (*Commentary* II: 199). But Polybius's point in that latter passage seems to be that Philopoemen, as the commanding general, was everywhere among his troops—thus not only in the rear (10.24.4), but in the front line as well (ποτὲ μὲν ἐν πρώτοις, ibid.).

5. See esp. Pédech, *Méthode*, 219 (in a context that emphasizes Polybius's lack of scruples). Not surprisingly, Pédech also argues that Polybius rarely employes the term ἀνδρεία—"manliness," or "courage" (251 and n. 204). But there are 16 examples in the extant text, to which should be added 19 examples of the parallel term ἀνδρώδης (see Mauersberger, *Polybios-Lexikon* I:1, cols. 117–18).

10.32.9). As for Scipio Africanus, Polybius does not say that Scipio *never* risked his life, only that he rarely did so (σπανίως, 10.3.7).[6] And in Hannibal's case, it may be that in 10.32–33 Polybius is rhetorically sharpening the contrast with the reckless and irresponsible Marcellus, for Polybius is well aware that even Hannibal, at moments he deemed crucial, did risk his life in battle. Polybius himself records this as happening during the siege of Saguntum (3.17.8), and again at Cannae (3.116.3–4).

In sum, Polybius's attitude toward generals' risking their lives in the passages in Books 10 and 11 is a complex one. But beyond these famous passages—which are famous only because scholars have focused so much attention on them—there exists a very large number of texts where Polybius's attitude toward the display of battlefield bravery by a general is far more traditional.

A good beginning is provided by the example of Philopoemen. One of Polybius's early works was a laudatory biography of this Achaean statesman and general.[7] It is clear that Plutarch's biography is directly based on Polybius's encomium,[8] and one of the striking features of the Plutarchean biography is the number of times Philopoemen is presented in a positive light as he risks his life in battle while in command of large numbers of troops.

The use of the *Philopoemen*, of course, presents a special problem. An encomium is not the same as true *historia,* as Polybius himself says; harsh criticism of the subject cannot be expected (10.21.8).[9] Still, if Polybius had disapproved of Philopoemen's risking his life in battle while a commanding general, the theme would not play such a large part in Plutarch—for Polybius then would simply have passed over these incidents in silence. Further, in the most famous of these incidents the tone of the *Philopoemen* can be checked against the text of *The Histories* (and/or texts derived from *The Histories*). No difference in the positive evaluation of these incidents is detectable.

Philopoemen first demonstrated his great physical courage when as a junior officer at the battle of Sellasia in 222 he personally led his cavalry force in a crucial attack despite receiving a very severe wound. Plutarch's account of this incident (*Phil.* 6.4–6) and Polybius himself in *The Histories*

6. On the manuscript reading here, see Walbank, *Commentary* II: 199. Scipio risked his life in going with only a small escort on a diplomatic mission to the Numidian prince Syphax in 206; he was almost captured by the Carthaginians (Livy 28.27.13–16; App. *Ib.* 29–30). Polybius included the story in *The Histories* (see 14.1.4, a retrospective).

7. On the biography, see above all Pédech, "Polybe et l'éloge," 82–103.

8. The basic discussion remains Nissen, *Kritische Untersuchungen,* 280–87. See also Walbank, *Commentary* II: 222–23; Pédech, "Polybe et l'éloge," 83.

9. On the sharp distinction between encomium and true ἱστορία, see also Polyb. 8.8.3–9. A good modern discussion: Avenarius, *Lukians Schrift,* 13–15.

(2.67.4–68.2, and 69.2) are completely parallel in their stress on Philopoemen's personal bravery here.[10] A decade or so after Sellasia, Philopoemen was elected Achaean hipparch (210/209), and led the League cavalry into battle against a combined Aetolian-Elean army.[11] The battle, Plutarch says, was a fierce one (*Phil.* 7.6)—and in the midst of it Philopoemen accepted a challenge to personal combat from Damophantus, the Elean cavalry commander. Philopoemen was victorious, killing Damophantus outright with a lance; the enemy forces were demoralized, and retreated (7.6–7). Plutarch's account ends once more with strong praise of Philopoemen: he was viewed as without equal among the Achaeans, either in physical prowess or military sagacity (7.7). Something similar must have stood in the Polybian encomium—which therefore apparently failed to deal with what might have happened to the hard-pressed Achaean cavalry if it had been Philopoemen rather than Damophantus who was killed in the glorious single combat.[12]

Soon thereafter, Philopoemen was elected League *stratēgos* (208/207). He completed the reorganization of the Achaean army that he had begun as hipparch,[13] and then led the army into battle at Mantineia against the Spartan tyrant Machanidas, who had been a thorn in the Achaean side for several years.[14] In the battle, the Spartan ruler's mercenaries broke the Achaean left wing, but Machanidas mistakenly pursued the defeated wing too far, and meanwhile the new Achaean phalanx in the center triumphantly held off the charge of the Spartan infantry. The battle was now essentially won, with Machanidas cut off (Polyb. 11.17.1–2). Yet it is still remarkable that at this point Philopoemen left a subordinate to deal with Machanidas's mercenaries—described as the backbone of the Spartan regime (11.18.1)—while the *stratēgos* himself set off on horseback along the battle line, seeking personal combat with Machanidas. He eventually found it, and slew the Spartan in a spectacular single combat in the ditch separating the two armies. The story is told in detail in Polybius's *Histories* (11.17–18), and there was apparently even more detail in Polybius's encomium: Plutarch says that in his eagerness for personal combat

10. For discussion of Philopoemen at Sellasia, see Errington, *Philopoemen*, 21–22.

11. For the military-diplomatic circumstances surrounding this campaign (a subsidiary action of the First Macedonian War), see Errington, *Philopoemen*, 47–58.

12. It is unclear how Polybius dealt with this incident in *The Histories* (as opposed to the encomium), since Livy 27.29ff., although it gives an account of events in Greece in 209 that is clearly based on Polybius, leaves out the Achaean cavalry battle entirely. But to judge from Polyb. 11.17–18 and 23.12 (discussed below), Polybius in *The Histories* was perfectly comfortable praising Philopoemen's personal bravery in the battle line even when Philopoemen was commander-in-chief.

13. On the army reorganization, see Anderson, "Philopoemen's Reform," 104–5; and Errington, *Philopoemen*, 63–65.

14. On the military-diplomatic background here, see Errington, *Philopoemen*, 58–65.

with Machanidas, Philopoemen even outrode his shield bearers, Simmias and Polyaenus (*Phil.* 10.7). Plutarch's account ends on a most positive note, with a description of the equestrian statue set up by the Achaeans to commemorate Philopoemen's great feat of arms in killing Machanidas (10.8).[15] And in *The Histories*, Polybius has nothing to say about what might have happened to the unstable morale of the newly organized Achaean army (cf. 11.8.7) if Philopoemen, rather than Machanidas, had died in the famous ditch—although earlier he had stressed that Philopoemen was the one man upon whom everything rested (cf. 11.10.1–6).[16]

The final appearance of Philopoemen in personal combat is the most intriguing—for it led directly to his death. By 183/182 he was over seventy, and *stratēgos* of the League for the eighth time. He now learned that the Messenians under their leader Deinocrates—a personal enemy (*Phil.* 18.3)—had seized Corone, on the Arcadian frontier. He thereupon arose from his sickbed at Argos (ibid.) and, in his eagerness to confront Deinocrates and the Messenians, rode all the way to Megalopolis in a single day (ibid.). At Megalopolis the *stratēgos* gathered a scratch force of some sixty aristocratic cavalrymen, supported by a few mercenaries, and rode off toward Corone. But he fell into an ambush set by Deinocrates; and, overwhelmed by numbers, Philopoemen sacrificed himself, drawing the attention of the Messenian soldiers to himself so that the rest of the Megalopolitan force could escape. In the end his tired horse stumbled and threw him. Philopoemen was seriously injured, captured by the Messenians—and later executed.[17]

The story of Philopoemen's self-sacrifice certainly has its noble aspect. And that is clearly the way Polybius chose to present it—as a moment of grandeur. The extant text of *The Histories* is lacking Polybius's account of the ambush, but it does contain an obituary of Philopoemen in which he is depicted as a man overwhelmed by Fortune after a long life of accom-

15. Walbank is unsure whether the story of the equestian statue comes from Polybius's encomium (*Commentary* II: 294). But Polybius was interested in Philopoemen's statues: see 39.3.

16. Note that Polybius specifically defends Philopoemen from a charge of cowardice regarding his dispositions for this battle (11.16.4–5).

17. Errington, *Philopoemen*, 191–93, doubts the story of Philopoemen's execution (Polyb. 23.12.3; cf. Livy 39.50.7–8, Plut. *Phil.* 20, and Paus. 8.51.7). He suggests that Philopoemen actually died of injuries sustained in the fighting, and that the execution story was developed by the Messenians in self-defense, in order to blacken Deinocrates and his friends—who allegedly pushed the execution through, upon an unwilling Messenian populace. But surely the story that Philopoemen died of his injuries would have been an even better Messenian defense, and especially if it were the truth; yet nowhere is there a hint of any tradition other than the execution. Errington is rightly rejected by Walbank, *Commentary* III: 240–41.

plishment and success (23.12). And to judge from Livy (39.49–50), what stood immediately before the obituary was a panegyric to Philopoemen's personal bravery: he could have escaped from the ambush with the help of his Cretan and Thracian mercenaries, but chose to stay and protect the Megalopolitan cavalrymen instead.[18]

Nevertheless, the events surrounding Philopoemen's death could have been presented quite differently. To ride off against the Messenians at Corone with a handful of troops: this is extraordinary conduct for a general of wide experience and mature years. And while Philopoemen's subsequent decision to sacrifice himself for the sake of the young Megalopolitans is a memorable and "shining" deed, it is also an example of a *stratēgos* of the League abandoning the heavy responsibilities he owed to the broader Achaean community. This is especially so because Philopoemen did not yet know the whereabouts—or even the fate—of the hipparch Lycortas and the main body of the Achaean cavalry, whom he had sent into Messenia.[19] Indeed, Philopoemen's death is not all that different from the death of Marcellus—an old general recklessly leads a troop of cavalry into a fatal ambush. The difference is that Polybius's tone is not condemnatory here but admiring. Yet certainly no deeply utilitarian purpose was being served by Philopoemen's self-sacrifice; for to put it ruthlessly, sixty Megalopolitan cavalrymen were not worth the life of the greatest general in the Achaean League.

The point, of course, is that Polybius was *not* ruthlessly utilitarian here; his focus is on the nobility of Philopoemen's display of personal bravery. And this point is strongly underscored by the fact that not only can one theoretically see how Philopoemen's behavior in 183/182 might have been condemned; in antiquity it actually *was* condemned. The condemnation is Plutarch's, in his *Comparison of Flamininus and Philopoemen.* Now free of his sources and making his own independent evaluation of his biographical subjects, Plutarch remarks that Philopoemen's great fault as a general lay in his contentious spirit and susceptibility to anger (*Comp.* 1.2).[20] Moreover, Plutarch specifically censures Philopoemen's last actions (*Comp.* 1.3):

> It would appear that he threw his life away in a fit of anger and contentiousness [τὸν βίον ὀργῇ προέσθαι καὶ φιλονεικίᾳ], hastening to attack Messene before occasion truly offered and more quickly than was appropriate;

18. On Livy 39.49–50 as deriving from Polybian material, see Errington, *Philopoemen*, 190 and n. 1.

19. Note his question to his Messenian captors concerning whether Lycortas and his men were in fact safe: Livy 30.50.7–8, Plut. *Phil.* 20.2–3.

20. φιλονεικία, ὀργή (1.2); these words in themselves show Plutarch's independence of judgment here, since Polybius's obituary strove to give exactly the opposite impression of Philopoemen's personality (see Polyb. 23.12.9).

for unlike Flamininus, he did not conduct all his military operations with due deliberation and a regard to safety.

We can understand how Plutarch arrived at this evaluation—but it is not Polybius's evaluation. One might argue that this is because for Polybius, Philopoemen could do no wrong; he was a fellow Megalopolitan, a family friend, a childhood idol. Yet Polybius was perfectly capable of strongly criticizing Philopoemen's behavior elsewhere (cf. 22.19).[21] And such an argument also avoids the question of what qualities the young Polybius saw in Philopoemen that made him into an idol in the first place. The answer seems to be that it was not only Philopoemen's sagacious generalship—of which Polybius both in the encomium and *The Histories* certainly provided many examples.[22] Rather, it would also appear that the young Polybius was attracted by what one might call Philopoemen's "Homeric" qualities: his spirit of action and his great physical courage, which led him persistently to risk his life in battle even when he was a commanding general.

In other words, Polybius's admiration for Philopoemen's conduct in the battle line was sincere. But if so, then we have an insight into the traditional aristocratic ethos of honor and valor in which Polybius grew up—and which to some extent he never outgrew.[23]

This hypothesis in fact finds much support in other texts where Polybius describes generals as they risk their lives in combat. A good example is his attitude toward the demise of Hamilcar Barca, the father of Hannibal. Hamilcar's shrewd generalship consistently wins Polybius's praise throughout the earliest portions of *The Histories,* and it appears that Polybius is the originator of a pro-Hamilcar tradition so powerful that it penetrated even Roman historiography.[24] But in winter 229/228 Hamilcar met his end near Alicante in Spain, attempting to cover the retreat of his army in the face of fierce attacks by the barbarian Oretani. Polybius again commends his conduct, but it is not his sagaciousness that is praised (2.1.7–8):

> He ended his life in a manner worthy of his previous achievements; for he died bravely in battle [ἐρρώμενως] . . . after exposing his person stoutly and very courageously to danger in the field [τολμηρῶς καὶ παραβόλως].

21. On this passage, see the detailed discussion in Chap. IV, below.
22. See, e.g., Polyb. 11.14.2–15.2 and 16.4–5, or Plut. *Phil.* 14.4–7 (surely from the encomium).
23. On the atmosphere in which Polybius was raised, and the education he received, see above all von Scala, *Studien,* 11–63 (old but indispensable). Cf. also Chap. I, above.
24. For Polybius's praise of Hamilcar Barca's generalship, see, e.g., 1.75–76 and 84.5–8. For Polybius as the source of a lasting pro-Hamilcar tradition, see Walbank, *Commentary* I: 152.

The other, more detailed accounts of this incident indicate that Hamilcar did not actually die in battle—which is the impression Polybius leaves; rather, he was swept away in a flooding river.[25] But this incongruity only underlines the warmth of Polybius's praise of Hamilcar for risking his life in direct battle. Even though the result was his death, and even though Hamilcar was the commanding general, it was the sort of heroic death that Polybius evidently found morally satisfying.

Another commander-in-chief who in Polybius's opinion gained a glorious death in the battle line was the Rhodian admiral Theophiliscus. During the naval battle of Chios in 201, Theophiliscus's ship performed "brilliantly" (16.5.1), while Theophiliscus himself displayed "remarkable bravery" (παραβόλως τῇ τόλμῃ)—and was severely wounded (5.6). But he continued to lead the attack, thereby demonstrating his "noble" and "brilliant" nature (γενναῖος, λαμπρός, 5.7). The battle was a draw (which actually constituted a strategic defeat for Macedon).[26] But Theophiliscus died of his wounds the next day—thereby depriving Rhodes of her finest naval commander. Polybius's evaluation is only positive: here was a man of great personal bravery in battle, a man of general vigor, a personage worthy of remembrance (16.9.1–4).[27]

Even monarchs who risk their lives in the battle line—men whose deaths could spell catastrophe for their states—receive Polybius's hearty praise. A good example here is Antiochus III ("the Great"). Antiochus was a redoubtable warrior in personal combat; but his greatest exploit, according to Polybius, occurred in Bactria (in 208). Learning that the Bactrians were marching to the relief of a town he was besieging (the name has been lost), Antiochus sought to deny them the crossing of the Arius River, seizing it himself with his light-armed troops (10.49.1–5). Antiochus then personally led the successful defense of the bridgehead (49.8), and in combat fought more brilliantly (διαπρεπέστατα) than anyone else (49.9). The fierceness of the battle is shown by the fact that not only was Antiochus's horse shot out from under him, but Antiochus himself received a severe head wound (49.13). Polybius's comment is respectful, and expressed in a tone of satisfaction: Antiochus's conduct in this action gained him a very great reputation for personal courage and manliness (ἀνδρεία, ibid.). Yet it is obvious from the severe head wound Anti-

25. For discussion, see Walbank, *Commentary* I: 152.

26. On the battle of Chios and its strategic impact, see now Walbank, "Sea Power and the Antigonids," 228–33.

27. Polybius's source for the battle of Chios is very likely to have been a Rhodian one (see Walbank, *Commentary* II: 508). But even if this positive evaluation of Theophiliscus was in origin that of a patriotic Rhodian, it was still Polybius who chose to include it, with emphasis, in *The Histories*. Theophiliscus's obituary therefore gives us an insight into Polybius's ideology of physical bravery in a commander.

ochus received that the king could easily have lost his life in what was essentially a subsidiary (if glorious) cavalry engagement.[28]

Indeed, for Polybius a brave death in battle could even partially redeem a life otherwise totally misspent. Thus Lyciscus of Stratus, the leading Aetolian politician of the 160s, was for Polybius a thoroughly destructive and evil figure (32.4.1–2). Yet his death—evidently in some sort of battle (4.1)—was a noble one (καλῶς, 4.3). And the historian appends this comment: "Fortune sometimes grants to the worst of men the fine death that is the reward due the good and the brave" (ibid.).[29]

Other examples of this ideology could easily be multiplied: the praise of the physical bravery of Philip V of Macedon, which often endangered his life; the praise of the bravery of Ptolemy VI of Egypt, who died of wounds received in a cavalry charge in 145; the praise of the fine deaths in battle of Epaminondas, Pelopidas, Brasidas, and Cleombrotus.[30] But the point has been made: Polybius often heartily commended the appearance of commanders-in-chief in the battle line. It was a sign of bravery, of manliness.

Not surprisingly, then, Polybius also displays outright contempt for those commanding generals whom he suspects of being lacking in physical courage. A striking example here is Aratus of Sicyon, the great statesman who was the true founder of the Achaean League. He was certainly one of the special heroes of *The Histories*.[31] Yet at the beginning of Book 4, while listing Aratus's many virtues, Polybius adds that when faced with set-piece battle, Aratus was slow in planning, lacking in daring in execution, and devoid of physical courage (4.8.5).[32] Polybius is probably drawing here on a tradition about Aratus that is found in more detail in Plutarch: when confronted with battle, Aratus tended to have severe cramps in his bowels, to become dizzy and overcome with torpor when the signal

28. It was Antiochus's siege of the city of Bactra itself that was the centerpiece of this campaign (see Polyb. 29.12.6). Walbank's discussion of Polybius's depiction of the action at the Arius has no mention of Polybius's moralizing remarks about Antiochus's bravery, and is limited to the question of geographical location (*Commentary* II: 264–65). But for personal valor as generally a central element in the ideology of Hellenistic kingship, see his own comments in "Monarchies and Monarchic Ideas," 82.

29. The details of Lyciscus's death are lost; but see the discussion in Walbank, *Commentary* III: 522.

30. Philip V: see the depictions in Livy 27.32–33 (in Elis and Achaea in 208; for Polybian derivation, see Walbank, *Philip V,* 91–92), and Livy 32.24 (at Athens in 200; for Polybian derivation, see Briscoe, *Commentary* I: 115–120). Ptolemy VI: see Polyb. 28.21 and 39.7.1; note that Ptolemy's death in battle was actually a strategic disaster for Egypt (see Gruen, *Hellenistic World and the Coming of Rome* II: 711–12). Epaminondas, Pelopidas, Brasidas, Cleombrotus: see frg. 139 B-W; for speculation on the context, see Büttner-Wobst, *Polybii Historiae* IV: 534.

31. See Chap. I, p. 2 and n. 3, above.

32. νωθρὸς . . . ἄτολμος . . . ἐν ὄψει δ᾽ οὐ μένων τὸ δεινόν.

to advance was given, and to go off to await the issue in a place of safety (*Arat.* 29.5). Polybius, for his part, concludes his delineation of Aratus's character with a remark about severe cowardice (δειλότατον, 4.8.7).[33]

If not even Aratus could escape Polybius's strictures on this issue, it stands to reason that Polybius is even harsher toward the failings here of men he does not like. Hence his portrait of Agathocles of Alexandria: a worthless person, not only for his general incapacity and indolence (15.34.3 and 34.6), but also for his inability to show courage in war (34.4), and his physical cowardice (ἀνανδρία, 34.6). King Prusias II of Bithynia was just as bad. Like Agathocles, he was a conglomeration of evil traits; but he was especially lacking in the military virtues: in military affairs he was "ignoble and womanish" (ἀγεννὴς καὶ γυναικώδης, 36.15.1), a physical coward (δειλός), incapable of putting up with hardship (15.2). These are traits, Polybius says, that no one wishes to see in a king (15.3).[34]

The sincerity of that latter statement is borne out by the bitter attack Polybius makes on King Perseus of Macedon for having displayed personal cowardice against the Romans at Pydna in 168:

> Perseus's one determination had been to conquer or die; yet he did not retain his courage, but fled the battlefield. . . . When the time of danger approached, and it was his duty to fight the decisive battle, his courage broke down. . . . The king of the Macedonians turned tail at the very beginning of the battle. (29.17.3–4; 29.18)

This could hardly be clearer. Polybius expected King Perseus to lead his troops personally into combat, and to die there if necessary—if he lost to the Romans.[35]

Again, Polybius cannot resist condemning the conduct of one of the Roman consuls at Cannae, C. Terentius Varro: when the final disaster occurred, Varro disgraced himself by fleeing (ἀνὴρ αἰσχρὰν μὲν τὴν φυγήν, 3.116.3). Walbank may be right that this assessment ultimately derives

33. This does not mean that Polybius's overall portrait of Aratus was negative; far from it. Indeed, one might have expected Polybius simply not to remark on the great Achaean's one major defect at all—but he is not prepared to pass it by. He explicitly defends the resulting complexity of the portrait he draws (4.8.7 and 11).

34. For an example of Prusias's warmaking, see the savage picture in Polyb. 32.15. On the misogyny of the historian's remarks here, see the detailed discussion in Chap. V.

35. The passage marked Polyb. 29.17–18 is partially drawn from Plut. *Aem.* 19, but there is no doubt that Polybius is Plutarch's source here (see Walbank, *Commentary* III: 389). The accuracy of Polybius's story of Perseus's panic has been doubted (see Walbank, ibid. 390). But even Perseus's defenders in antiquity admitted that he withdrew from the battlefield precipitously, and they were embarrassed by this (see Plut. *Aem.* 19.4–5). Note Polybius's similar harsh criticism of the ex-consul A. Postumius Albinus for withdrawing personally from battle in Phocis in 146, feigning (so the historian contemptuously says) an illness (39.1.11). On Polybius's attitude toward Postumius (based partly, perhaps, on personal animosity), see also p. 278 n. 22, below.

from Fabius Pictor, who clearly disliked Varro.[36] But if so, it was still Polybius himself who chose to use the assessment in *The Histories*—and it can now be seen how well it fits with his general expectations regarding a commander's behavior. There is no doubt that Terentius eventually left the Cannae battlefield; but other ancient sources render a much milder judgment on his conduct.[37]

In fact, Polybius draws a contrast between the cowardly Varro and the other consul at Cannae, L. Aemilius Paullus (father of the Aemilius Paullus who won at Pydna). Polybius has already had Aemilius, in a dramatic speech before Cannae, promise the troops that both consuls would share their perils in the upcoming battle (3.109.1); and, Polybius says, Aemilius made sure to fulfill that vow (3.116.2). Aemilius personally fought in the initial cavalry action on the right wing (116.1); then, seeing that in the crisis of the battle the decision would lie with the legions, he rode along to the center, where he again threw himself directly into combat, cheering on his men and personally exchanging blows with the enemy (116.3). Polybius has Hannibal do likewise (116.4)—so that in the end the moral contrast here is almost between the courageous Aemilius and the courageous Hannibal on the one hand, and the "cowardly" Varro on the other. Aemilius eventually died in the thick of the fighting, after receiving numerous dreadful wounds (116.3). As with Varro, Polybius provides his audience with an assessment of Aemilius, but how different it is: Aemilius was a man who had steadfastly done his duty for the state, both throughout his life and at the last (ibid.).

Prominent scholars have sometimes argued, of course, that since Polybius had close ties of friendship and obligation to the family of Aemilius Paullus the victor of Pydna, the historian would have felt called upon to depict the Paullus of Cannae—and every other member of this family— in as positive a light as possible. But in Chapter I it was shown how often Polybius in fact criticized members of the Aemilian and Scipionic families if they did not meet his standards of conduct—and this included Paullus of Pydna himself. Thus membership in the Aemilian house did not automatically ensure that the Paullus who fell at Cannae would receive a positive depiction in Polybius; something more is involved.[38]

---

36. *Commentary* I: 448.

37. Compare Polybius with Livy 22.49 and Plut. *Fab.* 18.4–5. The Senate in fact entrusted Varro with a series of important commands after Cannae—an action impossible to believe if Varro had shown himself a coward at the battle; see the comments of Dorey, "Livy and the Popular Leaders," 55–60.

38. On Polybius's criticism of the Aemilii and the Scipiones, see pp. 9–10, above, with much evidence from *The Histories*. Particularly relevant here are Polybius's nasty remarks imputing cowardice to Cn. Cornelius Scipio Asina, the grandfather of Scipio Africanus (1.21.7).

It might perhaps be argued that Polybius's praise of the consul of Cannae stems from the fact that in joining personally in the fighting in the
infantry line, Paullus was only acting in accordance with the maxim of
Polyb. 10.32.9—that it is permissible for a commanding general to risk
his life, though only at a crucial point in battle. But what then should be
done with Paullus's earlier personal combat during the initial cavalry action (3.116.1)? Such cavalry combat helped protect the flanks of the infantry as it advanced,[39] but in Polybius's conception of Cannae it was certainly subordinate to the main fighting, which was with the infantry itself
(3.116.1–2). It is therefore hard to see how the consul's risking his life in
the preliminary engagement could have been considered wise. Indeed,
in both Livy and Plutarch the consul's personal participation in the cavalry action actually leads to confusion and defeat, because of the desire
of the Roman cavalry to protect him after he is unhorsed.[40] Moreover, in
Plutarch's *Fabius,* Paullus in his last moments is presented as giving up
his life in despair, whereas his colleague, Varro, escapes to begin the practical task of reorganizing the Roman resistance to Hannibal (16.5–6). This
is hardly the picture Polybius draws—a picture that emphasizes, with
great satisfaction, Paullus's physical bravery from the beginning of the
battle right through to the end.[41]

If traditions on the crucial moments at Cannae were somewhat diver-
gent, however, what has been shown so far in this chapter is how consistent Polybius is in his admiration for the physical courage in battle displayed by commanding generals—and how unforgiving he is when he
suspects (even in someone like Aratus of Sicyon) the presence of physical
cowardice. I would conclude that whatever ties Polybius had with the
Aemilii, and whatever sources the historian had at his disposal concerning the behavior of Varro and Paullus at Cannae, his account is not intended as mere pro-Aemilian propaganda. The moralizing contrast between the two men is sincere and meant to be taken seriously. It is
congenial to Polybius's general conception of a commander's duty.

One final example will help bear this out. As already noted in Chapter
I, Polybius and his friend Scipio Aemilianus participated—while Aemilianus was commander-in-chief of the Roman siege—in a dangerous small-
unit attack on one of the gates of Carthage (Amm. Marc. 24.2.16–17).
The storming of the gate was presented by Polybius as a glorious act—so
glorious that it gave inspiration to the Emperor Julian some five hundred
years later (ibid.). Yet it was not even part of the culminating Roman

39. For discussion of Hellenistic tactics, see now Bar-Kochva, *Judas Maccabaeus,* chap. 1.
40. Livy 22.49.1–2; Plut. *Fab.* 16.4. This tradition is totally missing from Polybius's account (cf. 3.116.1).
41. Elsewhere, however, Plutarch does present a more "Polybian" picture of Cannae,
with Paullus's bravery contrasted with Varro's shameful flight (*Aem.* 2.2).

assault on the city, for it is missing from the sources that narrate the general course of the siege; it was merely a subsidiary event.[42] Aemilianus's conduct would thus seem to diverge sharply from Polybius's advice in Books 10 and 11 that a general should be very concerned for his own physical safety, especially when the fate of his army is not at risk. But we have seen that despite the comments in Books 10 and 11, the *overall* trend in Polybius's attitude toward generals who place themselves in the battle line is the other way: in fact he can rarely resist praising such valorous behavior on their part, even when highly dangerous (or even fatal). Thus the story in Ammianus fits remarkably well with what we have adduced concerning Polybius's deep adherence to the "warrior ethos." And the sincerity of Polybius's attitude here is proven by a simple fact: he himself chose to share with Aemilianus in the glorious deed of the storming of the Carthaginian gate (cf. Amm. Marc. 24.2.16).

HEROIC SUICIDE

If considerations of honor might, according to Polybius, require even a general (or a historian) to risk his life in the battle line, considerations of honor might equally require one actually to *end* one's life. Polybius in fact devoted considerable attention in *The Histories* to the idea of honorable or heroic suicide. But insofar as modern scholars have discussed this issue at all, they have not done justice to his position.[43]

The primary example of scholarly misreading of Polybius on suicide is 30.6–9, his discussion of the behavior of the neutral and anti-Roman politicians of Greece after the Third Macedonian War. The war, of course, had ended in 168 with a complete Roman victory. After it, Polybius says, there were three categories of Greek politicians who fell into trouble because of their previous conduct: those who had remained neutral; those who had sided with King Perseus but had been unable to convince their fellow citizens to follow them; and those who had sided with Perseus and had been able to bring their states into alliance with Macedon (30.6.5–8). Polybius's discussion here is lengthy. Its explicit purpose is to instruct his readers on their duty, and on how to avoid dishonor.[44]

From the group of politicians who had successfully brought their states

42. For the placement of Aemilianus's attack on the gate within the chronology of the Roman siege, see Walbank, *Commentary* III: 718.
43. To my knowledge, no systematic analysis of Polybius's attitude toward suicide has ever been published; there is only a scattering of scholarly remarks about various individual passages. In the major new study by van Hooff, *From Autothanasia to Suicide: Self-killing in Classical Antiquity,* Polybius is not even mentioned.
44. On the purpose of the discussion, see 30.6.4 (from the introduction) and 30.9.21 (from the conclusion). On duty and honor, note τὸ καθῆκον at 30.6.3 and τὸ πρέπον at 6.4.

into alliance with Macedon, Polybius singles out three Epirote statesmen: Antinous, Theodotus, and Cephalus. They deserve praise, Polybius says (30.7.3–4), because when Perseus fell they did not abandon their previous principles of life, but faced the situation squarely, and perished nobly and bravely (γενναίως). More detail is found in Livy 45.26.5–11, a passage clearly based on Polybian material.[45] It seems that Antinous and Theodotus took refuge in the town of Passaron; but when the Romans besieged it, the two men resolved to spare the townspeople by charging out alone into the Roman army, and dying in battle. To judge from the first section of this chapter, such a decision would have been especially appealing to the "Homeric" side of Polybian ethics (γενναίως, 30.7.3). Cephalus died under rather more mysterious circumstances, during the Roman siege of the town of Tecmon.[46]

Polybius then turns to those men who had remained neutral in the war. Many of them were accused of having secretly sided with Perseus. But, Polybius says, no proof was ever adduced, and so he praises them for submitting to trial and employing every means to defend themselves, rather than committing suicide (30.7.8): "For to end one's life when one is not conscious of having done anything unworthy . . . is no less a sign of ignobility [ἀγεννία] than to cling to life beyond the point of honor [παρὰ τὸ καθῆκον φιλοζωεῖν]."[47]

Finally, Polybius turns to those men who had tried but failed to win their states over to Macedon; now, for the first time, his tone turns critical. He singles out two Rhodians: Deinon and Polyaratus. Deinon, though the evidence of his contacts with Perseus was overwhelming, senselessly tried to defend himself against the charges (30.8.4–8). But Polyaratus's conduct was even worse: he ran away, begging for sanctuary from Rome

45. On the Polybian derivation, see Nissen, *Kritische Untersuchungen*, 276–277.

46. There does seem an incongruity in Polybius's presentation here. The deaths of Antinous and Theodotus are considered noble (30.7.3); yet Theodotus, for one, *had* no worthy principles to which his noble death adhered (7.4), since in his previous appearance in the (extant) text, his conduct had been condemned as "evil and treacherous" (27.16.1). On the other hand, Cephalus's political principles were ones that Polybius did consider noble (27.15.10–12)—yet, to judge from Livy, his *death* was not particularly noble, despite Polybius's remarks at 30.7.3–4 (cf. Livy 45.26.11, with the comments of Oost, *Roman Policy in Epirus and Acarnania*, 81). Perhaps Polybius fitted Cephalus into 30.7.3–4 simply because the Epirote accepted his fate and died resisting Rome to the last. Or perhaps at 30.7.3–4 Polybius was simplifying and schematicizing in order to make his rhetorical point about valor.

47. Some scholars suggest that this passage is actually a defense of Polybius's own failure to commit suicide when charged with anti-Roman behavior in 168/167, and perhaps is even a direct response to direct accusations made against him in this respect: so Pédech, *Méthode*, 419 n. 68; Walbank, *Commentary* III: 429. But Polybius's public position during the Third Macedonian War had been pro-Roman, not neutral (see above, Chap. I). Thus Polybius's political situation both during and after the war was different from *any* of the three categories of politicians discussed in 30.6–9.

at one Greek town after another; thus he not only placed many other people in danger, but also made himself look ridiculous (30.9.1–20).

Walbank has remarked that this passage on the fate of the Greek politicians of 168/167 "must appear to a modern reader as one of the most despicable Polybius ever wrote"; further, it shows Polybius as "first and foremost a political realist with no sympathy at all for the man who proves to have backed the wrong horse." Similarly, Walbank agrees with Wilhelm Otto in strongly condemning "the icy calm" with which Polybius describes the pathetic wanderings of Polyaratus. Prominent scholars thus depict Polybius's discussion in 30.6–9 as a prime example of his "Machiavellianism."[48] By contrast, K.-E. Petzold has argued that throughout 30.6–9 we actually find ourselves in the traditional Greek ethical world of "the honorable" versus "the shameful," the καλόν and the αἰσχρόν.[49] Petzold has not been followed.[50] But he is surely correct.

Thus Antinous, Theodotus, and Cephalus certainly "backed the wrong horse"; but Polybius, instead of being "unsympathetic" to them, warmly praises their principles, and their adherence to those principles even in circumstances of extreme adversity (30.7.3–4). The only men for whom Polybius lacks sympathy are Deinon and Polyaratus—on account especially of their "cowardice" (ἀγεννία, 30.9.1 and 21), also their "lack of wisdom" (ἀβουλία, 9.1). But the problem is not their having chosen the losing side in the war. It is that they added *shame* to defeat, by clinging desperately to life after the war (φιλοζωοῦντες), when they should not have (30.8.3; cf. παρὰ τὸ καθῆκον φιλοζωεῖν, 30.7.8). Since Polybius also says that it was this cowardly behavior, and this alone, that removed Deinon and Polyaratus from the pity and pardon of posterity (30.8.3), it follows that Polybius believed the other men discussed in 30.6–9 *were* fully deserving of those tender feelings—despite having lost the war. Indeed, Polybius was explicitly worried that he would be misinterpreted here, and thus appended to 30.9 the comment that in recounting the tale of Polyaratus's pathetic wanderings, his point was not to gloat over Polyaratus's misfortunes—which would, he says, be "completely inappropriate"

48. Walbank, "Polybius and Macedonia," 304; cf. "Political Morality," 11; *Polybius,* 87 (where Polybius's attitude toward the pro-Macedonian politicians of 171–168 is termed "brutally uncompromising," for they had "committed the ultimate sin—they had failed"); and *Commentary* III: 430, with Otto, *Zeit des 6. Ptolemaers,* 89 n. 6 (on Polyaratus). See also Sacks, *Polybius on the Writing of History,* 136 and n. 30; and now Ferrary, *Philhellénisme et impérialisme,* 549 and n. 9. Gruen, "Rome and Rhodes in the Second Century," 61 and 81, argues that the main point of the negative depiction of the two Rhodian politicians for Polybius was to make his own conduct during the Third Macedonian War look better to the Romans.

49. *Methode des Polybios,* 60 (a brief but cogent discussion, based on 30.7.4, 7.8, 8.3, 9.10, and 9.21). A similar earlier judgment: Wunderer, *Polybios,* 13 (citing the first three passages).

50. See the authors cited in n. 48. An exception is Petzold's own student Meissner, for whom the heavily moralizing tone of 30.6–9 seems self-evident ("Polybios," 334 and n. 223).

(ἄτοπόν γε . . . τελέως)—but rather to demonstrate to his audience which course of conduct in such unfortunate circumstances was the better (βέλτιον, 9.21).

In what sense does Polybius mean "better"? Sacks in particular has argued that any benefit to the reader from contemplation of 30.6–9 is intended by Polybius to be in terms of practical politics, not ethics; the seeming focus on the preservation of "honor" is in fact pragmatic—a utilitarian political stroke, intended as a way of substantiating one's previous political success and reputation.[51] But it is rather hard to see how suicide would—in *practical* terms—substantiate one's previous political success. Moreover, the previous political success of Deinon and Polyaratus was itself, Polybius's view, based on courage and daring (τόλμη, παράβολος): ethical principles (30.8.3), which they now betrayed. Polybius in 30.6–9 was certainly concerned with the preservation of reputation (τὸ δοκοῦν, 30.8.3), but—once again—for Polybius, reputation does not accumulate in a vacuum. It is based on actual previous behavior, undertaken within an ethical framework. By "better" at 30.9.21, Polybius is therefore most likely to mean not merely "wiser" but "more honorable"—morally better. It is not "Machiavellian" for Polybius to investigate how a statesman faced with political catastrophe can nevertheless preserve a modicum of dignity and honor amid the wreck.

The point that Polybius was attempting to make in 30.6–9, and that— as he feared—has often been misinterpreted, is further clarified by an examination of other passages in *The Histories* where Polybius discusses the relationship between honor and suicide.[52]

An interesting beginning here can be made with a Carthaginian. Polybius warmly praises Hasdrubal, the brother of Hannibal, for the way he faced catastrophe at the battle of the Metaurus in 207. As long as the outcome of the battle was in doubt, Hasdrubal neglected no action that might lead to victory (11.2.1–11); but when total defeat loomed, he chose to die fighting (2.11). Polybius strongly approves: this was congruent with the forcefulness of Hasdrubal's entire personality; he was a man who always acted "with noble spirit and courage" (καλῶς καὶ γενναίως), just like

---

51. *Polybius on the Writing of History*, 136 and n. 30.

52. The sources of Polybius's ideas on the justification for suicide are likely to have been varied and eclectic, and are not recoverable now. He was the product of a good but rather old-fashioned education (see Chap. I)—and, of course, had a highly varied life experience. Some of his ideas seem to parallel those of the Stoics (compare Polyb. 30.4.16, and perhaps Livy [P] 45.26 on Antinous and Theodotus, with Diog. Laert. 7.130: suicide in defense of one's country or one's friends). Some of his ideas seem to parallel those of the Platonists (compare Polyb. 5.38–39, 11.2, and 38.20 with Pl. *Laws* 873C–D, cf. *Phaedo* 61B–62D: suicide to avoid dishonor). But at 5.38–39, Polybius draws explicitly on Homer himself for the justification (*Il.* 22.304–5; see below). Polybius was certainly a man capable of making his own unique (and perhaps not totally systematic) synthesis on this issue.

his father, Hamilcar (2.3). And Polybius is explicit that his audience should take Hasdrubal's suicide at the Metaurus as exemplary behavior (2.4). He explains that most commanders consider only the pleasant consequences of success and victory; but they should also keep before their eyes what to do in the event of total disaster—although this requires the greatest forethought (2.6). As a result of their failure to look ahead, he continues, most act in defeat with cowardice and foolishness (ἀγεννίαν καὶ ... ἀβουλίαν), and therefore they make defeat shameful (αἰσχράς, 2.7).

Polybius will employ precisely the same phraseology (ἀγεννία, ἀβουλία) some twenty volumes later, in condemning the behavior of Polyaratus (30.9.1 and 21; see above). The difference is that here in 11.2 Polybius is *completely* explicit that he is intent on the avoidance of shameful conduct (αἰσχράς, 11.2.7)—that is, practical politics is not involved—and that defeat is not shameful *per se;* it is how one reacts to defeat that may be shameful. Thus he clearly feels that Hasdrubal dealt with his own situation in a most honorable fashion. And so that readers will not miss the point, at the end of his discussion of Hasdrubal (11.2.11) he reiterates the sentiments of 11.2.7: those who engage in public affairs should not *make* disaster disgraceful and subject to reproach (αἰσχρὰς ... ποιῶσι) by clinging to life when duty forbids it (φιλοζωοῦντες παρὰ τὸ δέον).[53]

The idea that it is not defeat that is shameful but rather one's possible reactions to it also appears at another dramatic high point in Polybius's account of the Second Punic War: the depiction of Scipio Africanus's speech to his troops before the great battle of Zama in 202. Polybius here presents Scipio as saying that if the Romans win they will win mastery of the world, but if they lose, then those who have fallen bravely in battle will still have the noblest of burial shrouds (κάλλιστον ἐντάφιον), that of having died for their country (15.10.3). Only those who run away will suffer horrid misery and great shame (αἰσχίστων, ibid.). Therefore, how base and foolish these men would be (ἀγεννέστατοι, ἀφρονέστατοι, 10.5) who would reject the greatest of goods—by which Scipio evidently means either victory or glorious death—and choose instead the greatest of evils (i.e., disgrace), out of mere love of life (φιλοζωία, ibid.).

Whether Scipio actually said something like this before Zama is uncertain.[54] Clearly, however, Scipio's speech as Polybius presents it emphasizes the same constellation of ideas found in both 11.2 and 30.6–9, including

53. Note the parallel, again, with 30.7.8 and 8.3., even to phraseology. Polybius's attitude is consistent. The heavily moralizing tone of 11.2.7–11 is recognized by A. J. Pomeroy, "Polybius's Death Notices," 414.

54. For discussion, compare Walbank, *Commentary* II: 456 (doubtful that much is authentic), with Harris, *War and Imperialism in Republican Rome,* 188 (arguing for basic authenticity). Polybius, of course, claims that the speeches in *The Histories* are all closely reflective of what

the ignobility and foolishness of clinging desperately to life in dishonorable circumstances. The sentiment that not defeat but shameful reaction to defeat was "the greatest evil" (τὰ μέγιστα τῶν κακῶν, 10.15.5) was obviously a sentiment that Polybius found congenial. Rather than run away in battle, it was better to die.[55]

The same admiring tone that pervades Polybius's depiction of Hasdrubal's actions at the Metaurus also pervades his account of the death of King Cleomenes III of Sparta (5.38–39). One would have thought that the ruler who had sacked Megalopolis in 223 could hardly be one of Polybius's favorite figures. Yet Polybius's narrative of the last actions of Cleomenes as a hard-pressed exile in Alexandria are positive indeed— on moralizing grounds.

Knowing he was suspected of being a potential plotter against the ineffectual Ptolemy IV, Cleomenes resolved to attempt an escape, though he knew his chances were poor (5.38.8–9). Polybius comments (38.9):

> Not that he believed that he would gain his object (for he had nothing on his side conducive to success), but rather, he wished to die a death of honor, without submitting to anything unworthy of the high courage he had always previously shown.

This is obviously Polybius's personal (and of course highly approving) interpretation of what was going through Cleomenes' mind at Alexandria in 219. And the statement at 5.38.9 is followed by a still more personal rumination (38.10):

> And I suppose that there dwelt in his mind and inspired him those words that are wont to commend themselves to men of brave spirit: "Let me not perish without a struggle or ingloriously—but rather in the working of some great deed for the hearing of men yet to be."

The quotation is from *Iliad* 22.304–5: Hector's last speech before his fatal confrontation with Achilles.

Walbank sees this whole passage, and particularly the quotation from Homer, as mere ostentatious literary ornamentation, adding little to the narrative.[56] I would argue that, on the contrary, Polybius here is actively entering in his imagination into Cleomenes' situation, and identifying with him in a most personal way. As for the use of the lines from Homer,

---

had actually been said, and are not mere rhetorical exercises (cf. 2.56.11–12; 12.25b.4; 12.25i.8; and 36.1.7).

55. Cf. the very similar sentiment in frg. 164 B-W: "To yearn for life and to cling to it [φιλοζωεῖν] is the greatest sign of ignobility and baseness [ἀγεννία, κακία]"; the context is unknown. The sentiment that the role of the hero was to stand his ground, win or lose, and not run away, was of course very old in Greek culture; see esp. *Il.* 12.310–28, with the comments of Griffin, *Homer on Life and Death*, 92 and n. 35.

56. *Commentary* I: 569; cf. 430.

this is hardly ostentatious; the lines were famous, and what Polybius seems to be doing with them is sincerely reaching out to his audience, on common ground, to underline and even ennoble the scene he is describing.[57] Finally, it is important to realize that what results in 5.38.9–10 is yet another passage where the standard of historical judgment is not mere success, but heroic action—win or lose.

Indeed, Cleomenes' efforts at Alexandria were unsuccessful. Hopelessly surrounded, in the end he and his men decided to take their own lives (5.39.5). Polybius once more injects a personal comment: "They died by their own hands, like brave men and Spartans" (εὐψύχως πάνυ καὶ Λακωνικῶς, ibid.). A final summation of Cleomenes' personality immediately follows, and is equally positive: "In a word, he seemed designed by nature to be a leader and a king" (39.6). And Polybius's favorable assessment of Cleomenes' final conduct appears again in a retrospective comment more than a dozen volumes later: Cleomenes, Polybius says, far preferred a glorious and noble death (καλῶς) to a life lived in disgrace (αἰσχρῶς, 18.53.3).[58]

Nor is Polybius's depiction of suicide as heroic in certain circumstances limited to the actions of males. This is shown by his presentation of the suicide of the wife of Hasdrubal, the leader of Carthage during the Third Punic War, at the moment of the Roman destruction of the city.

It was Hasdrubal himself who had vowed that the same day would see the end of Carthage and his own death; for, he said, "it is a noble funeral (καλὸν . . . ἐντάφιον) for right-thinking men to perish amid the flames of their native city" (Polyb. 38.8.9). Polybius comments that it is right to admire the noble spirit of Hasdrubal's words (τὸ μεγαλόψυχον).[59] However, "when we turn to Hasdrubal's actual conduct, we are amazed at his baseness and cowardice" (ἀγεννία, ἀνανδρία, 38.8.10). For Hasdrubal—a

57. *Il.* 22.304–5 a well-known passage: see the comments of Griffin, *Homer on Life and Death*, 95–98. The passage is quoted by Cicero, in commenting upon a crucial decision in his own political career (*Fam.* 13.15.1–2); and even, later, by a Christian bishop, who stresses—in Polybian style—Hector's bravery and manliness (ἀνδρεία) in the face of death: see *Eustathii Commentarii ad Homeri Iliadem Pertinentes*, ed. M. van der Valk, 618. Polybius himself considered Homer a "philosopher" (see 34.4.4), and evidently presented the young Philopoemen as studying Homer to inspire the desire for deeds of valor (ἀνδρεία again: Plut. *Phil.* 4.4). Von Scala suggests that Polybius personally did the same (*Studien*, 65).

58. Conversely, Polybius's very favorable portrait of Cleomenes' final conduct in Book 5 shows that this comment in Book 18 (in the context of an attack upon the sloth of the Aetolian general Scopas) is not mere anti-Aetolian propaganda. One may wish to view it, perhaps, as anti-*sloth* propaganda (see Chap. VIII). Another Polybian example of a commander who chose death over what he considered dishonor, and thus died at his post—an example evidently intended to be inspiring—is the story of Aenesidemus of Dyme, in Livy [P] 32.25. On the Polybian derivation of this passage, see Briscoe, *Commentary* I: 1–2.

59. Hasdrubal's phrase recalls that given Scipio Africanus in his speech before Zama: to die for one's country is a κάλλιστον ἐντάφιον (Polyb. 15.10.3, discussed above, p. 44).

tyrant and a glutton (8.11–13)—failed to fulfill his noble vow; instead, he saved his life by surrendering to Scipio Aemilianus (38.20). Polybius clearly delights in detailing the taunts to which Hasdrubal was subsequently subjected both by Romans (including Aemilianus himself) and by Carthaginians (38.20.1–10). Once more, as with King Perseus and even Aratus of Sicyon (see above), the specter of physical cowardice incites Polybius to instant disapproval. And among those who berate Hasdrubal for cowardice is his wife, a Punic noble: her bitter speech is reported in full (38.20.7–10). The text now becomes very fragmentary; but it is clear from Appian's parallel account that she followed up her speech by throwing herself and her children into the flames of the burning city— doing, Appian says, what Hasdrubal ought to have done (*Lib.* 131–32). Moreover, even from the fragments of the Polybian manuscript, it is obvious how Polybius described this scene: the onlookers are deeply moved by her act (συμπαθεῖς, 38.20.11). And this makes sense. Polybius had explicitly praised Hasdrubal's vow of suicide as an example of greatness of soul (38.8.10). The historian evidently concluded that it was Hasdrubal's wife who turned out to possess this noble quality.[60]

The above survey demonstrates that Polybius's praise in Book 30 of the Epirote statesmen who went bravely to their deaths in 168/167, as well as his criticism of the desperate and/or cowardly behavior of Deinon and Polyaratus of Rhodes, was no sudden departure in Polybian thought—a momentary rhetorical stance. On the contrary: both the commendations and the criticisms in Book 30 exemplify consistent Polybian themes, themes that appear in *The Histories* from the first (in Books 5 and 11), and that continue right through to their end (in Book 38). Those themes emphasize the struggle to achieve the καλόν in one's conduct— and the deep desire to avoid the αἰσχρόν. This is the traditional aristocratic world of honor and shame.[61]

But even more striking to modern eyes is Polybius's approbation of the mass suicide of whole communities. In *The Histories* there were at least four such incidents. One concerned the decision of the Phocians, when threatened by Thessalian invasion in the 480s, either to be victorious against the Thessalians or else die on the battlefield—and to arrange the slaughter of their families if they lost.[62] The story of the Phocians may

---

60. On how the fragments of Polyb. 38.20.11 fit into the story of the suicide of Hasdrubal's wife, see Walbank, *Commentary* III: 722. Polybius may well have been an eyewitness to this scene, for he was right at Aemilianus's side during the climactic stages of the siege and burning of the city (38.21–22, *passim*).

61. Cf. Petzold, *Methode des Polybios*, 60 (with the comments on p. 42, above).

62. The only remaining Polybian reference to the Phocian incident is at 16.32.1, where he mentions his previous discussion. Its approximate date can be established from other sources: see Walbank, *Commentary* II: 541–42.

well have been used by Polybius as an introduction to his account of the similar decision by the Acarnanians when they were threatened by Aetolian invasion in 211.[63] There is only one extant fragment of Polybius's account of the Acarnanian incident (9.40), but we know that he approved of their decision, since at 16.32.1 he refers to their courage (εὐψυχία) at that time. It follows that Polybius's judgment of the stern resolve of the Phocians was similarly positive.[64]

The third case of mass suicide is that of Astapa in Spain in 206. The original Polybian text here is almost wholly lost; detailed versions of the story only appear in Livy and Appian. For our purposes, what is important is the explicit intellectual rationale for mass suicide given by the Astapans when faced with the successful siege of the Romans (Livy 28.22.9–10):

> Remember, by the gods above and below, that liberty would have to be brought to an end that day, either by honorable death or by shameful slavery. . . . Let indigenous and loyal hands destroy all that was doomed to perish, rather than have the enemy offer indignities and insolent mockery.

The Astapans chose fifty men, under oath, to burn the wealth of the town, slaughter the wives and children, then kill themselves, if the battle were finally lost (22.7–8). And this is what occurred (23.1–2).

The point made by the Astapans in Livy 28.22 is that once their battle—and hence their liberty—has been lost, a choice still remains. It is a choice heavy with moral resonance for ancient Mediterranean people: the choice between honor and shame. In this case, honor can be obtained only by a voluntary death, which cheats the victor (and/or the situation) of the opportunity to impose shame. The sentiment is quite similar to those in the Polybian narratives of heroic suicide discussed above. The question is whether something like it existed in the original Polybian account of Astapa. The probability is high that it did.

Here the problem is complicated by the fact that Walsh, Walbank, and Luce all suggest that Livy's description of the siege of Astapa was heavily influenced both by the traditions surrounding Hannibal's siege of Saguntum in 218 (described by Livy some seven books previously), and by Polybius's account of the siege of Abydus by Philip V (which occurred some six years after Astapa, and much farther along in the Polybian text). In other words: Livy's narrative of Astapa is a conscious conflation of various

---

63. So, persuasively, Walbank, *Commentary* II: 542.

64. Hence Polybius's reference at 16.32.1 to the Phocians' ἀπόνοια—normally a negative word to him—should probably be translated here merely as "boldness" or "intrepidity" ("Kühnheit": Mauersberger, *Polybios-Lexikon* I:1, col. 196).

other siege narratives, and hence pretty much a free composition.[65] If so, then obviously nothing in Livy 28.22–23 can be postulated as having been derived from Polybius.

The Walsh-Walbank-Luce thesis has gone essentially unchallenged.[66] Yet it is based merely on certain similarities between the siege of Astapa and the descriptions of the sieges of Saguntum and Abydus: the choosing of fifty men bound by oath to kill the noncombatants in case of defeat; the eventual burning of the town.[67] But incidents such as Astapa happened in similar fashion throughout antiquity, so that too much can be made of the general similarity of these descriptions.[68] And on the other hand, the similarity of the three narratives is balanced by significant differences: at Saguntum, while there was a burning of the town, there was not—as at Astapa—a conscious and carefully considered decision for mass suicide (see Livy 21.14.1–2); at Abydus there was a conscious decision for mass suicide (which was not—as at Astapa—fully carried out), but no burning of the town (see Polyb. 16.30–34). Moreover, the Walsh-Walbank-Luce thesis requires Livy to have been reading far ahead in his sources, so that he used an event from well beyond the Hannibalic War (the siege of Abydus) as a model for his account of an event within the war. Yet Livy complains at 31.1.5 at the sheer amount of material on the Punic Wars he has ended up giving his readers—a fact that argues *prima facie* against the idea that he simultaneously engaged in supplementing his information on the Hannibalic conflict by reading far ahead.[69]

The strongest objection to Walsh, Walbank, and Luce, however, is that a much better candidate to be the source of Livy's Astapa narrative is the account of Astapa given by Polybius himself. Thus the fragmentary Polyb. 11.24.11, a description of Roman soldiers perishing in their greedy search for gold and silver amid the flames of a burning town, closely parallels Livy 28.23.4—the description of how Roman soldiers, in their

65. Walsh, *Livy*, 194–95; Walbank, "Livy's Fourth and Fifth Decades," 60 and no. 101; Luce, *Livy*, 188 n. 5.

66. It is briefly doubted by Briscoe, *Commentary* I: 103; but he offers no specific arguments, or alternative sources for the Astapa narrative.

67. Walsh, *Livy*, 194–95; Walbank, "Livy's Fourth and Fifth Decades," 60; Luce, *Livy*, 188 n. 5.

68. Cf. the comments of Catin, *En lisant Tite-Live*, 102.

69. This is why Walbank, "Livy's Fourth and Fifth Decades," 71 n. 101, opts instead for the idea that Livy drew his account of Astapa not directly from Polybius's account of Abydus, but from a source that had read Polybius and then applied Abydus as a model for Astapa. But this only recreates the problem at one remove—the stage of the unknown but Polybius-influenced source of Livy on Astapa; why should *that* source have read so far ahead in Polybius as to apply the model of Abydus to events long preceding it? Luce, *Livy*, 188, has to assume that Livy's complaint at 31.1.5 should not be taken at face value.

greed for gold and silver, perished in the looting of burning Astapa that followed the mass suicide. This shows that Polybius covered the Astapa incident—and in dramatic detail.[70] Just as importantly, the parallel in detail between Polyb. 11.24.11 and Livy 28.23.4 suggests that Livy here was in fact very closely following the Polybian narrative.[71] This hypothesis is supported by App. *Ib.* 33, an account of Astapa that closely parallels Livy, but is clearly based on a Greek source. Moreover, Appian's account of Astapa contains a reference to the idea that mass suicide under certain circumstances is to be applauded as a sign of courage and excellence— and because it cheats the enemy of total victory.

It seems far more likely, then, that in 28.22–23 Livy was closely following the Polybian narrative of Astapa rather than conflating accounts of the sieges of Saguntum and Abydus into a composition of his own. This Polybian narrative of Astapa was detailed, dramatic—and included praise of the Astapans for committing mass suicide rather than submitting to potential dishonor (e.g., enslavement).

We now come to the fourth case of mass suicide in *The Histories,* and the only one with a narrative that is fairly complete: the mass suicide at Abydus in Book 16. Here for once Polybius's attitude can be observed in detail. Yet—once more—it has been persistently misinterpreted.

In the autumn of 200 the people of Abydus were encouraged by Pergamum and Rhodes (then at war with Philip V of Macedon) to resist Philip's current advance into the Hellespont. The Abydenes initially held their own; but aid from Pergamum and Rhodes was insufficient, and eventually they opened negotiations. Philip's demand, however, was unusually harsh: unconditional surrender. The response of the Abydenes was at first despair, then determination. They swore an oath to conquer or die in battle, and delegated fifty men, under oath, to destroy the women, the children, and the wealth of the town should it ever appear that the Macedonians were on the verge of victory.[72] The ensuing Macedonian assault eventually brought Philip to the brink of success; but at this point the Abydene leaders, instead of beginning their task of slaughter and

70. See Walbank, *Commentary* II: 305 (very persuasive). Walsh (Livy, 195) argues that the obscure Astapa campaign of 206 needed to be "filled out" by Livy, by drawing in the Polybian material based on the story of Abydus; but Polyb. 11.24.11 suggests strongly that no "filling out" was necessary.

71. This implication of Walbank, *Commentary* II: 305 (see above), is—oddly enough— not drawn out by Walbank himself in "Livy's Fourth and Fifth Decades."

72. Philip's harsh attitude toward the Abydenes may well have come as a surprise. Not long before, he had been willing to grant negotiated surrenders to towns on terms similar to those proposed by the Abydene envoys and now rejected: compare Polyb. 16.11.5 (Prinassus) with 16.30.7 (the Abydenes); cf. also Livy [P] 31.16.5 (Elaeus and Alopeconnessus). The attempt by Golan, "The Events of Abydus," 400–401, to whitewash Philip is unconvincing (indeed, Philip's demand for unconditional surrender is never mentioned).

destruction, surrendered to Philip. The king took possession of the town; but when he saw most of the remaining Abydenes now committing suicide in a frenzy, he allowed them to continue, and few fell alive into his hands.

A grim story, and we have two detailed versions of it: Polybius's original account (16.30–34), and Livy's account (31.17–18), which is based on Polybius, but to which Livy brings his own perspective. The two versions differ markedly in tone. To Livy, the actions of the Abydenes are a shocking example of insanity, desperation, and mass hysteria—presented within a highly dramatic narrative structure and in a highly rhetorical Latin style.[73] By contrast, it is usually alleged that Polybius's presentation of the Abydus story is dry, detached, objective.[74] And Ladouceur has recently strongly reasserted Walbank's 1965 contrast that to Livy's Augustan sensibility the Abydus story is one of unrelieved horror, but that Polybius on Abydus "writes as a ruthless pragmatic historian whose criteria in judging an action are success and consistency."[75]

This is also Walbank's evaluation of the Abydus incident in his 1972 monograph on Polybius, where in fact he uses Polybius on Abydus as a good example of the historian's mental disposition: "ruthless, hard, realistic."[76] It is the purpose of the rest of this section of the chapter to demonstrate, however, that Polybius on Abydus is neither dry and detached, nor ruthless and hard. Though the emotions of Polybius concerning Abydus are different from those in Livy, his text is as dramatic in its own way as the passage Livy fashioned from it, and it is equally intended to move his audience—although in a direction opposite to the one Livy had in mind.

The predominant emotions within Polyb. 16.30–34 are profound admiration for the courage and determination of the Abydenes, combined with pity that they could not be victorious, and discontent with Tyche (Fortune) for allowing them neither the victory they deserved for their valor, nor even the fulfillment of their stern but glorious plan of self-destruction in defeat. Further, Polybius expresses deep anger at the Abydene leaders who betrayed the plan of self-destruction—and hence the chance for undying glory—by surrendering at the last moment to Philip.[77]

73. The groundbreaking discussion of the narrative structure and Latin style of Livy 31.17–18 is McDonald, "The Style of Livy," 168–70.

74. McDonald, "The Style of Livy," 168; Walbank, "Livy's Fourth and Fifth Decades," 60; cf. Briscoe, *Commentary* I: 107, and Walsh, *Livy*, 193.

75. Ladouceur, "Josephus and Masada," 108 and n. 42, citing Walbank, "Political Morality," 11.

76. *Polybius*, 178.

77. It is possible that Polybius also reported the governments of Pergamum and Rhodes for failing to provide Abydus with adequate military aid; that is the implication of Livy

Polybius's admiration for the Abydenes could not be more straightforward. His introduction to the account of the siege is simply a massing of compliments (16.30.3). The siege of Abydus, he says, was remarkable "for the noble spirit and the outstanding courage displayed by the besieged, which renders it worthy of memory and of description to posterity."[78] Throughout the narrative of the siege itself, Polybius then consistently praises the energy, valor, and ferocity of the Abydene soldiery, both at the beginning (16.30.4–5) and then in the last climactic assault on the town (33.1–3).[79] The historian's admiration for the Abydenes is repeated in 16.32.1–4, his general commentary on the decision for mass suicide. To Polybius their courage (τόλμα) surpassed even that of the Phocians (in the 480s) and the Acarnanians (in 211), which he had previously discussed: the latter peoples had valiantly resolved to conquer or all die when there yet remained hope to them of actual victory (32.1–3); but the Abydenes made their similarly valiant resolve at a time when they had no real hope of victory (32.4).

It is Polybius's wholehearted admiration for what he perceives as the courage and nobility of the Abydenes that forms the basis for his subsequent criticism of Tyche (16.32.5–6).[80] Polybius chastises the behavior of Tyche at Abydus because, as if in pity, she had set right the misfortunes of the Phocians and Acarnanians, granting them victory and safety, but she had chosen to do the opposite with the Abydenes: for the cream of the men died in battle, the city was taken, and the women and children fell into the hands of the enemy anyway (32.5–6). Polybius concludes that Fortune was grievously at fault to allow such a total catastrophe (32.5).

Polybius's statement that Tyche should have taken pity on the Abydenes (ἐλεήσασα, 16.32.5) is clearly intended to awaken similar feelings of pity in his audience. Such valiant people should have been given vic-

---

31.16.10–11, which is *prima facie* based on Polybian material, and which conforms to Polybius's previous criticisms of the sloth of Attalus I and the Rhodians in their war against Philip (see Polyb. 16.28). Golan, "The Events at Abydus," 389–404, esp. 404, argues that the resistance of Abydus to Philip was intentionally instigated by the Roman envoys present at Rhodes in 200, that the Abydenes were then intentionally left in the lurch at Roman insistence in order to create an "atrocity" useful for propaganda against Philip in Greece, and that, further, Polybius expected his readers to draw just these conclusions from a perusal of *The Histories*. None of this finds support in the ancient evidence.

78. θαυμάσιος, γενναῖος, εὐψυχία, μνήμης ἀξία καὶ παραδόσεως.

79. See the description of the Abydenes as fighting ἐρρωμένος (16.30.4), εὐψύχως (30.5), τετολμηκότως (33.1, part of a very dramatic account of the fierce fighting for the ruined wall of the town: 33.1–3).

80. Polybius's praise of the Abydenes is only reluctantly referred to by McDonald: "detached and objective" ("The Style of Livy," 168). Walbank, too, implies that Polybius's praise of the Abydenes is unemotional ("Livy's Fourth and Fifth Decades," 60). Contrast von Scala, *Studien*, 213, who (rightly) describes Polybius's admiration for the town's defenders as "unverkennbarer Hochachtung."

tory—or if not, should have been allowed to carry out their noble intention of mass suicide rather than surrender. But they were permitted to do neither.

The historian then explains how what he considers the second aspect of the Abydene disaster occurred. When the battle for the town wall ended with the Macedonians once more repelled but most of the defenders dead, so that the success of the next assault was assured, the time had come to fulfill the oaths of self-destruction (16.33.4–5; cf. 31.5). Instead, two of the Abydene leaders—Polybius makes sure to give us their names (Glaucides and Theognetus)—called a meeting of the town elders where they arranged to surrender to Philip, begging him for mercy (16.33.5). Polybius expresses bitter anger toward these men (33.4): "They threw away all that was splendid and admirable [τὸ σεμνὸν καὶ θαυμάσιον] in the original resolve of the citizens—in the hope for personal advantage."[81]

The idea that even in hopeless circumstances one ought to attempt the performance of some deed that would be "splendid and admirable" (σεμνὸν καὶ θαυμάσιον)—even if that deed can only be suicide—is, of course, a consistent Polybian theme. It formed the basis for his praise of Cleomenes in 5.38–39, and would form the basis of his evaluation of the Epirote versus the Rhodian statesmen in Book 30, or of Hasdrubal's wife in Book 38.[82]

One mystery does remain here. It cannot really be part of Polybius's indictment of Tyche in 16.30–34 that the Abydene noncombatants were ultimately prevented from death, since when Philip occupied the town, he did not stop the survivors from killing themselves (34.8). Indeed, Polybius describes the resulting scenes of slaughter in great detail (34.9–12). Why, then, is Tyche criticized, and why are the Abydene elders excoriated, for allowing the wives and children to fall alive into the hands of the enemy? The answer seems to be that whatever the nature of Philip's decision, the fate of the Abydenes had become, with the surrender, *his* decision—not theirs. His troops had taken control of the town, and could have stopped the mass suicide if the king had wished.[83] That is: the Aby-

81. Polybius may be implying that these men were cowards, or perhaps that they hoped for a reward for their action from Philip.

82. See above, pp. 42–43 and 47. Walbank, "Political Morality," 11, argues that Polybius's criticism of the Abydene elders for surrendering to Philip reveals "Polybius's ruthlessness in demanding consistency of action." But the source of Polybius's anger in 16.33.4–5 is surely not the mere failure of the Abydene elders to be, in general, politically consistent. Rather, it is their failure to hold specifically to the σεμνὸν καὶ θαυμάσιον (16.33.4), and to sacrifice this for some transient personal advantage (τὰς ἰδίας ἐλπίδας).

83. They could have rounded up the townspeople and put them in a place for safekeeping; if necessary, they could even have chained them in order to prevent them from doing injury to themselves (chains being readily available from the slave-dealers who followed behind every ancient army).

denes had been robbed of autonomy by the cowardice of the elders and the cruelty of Fortune; and having been robbed of autonomy, they had been robbed of honor. It was the fact that the Abydenes had become totally dependent upon Philip's "benevolence" that was, to Polybius, an intolerable and shameful outcome for a valiant people.

To sum up: far from being a "dry, detached and objective" account, and farther yet from being a "ruthless" narrative in which the sole criterion of historical judgment is success in the real world (in which case one might have expected the Abydenes to have been taken to task for resisting Philip in the first place), Polybius's account of the fall of Abydus was written to move his audience to admiration for—and sympathy toward—the besieged. But at this point in our discussion of Polybius's admiring and sympathetic attitude toward physical courage, none of this should be surprising.[84]

CONCLUSION

This chapter has had both a general purpose and a specific one. The specific purpose has been the reinterpretation of two types of behavior depicted in *The Histories* where Polybius's attitude has been deemed to be "Machiavellian": namely, commanding generals' fighting personally in the battle line, and the issue of suicide in circumstances of military and/ or political defeat. The reinterpretation of Polybius's presentation of these two types of behavior has in turn served to raise the broader prospect that the historian—far from being a consistent proponent of a ruthless standard of judgment based solely on success or failure in the real world—was often an enthusiastic purveyor of a rather traditional moral code of heroism, glory, honor, and duty.

In the case of commanding generals risking their lives in direct battle, it has been shown that despite some famous comments (which themselves turn out to be somewhat complex and ambiguous), by far the predominant trend in Polybius's thinking is toward hearty approval of commanders who engage in personal combat. Polybius metes out such approval to

---

84. Walsh, *Livy*, 196, praises Livy's literary artistry in structuring the Abydene narrative so that a dramatic hiatus is created between the surrender of the town and its final fate, by means of the appearance of the Roman envoy M. Aemilius Lepidus, come to deliver an ultimatum of war against Philip. But in fact Livy here is merely following the literary artistry of the original Polybian text (cf. 16.34.1–7). The appearance of a Nemesis figure (here in the person of M. Aemilius) at a moment of seemingly approaching triumph is, of course, a classic Greek literary-moral motif; and Polybius's audience has already been told that this confrontation with Rome will in fact set in train the eventual destruction of Macedon itself (see 15.20). Polybius's highlighting of M. Aemilius in this fashion (although something like this probably did happen historically) is yet another demonstration of the moral seriousness and literary care with which Polybius approached the whole Abydene episode.

the physical courage in battle of Philopoemen, Hamilcar Barca, Theophi-liscus, Antiochus III, L. Aemilius Paullus of Cannae—and many other commanders. Moreover, he extends this praise even though in some of these cases the commander's decision to engage in personal combat led directly to his death—with negative practical consequences for his com-munity. Conversely, Polybius condemns not only King Perseus of Macedon but even the Achaean leader Aratus of Sicyon (otherwise a Po-lybian hero) for what the historian perceives as their unwillingness to go into the battle line.

Polybius's attitude toward suicide is similar. Despite modern assertions that Polybius was "ruthless" and "pragmatic" on this issue, the idea he seems consistently to have advocated was that even in defeat and extrem-ity it was still possible (and hence required) to attempt, through suicide, the performance of the καλόν, the "noble," the "brilliant"—and that, con-versely, it was especially necessary here to avoid the kind of shameful conduct that made defeat truly shameful. This comes through in his ad-miring accounts of the deaths of Cleomenes III and Hannibal's brother, Hasdrubal; in the comparison he draws between the noble behavior of the three Epirote politicians in 168/167 as opposed to the base and cow-ardly behavior of the two Rhodians (a passage that has been much misun-derstood); in the comparison between the cowardice of Hasdrubal the Punic leader of 146 and the noble conduct of his wife; and in the praise heaped upon the Phocians, the Acarnanians, or the Abydenes (another text that has often been misinterpreted) for their plans of mass suicide in defeat.

Heroic suicide, suicide to avoid shame, to avoid adding the burden of shame to an already-existing defeat or disaster, or to make a last defiant gesture of stubborn autonomy in the face of overwhelming power: such action Polybius always found praiseworthy and moving. And insofar as he saw such action as a means of preserving and even enhancing personal reputation in the eyes of posterity, and saw part of the historian's duty to be the preservation and presentation of wholesome *exempla*, Polybius turns out to be the heir of a Homeric attitude toward life—not the pre-cursor of a "Machiavellian" one. This theme will be pursued further in the next chapter, as we turn from physical heroism *per se* to Polybius's attitude toward more general "deeds of honor," and to his attitude toward the acquisition and use of wealth.

THREE

Polybius's Aristocratic Ethos: Honor, War, and Wealth

The bookkeeping considerations of profit and loss ignore the fact that some issues can only be decided upon considerations of duty, dignity and honor.
—WINSTON S. CHURCHILL

INTRODUCTION

The purpose of the previous chapter was to establish that Polybius evaluated important categories of behavior, where people directly risked (or actually lost) their lives, on traditional Greek ethical grounds. The present chapter deals with his evaluation of behavior in somewhat less extreme circumstances, but circumstances where the dominant trend of his judgment remains rooted in the aristocratic traditions of honor and shame (the καλόν and the αἰσχρόν), rather than in pure utilitarianism. Two categories of behavior will be covered: the undertaking of war "for honor's sake"; and the acquisition and use of wealth, where rationalistic gain and loss are at their most concrete. If it can be shown that in these areas, too, the ideology of stern utilitarianism with which Polybius has been credited is mostly missing, then another significant step will have been taken in the transformation of our understanding of the way he perceived his world, and the kind of advice he was actually offering his audience.

WAR FOR HONOR'S SAKE

Like Herodotus and Thucydides, Polybius took warfare between states to be the fundamental and most important fact of international life, and the natural theme of historical writing.[1] This perception did not prevent

1. On war as the normal condition of relations between Greek states, with peace as the unusual exception, see de Romilly, "Guerre et paix entre cités," 207–20; Veyne, "Y a-t-il eu un impérialisme romain?" 796–801; and the remarks in Schmitt, "Polybios und die Gleich-

Polybius from attempting to analyze the specific causes of particular wars; indeed, such analyses are a famous aspect of *The Histories*.[2] Moreover, at the beginning of the main body of *The Histories* (in Book 3), Polybius presents a theoretical discussion of the causes of war, and here he evolves two general paradigms. First, there was the war begun by thoughtful statesmen, out of cold, rational calculation of the advantages to be gained balanced against the risks to be run, and founded on an understanding of the realities of existing international relationships of power. Polybius's example is the war against Persia conceived by Philip II of Macedon and carried out so successfully by Philip's son, the great Alexander; and the historian's tone is very positive (3.6). Second, there was the war undertaken without rational calculation, but emerging from sheer, unrestrained emotion. Polybius's example is how the anger of the Aetolians brought on their catastrophic war with Rome in 191–189; and his tone is very negative (3.7.1–3). When one adds Polybius's earlier statement that "no man of sound mind goes to war merely for the sake of crushing an adversary" (3.4.10)—that is, what counts are the practical advantages to be gained from such acts (4.11)—it is clear why some scholars emphasize these passages as characteristic of a hard Polybian pragmatism.[3]

Yet there exists another trend in Polybius's thought that deserves some emphasis: war undertaken not out of cold calculation, nor out of uncalculating emotion, but simply for the sake of honor. And it is important that such wars receive Polybius's strong approbation.

Polybius's most striking statements in this regard occur in 4.30–33, his review of the attitude of various Greek states at the start of the Social War. The Acarnanians, members of the Hellenic Symmachy, agreed to join the fighting against Aetolia immediately. In doing so, Polybius says, they acted nobly (γνησίως), for it would have been excusable if they had hesitated out of fear, or had deferred their decision (4.30.2): the Aetolians were their immediate neighbors, far more powerful—and the Acarnanians were isolated from any potential help from the rest of the Symmachy. In fact, the Aetolians had inflicted terrible damage upon Acarnania not long before (in the 240s and 230s).[4] Polybius offers a personal explanation for the Acarnanian decision (4.30.4): they were men of honor

---

gewicht der Mächte," 90–92. For warfare seen as the most natural theme of Greek historical writing, see esp. Havelock, "Heroism and History," 19–55.

2. For discussion, see esp. Pédech, *Méthode*, 99–203; and Mohm, *Anschauungen des Polybios*, 183–89.

3. Cf. Harris, *War and Imperialism*, 1; Mohm, *Anschaungen des Polybios*, 138; and Walbank, *Commentary* I: 301 (where the emphasis is on Polybius's strictly utilitarian attitude in 3.4 toward knowledge in general).

4. For discussion, see Walbank, *Commentary* I: 477, with 239–40.

(γνήσιοι), and such men place nothing before the performance of their duty (τὸ καθῆκον). Therefore, one should take the Acarnanians into any alliance (30.4–5), for although their military resources are slender, their adherence to principle and their love of freedom is great.

Polybius's highly positive evaluation of the Acarnanian decision is not connected with any enduring practical benefits they derived from it. It is true that they made territorial gains during the Social War itself, but within a few years the bitter enmity of the Aetolians would involve the Acarnanians in war with Rome—and an Aetolian invasion (211) that threatened the very existence of the Acarnanian people.[5]

Polybius continues his review of the attitude of the Greek states in 220 by contrasting the courageous behavior of the Acarnanians with the deceitful conduct of the Epirotes (4.30.6–8).[6] Then he chastises the Messenians as well (4.31–32). Although the Social War was begun because of Aetolian aggression against Messenia,[7] when the Symmachy declared war the oligarchical faction in Messenia persuaded the government actually to remain at peace, out of fear of Aetolian raids (4.31.1–3). Polybius now once again injects himself directly into the narrative. The Messenian oligarchs, he says (4.31.3), "were, in my opinion, mistaken, and strayed far from the proper course [τὸ δέον]." He means the *morally* proper course, since what follows is a disquisition in praise of risking war for the sake of honor and freedom (31.4):

> I myself say that war is a terrible thing—but not so terrible that we should submit to anything in order to avoid it. For why do we extol civic equality and freedom of speech, and all that is inherent in the very word "freedom" [ἐλευθερία], if nothing is more advantageous than peace?

To support this idea, Polybius then adduces the example of Thebes during the Persian invasion of 480. We do not praise the Thebans, he says (4.31.5), for having deserted the Greeks out of fear when the moment of danger came; the advice to remain neutral seemed plausible at the time (31.6), but was soon shown to be deeply disgraceful (αἰσχίστην) and harmful (31.7). He concludes with another volley of moralizing language (31.8): "For peace with justice and honor is the noblest and most advanta-

---

5. Eventual Acarnanian territorial gains from the Social War: see Walbank, *Aratos,* 123–24. The desperate Acarnanian situation when confronted by the Roman-Aetolian alliance in 212/211: Polyb. 9.40.4–6 with Livy 26.25, and Walbank, *Commentary* II: 182–83.

6. This incident, and Polybius's attitude toward it, will be discussed in detail in Chap. IV, below.

7. For the background to the outbreak of the Social War, see conveniently Walbank, *Philip V,* 24–32.

geous of possessions, but when achieved by baseness and disgraceful cowardice it is the most shameful and harmful of all." In a practical sense Thebes did suffer some harm as a result of its neutrality in 480—the Boeotian League was temporarily broken up—but this cannot be the "terrible harm" Polybius means. In good part, that is because the catastrophe is not physical but moral: the taint of baseness and disgraceful cowardice (31.8), the acquisition of deep shame (31.7 and 8). But deep shame would be a "terrible harm" only to someone for whom the concepts of the καλόν and the αἰσχρόν remained deeply meaningful.[8]

The Messenians ultimately fell into difficulties even on practical grounds—for because of their own undependable behavior they failed to secure any dependable friendships against their traditional enemy, Sparta (4.32.4–9). But Polybius's point here is merely that the policy of the Messenians in 220 was *both* ethically improper (4.31.2), and *also* self-defeating in practical terms.

Polybius believes the Messenians can be reformed. Thus while he hopes the present tranquility of the Peloponnese will last (4.32.9), he ends by urging the Messenians and his own Arcadians to cooperate wholeheartedly with each other should there ever be new trouble with Sparta (32.10–33.12). This advice *is* certainly utilitarian—but (once again) not only utilitarian.[9] It is in good part founded on the morality of obligation (the many good deeds that the Arcadians have performed for Messenia, 4.31.1–10)—and on the morality of courage and honor in a crisis, the disdain of fear and of peace at any price (33.12, repeating the idea in 31.4 and 8).

Walbank has rightly drawn a connection between 4.31–33 and a later passage in Book 4, on Elis. The Eleans had long enjoyed *asylia* (inviolability) because of the presence of the Olympic sanctuary, but it had lapsed when the Eleans themselves began to wage war, originally against Arcadia (4.73.5–74.2). Polybius advises the Eleans that now is a most propitious moment to petition the Greeks for reinstitution of *asylia* (4.74.8). For, he says, everyone would deem those people wrong who neglect a chance to obtain peace, a very great blessing, "with justice and honor" (μετὰ δικαίου καὶ καθήκοντος, 4.74.3). The idea recalls 4.31.8, and Polybius's point is apparently that given the present political conditions, the Eleans (unlike,

---

8. In addition to the temporary abolition of the Boeotian League (it was back in operation by the mid-440s), the Thebans were also forced (after a short siege) to turn over their pro-Persian leaders for execution. For discussion, see conveniently Sealey, *A History of the Greek City-States*, 270, 325. Whether the Thebans also had to pay a monetary penalty is uncertain, and hotly debated: for discussion, see Walbank, *Commentary* II: 180–82.

9. *Contra*: Sacks, *Polybius on the Writing of History*, 136 n. 30.

say, the Thebans in 480) can now have permanent peace in an *honorable* fashion.[10]

The moralizing tone of 4.31–33 and 73–74 is obvious; the problem is that most scholars have tended to view it as hypocritical. Insofar as Polybius's comments have been seen as more than clichés about war deriving from earlier writers (especially Thucydides),[11] they have been taken to be in actuality clever strokes of policy all aimed at strengthening the Achaean League against Sparta. His championing of Arcadian-Messenian cooperation has the explicit goal of balancing Spartan power (4.33.11), and the advice to Elis to become a permanent neutral subtly achieves the same effect, for the Eleans had often pursued a pro-Spartan policy; their permanent neutrality would thus deprive Sparta of an ally. In other words, behind the moralist stands only a shrewd and practical Achaean patriot.[12]

I do not think this interpretation of 4.31–33 and 73–74 should be accepted. To begin with, Polybius's ideas in these passages are not clichés. Thus Marsden has shown that the parallels between Polybius's ideas here and those of Thucydides are actually not very close. Of the Thucydidean passages most often cited, one (1.80.1) simply says that war is more dangerous than the uninitiated expect, and the other (1.124.2) that war sometimes leads to a more stable and lasting peace. But neither of these statements has an exact counterpart in Polybius; and the latter statement (a self-serving remark of the Corinthians in autumn 432) is in any case clearly proven false.[13] Other statements by earlier Greek writers, to the effect that everyone (or all good men) agree that war is bad and should be shunned, and that peace is good,[14] are exactly what Polybius does *not* say: for him, war is terrible but not the worst thing, and only a peace achieved with justice and honor is good.[15] Thus it is likely that in 4.31–33 and 73–74 Polybius was expressing his own personal and carefully thought-out opinions about the ethics of peace and war.[16] But if so, then

10. The connection between 4.31–33 and 4.73–74: Walbank, *Commentary* I: 527. The Arcadian-Elean border conflicts, starting in the fourth century: see *RE* 5:2, s.v. "Elis," cols. 2398–99. In fact, it is doubtful that Elean *asylia* ever really existed: see now Bauslaugh, *The Concept of Neutrality in Classical Greece*, 42–43.

11. First suggested by von Scala, *Studien*, 306; cf. Walbank, *Commentary* I: 478.

12. So Walbank, *Commentary* I: 478 and 527; *id.*, *Polybius*, 20; accepted with variations by Pédech, *Méthode*, 547; Petzold, *Methode des Polybios*, 100 and n. 1; Lehmann, "Polybios," 189–92.

13. Marsden, "Polybius as Military Historian," 282–84.

14. Eurip. *Troad.* 400; Thuc. 4.62.6; Xen. *Hieron* 2.7 (cf. von Scala, *Studien*, 306).

15. Walbank, *Commentary* I: 478, recognizes that the passage from Euripides is not a parallel to Polybius.

16. Cf. Marsden, "Polybius as Military Historian," 283. Note also the sentiment in frg. 5 B-W (the context is unknown), which implies that death is preferable to loss of honor and freedom of speech. The parallel with 4.31.3–4 is clear.

it becomes much less probable that his statements were simultaneously meant only as a camouflage for what was in reality a sinister grand strategy aimed at Sparta.

Further, although the proponents of the "anti-Sparta" thesis agree that Polyb. 4.31–33 and 73–74 are cleverly coordinated insertions into the original text of Book 4, they are unable to agree on what caused Polybius to insert these passages. A period of increased Spartan-Achaean tensions seems required; hence Walbank suggests that 4.31–33 and 73–74 were written around 150/149 and reflect the sudden growth of Spartan-Achaean tensions after 150.[17] Yet Polybius was extremely busy between 150 and 145, his attention focused overwhelmingly on the West (Spain, then Africa), and only briefly in the Peloponnese at all. During these busy years, how much time would he have had for deep considerations of Peloponnesian conditions, and to revise the early text of his *Histories* accordingly? On the other hand, before 151—when Polybius did have time to write—Spartan relations with Achaea were not yet a major issue.[18]

Alternative reconstructions are no more satisfactory. Lehmann suggests that 4.31–33 and 73–74 are coordinated insertions written shortly after 145.[19] But while Polybius had the leisure once more to write after 145, the passages in question assume a Greek freedom of political maneuver that no longer existed at that time. Indeed, after Rome's settlement of Peloponnesian affairs in 145/144, any attempt to create a new anti-Spartan combination in the Peloponnese would have been little short of suicidal.[20] By contrast, Petzold suggests that the passages were originally part of Polybius's encomiastic biography of Philopoemen, and would date their composition—and hence the circumstances in the Peloponnese which the passages reflect—to the 180s.[21] But it is not clear that the *Philopoemen* should be dated as early as the 180s; and in any case, Polybius's friendly (if also admonishing) tone toward the Messenians—the executioners of Philopoemen in 182—ill fits such a context.[22]

There is another, simpler possibility. Perhaps 4.31–33 and 73–74 are not clever insertions at all, but rather were part of the original draft of Book 4. Thus Polybius's comments on "the present" (νῦν, 4.32.9 and 74.8) would reflect the relatively peaceful conditions in the Peloponnese

17. *Commentary* I: 478; *Polybius,* 20.
18. See the comments of Pédech, *Méthode,* 547 n. 181; Lehmann, "Polybios," 190.
19. "Polybios," 189–92.
20. This was pointed out long ago by Thommen, "Über die Abfassungszeit der Geschichten des Polybius," 219; cf. Pédech, *Méthode,* 547 n. 181.
21. *Methode des Polybios,* 100 and n. 1; Petzold believes, however, that a date of composition in the late 140s is also possible (100 n. 1).
22. For the execution of Philopoemen by the Messenians, see above, Chap. II, p. 32 and n. 17.

in (say) 160. But the main point is that the historian's comments would then simply be his momentary reaction to the actual historical events of the Social War, as he was describing them step by step: Acarnania and Messenia early in the volume (events of 220), Elis somewhat later (events of winter 219/218). One should remember, after all, that the Acarnanians *did* take a great risk in joining the Hellenic Symmachy in its war against Aetolia; the Messenians *did* refuse, oddly enough, to partake in a war begun in good part because of Aetolian aggression against Messenia; and the Eleans *were* severely plundered by Philip V's army in winter 219/218 (4.73.4–5), which might not have happened if they had been neutral at the time, instead of allies of Aetolia. There is no need for any oversubtle "anti-Spartan" interpretation. In other words: while Walbank was correct to posit a philosophical or ethical link between 4.31–33 and 73–74, the philosophical-ethical link is the only link that exists.

One might still want to argue, however, that Polybius's praise of the Acarnanians and his admonitions to the Messenians—though *encoded* in moralizing language—are ultimately founded merely on the extent of their support for Achaea in the specific crisis of 220. No one, so far as I know, has suggested this, because scholars have been too intrigued with the clever "anti-Spartan" hypothesis instead. Like the latter, this interpretation of course requires Polybius to be a hypocrite—though now perhaps an unconscious one. The final test of the moral seriousness and sincerity of 4.31–33 and 73–74 will thus have to depend on the frequency of passages elsewhere in *The Histories* where the themes of war for honor's sake, and/or peace achieved but only with honor, are raised.

Polybius in fact passes this test. These themes do appear both before and after Book 4, and often in circumstances far removed from the politics of the Peloponnese.

The earliest example is the behavior of the Carthaginians in rejecting peace with Rome in winter 256/255 (Polyb. 1.31). The campaign of 256 had been disastrous for Carthage: the great naval defeat at Ecnomus, the subsequent Roman invasion of Africa itself, the defeat of the Punic armies there, and the growing prospect of a Roman siege of the now-isolated and weakened capital.[23] When the Roman commander M. Atilius Regulus offered peace negotiations, the Carthaginians willingly accepted (Polyb. 1.31.4–5). But Regulus's terms for peace were so harsh—they probably included the Punic evacuation of Sicily and Sardinia, the payment of a war indemnity, and the demilitarization of Carthage—and his personal demeanor was so arrogant and insulting, that the envoys reported back

---

23. For detailed discussion of the campaign of 256/255, see esp. de Sanctis, *Storia dei Romani* III:1, 136–48.

to the Carthaginian senate negatively (31.5–7).[24] The envoys argued that Regulus was offering not peace but subjection, and Polybius continues (1.31.8):

> The senate of the Carthaginians, upon hearing the peace proposals, though they had given up all hope of safety, nevertheless took a stand of such manliness and nobility [ἀνδρώδως . . . καὶ γενναίως] that they chose to undertake any and all hardships and any kind of toil and exertion, rather than submit to anything ignoble [ἀγεννές], or unworthy of their previous achievements.

That is: the Carthaginians chose to fight on, in apparently hopeless circumstances, rather than accept a peace viewed as disgraceful. And Polybius praises them for it.[25]

Walbank downplays the ethical significance of this passage, arguing that Polybius's praise of Punic behavior here merely reflects the bias of his source, the pro-Punic writer Philinus of Agrigentum.[26] But even if Polybius based his account of 256/255 on Philinus, Polybius was a sophisticated intellectual, not a copying machine—and he was well aware of Philinus's biases (see 1.14.3).[27] Indeed, the praise of the Carthaginians for not doing anything unworthy of their previous achievements exactly parallels Polybius's praise of the Epirote statesmen of 168/167 and of Cleomenes III of Sparta, discussed in Chapter II, above. Thus even if Polybius did find praise of the Carthaginian action in Philinus, he must have used it because he found its basic ideas congenial to his own view of proper behavior.[28]

A similar Polybian attitude toward a refusal to make peace in a less than honorable situation appears in his depiction of the Roman decision, crucial for world history, to continue the war against Hannibal after the Roman defeat at Cannae (summer 216). Polybius carefully arranges his narrative and rhetoric to underscore the extent of the Roman catastrophe (3.118.1–8). This is accomplished in part by passing over in silence what seems to have been a quite significant victory won in Spain by P.

---

24. For the details of Regulus's terms, see Dio frg. 43.22–23, with the comments of Schmitt, *Staatsverträge* III: 154. On the theme of Regulus's arrogance, see Mix, *Marcus Atilius Regulus: Exemplum Historicum*, chap. 1.

25. The Carthaginians, of course, would go on to defeat Regulus unexpectedly; but since they still eventually lost the war—after 15 more years of expense and suffering—the decision of 256/255 would appear highly problematic from a purely utilitarian perspective.

26. *Commentary* I: 91.

27. Polybius no copying machine: see esp. Badian, "Review of La Bua," 208. Polybius's awareness of Philinus's bias: see Meister, *Historische Kritik bei Polybios*, 127–42.

28. Note that the Punic resolve to *act* (1.31.8)—even in desperate circumstances—is especially parallel to Polybius's positive depiction of Cleomenes III's attitude in his last desperate days (5.38–39).

and Cn. Cornelius Scipio sometime after Cannae.[29] In addition, Polybius chronologically links Cannae itself with the annihilation of a second large Roman army, by Celts in the Po Valley (3.118.6)—a calamity that in reality occurred much later in 216.[30] Finally, Polybius offers explicit comments consistently emphasizing Rome's almost helpless situation. Thus after Cannae "all eyes were now turned toward the Carthaginians," while the Romans, abandoning hope of maintaining any supremacy in Italy, were instead in great fear that the city itself would soon be taken (3.118.3–5); "it seemed to the Romans as if Fortune herself were fighting in league with the enemy," and the city was convulsed with panic (118.6); "the Romans seemed now beyond question to be beaten, and had lost their reputation for skill in war" (ibid.).

Yet Polybius also informs his audience that Rome would survive, go on to defeat Carthage, and soon become master of the world (3.118.9). He says this startling reversal occurred because of the unique qualities of the Roman state—and by means of "the brave, noble counsels" of the Senate (βουλεύεσθαι καλῶς, ibid.). Indeed, Polybius has already depicted the Senate as deliberating about the terrible situation "in manly fashion" (ἀνδρώδως, 118.7). Walbank would ascribe the praise of senatorial courage here to Q. Fabius Pictor, the Roman historian, whom Polybius may have been following.[31] But (once more) Polybius was no mere copyist—and he was as aware of Fabius's biases as he was of the biases of Philinus (see 1.14.3).[32] Moreover, ἀνδρώδως happens to be the very same term Polybius uses to describe the courageous behavior of the Carthaginian senate in refusing to make peace under "dishonorable" circumstances in 256/255—a passage that Walbank ascribes to the influence of the pro-Punic Philinus![33] Surely, what we have instead in 3.118.7 is Polybius's own personal and sincere opinion concerning the Roman Senate's conduct.

It is not until Book 6 that the audience fully learns what Polybius means by βουλεύεσθαι καλῶς and ἀνδρώδως. The deliberations of the Senate in this crisis, Polybius makes clear, included the rejection of any peace with Carthage—despite the Cannae disaster.[34]

29. On the implications of this silence in terms of Polybius's alleged pro-Scipionic *Tendenz*, see Chap. I, above. On the strategic importance of the Scipionic victory in Spain, see de Sanctis, *Storia dei Romani* III:2, 246; Lazenby, *Hannibal's War*, 128–29.

30. For discussion of the actual date of this Roman defeat, see Walbank, *Commentary* I: 448–49.

31. *Commentary* I: 449.

32. Polybius's sophisticated use of his sources: see above, n. 27. His awareness of Fabius's bias: see Meister, *Historische Kritik bei Polybios*, 142–49.

33. *Commentary* I: 91 (see above, p. 63).

34. This delay in detailed explanation is caused by the shifting of the geographical arena of Books 4 and 5 to the Greek East. The shift makes sense in terms of Polybius's chosen genre of "universal history"; but no doubt the delay also serves to create a certain dramatic

Book 6 is famous, of course, for its exposition of the virtues of "the mixed constitution." Polybius ascribes Rome's survival in the Hannibalic War (and specifically the survival of the governmental structure in the face of military catastrophe) in good part to the stability provided by the "balance" of Rome's three coequal branches of government (6.3–18). Nothing in the following discussion minimizes that point.[35] But Book 6 also contained much more than an exposition of Roman political institutions; it was a description of Rome's entire way of life.[36] And in the later part of the volume, Polybius's special emphasis is on how the institutions of Roman society in the Hannibalic period produced not only honest men (6.56) but courageous men. That is the point of his description of the pomp and ceremony surrounding Roman aristocratic funerals (6.52.11–54.6), as well as his recounting of the heroic tale of Horatius at the bridge (6.55): to show how Rome's institutions and traditions inspired men to seek the καλόν (55.4).

And in fact even Polybius's description of Rome's political institutions is not merely for the purpose of political science. In the introduction to the volume, he says that the test of any polity is its ability to act with dignity and nobility (μεγαλοψύχως καὶ γενναίως) during the deepest misfortune or the greatest success (6.2.6)—which is the story of the Romans since Cannae (2.7). This is not just a test of governmental political stability, then; Book 6 is about a test of character.[37]

The ability of a polity to act with dignity and nobility is in part based on its political institutions (cf. 6.3–18), but also on the moral qualities of the leaders produced by society (cf. 6.51–56). And the political, social, and even moral analysis of Book 6 leads eventually to a single incident (6.58). Polybius is emphatic as to its importance. In 6.51.5–8, he has already said that the superiority of the Roman state over the Punic state in the age of Hannibal was demonstrated by the fact that although the Romans after Cannae had met with complete disaster, the Senate by brave and noble counsel (βουλεύεσθαι καλῶς) won through in the end to victory. This phrase is an exact repetition of Polybius's description of the Senate in the Cannae crisis at 3.118.9. Now Polybius says that he will draw

---

tension. It was a well-known Greek literary technique: see Havelock, "Heroism and History," 40–41.

35. For discussion of this famous aspect of Book 6, see von Fritz, *Mixed Constitution*, esp. chaps. 4 and 6.

36. See von Fritz, *Mixed Constitution*, chap. 6. Also: Walbank, *Polybius*, 130 and 147–49.

37. *Contra*: Sacks, *Polybius on the Writing of History*, 136 and n. 30, who sees Polybius's judgment in 6.2 as sternly utilitarian, focused simply on how effectively the Roman constitution can perform amid rapid fluctuations of fortune. So also Eisen, *Interpretationen*, 74 n. 164 ("Der Nutzen des Staates ist das Wichtigste"). For 6.2 as emphasizing success or failure as a test of character as well as of political structure, see, rightly, Wunderer, *Psychologische Anschauungen*, 30; *Polybios*, 13; and now Meissner, "Polybios," 336–37.

together all the threads of his discussion of the Roman state and society, "making manifest its maturity and strength in the period under review" (6.58.1). That action is the refusal of the Senate to entertain any possible Punic overtures toward peace.[38]

After Cannae, Polybius says, Hannibal held about eight thousand Roman prisoners of war (6.58.2). He now sent a delegation to the Senate, offering to ransom these prisoners for cash. The delegation even included ten prisoners of high rank, who spoke on behalf of their fellows— but the *Patres* totally refused the offer (58.2–11). Thousands of Roman prisoners were thus sold into slavery, many in Greece.[39] Polybius says that he is giving only a brief summary of these events (6.58.1). Livy adds more detail: if the Senate's response to the offer about the prisoners had been positive, then Hannibal's chief envoy, Carthalo, had instructions to suggest full peace terms (22.48.7–9).[40] Moreover, Polybius himself says that the Senate answered the Punic embassy by declaring to the remaining Roman armies that they must either conquer, or die on the battlefield (6.58.11): that is, there would be no negotiations.

"Conquer or die" (ἢ νικᾶν μαχομένους ἢ θνῄσκειν, 6.58.11): such stern resolve on the part of communities in difficult straits wins Polybius's strong approbation elsewhere in *The Histories*, and it wins it here.[41] The Roman Senate, he says (6.58.8 and 13),

> neither yielded so far to catastrophe as to disregard the conduct proper to their own dignity [τοῦ πρέποντος αὐτοῖς], nor omitted anything required by

38. The intellectual link between 6.51.5–8 and 6.58 is noted briefly by Walbank, *Commentary* I: 736. The intellectual link among 3.118.9, 6.51.5–8, and 6.58 is noted briefly by Petzold, *Methode des Polybios*, 65 and n. 5.

39. These people were returned to Italy only in the mid-190s—twenty years later—as a result of efforts to please T. Quinctius Flamininus after the Second Macedonian War. See Livy 34.50.1–7, Diod. 28.13, and Plut. *Flam.* 13.4–6 (all based on Polybius); cf. Val. Max. 5.2.6. For discussion: Decrey, *Le traitement des prisonniers de guerre dans la Grèce ancienne*, 249; cf. Briscoe, *Commentary* II: 126.

40. Polyb. 7.9.12 (the text of Hannibal's treaty with Philip V) also makes it clear that in Polybius, Hannibal was hoping to conclude peace with Rome after Cannae. On the embassy of Carthalo, see Hoffmann, "Hannibal und Rom," 56–57—who notes the existence of *hospitium* between Carthalo and the family of Q. Fabius Maximus (Livy 27.16.5). Such personal ties with the Roman aristocracy would have made Carthalo a logical choice to lead an embassy that had as a task the presentation of overtures of peace.

41. See Chap. II, above, on the Phocians in the 480s, the Acarnanians in 211, and the Abydenes in 200. Cf. also Polybius's praise of his own Megalopolitans for their staunch refusal to make peace with Cleomenes III in 223/222—though the result was the destruction of their city (2.55.5–7 and 61.7–8). Polybian local patriotism is naturally suspected to be at work here—and perhaps even some exaggeration of Megalopolitan staunchness (see Meister, *Historische Kritik bei Polybios*, 104–7, and Urban, *Wachstum und Krise*, 193–200); so the incident is best not stressed. Yet even if Polybius exaggerated Megalopolitan staunchness in 223/222, that is an indication of the high value he placed on this quality.

the situation. . . . So Hannibal was struck with astonishment by the un-shaken firmness and the nobility of spirit [τὸ μεγαλόψυχον] displayed by the Romans.

Polybius does refer briefly here to the practical steps the Senate could take in this crisis (6.58.8). But his focus is really elsewhere: on the sheer moral nobility of the Roman decision to continue the fight. Given Polybius's reputation for practicality, one might have expected in 6.58 an examination of the great resources still available to the Roman state after Cannae. But Polybius's emphasis is entirely the other way: on Rome's *lack* of resources (3.118.4–8, repeated in 6.58.7). Thus in this truly climactic moment of *The Histories,* in the single action that will for Polybius exemplify all the virtues of the Roman state and the Romans' way of life (6.58.1), what wins Polybius's praise is not Roman rational calculation of physical resources, but rather Roman firmness and courage in the face of the most terrible adversity.[42]

In 6.58.13 Polybius sums up the Roman attitude in one word, a word heavily freighted with traditional aristocratic ideology: μεγαλοψυχία (nobility of spirit). The appearance of the term μεγαλοψυχία here is in fact a recapitulation of the point Polybius had made back in the introduction: that the true test of a polity (or a man) is the ability to bear the sharpest reversals of fortune, good or bad, "with dignity and nobility" (μεγαλο-ψύχως . . . καὶ γενναίως, 6.2.6). It is thus a concept that ties together this entire volume of *The Histories.*[43] The Romans' stern resolve to "conquer or die" (6.58.11) exemplifies for Polybius the *moral* superiority (μεγαλο-ψυχία) of the Romans, and from 6.51–52 this moral superiority begins to take on explanatory force. Combined with the stability of the Roman constitution, it helps provide a reason for Roman survival in 216; and it may even have implications regarding the eventual Roman success in competition with the other great states of the Mediterranean world.[44]

Of course, it might be argued that Polybius's evaluation of Roman conduct here, though again encoded in moralizing terminology, is in fact informed by political bias. After all, this section of *The Histories* was most probably composed before 150, at a time when Polybius was a political

42. For this latter theme as one that is prominent in *The Histories* (and typically aristocratic), see n. 28 above.

43. It is therefore worth interest that the word μεγαλοψυχία is missing from the lists of important Polybian terms presented in the index of Pédech, *Méthode* (cf. 634); Petzold, *Methode des Polybios* (cf. 206); and Walbank, *Polybius* (cf. 200).

44. Walbank, *Polybius,* 133, recognizes the moralizing tone of 6.58, but downplays the ideological importance of the passage, arguing that it merely functions as a convenient way for Polybius to reenter his narrative of the Second Punic War following his digression on Rome; so, too, Roveri, *Studi su Polibio,* 165. But cf. (briefly) Petzold, *Methode des Polybios,* 65 and n. 5.

detainee in Rome: what else could he do but praise the Romans?[45] Yet
Polybius's earlier praise of the Carthaginians—and in exactly the same
language (1.31; see above)—argues strongly against this hypothesis. As a
final test of Polybius's sincerity in underlining the theme of war for the
sake of duty and honor, three more case studies are therefore now offered. They deal with incidents of relatively small historical importance
where Polybian political bias is not likely to have been a factor in his evaluation of conduct, and they round out this section of the chapter.

First, as we saw in Chapter I, Polybius appended to his account of the
Seleucid siege of Gaza in 202/201 an essay praising the character of the
Gazan people (16.22a). They were outstanding, he says, in their willingness to keep faith (πίστις, 22a.3 and 6)—in this case, with the Ptolemies.
Against Antiochus III, however, their efforts failed; the city was taken
and sacked. Nevertheless, Polybius concludes that—as with all noble and
virtuous men and cities—the Gazans deserve special mention (22a.7).
That is: the Gazans fought their war against Antiochus for honor's sake
(to preserve πίστις)—and Polybius honors them for it.[46]

Yet so broadly apolitical are Polybius's standards of judging conduct
that just five volumes later he can also present a positive picture of loyalty
to Antiochus. In spring 188, the proconsul Cn. Manlius Vulso marched
on the strategic town of Perge, for he had learned that the Seleucid commander there had not yet withdrawn his troops, as was required under
the preliminary peace agreement now in effect between Antiochus and
Rome (Polyb. 21.42). Manlius intended to storm the town if necessary
(42.1). The Seleucid commander entered into talks, and explained his
situation: he was only doing his duty (ποιεῖν γὰρ . . . τῶν καθηκόντων,
42.2); he had been entrusted by Antiochus with the town (ἐν πίστει), and
he was holding it until informed what to do by the person who had be-
stowed this trust upon him (παρὰ τοῦ πιστεύσαντος, 42.3); but so far, he
had received no instructions (ibid.). The commander asked for a truce of
thirty days, to send to the king to find out what he should do, and Manlius agreed (42.4). When the commander finally received an answer, he
surrendered the town (42.5).

Polybius clearly presents the Seleucid commander at Perge as an honorable man who did his duty under difficult circumstances. He did not
surrender the town upon the arrival of Manlius with a Roman army, and
the implication is that he would not have surrendered the town without
explicit orders, preferring to withstand a siege or assault. As it happened,
the outcome of the incident was peaceful. It is a small story—but it dem-

45. Cf. Shimron, "Polybius on Rome," 99; and now Reiter, *Aemilius Paullus*, 20–21 and
32; and Green, *Alexander to Actium*, 278.
46. On the importance of 16.22a.7 for establishing the sincerity of Polybius's stated belief
that a major goal of history writing is inspiration to noble deeds, see Chap. I, above.

onstrates the pervasiveness of the ideology of honor, duty, and good faith (καθῆκον, πίστις) within Polybius's thought.[47]

The final case of war for honor's sake is that of Priene in Ionia in 155/ 153 (Polyb. 33.6).[48] Some years previously, Ariarathes V of Cappadocia had been driven from the throne by his half-brother Orophernes. King Orophernes later deposited some four hundred talents for safekeeping in Priene (Polyb. 33.6.2). But then Ariarathes—helped by Attalus II of Pergamum—drove Orophernes out; and as king, Ariarathes demanded back the money Orophernes had deposited (ibid.). The Prienians, however, refused to surrender the money to anyone but the original depositor, Orophernes (6.3; he was in exile at the court of Demetrius I of Syria: Justin 30.1.1–4). The result was that the armies of Ariarathes and Attalus devastated the territory of Priene, right up to the walls of the city (cf. Polyb. 33.6.6–7). The Prienians still did not give the money to Ariarathes, but appealed first to Rhodes, then to Rome (33.6.7). Polybius says that the appeal was fruitless (6.8). But an inscription from the temple of Athena Polias in Priene records a formal Roman note of protest to Ariarathes and Attalus over their attack, and since a copy of the decree was put up officially by the Prienians, perhaps it helped defuse the situation.[49] Meanwhile, at some point after Priene refused Ariarathes' demand, the money was actually turned over to Orophernes (Polyb. 33.6.9).[50]

It is clear that Priene suffered heavily for its loyalty to Orophernes; both Polybius and the decree of the Roman senate indicate that the extent of damage in the countryside was large.[51] Yet Polybius, injecting himself personally into the narrative, says that in his opinion the Prienians acted correctly (ὀρθῶς) in refusing to give the money to Ariarathes (33.6.2). Obviously, by ὀρθῶς here Polybius does not mean "in a politically advantageous manner"—since that was hardly the case (as Polybius explicitly says, 33.8.6–9). Rather, Polybius means that the refusal to give money to anyone but the original depositor was a *morally* correct act, and he approves of this act despite the destructive war against Priene that developed as a result.[52]

But at this stage of discussion, it should cause no surprise to find that

47. See the comments of Wunderer, *Polybios*, 15 n. 25. The story of the Seleucid commander at Perge has its parallel in the story of Aenesidemus of Dyme, who died at his post rather than formally surrender Argos to the enemies of the Achaean League in 198; this incident was evidently covered in detail by Polybius in the lost Book 17: see Livy [P] 32.25.

48. For the date, see Walbank, *Commentary* III: 547.

49. The Prienian decree: *OGIS* 351 = Sherk, *Roman Documents from the Greek East*, no. 6b (with a useful historical commentary).

50. For the relative chronology of events, see Walbank, *Commentary* III: 548.

51. See Polyb. 33.6.6–7; Sherk, *Roman Documents*, no. 6B, lines 1–3.

52. Perhaps cynical modern scholars would seek to detect a hidden political bias behind Polybius's moralizing here, since Orophernes was a political ally of Demetrius of Syria

war simply for the sake of honor (even a disastrous war) wins Polybius's praise. With a remarkable stability of outlook extending right from Book 1 (the Carthaginians in 256/255) to Book 33 (the Prienians)—with the most explicit ideological statement coming in Book 4 (the example of Acarnania set against that of Messenia in 220)—Polybius adheres to the idea of the moral correctness of war engaged in purely for honor's sake. Whatever complicating factors exist in any of the passages presented above, the evidence taken as a whole conclusively demonstrates that Polybius considered the willingness to undertake such wars—and/or the willingness to refuse to make peace except under conditions perceived as completely honorable—as a sign of high character (as with the Acarnanians), or even of national greatness (as in the example of Rome in 216).

WEALTH AND ITS TEMPTATIONS

For a personage taking a strictly utilitarian approach to human conduct, the realm of wealth offers an easy, accurate, and very concrete measure of success or failure: namely, profit and loss. But this is exactly the standard that Polybius does not apply to financial affairs. On the contrary: he views with firm approval acts of honesty, generosity, and/or self-restraint, even when financially disadvantageous; and he views with prim disapproval financial conduct that, while successful in terms of profits, violates his understanding of the καλόν.

Polybius's socioeconomic background was discussed in detail in Chapter I; here it is enough merely to note that he brings to these issues the perspective of the man of inherited, landed, and very substantial wealth. In a word, Polybius's socioeconomic background, his education, and his point of view were aristocratic—as was his audience. And this comes through in his heavily moralizing comments on wealth, and the temptations to which it is heir. As with most traditional aristocratic men, men for whom wealth was assured and existed as a given, honor—both in the public sense and as an inner feeling—was to Polybius more important.[53]

The historian's criticism of financial greed (even when such greed is successful) is in fact a constant. We have already seen a good example of

---

(Diod. 31.32; Justin 30.1.1–4), and Demetrius was Polybius's personal friend. Yet the picture of Orophernes in Polybius is itself harshly critical (32.11.1 and 10), and Polybius believes that Orophernes' right to the Cappadocian throne—though supported strongly by Demetrius—was in fact very doubtful (32.10.4–8). This is enough to show that the story of Priene in 33.6 is not likely to be motivated by any political bias in favor of Orophernes or the policy of Demetrius. It is the action of the Prienians, *per se*, that wins Polybius's positive assessment.

53. On this aristocratic attitude, as found in a wide range of traditional societies, see Kautsky, *Politics of Aristocratic Empires*, 187–97.

this attitude in Chapter I: Polybius's harsh disapproval of what he viewed as the irrational (though eventually successful) avarice of Alexander of Isus, the Aetolian statesman. It was disgraceful, according to Polybius, for a major political figure to act in this way (21.26). A similar point of view informs Polybius's criticism of the Rhodians ten volumes later. They had accepted an enormous gift from Eumenes II of Pergamum, which was to be used to support the Rhodian system of public education (31.31.1). Politically the Rhodians came out ahead here, since all Eumenes received in return for his generosity was a continuation of informal friendly relations—that is, nothing binding on Rhodes.[54] Yet Polybius rebukes the Rhodians for accepting the gift: they themselves were wealthy enough not to have to accept the subsidy, and therefore they should not have done so (31.31.2); it was an act lacking in pride and dignity, a violation of propriety (τὸ πρέπον, 31.31.3). In other words, avarice had won out over what Polybius considered fitting and proper behavior for an independent and prosperous polity. This was to be condemned.

Indeed, Polybius throughout *The Histories* consistently warns his audience of the conflict between avarice and honor. Thus he expresses disgust at the behavior of the Spartan ephors who in 219 were bribed one talent each to put the pretender Lycurgus on the Spartan throne—"so cheap had τὰ καλά become everywhere"—and he expresses satisfaction when these men soon paid for this act with their lives (4.35.15).[55] But then, Polybius is in general disgusted with the Greek attitude toward money: no one there, he says, ever does anything without a bribe (18.34.7).[56] The mores of Cretan society are particularly condemned in this respect, in a volley of moralizing language (6.46.3): "So much does the shameful love of gain and lust for wealth prevail among them [αἰσχροκέρδεια, πλεονεξία], that the Cretans are the only people in the world in whose eyes no gain is disgraceful [αἰσχρόν]." Again, Polybius believes that the customs relating to the acquisition of wealth are better at Rome than at Carthage (6.56.1), because at Carthage nothing that results in profit is viewed as shameful (αἰσχρόν, 56.2). Hence bribery, and the acquisition of wealth by improper means (ἀπὸ τῶν μὴ καθηκόντων), are common (ibid.), whereas at Rome the members of the governing class adhere to proper conduct (τὸ καθῆκον, 56.14).[57]

54. On this transaction, see now Berthold, *Rhodes in the Hellenistic Age*, 221 and n. 22.

55. On the moralizing tone of Polyb. 4.35.8–15, see esp. Wunderer, *Polybios*, 12.

56. For more Polybian castigation of Greek avarice and financial corruption, see 6.56.13–15 and 36.17.7. The stability of outlook, from early in the text of *The Histories* right through to the final volumes, is very striking.

57. Polybius's statement about the Punic attitude toward gaining wealth (nothing is disgraceful: 6.56.2) obviously contradicts his earlier statement that the Cretans were the only people in the world who suffered from that defect (6.46.3)—which only shows the rhetorical and ideological power that such an accusation about greed held for the historian. At 9.38.6

No doubt in the discussions comparing the forms of states here late in Book 6, Polybius is in part making a utilitarian point. The restraint on avarice exercised by the Roman ruling class was one of the reasons Rome in the period of the Hannibalic War was a strongly cohesive state (cf. 6.56.7), and hence able to withstand the stress of disaster. But the overall ethicizing tendency of Polybius's remarks is also difficult to miss.

This tendency also strongly appears in the long commentary that Polybius appends to his description of the turbulence of Cretan social life, a turbulence that he ascribes to the innate and shameful Cretan lust for gain (6.46.3; see above). For, Polybius asserts, there is an intimate connection between the customs of social life and the laws and the character of a polity as a whole (6.47). And those customs and laws are desirable that make people's private lives "righteous and moderate" (ἀποτελεῖ καὶ σώφρονας), and the public life of a polity "humane and just" (ἥμερον . . . καὶ δίκαιον, 6.47.2): customs and laws that are praiseworthy produce men who are praiseworthy (47.3). Conversely, disreputable customs and laws produce disreputable men—and therefore are to be shunned (47.2). Polybius continues:

> And when we see men whose private lives are filled with lust for gain [πλεονεκτικούς], and whose public behavior is unjust [ἀδίκους], then we have clear reason to say that these men's actions, their laws, and their whole polity is evil and ignoble [φαύλην].

Thus it is with the Cretans: their personal conduct is steeped in treachery (δολιώτερα); their public conduct, in injustice (ἀδικώτερα, 47.5).

Polybius's point in 6.46–47 is clearly not that such an ethos is the source of military and political weakness for the Cretan states in the international arena. His vision is much broader: he is expounding the principles by which to judge the moral stature of a community, and he is explaining what he sees as the origins of correct and incorrect conduct, both at the personal and at the state level. He draws a close connection between turbulence, injustice, and ignoble behavior; and at the center of this web of evil he places, in this case at least, uncontrolled avarice and lust for gain (αἰσχροκέρδεια, πλεονεξία)—the besetting Cretan vice.[58]

The close conceptual connection between avarice and general ignobility throughout this theoretical discussion of politics in Book 6 is shown

---

Polybius has the Acarnanian statesman Lyciscus make the same accusation against the Aetolians: "They think nothing disgraceful [αἰσχρόν] if only they gain from it."

58. Polyb. 6.46.3, 46.9, 47.4. Walbank (*Commentary* I: 732) sees Polyb. 6.46–47 primarily as evidence that Polybius was persistently hostile toward Crete. Contrast Roveri, *Studi su Polibio*, 191–92; and Nicolet, "Polybe et les institutions romaines," 243–44. For an example of Polybius's disgust at an act of Cretan treachery that yet was financially highly profitable for its perpetrators, see 8.36.9 (the case of Bolis and Cambyses).

also by Polybius's discussion of the degeneration of aristocracies (6.8). Here one of the major signs of the change from aristocracy into its evil twin, oligarchy, is the addiction of the elite to "lust for gain, and unscrupulous acquisition of wealth" (πλεονεξίαν καὶ φιλαργυρίαν ἄδικον, 6.8.5). And Polybius associates these evils with a more general corruption, including drunkenness, gluttony, debauchery, and the rape of women and young boys (ibid.).[59]

Polybius gives a further full exposition of what he considers the ignobility of avarice in his discussion of the monarchs Perseus of Macedon and Eumenes of Pergamum during the Third Macedonian War (29.7–9). He says that Eumenes offered Perseus the neutrality of Pergamum for a payment of five hundred talents, and offered to mediate an end to Perseus's war with Rome for fifteen hundred. An offer to bend state policy for the sake of money was, according to Polybius, something that even the miserly Perseus thought disgraceful (αἰσχρόν, 29.8.7). The two kings, he continues bitterly, now "fought to a draw in the contest for first prize in avarice" (8.9; cf. 8.3 and 9.1): Eumenes, in his lust for wealth, risked his kingdom via a potential quarrel with Rome, in order to receive a bribe that dishonored him as a king (τὰ μὴ καθήκοντα, 9.12), whereas Perseus in the end was too much a skinflint to risk the money Eumenes was demanding, even though the transaction would probably have helped him strategically and diplomatically (8.9; cf. 9.11). The historian cannot forbear a direct and personal comment: this dishonorable financial intrigue convinces him that "avarice is the peg of all evil" (8.10).[60]

In this discussion, Polybius connects avarice not only with ignobility but with folly.[61] The theme that lust for wealth drives men to folly, irrational risks, is in fact another consistent theme in *The Histories*. Not surprisingly: for Polybius pronounced it a general rule of human behavior.

Thus it is this compulsion of greed that explains why disciplined armies so quickly degenerate into pillaging mobs, neglecting every concern for military safety; "for most men risk their lives for the sake of gain" (Polyb. 10.17.1). Similarly, the stupid avarice of the masses at Cius for the property of others led them into the disaster of violent revolution and then tyranny; they should have known better, since this is what always

59. It is precisely this close conceptual connection in Polybius's mind between avarice and general ignobility that makes him so uncomfortable with the accusations of avarice made against Hannibal (9.25–26)—for he views Hannibal as a heroic figure (9.22.1–6 and 10; 11.19 *passim*).

60. πάσης κακίας . . . πατταλεῖόν ἐστιν ἡ φιλαργυρία. For the correct translation of this phrase, see Walbank, *Commentary* III: 369. The truth of Polybius's allegations concerning the financial intrigue between Eumenes and Perseus is debated: see Schleussner, "Pergamenisch-makedonischen Kontakte," 119–23. But that is immaterial here: Polybius believed the allegations, and his moralizing is based on that belief.

61. "Ignoble" behavior in general: 29.9.12. Folly: 29.9.1 and 12.

happens (15.21.3–8).[62] Polybius here is dealing with the greed of ordinary people; but it is clear that in his world, aristocrats and even kings are by no means immune. That is already shown by the examples above of Alexander of Isus, and of Eumenes and Perseus. And when at 32.11.1 Polybius once more pronounces a general rule that "not a few men, from lust for wealth, have delivered up their own lives in the hunt for money," his example is King Orophernes of Cappadocia—who lost his throne because of his oppressive greed.[63]

In connecting avarice with folly, Polybius is clearly concerned in good part with pragmatic outcomes; folly caused by lust for wealth can lead to political disaster, as happened to Orophernes, or the populace of Cius. Nevertheless, Polybius is equally condemnatory of Alexander of Isus (whose grasping behavior brought him a famous success), or the Rhodian dealings with Pergamum about 160 (which were equally profitable). Polybius's perspective here is thus broader than mere failure versus success. What he is disturbed by in all these cases is, rather, the lack of self-restraint or decorum displayed by those who seek wealth and profit above all else. Whether disastrous or successful, greed like this is deeply suspect to him as conduct that is *inherently* ignoble or "low" (φαύλη; cf. 6.47.4).

Polybius's concern over lack of self-control in regard to wealth comes out not only where unscrupulous greed is displayed in its acquisition, but also in his consistent emphasis on the perils of prosperity once wealth itself has been achieved. The employment—or enjoyment—of wealth in a suitable honorable fashion is viewed by him as an inherently difficult task.

The historian establishes the general rule early on. At 5.88.3 he announces as a simple fact that unless prosperity is handled with care and wisdom, it can actually inflict severe damage on states and individuals.[64] More detail is added in the next volume (6.18.5; cf. 57.5–7): polities that become exceedingly prosperous are immediately susceptible to moral corruption, for they become open to flattery, idleness, arrogance, overweening pride.[65] Specific examples of this phenomenon follow in the succeeding books: the Capuans (7.1.1–2); Tarentum (8.24.1).[66] And the dan-

---

62. The first passage is discussed in detail in Chap. VI, below; the second is discussed in detail in Chap. V, below.

63. Other examples: Polyb. 33.5.2–4 (Archias, the Ptolemaic governor of Cyprus, who destroyed himself by greed); frg. 96 B-W, cf. Diod. 29.24 (Seleucus IV).

64. For this idea, see also Polyb. 10.36.1, with its emphasis on caution (φυλακή) in success—discussed in detail in Chap. VII, below.

65. On the heavy moralism of Polyb. 6.18.5, see the comments of Wunderer, *Psychologische Anschauungen*, 17.

66. On the context and tradition behind Polyb. 7.1.1–2, see von Ungarn-Sternberg, *Capua in zweiten punischen Krieg*, 39–41. On the context and tradition behind 8.24.1, see Hoffmann, "Kampf zwischen Rom und Tarent," 11–24.

gers inherent in prosperity and ease are repeated in 11.25, where Polybius asserts as a maxim that internal corruption immediately follows upon the indolence that is the all-too-natural result of good fortune and plenty.

Polybius's theory connecting prosperity with the growth of indolence and corruption has implications, of course, for the fate of Rome itself. This will be discussed in detail in Chapter VII. But for now, note that Polybius directly predicts the growth of arrogance and extravagance as a result of Roman success and prosperity—in conformity with his general rules of human behavior (6.57.5–7).

But Polybius was not only concerned with the impact of great wealth upon polities; he was equally worried about its impact upon individuals. His general finding is similar: the possession of great wealth carries with it great temptation, and a severe danger of moral corruption. Thus it was because the middle period of Ptolemy IV's reign was peaceful and prosperous that the king at that time "abandoned the path of the καλόν" and instead led a life of dissipation and debauchery (βίον ἀσώτον, 14.12.3; cf. 11.2–5).[67] The Aetolian general Scopas—whom Polybius believes had a much better chance of staging a successful coup in Alexandria than had Cleomenes III some twenty years earlier—was apparently lacking in the correct energy because of his wealth (18.53.1–4; cf. 55.1–2).[68] The Ptolemaic official Polycrates had once been honest and energetic (18.55.5–6), but having amassed a huge fortune, in old age he wrecked his reputation by yielding to a licentious and depraved style of life (βίον ἀσυρῆ, 55.7). A very similar fate—indulgence in disgraceful conduct (ἀπρεπῆ)—befell Ptolemy of Megalopolis as a rich old man (18.55.8–9).[69] And Ptolemy VI, according to Polybius, became mentally distracted in times of success and good fortune, indulging in a life of debauchery and indolence (ἀσωτία καὶ ῥᾳθυμία, 39.7.7).

It is noticeable that in many of the above cases the indolence, arrogance, and dissipation caused by possession of great wealth leads to pragmatic political or military reverses. That might suggest (once more) that Polybius is applying a strictly utilitarian standard of judgment to the issue

---

67. It is possible that Polybius's picture of Ptolemy IV's dissoluteness and indolence is overdrawn: so esp. Huss, *Aussenpolitik Ptolemaios' IV.* But if so, this only serves to underline the historian's moralistic ideology: see Préaux, "Polybe et Ptolemée Philopator," 364–75. Not everyone accepts Huss's defense of Ptolemy's regime: see now Hauben, "A Neglected Detail of Philopator's Policy," 389–403, who emphasizes Ptolemy's megalomania and wastefulness.

68. On Scopas's greed, see also Polyb. 13.2.2. On Cleomenes' attempted coup at Alexandria in 221, see Polyb. 5.38–39 (discussed in detail in Chap. II).

69. Polybius evidently covered the delicts of Ptolemy of Megalopolis in detail, in a passage now lost (cf. 18.55.9). On the moralizing here, see Wunderer, *Psychologische Anschauungen,* 17.

of the "corruption" caused by prosperity. But in other cases, it is quite clear that to Polybius, indolence and debauchery constitute in and of themselves an abandonment of the καλόν (cf. 14.12.3)—and are to be condemned on that ground alone. Thus while Polycrates and Ptolemy of Megalopolis do not appear to have suffered any terrible practical consequences as a result of their dissipate styles of life, Polybius's account of their behavior is nevertheless harshly disapproving.

Given the above findings, it is not surprising to learn that Polybius in *The Histories* consistently gives praise to those who show self-restraint in activities connected with acquiring wealth. Similarly, self-restraint and moderation in the employment of wealth once it is gained also win the historian's explicit approval.

The most prominent personages in the first category are, of course, L. Aemilius Paullus the conqueror of Macedon, and his son Scipio Aemilianus. Polybius, in a discussion involving the decline of old-fashioned Roman morality in the age of overseas expansion, cites Paullus as an example of the original Roman ways of financial honesty and good faith (18.35.1–2).[70] After his victory at Pydna in 168, Paullus became master of Perseus's royal treasure of some six thousand talents (Polyb. 18.35.5), but he had not the slightest avaricious appetite (ibid.), and did not even wish to look upon the treasure; he handled its disposition through intermediaries—and this although his own personal fortune was not large (35.5–7). Later, in the obituary Polybius gives Paullus in Book 31, the historian even takes the fact that Paullus died in relatively moderate circumstances as one important proof of his moral excellence (ἀρετή, 31.22.2). Polybius also returns here to the theme of how very admirable it was that Paullus, although he had the entire kingdom of Macedon at his disposal, had displayed not the slightest lust for financial gain (μηδενὸς ἐπιθυμῆσαι, 22.7). And he presents Paullus's son Scipio Aemilianus as having the same self-disciplined attitude regarding money as his father (18.35.9–11). Thus when Aemilianus captured Carthage, the richest city in the world, he took nothing from it to add to his own fortune—which was a modest one for a Roman (35.10). The parallel between father and son was no accident, according to Polybius; for Scipio Aemilianus had learned "purity and nobility of spirit" regarding money (τὸ καθαρόν, μεγαλοψυχία) at his father's knee (31.25.9–10).[71]

Paullus and Scipio were, of course, Polybius's friends and even protectors, so it is easy to suspect that a favorable personal bias informs these

70. On the place of this passage in the development of Polybius's ideas on the decline of Roman morals, see esp. Petzold, *Methode des Polybios*, 91.

71. On Aemilius Paullus as a model for his son Scipio, see also Diod. 31.27.1 (Polybian).

passages.[72] Certainly Paullus, who left an estate with comparatively little cash but valued overall at some sixty talents (Polyb. 31.28.3), can hardly be thought of as having lived a life of virtuous poverty.[73] But it is Polybius himself who provides the evidence on the scale of Paullus's property; he clearly was not trying to fool anyone. As with Scipio Aemilianus, the historian's point is merely that Paullus was a person of comparatively modest means for a Roman noble (ὡς Ῥωμαῖος), who had refused to enrich himself grossly through public service.[74] There is precious little evidence to contradict Polybius here.[75] In any case, the main point for our purposes is the *type* of behavior Polybius told his audience was outstanding and worthy of praise.

Here one should note that Paullus and his son do not stand alone. L. Mummius, the conquerer of Corinth in 146, receives Polybius's approval for "the self-restrained and completely pure manner" in which he had conducted himself after the fall of the city (ἐγκρατῶς καὶ καθαρῶς, 39.6.3). Polybius's point is apparently that Mummius chose not to enrich himself from the spoils of Corinth (indeed, he became famous for that action); yet Mummius was not well off financially.[76] Similarly, Polybius praises Philopoemen for having refused a gift of 120 talents from the post-Nabis regime in Sparta in 192, because he took it to be a bribe (20.12.6–7). In the encomium, this was evidently presented as a demonstration of Philopoemen's "great dignity, and simplicity of living" (Plut. *Phil.* 15.4–6).[77]

Since Philopoemen was a family friend, and one of the young Polybius's heroes, the story of the refusal of the Spartan gift obviously has its propagandistic aspect. Certainly Polybius enjoyed telling it, since it appeared both in the encomium and in *The Histories*. But the basic facts of the incident are not doubted.[78] And what is important for us, once more, is the *type* of praiseworthy conduct Polybius was concerned to underline

72. Reiter, *Aemilius Paullus*, 115–16, is especially ready to see Polybius's picture of Paullus's moderate style of life and modest financial circumstances as greatly idealized (cf. also 39–40).

73. So, correctly, Reiter, ibid. 116.

74. ὡς Ῥωμαῖος: Scipio Aemilianus's fortune is so labeled by Polybius at 18.35.10, and Aemilianus's fortune was about equal to that of his father (cf. Polyb. 31.28.3).

75. Thus Reiter, *Aemilius Paullus*, 115–16, stresses that after Pydna, Paullus took the library of the Antigonid kings as his own (Plut. *Aem.* 28.11), and allowed his son Aemilianus the run of the royal hunting preserves (Polyb. 31.29.3–5). But this is not "lusting after financial gain"—which is what Polybius denies about Paullus's conduct (18.35.5, 31.22.7).

76. Mummius's self-denial at Corinth famous: see Livy *Per.* 52. The resultant poverty of his family: see Front. *Strat.* 4.3.15, Plin. *NH* 34.36.

77. Plutarch based on Polybius: proven by the exact parallel between the Plutarch passage and Polyb. 20.12. See Pédech, "Polybe et l'éloge," 95.

78. For detailed discussion of the episode, see Errington, *Philopoemen*, 110–12.

for his audience. Perhaps it was the type of conduct that had attracted Polybius to Philopoemen—or Aemilius Paullus and Scipio Aemilianus—in the first place.[79]

What particularly impresses Polybius in all the above cases is that none of these men took advantage of their public positions in order to reap large financial benefits.[80] This attitude in itself demonstrates the nature of the audience for whom such depictions were meant to be inspiring; they came, like Polybius himself, from the prosperous local aristocracies—the office-holding class.[81]

Polybius thus both perceived and expounded a sharp dichotomy between dishonorable and honorable means of gaining wealth—between τὸ μὴ καθῆκον and wealth gained ἐν καλῷ (cf. 6.56.2–3).[82] And just as Polybius praises those men who exercise self-discipline in the means of acquiring wealth, avoiding τὸ μὴ καθῆκον, so too he expresses special approbation for those men who can manage the temptations that the possession of great wealth poses—especially the temptations toward dissipation.

An excellent summary of Polybius's ideology here appears in his approving discussion of the marshals of Alexander the Great (8.10.9–11). In this passage the reader is confronted once more with a mass of moralizing terminology. These men undertook extraordinary toil, danger, and hardship (8.10.9); yet, having become masters of great wealth and the resources to satisfy every lust (ἐπιθυμία), not a single one of them sought to gratify his passions through unjust or licentious behavior (ἄδικον, ἀσελγές, ibid.). On the contrary: in prosperity all of them conducted themselves with moderation and nobility of spirit (σωφροσύνη, μεγαλοψυχία, 10.10). Thus they left behind a record of great glory (10.11).[83] The historian is similarly approving of the moderation in style of life led by

---

79. Cf. Polyb. 18.35 and 31.22 on the character of Paullus, and 31.25.2 and 9–10 on the character of Aemilianus.

80. Cf. the comments of Reiter, *Aemilius Paullus*, 33–35 (important, though limited to the case of Paullus himself).

81. They were the type of men who would appreciate a Polybian sentiment such as "what a great and fine possession [μέγα τι καὶ καλόν] is the quality of moderation" (8.12.6). For the ideological importance of this passage (on the death of Aratus of Sicyon), see Wunderer, *Polybios*, 14. Cf. also the similar sentiment (honor is a better possession than mere wealth) at 21.23.9–12.

82. To judge from Plut. *Phil.* 3.4, Polybius believed that the most honorable way (δικαιοτάτῳ) of acquiring wealth was through energetic work at investment farming. This was the traditional ideal of the aristocracies of the ancient Mediterranean. Cato agreed: it was wealth gained through farming that was truly *honestum* (see Astin, *Cato the Censor*, 255). Polybius and Cato, of course, knew each other (Polyb. 35.6), and in 31.25.5a Polybius approves of Cato's moral positions—including references to farming.

83. For discussion of the context and ideological importance of this portrayal of the marshals of Alexander, see Eckstein, "The Power of Irrationality," 3–4.

Hiero II of Syracuse (7.8.7–8). Attalus I of Pergamum (18.41.4–8), and Massinissa of Numidia (36.16). Only the noblest of souls, he writes, can resist the corruption inherent in the possession of great wealth (18.41.3–5).[84]

But self-restraint and self-discipline are not the only elements in Polybius's ideology of the proper use or enjoyment of wealth. Equally important here was a strong feeling that "nobility of behavior" required, in those of wealth, an open-handed generosity. This, too, is an outlook typical of traditional aristocracies.[85] Thus Polybius expects that true kings will distinguish themselves from mere despots through their great benefactions to others (5.11.6).[86] One of the marks of Attalus I's μεγαλοψυχία was his manifold gifts to others (18.41.5–6)—and the same holds true for Hiero II of Syracuse (1.16.10; 7.8.6).[87] The expectations here are not limited to kings; to Polybius, one of the signs of Scipio Africanus's greatness was that he was generous with gifts (10.5.6).[88]

The most extensive expression of Polybius's ideology of aristocratic generosity comes, in fact, in his disapproving discussion of the general stinginess of the Roman nobility. It is true enough that they seemed to him to be honest in the acquisition of wealth (or that they used to be: 6.56.2–3). But he also found the Roman aristocracy to be extraordinarily tight-fisted—and he did not hesitate to criticize them for it. This is a perception that thoroughly imbues his detailed account of how Scipio Aemilianus gained a great reputation in Rome for generosity: according to Polybius, it did not take much.

When Polybius became Scipio's mentor (ca. 167/166),[89] one of their major goals was to distinguish Scipio from other Roman aristocrats in terms of "nobility of spirit and purity regarding money matters" (μεγαλοψυχία, τὸ καθαρόν, 31.25.9; cf. Diod. 31.27.1). Polybius says that Aemilianus was helped toward this goal by the fine example set by his father, Paullus (see above), and because Aemilianus himself had "an eager disposition to lead a life of virtue" (τὸ καλόν, 31.25.2), and "good natural inclinations toward what was right and proper" (ἐπὶ τὸ δέον, 25.10). The ques-

84. On the tone of these latter passages, see the comments of Welwei, *Könige und Königtum*, 89–99, 116, and 146–47.
85. For convenient discussion, see Kautsky, *Politics of Aristocratic Empires*, 193–95.
86. Cf. the comments of Welwei, *Könige und Königtum*, 162. This ideological expectation concerning the conduct of royalty antedates the Hellenistic period, but becomes very strong in Greek political thought after Philip II and Alexander: see Welwei, 165; and now Austin, "Hellenistic Kings," 462–63.
87. Cf. Welwei, *Könige und Königtum*, 96 and 162.
88. Ibid. 162.
89. On the date and origins of this relationship, see esp. Walbank, *Commentary* III: 497–99.

tion is: What did Polybius think was both "right and proper," "noble and virtuous," and yet so generous as to set Scipio apart from other aristocratic Romans?

First, when Scipio inherited the fortune of Aemilia, widow of the great Africanus (ca. 163/162), he gave not the whole fortune but Aemilia's magnificent personal effects (and her staff of household slaves) to his natural mother, Papiria.[90] Papiria had long been separated from Scipio's father, Paullus, and her private means had not been sufficient to maintain her in a state suitable to her rank (Polyb. 31.26.6). But now when she went out in her new splendor to public sacrifices, "all the women were struck with amazement at Scipio's good nature and nobility of spirit" (μεγαλο-ψυχία, 31.26.8). Polybius explains the reason for the amazement (26.9): "For such conduct as Scipio's would have seemed noble [καλόν] anywhere, but in Rome it seemed a real marvel; for at Rome no one ever readily and of his own free will gives away anything of his own to anybody."

Somewhat later, Aemilianus completely paid off the dowries of his two step-aunts (the daughters of Africanus) in one installment, amounting to some fifty talents, rather than giving only the legally required annual minimum of one-third of the total (Polyb. 31.27.1–5).[91] Polybius says that when the husbands of the aunts (Ti. Sempronius Gracchus, consul 177, and P. Cornelius Scipio Nasica, consul 162) went to the banker to receive their minimum legal payments, they were astounded to learn that they would be receiving the dowries in full. And Polybius explains the reason for their astonishment (31.27.10–11):

> For at Rome, far from anyone paying fifty talents three years before it was due, no one will pay even *one* talent before the appointed day—so unusual and extreme [τοιαύτη . . . καὶ τηλικαύτη] is the Roman exactitude about money, and their concern to gain profit from holding on to it down to the very last moment.

Indeed, Gracchus and Nasica went straight to Aemilianus and urged him to keep the money that was not immediately legally due, to look after his own interests, and to use the money for the considerable time left (Polyb. 31.27.12–13). But, Polybius continues, Aemilianus replied that while with strangers he insisted on the letter of the law, with relatives and friends he chose to behave, as far as possible, "in a ready and noble manner" (γενναίως, 27.14). Polybius concludes that Gracchus and Nasica went

90. Polyb. 31.26.6; on the date of Aemilia's death, see Walbank, *Commentary* III: 503 and 507. On the complex family relations of Scipio, see Astin, *Scipio Aemilianus*, 12–15.

91. On the legalities involved, see Walbank, *Commentary* III: 506–7; and now Dixon, "Polybius on Roman Women and Property," 152–56. The annual payments were apparently to date from the death of Aemilia the widow of Africanus (Dixon, 155–56).

away struck with amazement at Scipio's nobility of spirit (μεγλοψυχία, 27.16)—and abashed at their own small-mindedness concerning money matters (μικρολογία, ibid.).[92]

Two years later (ca. 160), L. Aemilius Paullus himself passed away, leaving Scipio and his brother Q. Fabius Maximus Aemilianus as joint heirs to his estate, which was valued at some sixty talents (Polyb. 31.28.1–3). But Scipio, seeing that Fabius was not well off, voluntarily turned over his own share of the inheritance to him (ibid.). It was an act of generosity that Polybius describes as "noble, and worthy of memory" (καλόν, 28.1).[93] Soon thereafter, Scipio's mother, Papiria, also died. Rather than taking back the magnificent gifts he had given her from his inheritance from Aemilia, Scipio instead now turned all of Papiria's effects over to his own sisters—who, Polybius emphasizes, had no legal claim (31.28.7–8). This act, the historian says, helped spread Aemilianus's reputation for nobility and family affection (τὸ μεγαλόψυχον, 28.9).

No doubt these stories were told by Polybius in part to glorify his friend Scipio. But since in the passage concluding this account Polybius explicitly emphasizes that Scipio gained a great reputation at Rome *without* displaying really extraordinary generosity as Polybius conceives it (31.28.10–11), there is not much reason to suspect exaggeration here.[94]

The purely utilitarian aspect both of Polybius's advice to Scipio on these matters and of his assessment of the latter's actions cannot be doubted. Polybius and Scipio intended Scipio's growing reputation for generosity (as well as for other virtues such as courage and a moderate style of life) to be a useful tool for Scipio's political advancement.[95] And more broadly, some scholars have argued that the virtues that Polybius praises in Aemilianus are precisely the virtues that the historian thinks necessary for the preservation of political stability within a state, as well as for its imperial expansion abroad: pragmatic considerations indeed.[96]

Nevertheless, I would underline a different aspect of these passages. To Polybius, the exacting attitude of most Roman aristocrats toward money was "unusual and extreme" (31.27.11). This Roman state of mind

92. Compare Polybius's criticism of Perseus's attitude toward money: μικρολογία (29.8.8).

93. The money went in good part to defray the cost of Paullus's funeral, which ran to some 30 talents (Polyb. 31.28.6); the point was that the funeral games had to be performed on an honorable scale (μεγαλομερῶς, ibid.).

94. Polybius's bias is stressed by Astin, *Scipio Aemilianus*, 3, although—like Walbank (*Polybius*, 173)—he accepts the basic facts of Scipio's early conduct as Polybius sets them forth. Polybius's favorable bias toward Aemilianus probably finds expression not in any exaggeration or distortion of his conduct, but rather in the prominence and great detail with which this conduct is presented to the audience.

95. For the emphasis on reputation, see esp. Walbank, *Commentary* III: 449.

96. For this interpretation, see esp. Walbank, *Polybius*, 173 and n. 106.

had its origin in the deep legalism of Roman culture, and perhaps in the deep Roman desire for orderliness; but to Polybius it was "not fitting and proper" (cf. 25.10). This perception forms the basis for Polybius's depiction of Scipio's conduct regarding money, and in itself reveals much about Polybius's own aristocratic ethos. Secondly, reputation alone is not the issue in 31.25–30. Polybius twice emphasizes at the beginning that Scipio had in fact a good character—an eager disposition to lead a life of virtue (25.2 and 10). Throughout his account, Scipio's true μεγαλοψυχία is then repeatedly stressed.[97] And at the end, Polybius expresses his hope that the discussion will have proved pleasant for older readers, and salutary for the young (31.30.1). Surely, more than a cynical appreciation of Scipio's political maneuvers is meant. As Polybius says at 31.28.1, it is the noble (the καλόν) that is worthy of memory.[98]

Nor should one dismiss Polybius's warm statements of approval for Scipio's conduct as merely an expected moralizing trope, or a literary artifice. His sincerity here can be shown by his own conduct. The incident was discussed in detail in Chapter I, and need only be summarized: in 146/145 Polybius refused the Roman offer of loot from the confiscated property of anti-Roman Achaeans, and he counseled his friends to avoid buying up such confiscated property (39.4)—although presumably much financial profit was thereby missed.[99] But to engage in this behavior— or even to think of doing it—was to dishonor oneself (καθόλου μηδενὸς ἐπιθυμῆσαι, Polybius warns: 39.4.2). And honorable behavior, to Polybius, was more important than financial gain.[100]

CONCLUSION

The values typically asserted in traditional aristocratic cultures include honor, moral courage, generosity, equanimity in the face both of disaster and temptation.[101] Just as Chapter II demonstrated that Polybius is a strong exponent of the aristocratic value of sheer physical courage, so the present chapter has shown that the historian is a strong exponent of these other traditional aristocratic values as well. Hence Polybius's praise throughout *The Histories* for communities that undertake war (or that continue to fight) primarily for the sake of honor—to maintain their own

97. Polyb. 31.25.9, 26.6, 27.16, 28.9.

98. For Polybius's emphasis on the καλόν in regard to the conduct of the young Scipio Aemilianus, see, rightly but briefly, Petzold, *Methode des Polybios,* 91–92.

99. The profits would accrue from the fact that the confiscated property would be selling for much below its real value, because of the prevailing situation of a glut on the market, combined with few available buyers (as a result of the wrecked economy of Achaea).

100. Cf. the comments of Wunderer, *Polybios,* 3 and 13.

101. See the survey in Kautsky, *Politics of Aristocratic Empires,* 169–77, 193–95.

sense of dignity. The Carthaginian decision to continue the war against Rome in 256/255, the Acarnanian decision for open war against Aetolia in 220, the Roman decision to continue the war against Carthage in 216, the Prienian decision to resist the demands of Ariarathes and Eumenes in 155/153: these are only some of the many examples of Polybius's ideologically loaded presentations of such incidents. Hence, too, Polybius's condemnation of avarice (Perseus and Eumenes), and of immoderation and dissoluteness when in possession of great wealth (Ptolemy IV, or Ptolemy of Megalopolis). This also explains the historian's praise of honesty and self-discipline regarding money on the one hand (L. Aemilius Paullus), and generosity with it on the other (Attalus I; Scipio Aemilianus). For wealth, like war, presented a challenge to honorable conduct.

Moreover, although Polybius has a wide reputation among modern scholars as a historian whose standards for evaluating conduct are utterly utilitarian, on the subjects covered above he often distributes praise or blame with little regard for the effect of such behavior in a utilitarian sense. Thus he praises the Roman decision to fight on after Cannae as an example of steadfastness and nobility of spirit (μεγαλοψυχία); but he equally praises the steadfastness and nobility of spirit of the Carthaginians in 256/255 or the Gazans in 201/200—though they ultimately lost. Conversely, the historian condemns the financial behavior of Alexander of Isus and the Rhodians as dishonorable, even though their desire for profit worked out well when viewed in utterly pragmatic terms. And Polybius's own conduct in Achaea in 146/145 strongly supports the sincerity of the latter judgments.

All in all, the portrait of Polybius that emerges from this chapter is of a man much concerned with the advocacy of traditional ethics, as his elite stratum of society understood them. In the next chapter, this aspect of *The Histories* will be examined from yet another angle: the question of the employment of good faith and deceit in political life.

FOUR

Polybius's Aristocratic Ethos: Deceit and Good Faith

As for trickery, cunning, and that which in sovereigns they call Kingcraft, and reason of State in Commonwealths, to them he is an open Enemy.
—JOHN DRYDEN ON POLYBIUS (1691)

INTRODUCTION

One test of "Machiavellianism" in *The Histories* would be Polybius's willingness to accept double-dealing, on utilitarian grounds, as a normal and reasonable part of public life. In other words, the ends justify the means. Polybius was well aware of the moral dilemma here. At 21.32c.1 he explains it to his audience:

> What is noble [καλόν] rarely coincides with what is pragmatically advantageous [συμφέρον], and rare are those men who can combine the two. . . . Indeed, as we all know, for the most part noble action [καλόν] by its very nature shuns immediate advantage, while actions taken for profit, by their very nature, shun the noble.

From this passage it would appear that for Polybius an ideal political-military decision would be one that results both in the achievement of the καλόν *and* in utilitarian advantage: he indicates respect for those rare individuals whose policies can combine the two. Hence his praise in this very passage for Philopoemen's policy of restoring exiles to Sparta—an act that was morally correct (καλόν), as well as advantageous to Achaea (32c.3).[1] Similar is Polybius's praise for the policies of Philip II after Chaeronea in 338 (including the sparing of Athens), of Antigonus Doson after Sellasia in 222 (sparing the Spartans), and of Antiochus III at Armosata in 212 (sparing that city from destruction): these policies were indeed politically effective, but also "noble-minded and humane."[2]

1. For the (complex) political background to Philopoemen's restoration of the Spartan exiles, see Walbank, *Commentary* III: 137–38; and Errington, *Philopoemen*, 137–43.
2. Philip II and Antigonus III: see Polyb. 5.9.8–10.5. Antiochus III: 8.23.3–5. Note that although Welwei, *Könige und Königtum*, 26–27 and 36–37, offers a completely cynical inter-

84

Nevertheless, Polybius's general opinion, forcefully expressed in 21.32c twice, is that opportunities for acting simultaneously in both a moral fashion and a pragmatically advantageous one are rare. What, then, is the basis for the historian's evaluation of action when such simultaneously moral and pragmatic conduct will not be possible? Several aspects of this question have already been addressed in the previous two chapters; and an answer is obviously evolving. But the special case of acts of good faith or deception offers a further entry into Polybius's thinking, and forms the subject of the present chapter.

"MACHIAVELLIAN" PASSAGES

Several passages in *The Histories* might be taken to indicate that Polybius approved of acts of deceit in political-military affairs, or at best took a morally neutral stance. But even if the "Machiavellian" interpretation of these passages is correct (which is open to severe doubt), they still will have to be considered within the context of the many other passages that point in the opposite direction.

One of Polybius's heroes in *The Histories* is Scipio Africanus, and three episodes from Scipio's career may be adduced as indicating Polybius's approval or acceptance of Scipionic deceit. First, Polybius says that Scipio persuaded his mother to allow him to run for the aedileship by telling her of a dream, and allowed the impression to be gotten in Rome that the dream represented his being summoned to office by the gods; but in reality, Scipio won election by carefully reckoning upon his popularity, and exploiting the opportunity provided by the people and his mother (10.4–5). Second, according to Polybius, Scipio as Roman commander in Spain used the story of a dream he had allegedly received from the god of the sea to bolster the morale of his troops, especially regarding an amphibious assault across the lagoon at New Carthage (10.14.11–12; cf. 11.7). But in reality Scipio had learned by energetic inquiry that the tide in the lagoon fell naturally at a certain point during the day (10.8).

Polybius certainly viewed these incidents positively: Scipio acted "with skill" in the first case (10.5.6), and provided needed bolstering of wavering army morale in the second. Nevertheless, these episodes are clearly not serious instances of deceit in military-political life. Nor is Polybius's main point here to commend to his audience whatever trickery is involved; rather, he is specifically seeking to counter the widespread view that Scipio owed his success to luck and to divine aid, and to assert instead

---

pretation of the passages on Philip and Antigonus, later (150–56) Welwei realizes that Polybius's code of behavior for rulers has its sternly moral aspects.

that Scipio's success was always the result of careful calculation, intellect, and hard work.³ Polybius's acceptance of Scipio's use of mild forms of trickery in Book 10 is thus only slight support for the hypothesis that the historian was a stern "Machiavellian."⁴

Much more serious is Scipio's conduct at the battle of the Camps (spring 203). Following the Roman invasion of Africa in 204, Scipio was blockaded by numerically superior Carthaginian-Numidian forces on a peninsula near Utica. During the subsequent winter, he made a pretense of entering into peace talks, but their real purpose was to spy out conditions in the enemy camps, and/or to win over the Numidian prince Syphax (14.1.3–7). Scipio failed to win over Syphax, but saw that a surprise attack on the enemy was possible (14.1.8). He therefore decided on what Polybius explicitly calls a "trick" (κατασκευή, ibid.).⁵ Scipio intensified the peace talks, thus making possible frequent visits to Syphax's camp and better spying-out of its approaches (14.1.9–15)—while Syphax and the Carthaginians relaxed their guard (2.7–8, 3.2–3). But at the very last moment, Scipio broke off the talks (2.11–12). Polybius explains that he did this so as not to appear to be breaking the truce when he attacked; Scipio considered that his conduct would now not be "open to blame" (2.13–14).

That very night he launched an attack on the enemy camps—a very difficult operation (cf. 14.4.3–4) that was a complete success. The camps were burned, great loss of enemy life was inflicted, and the blockade broken. After describing the night attack in great detail, Polybius comments approvingly (14.5.15): "This action, of all the many brilliant achievements of Scipio, seems to me to have been the most brilliant and hazardous [κάλλιστον . . . καὶ παραβολώτατον]."

Yet Scipio's action seems in many respects an example of thorough bad faith and deception, through the use of fraudulent peace talks. The conundrum here seems increased by the apparent contradiction—stressed by Walbank—between Polyb. 14.5 and the historian's long discussion in 13.3, just one volume earlier, where treachery and trickery in military-political affairs are twice explicitly called evildoing (κακοπραγμο-σύνη, 13.3.1 and 8), against which Polybius remonstrates. Such behavior

3. See 10.2.9, 5.9–10, 9.2–3, and (rightly) Walbank, *Commentary* II: 192. However, Polybius later admits that Tyche did play some part in Scipio's career: see 10.40.6 and 9, with Walbank, *Commentary* II: 201 and 253.
4. Polybius's interpretation of Scipio's conduct regarding his dreams has been suspected of being overly cynical; some scholars suggest that Scipio may have been a true mystic: see de Sanctis, *Storia dei Romani* III:2, 452; or the milder variant of Scullard, *Scipio Africanus,* 23–25. Scullard (24) rightly notes that Polybius never quite says that Scipio overtly lied about having these dreams.
5. For this translation of κατασκευή, see Walbank, *Commentary* II: 426.

was contrary to the honorable ways of the ancestors, and could never be called brilliant (λαμπρόν, 3.4).[6]

How can the apparently sharp divergence in moral outlook between Polyb. 13.3 and 14.5 be explained? Even Roman tradition was evidently uncomfortable with Scipio's conduct here.[7] By contrast, Pédech sees Scipio's public announcement of the suspension of negotiations before he attacked as an example of Polybius's presentation of Scipio's chivalric sense of honor.[8] Polybius certainly thought that if the Carthaginians and Syphax were taken by surprise that night, it was their own fault: since the truce was ended, war should have been expected at any time (14.3.2–3). Nevertheless, it is hard to see how a "trick" (κατασκευή)—the use of a truce to prepare for war—could be called καλόν (indeed, κάλλιστον: 14.5.15).

The answer is that it is not the "trick" that is receiving Polybius's praise in 14.5. The other adjective that Polybius applies to Scipio's conduct is "extremely hazardous" (παραβολώτατον). This word can hardly refer to the "trick," for there was nothing hazardous about that. The term clearly refers instead to the difficult character of Scipio's night attack itself. Polybius in fact found this type of military operation fascinating: the digression on generalship in Book 9 contains four full chapters on just a few of the problems inherent in such night attacks (9.14.6–18.4). And in his direct narrative of Scipio's attack on the Camps, Polybius again emphasizes its difficulty; operations such as this require skill combined with daring, careful organization combined with courage—but no rashness (14.4.3–4).

Thus it is the technical military achievement of the successful night assault on the Camps that Polybius enthusiastically praises in 14.5—not the "trick." It is true that the "trick" is there as a fact in the background, but it is not praised (indeed, κατασκευή can easily be seen as a pejorative term). And as Pédech notes, Scipio in any case was doing the opposite of a formal violation of the laws of war (the type of behavior excoriated in 13.3). The passage therefore cannot be considered strong evidence that Polybius considered outright deceit in military-political affairs as praiseworthy.[9]

6. Cf. also Polyb. 6.47.5, where the prevailing Cretan custom of treachery is linked closely in Polybius's mind with the idea of injustice (ἀδικώτερος); similar are Polybius's biting comments at 22.19 (discussed below). For the apparent contrast between Polyb. 13.3 and 14.4–5, see Walbank, *Commentary* II: 417 and 430.

7. Hence the stories in Livy (30.4.8) and Appian (*Lib.* 17–23) that it was Syphax (not Scipio) who at the last moment ruined the peace negotiations (see Scullard, *Scipio Africanus*, 121).

8. *Méthode*, 219.

9. Cf. Roveri, *Studi su Polibio* 61, who alludes briefly to the technical nature of Polybius's praise of Scipio at 14.5.15.

Just one volume later, Polybius makes a comment regarding Philip V of Macedon that similarly has been taken as "Machiavellian" concerning the use of trickery and deceit in military-political affairs. In 15.24 Polybius describes Philip's conquest of Thasos in the northern Aegean in 202. The Thasians proposed to surrender on terms (no garrison, no tribute, and left under their own laws), and Philip agreed; but once his forces had actually been admitted into the city, he enslaved the entire population (15.24.1–2). Polybius's comment on the betrayal of the Thasians seems to criticize the king merely for the inexpediency of this act in terms of his plans for imperial expansion (24.5–6):

> Who would not characterize a ruler as completely illogical and mad who, while engaged upon vast enterprises and aspiring to universal dominion, and with his chances for success still unimpaired . . . proclaimed to all his faithlessness and untrustworthiness in the very first matter he was called upon to deal with?

Thus Walbank remarks on this passage: "The absence of any moral criterion is noteworthy." [10]

But this is rather unfair, for Polyb. 15.24.5–6 does not stand in isolation. It is prefaced by a powerfully moralizing comment about kingship at 15.24.4: however liberal at the start of their reigns, kings often degenerate into tyrants, and through their tyrannical behavior they fail to maintain correct ethics (τοῦ μὲν καλοῦ διαψεύδονται), although they may not fail to gain immediate practical advantages (the συμφέρον).[11] Thus when one takes 15.24.4–6 as a whole, concern for practical advantage is certainly present (a reputation for trustworthiness would be helpful to Philip's imperial ambitions), but a moral criterion for behavior (Philip's failure to maintain the καλόν) seems strongly present, too.

Moreover, not only must 15.24.4–6 be taken as a whole, but the whole passage also needs to be read within the broader context of the avalanche of moral castigation that Polybius heaps on Philip beginning in 15.20. There Polybius attacks Philip's secret treaty with Antiochus III against the child Ptolemy V as "unjust, shameful, animallike" (ἀσεβής, αἰσχρά, θηριώδης, 15.20.3–4).[12] And Philip's subsequent behavior reflected those qualities. He acted unjustly (ἀδίκως) against the city of Cius (15.22.3); this sealed his universal and well-deserved reputation among the Greeks for cruelty and impiety (ὠμότης, ἀσέβεια, 22.4). Philip enslaved the Cians

10. *Commentary* II: 480.

11. For this translation of διαψεύδονται, see Mauersberger, *Polybios-Lexikon* I:2, cols. 530–31 ("eine Sache verfehlen," or "nicht erreichen").

12. The historicity of this alleged treaty is debatable (see below, Chap. VII, n. 5); but the point here is that Polybius firmly believed in its existence—and firmly condemns it on moral grounds.

after he captured the city—a cruel and treacherous act (ὠμότης, ἀθεσία, 23.3–4). In sum, Polybius says (23.5), Philip in this period betrayed not so much others as himself (παρασπονδήσας), having departed so far from proper conduct (τοῦ καθήκοντος) that he boasted of acts about which he ought to have felt the deepest shame (αἰσχύνεσθαι).[13]

Certainly there were practical political consequences to what Polybius in these passages sees as Philip's terrible misbehavior—the alienation of the Rhodians and the Aetolians from him (15.23.6–9). But this is not what Polybius means by "Philip had betrayed himself" (23.5). Rather, Polybius is summarizing and underlining here the king's utter moral degeneration, a theme that is reiterated in the story of Thasos as well (τοῦ μὲν καλοῦ διαψεύδονται, 15.24.4). The moral criterion is a formidable presence here.

A similar "utilitarian" interpretation of a Polybian judgment of Philip is also offered by Walbank concerning Philip's actions at Messene in 215. These led at first to a bloody massacre (Plut. Arat. 49.3–5; cf. Polyb. 7.12.6), and then to Philip's toying with the idea of seizing the great Messenian fortress of Ithome for himself. Philip's adviser Demetrius of Pharus urged him toward this "treachery" (as Polybius calls it: 7.12.8); he should seize the fortress "if he had the mind of a king" (12.2). But Aratus of Sicyon was able to dissuade Philip from taking Demetrius's cynical advice (12.9–10). Polybius says that he describes this incident in detail "so that men of politics can correct their conduct by means of the study of history" (11.2). Walbank takes Polybius to mean here merely that a study of history affords statesmen practical lessons in statecraft.[14]

No doubt practical considerations inform part of Polybius's outlook on the Messene incident, and part of the outlook of 7.11–14 taken as a whole. Polybius indicates that before this period, Philip had gained great influence among the Greeks through his honorable conduct and good faith, but now his increasingly harsh and treacherous policies began to undermine his political position (7.11.8–11; cf. 14.4–6). Yet, as in 15.20–24, the fact is that 7.11–14 is a passage that is also rife with heavily moralizing terminology. It is a discussion of Philip's "transformation for the worse" (ἐπὶ χεῖρον, 7.11.1). The bloody intervention at Messene was the first of Philip's "enormous impious crimes" (τῶν μεγίστων ἀσεβημάτων, 13.6), the first of his "wicked acts" (μοχθηρόν, 13.4), the first sign of a new and continuing "impiety and injustice" (ἠσέβει . . . ἀδικήσας, 14.3–4), his

13. The reference here is apparently to Philip's glorying in the conquest of Cius (cf. 15.22.1), perhaps because he was "helping" his in-law Prusias I of Bithynia—in which case, Polybius's point is that while it is a good deed to help a relative, it is perverted to help a relative in a deed of aggression that itself is ignoble.

14. Commentary II: 58; cf. Sacks, Polybius on the Writing of History, 135 (even more strongly on Polybian amorality here).

violation of the laws of war (ἡμάρτανε, 14.3). At Ithome, Philip could still be moved by a sense of shame (ἐνετράπη, 12.9), so that Aratus was able to block his strong penchant for treachery (παρασπονδεῖν, 12.8). But, Polybius continues (13.7):

> Philip henceforth, having now tasted of human blood and the slaughter and betrayal of allies, if he did not actually turn from a human being into a wolf (as in the Arcadian tale quoted by Plato), did turn from a true king into a savage tyrant [πικρός].

Philip as a werewolf: it is hard to believe that Polybius's point is merely that Philip's policies were counterproductive. Indeed, the intensity of Polybius's moral condemnation of Philip here gains a highly personal note by the employment of a hideous fable from the historian's native Arcadia.[15]

A fifth passage, however, seems explicit on the usefulness of deceitful conduct. In 166 a Roman embassy headed by the ex-consul Ti. Sempronius Gracchus visited Antiochus IV, who received them with hyperbolic courtesy (Polyb. 30.27.2–3). The envoys thus came away convinced of Antiochus's sincere friendship with Rome, and they criticized other Romans who suspected him of being hostile (27.2). Yet, Polybius emphasizes, Antiochus in fact *was* hostile, because of Roman interference in his attempted conquest of Ptolemaic Egypt (27.2 and 4).[16] Polybius describes Antiochus's conduct here as "clever" (ἐπιδεξίως, 30.27.2). And Antiochus certainly reaped pragmatic benefits from his deceitful actions, which Walbank terms "Machiavellian."[17]

Yet ambiguities must remain even in this passage. Polybius has just described Antiochus as a highly erratic ruler given to treachery and shameful acts (30.26.6–8). And at 30.27.3, he sneers at the king's servile behavior toward the Romans: he not only gave over his own palace to the envoys, but very nearly his crown as well. So the picture of Antiochus even in 30.27 is not completely positive. Pédech has even suggested that Polybius's main point in 30.27 is not the cleverness of Antiochus but rather the extreme naiveté of Ti. Sempronius.[18]

The historian definitely presents the unsavory conduct of a much earlier Greek ruler—Hiero of Syracuse in the 270s—in a neutral or even

---

15. Arcadian legend held that those who had tasted human flesh remained werewolves forever (Paus. 8.2.6, using the same verb Polybius uses of Philip at 7.13.7). Both von Scala (*Studien*, 20 n. 2, and 99) and Walbank (*Commentary* II: 61) see Polyb. 7.13.7 merely as a frigid intellectual criticism of Plato, *Rep.* 8.565D. This seems to me to miss the historian's point completely.

16. On the Roman intervention against Antiochus IV in Egypt, see now Morgan, "Antiochus Epiphanes," 37–76.

17. *Commentary* II: 454.

18. *Méthode*, 317. Note Polybius's heavy criticism of Gracchus's naiveté at 30.30.7–8.

approving tone. But there are special circumstances involved. Having seized Syracuse in a military coup—an action of which Polybius does not approve, but that he finds mitigated by Hiero's subsequent mildness toward the citizens (1.8.3–4; cf. 7.8.1–8)—Hiero set about consolidating his regime by the elimination of the mercenaries who formed a good part of the Syracusan army. In a battle with the Mamertines, Hiero therefore allowed his mercenaries to be slaughtered, while he intentionally kept back his citizen troops (1.9.4–6). And Polybius's assessment of this act of treachery is that Hiero had conducted himself πραγματικῶς (1.9.6). Perhaps this is merely a morally neutral judgment on the efficiency with which Hiero had achieved his goal; but the epithet generally has favorable connotations. The whole passage therefore seems to most moderns—in De Sanctis's words—infelice.[19]

The key to Polybius's attitude here, however, is the nature of Hiero's target. Polybius despised and feared mercenaries, and warned his readers against their use, precisely because he saw them as brutal and untrustworthy—a threat to civilized life. This is a theme that would dominate the entire last half of Book 1, where Polybius describes in detail the attempt of mercenaries hired by Carthage to seize Carthage itself (1.65–88); it is a war in which Polybius describes the mercenaries as semianimals, and presents their destroyer, Hamilcar Barca, as a hero.[20] Indeed, just before Polybius's account of Hiero and the mercenaries, he has informed his audience of how the Mamertines, former mercenaries of Syracuse, had seized the city of Messana with great violence and through treachery (1.7.2–4): an outrage (παρανομία, 1.7.4). And he implies that Syracuse faced a similar danger itself: for he twice says that the mercenaries destroyed by Hiero were "disaffected and rebellious" (1.9.3 and 6).

Against such a threat, Polybius evidently felt that Hiero's action was justified. Moderns may find uncongenial this attitude of Polybius toward hired soldiers who were, after all, themselves often the product of social dislocation. But it is not pure "Machiavellianism."[21]

In another case—the deception practices by Aratus of Sicyon on the Achaeans (2.47–52)—Polybius's depiction again appears to be neutral or even sympathetic, but again there are special circumstances involved.

19. Storia dei Romani III:1, 94 n. 8. On this battle, see now Hoyos, "The Rise of Hiero II," 48–51.

20. On Polybius's hostile portrait of the mercenaries during their war with Carthage, see Chap. V, below. On his depiction of their destroyer, Hamilcar, as a savior of civilization, see Chap. VI, below.

21. Certainly Polybius did not in general construct his judgment of Hiero's rule on criteria of utter pragmatism; note his emphasis on μεγαλοψυχία (nobility of spirit) and σωφροσύνη (moderation) in the depiction of Hiero, with the discussion of Welwei, Könige und Königtum, 91–94; cf. 148–49.

When war began in 228 between the Achaean League and Cleomenes III of Sparta, Aratus—the senior Achaean statesman—feared a deadly danger if Sparta formed an anti-Achaean alliance with Aetolia and Macedon. He was therefore forced to seek a reconciliation with the League's old enemy Macedon, in the person of King Antigonus III Doson (2.47.3–6). But Aratus at first operated in secret, through Megalopolitan intermediaries. The secrecy was necessary, Polybius says, in order to maintain current Achaean morale against Sparta (2.47.8).[22] Aratus's deception of the Achaeans regarding his own role in negotiations with Macedon even extended to blocking publicly the very alliance that in secret he was setting out to engineer—on the grounds that the Achaeans should seek a reconciliation with Macedon only as a last resort (2.50.11); in addition, he did not want to be seen as the man responsible for the reintroduction of Macedonian power into the Peloponnese (50.7–9). By winter 225/224 Cleomenes' continued victories over Achaea were indeed threatening the existence of the League; and now Aratus, with wide public support (2.51.4), entered into open negotiations with Antigonus (negotiations that had been secretly prepared back in 228). The result was the arrival of the Macedonian army, and the destruction of Spartan power at Sellasia in 222. If the price was high—renewed Macedonian domination of the Peloponnese—Polybius believes that Aratus's policy was the only way to save the League (cf. 2.51.4).

It is true that Polybius presents Aratus's tactic of deceiving the Achaeans without moral condemnation, and perhaps even sympathetically (although he also notes that Aratus was uncomfortable with what he had done: 2.47.10–11). But Polybius adopts this attitude because (1) Aratus's deceptions were clearly intended not to be destructive, but rather represented a "higher patriotism" on his part, and (2) they were the result of sheer necessity (2.47.8), like the general policy toward Macedon itself (51.4). Moreover, the themes of honor and shame (καλόν and αἰσχρόν) are plainly visible in this passage.[23] One should therefore be careful about using the story of Aratus in 2.47–52 as evidence that Polybius was a "Machiavellian," at ease with the general employment of deceit in military-political affairs.[24]

Finally, the most famous example of a possible "Machiavellian" attitude toward deceit in Polybius. In winter 198/197 T. Quinctius Flamininus was

22. Note the similarity between Aratus's motive here and the motive Polybius ascribes to Scipio Africanus in his manipulation of the story of his dream "from Poseidon" in Spain: to boost the morale of his troops (10.2.12, 11.7, 14.11–12).

23. See esp. 2.47.10–11; but cf. also 47.1 and 50.11.

24. Bickermann, "Notes sur Polybe, II: Les négociations entre Aratos et Antigone Doson," 287–88, argues that Polybius's account of this incident fits comfortably within the terms of Achaean as well as general Greek principles of politics (esp. juridical principles).

the Roman commander in Greece against Philip V. When Philip now offered peace talks, Flamininus accepted. His motives are given by Livy and Plutarch, drawing on Polybian material: if he were to be prorogued in command by the Senate, Flamininus certainly wanted the war to continue; but if he were not to be prorogued, then he wished the glory of having brought the war to an end.[25] Unsure of what the Senate would decide, Flamininus held out to Philip the possibility of a compromise peace—one that would not require the complete evacuation of the Macedonian possessions in Greece.[26] Such a peace, however, would mark a significant retreat from the demand for total Macedonian withdrawal from Greece that Flamininus himself had made in spring 198, and that was now the enthusiastic position of Rome's Greek allies. Perhaps Flamininus could have engineered such a compromise peace; but the Senate prorogued him instead. His political friends thereupon successfully sabotaged the possible compromise (Polyb. 18.11). The war continued, with Flamininus at its head. Polybius comments (18.12.2–4):

> Now all had fallen out as Titus had wished, a little by chance, but mostly as a result of his foresight. . . . For he was as sharply sagacious a man as Rome has ever produced, and had handled not only the public enterprises but also his private projects with a skill and intelligence that could not be surpassed, and this though he was quite a young man, not yet more than thirty.

Obviously, Polybius's remarks here could not be more laudatory.[27] Yet as Polybius reconstructs events, Flamininus seems to have been prepared to betray either King Philip (before whom he dangled the possibility of a compromise peace), or the Greek allies of Rome (who wanted complete Macedonian evacuation of Greece), depending on the senatorial decision regarding his prorogation. Moreover, since a compromise peace might be seen as compromising Rome's ultimate interest in restraining Macedonian power, it has even been suggested that Flamininus was apparently ready to betray Rome as well, rather than allow another man the glory of finishing the war. On this interpretation, Polybius was praising a political maneuver that was not only unsavory, but verged on the treasonous.[28]

25. Livy 32.32.5–8, Plut. *Flam.* 7.1; cf. Polyb. 18.10.7 and 12.1, which prove the Polybian derivation of this tradition. See Holleaux, "Politique de Flamininus," 155 n. 2; Briscoe, *Commentary* I: 227–28.

26. The basic negotiating terms are established by Polyb. 18.8.8–9.2. See Badian, *Flamininus*, 42–43.

27. Note that Polybius employs the same term, εὐστόχως ("in a skillful manner"), to describe Scipio Africanus's manipulation of the Roman populace (and his mother) during his campaign for the aedileship: see above, pp. 85–86.

28. See esp. Holleaux, "Politique de Flamininus," 164–76. Polybius certainly is not involved in an attack on Flamininus here—despite Wood, "The Tradition of Flamininus' 'Selfish Ambition' in Polybius and Later Historians," esp. 102–3. See, rightly, Badian, *Flamininus*, 22–23. Tempted by Wood: Briscoe, *Commentary* I: 23–24. ▪

The latter view, however, rests on a misunderstanding of ancient aristocratic political attitudes. Polybius, in viewing Flamininus's concern for his personal standing and glory as a legitimate basis for political maneuver, was not violating the ethical standards of his own culture, nor was he praising actions normally considered shameful.[29] Concern about prorogation was in fact the normal corollary of republican systems of government that severely limited tenure of office and command—as the historian well knew.[30]

Certainly Polybius did not think of Flamininus as betraying Rome, for he explicitly says that Flamininus handled Rome's public enterprise here as skillfully as his private projects (18.12.4). Flamininus, after all, successfully demanded from Philip the total Macedonian withdrawal from Phocis and Locris—prime defensive country—in exchange for the two-month truce during which the possible compromise peace would be tested at Rome (18.10.4).[31] It is worth remembering as well the tradition that the war against Philip had little support among the war-weary Roman people (Livy 31.13.2–4 and 33.25.8)—while Philip had proven himself a very tough opponent.[32] Thus a compromise peace involving significant Macedonian concessions, far from seeming a "betrayal" of Roman interests in winter 198/197, might well have seemed to many contemporaries—including Flamininus himself—a satisfactory outcome to a difficult and unpopular war. It is only from the perspective of Flamininus's great victory over Philip at Cynoscephalae the next year (197) that the proposed compromise peace looks weak—and in fact the great victory, when it came, was itself a very near-run thing. Polybius's judgment that Flamininus in winter 198/197 managed Rome's public affairs with great skill (18.12.4) thus makes good sense.

As for Rome's Greek allies, even under the terms of winter 198/197 they would have received substantial territorial concessions from Macedon (Polyb. 18.8.9).[33] They certainly preferred the complete Macedonian withdrawal from Greece (18.7.1, 9.1); but they also accepted the truce with Philip, and peace talks at Rome (18.10.1). Moreover, during the truce the allies would be sending independent diplomatic missions to the Senate, to state their own demands on Philip (10.2). Meanwhile, Po-

---

29. See Lehamnn, *Glaubwürdigkeit des Polybios*, 168–72; Badian, *Flamininus*, 25 and 47.

30. Cf. Walbank, *Commentary* I: 91. Polybius personally saw this process at work in the last stages of the Third Punic War, in the concern of Scipio Aemilianus that he might be superseded in the Carthage command; this led Aemilianus to moderate slightly the peace terms he was prepared to offer (38.8.3–4).

31. See, rightly, Badian, *Flamininus*, 41. The withdrawal from Phocis and Locris at Flamininus's demand may also have constituted a damaging blow to the prestige of Macedonian power in Greece—and to Philip's pride. See Holleaux, "Politique de Flamininus," 61.

32. On the fighting, see Eckstein, "Flamininus and the Campaign of 198 B.C.," 126–42.

33. Cf. Eckstein, *Senate and General*, 283–84.

lybius says, Flamininus took energetic care to protect the allies from any aggression by Philip during the truce (10.5). Thus one may seriously doubt that Polybius perceived Flamininus's actions as a violation of good faith toward the Greeks, or expected his readers to do so. But this means that his praise of Flamininus's sagacity in 18.12 does not imply approval of such violations.

King Philip is a somewhat different story. It is hard to avoid the idea that Flamininus in his private meetings with Philip at the peace talks (Polyb. 18.8.4–8) said things that led Philip to believe certain issues would simply not be on the agenda at Rome: specifically, Macedonian withdrawal from the famous fortresses of Demetrias, Chalcis, and Acrocorinth, "The Three Fetters of Greece." This would account for the high price Philip was willing to pay for the two-month truce—as well as for the fact that Philip's peace envoys at Rome had no instructions regarding Macedonian withdrawal from the fortresses.[34] Yet once Flamininus was assured of his prorogation, the issue of the fortresses suddenly became the central point pushed both by Flamininus's friends and by the Greeks, and on this issue the peace talks collapsed (Polyb. 18.11).

Such a reconstruction can be teased out of the Polybian evidence.[35] But whether this is actually what Polybius believed is quite another question. Polybius did not know what had occurred in the private meeting between Flamininus and Philip (cf. 18.8.4–8). Furthermore, in the Polybian narrative there is in fact no "promise" about the three fortresses—explicit or even implicit—from Flamininus, no promise for him to betray. And, of course, there may have been none in reality.[36] Indeed, the only element in the Polybian narrative that is explicit on the question of bad faith is the fear of Flamininus and the Greek allies that *Philip* would play the cheat during the truce (18.10.5). This, of course, conforms to the picture of a cruel and treacherous Philip that Polybius has been evolving since Book 7.[37]

In sum: while Flamininus's political maneuvers in winter 198/197 have appeared reprehensible to modern scholars, one may doubt that they appeared so to Polybius. Nor does this mean that Polybius simply had no moral standards. Rather, in Polybius's view it would seem that while Flamininus had been very clever in his handling of the delicate political-diplomatic-military situation he faced in winter 198/197, he had not by

34. See Badian, *Flamininus*, 41–42.
35. See Holleaux, "Politique de Flamininus," 164; Badian, *Flamininus*, 43; Eckstein, *Senate and General*, 278–84. An alternative reconstruction by Balsdon, "T. Quinctius Flamininus," 180–84, has rightly not found a wide following.
36. Perhaps what Flamininus held out as a hope, Philip chose to take as a promise. See Badian, *Flamininus*, 42.
37. See above, pp. 88–90.

any of his actions actually violated the canons of good faith. The question of how Polybius would react to conduct that he *did* perceive as a violation of good faith (or conversely, to actions he regarded as upholding the standards of good faith at utilitarian expense) therefore remains to be answered.

NON-"MACHIAVELLIAN" PASSAGES

Balanced against the above texts, all of which are ambiguous rather than truly "Machiavellian" (or else irrelevant to the real issue), there are a large number of passages in *The Histories* that indicate Polybius's deeply hostile attitude toward acts of deceit and violations of good faith. Sometimes his criticism of such acts—or, conversely, his praise of acts of good faith— combines moralism with pragmatic concerns. But Polybius's tone here is consistently negative even when deceitful or treacherous conduct brings no ill effects against the perpetrator, and consistently positive even when adherence to good faith leads to serious pragmatic difficulties.

A good place to begin is 30.4, a passage where Polybius directly enunciates an important general principle of ethical conduct. The Rhodian envoy Astymedes came to Rome in 166 in a desperate attempt to mend Roman-Rhodian relations, threatened by Rhodian actions during the Third Macedonian War.[38] In a famous speech (which Polybius had read: cf. 30.4.11), Astymedes not only exaggerated to the Senate the previous Rhodian services to Rome while belittling those of other Greek states, but also exaggerated the offenses against Rome of other Greek states, so that the Rhodian offenses would seem smaller (30.4.12–14). Astymedes was in fact successful: the *Patres* assailed Rhodian actions, but assured the envoy that there would be no war (4.7), and even said that his own behavior was in good part responsible for this (4.9).[39] Nevertheless, Polybius is highly critical of Astymedes' speech, on general ethical grounds (30.4.15–16):

> For it was by no means proper for a civilized man [οὐδαμῶς . . . πρέπειν], since surely with men who have partaken in a conspiracy we do not praise those who either from fear or for the sake of money turn informers and betray confidences, but rather we applaud and regard as good men and

38. The Senate was especially angered by an ill-timed Rhodian effort to mediate the war, which came (as it turned out) when Rome had virtually won it; this raised suspicions among the *Patres* that the Rhodians actually favored Macedon (Polyb. 29.19.6–9). For detailed discussion, see now Eckstein, "Rome, the War with Perseus, and Third Party Mediation," 429–33.

39. Walbank rightly emphasizes that Astymedes' mission was a success (*Commentary* III: 420–21). Note that the ambassador was proud enough of his speech before the Senate to have a version of it published (Polyb. 30.4.11).

true those who endure every torture and punishment without being the cause of similar suffering to the others involved.[40]

But Astymedes and the Rhodians, fearing a danger that was hardly certain, revealed to Rome's power the already-forgotten delicts of others. "How, then, can those who learn of this conduct fail to disapprove of it?" (30.4.17).

Walbank would interpret this passage purely politically. Despite the moralizing language, Polybius was judging Astymedes' speech not as a moralist but as an Achaean; he found Astymedes' public airing of old anti-Roman actions and attitudes—presumably including those of the Achaeans—to be a threat to his own interests.[41] By contrast, Petzold lists Polybius's criticism of Astymedes as self-evidently based on perceptions of honorable versus shameful behavior in difficult times: the καλόν against the αἰσχρόν.[42]

No doubt as a patriotic Achaean, Polybius found betrayal especially distasteful when it was Achaea that was being betrayed. And, of course, in 166 he himself was a detainee in Rome on charges of anti-Roman behavior, so Astymedes' speech might have touched a very sore spot. Yet Polybius always claimed that the charges against him were false, whereas he heavily implies that the incidents brought up by Astymedes were true. The issue involved here was therefore quite different.[43] Nor is it likely that Astymedes' speech was directed primarily against Achaea. Polybius attacks him for exposing previous anti-Roman conduct by Greeks (4.14–17)—but the Achaeans had never played a conspicuous role in such conduct. These are very shaky grounds on which to argue that Polybius in 30.4 is a hypocrite.

Moreover, Polybius's comments on the conduct of Philip V after Cynoscephalae, much earlier in The Histories (18.33), are completely consistent with what he says in 30.4. Polybius underlines the fact that even in the confused aftermath of the Cynoscephalae defeat, Philip still managed to order the correspondence from his secret Greek supporters destroyed; he was concerned that this material would fall into the hands of the Romans (18.33.1–3). From Book 7 onward, Polybius's treatment of Philip has been unfavorable—but now the historian turns laudatory. Philip, he says, even in the midst of catastrophe, acted in a kingly fashion and did

40. For "civilized man" as the correct translation of ἀνὴρ πολιτικός at 30.4.15, see Walbank, Commentary III: 421. For πόρον (money) rather than πόνον (pain) as the correct reading at 30.4.16, see Walbank, ibid.

41. Ibid., 420–21.

42. Methode des Polybios, 60.

43. For the (false) accusations of anti-Roman behavior made against Polybius and others in 167, and for Polybius's actual policy during the Third Macedonian War, see Chap. I, above.

not forget to do his duty (τὸ καϑῆκον, 33.2). Indeed, for Polybius this act of good faith toward his friends, protecting them from Roman power, is the first sign of a general change for the better in Philip's character (his good "third phase" of development).[44] But Philip's action in 197 is, of course, the exact opposite of the conduct of Astymedes in 166, which was an attempt to appease Rome by exposing others to Rome's wrath.[45]

The balance of evidence and argument thus favors the hypothesis that Polybius's criticism of Astymedes in 30.4 is sincerely based on Astymedes' violation of the important general principle of good faith toward others enunciated at 30.4.15–16. And this fits well into the much larger general pattern of praise for good faith, and condemnation of treachery and deceit, that is found throughout *The Histories*. Let us begin with deceitful behavior among the Greeks.

Polybius condemns the conduct of the Epirotes in the crisis of 220; they voted publicly to join the war of Macedon's Hellenic Symmachy against Aetolia—but simultaneously informed the Aetolians that Epirus had in fact resolved to remain at peace with them (4.30.6–7). This deceitful maneuver was apparently prompted by Epirote fear of having to face Aetolia without direct Macedonian support.[46] But the tactics of 220 did not do the Epirotes any political harm. On the contrary: thanks to Philip V, the Epirotes soon made substantial territorial gains at Aetolia's expense.[47] Yet this means nothing to Polybius's evaluation of Epirote conduct: it was, he says (4.30.7), as ignoble (ἀγεννῶς) as it was two-faced (ποικίλως).

Walbank, once more, doubts the sincerity of Polybius's moralizing judgment, arguing that the true basis of Polybius's condemnation of the Epirotes is political: Achaean hostility to the eventual diversion of Macedonian military resources to northwest Greece in the first year of the Social War, when those resources should have been used instead to help the Achaean League in the Peloponnese.[48] Yet this, too, is a weak argument. Philip in the first year of the war did spend much time aiding the Epirotes militarily; but he spent at least as much time aiding the Acarnanians (cf. Polyb. 4.62–63)—and Polybius has only praise for Acarnanian conduct in this period (4.30.1–5).[49] But if the strategic impact was the same, then the difference in Polybius's assessment must lie precisely in

44. The ethical content of Philip's "change of heart" after Cynoscephalae is also stressed in the retrospective judgment at 25.3.9. On Polybius's view of the various stages of Philip's career, see Welwei, *Könige und Königtum*, 38–53.

45. On the sincerity of Polybius's criticism of Astymedes, and the intellectual link between Polyb. 30.4 and 18.33, see (briefly but cogently) Wunderer, *Polybios*, 15.

46. See Oost, *Roman Policy in Epirus and Acarnania*, 25.

47. See Walbank, *Philip V,* 38–40.

48. *Commentary* I: 477.

49. On Polybius's praise of the Acarnanians, see Chap. II, above.

the difference between the one conduct and the other. Polybius was impressed with Acarnanian bravery in openly declaring war against Aetolia despite their exposed position (4.30.1–5), and he was equally impressed with Epirote hesitation and deceit, and told his readers so.[50]

Two episodes from later Epirote history show Polybius again condemning on moral grounds policies of deceit and treachery that were quite successful in the real world of statecraft.

First, an incident of 170. By the time of the Third Macedonian War, Epirus had a relationship of alliance with Rome; this relationship may have been sanctified by treaty, or (more likely) it was informal but traditional.[51] Nevertheless, the prominent politicians Theodotus and Philostratus plotted with King Perseus to violate this alliance by kidnapping the new Roman consul A. Hostilius Mancinus as he was passing through Epirus on his way to his Greek command (Polyb. 27.16). The plot failed, and Hostilius escaped capture (27.16.5–6). But since Epirote reputation with Rome was now ruined, most of the Epirotes soon felt forced to commit themselves to Macedon.[52] In this broader sense the plot was in fact a success—as scholars have emphasized.[53] Yet ultimate pragmatic success is immaterial to Polybius here. He judges the attempted kidnapping harshly: it was "wicked and treacherous" (ἀσεβής, παράσπονδον, 27.16.1).

But if Polybius, on moral grounds, judges this anti-Roman Epirote action harshly, he is equally ready to judge a *pro*-Roman Epirote politician harshly—and again on moral grounds. Charops, Polybius says, was a naturally ambitious young man, and filled "with every sort of wickedness" (πάσης πονηρίας, 27.15.6). When Rome's war with Macedon broke out, Charops began denouncing senior Epirote statesmen to the Romans. Polybius emphasizes that the charges were false; but the Romans became convinced that these men—prominent among them Cephalus, a person of great wisdom and nobility—were their enemies (15.8–12). The result was that they were eventually forced to flee to Perseus, while Charops ended up running Epirus.[54] Charops essentially ruled Epirus, with Ro-

---

50. Note that Polybius condemns the deceit of the Epirotes in 220 even though the primary victims of that deceit turned out to be the Aetolians—traditional enemies of Achaea, for whom Polybius normally has little sympathy.

51. For a formal treaty: Hammond, *Epirus,* 621; Walbank, *Commentary* III: 315. Against (with strong arguments): Gruen, *Hellenistic World and the Coming of Rome* I: 23. If Gruen is correct, the fact that Polybius views the incident described below as a violation of good faith becomes even more noteworthy, showing that he is not always tied to a strict legalism.

52. For discussion, see esp. Oost, *Roman Policy in Acarnania and Epirus,* 75–77.

53. See Meloni, *Perseo,* 257; Oost, *Roman Policy in Acarnania and Epirus,* 77; Hammond, *Epirus,* 627–28; Deininger, *Politische Widerstand gegen Rom,* 175; Walbank, *Commentary* III: 316.

54. Cephalus, meanwhile, took his own life after the Macedonian defeat—receiving from Polybius yet another encomium for his steadfastness and noble principles despite political failure. See Polyb. 30.7.1–4, discussed in detail in Chap. II, above.

man support, for the next ten years, and he died in power (cf. Polyb. 32.5–6).

And none of this political success impresses Polybius. He condemns Charops bitterly, as an evil man who rose to power through deceit and treachery (27.15.6–9). Similarly, Polybius condemns Charops's successful contemporary Lyciscus in Aetolia (cf. 32.4): he, too, brought false accusations of "anti-Roman" behavior against his rivals (30.13.11), and even massacred some of them, successfully defending himself with more "anti-Roman" accusations (Livy [P] 45.31.1–2).⁵⁵ Polybius calls the passing-away of this generation of ruthless pro-Roman politicians "a kind of purification of Greece" (καθαρμόν τινα . . . τῆς Ἑλλάδος, 32.5.3).

Of course, one might argue once more that these judgments are informed by mere personal bias, since Polybius himself had been the victim of a similar maneuver ("anti-Roman" accusations) in Achaea. But in fact Polybius's distaste and disdain for deceitful Greek politicians comes out as early as Book 5, in a context far removed from Rome. Here Polybius describes the contest between Epigenes and Hermeias for influence over the young Antiochus III around 220. He depicts Epigenes as wise and honest (5.49.1 and 6); Hermeias, by contrast, was consistently wrong (5.49.2–5; cf. 51.5), and, motivated by "thoughtless and violent passions" (49.3), placed his own interests over those of the state (49.2–5). Eventually, Hermeias's jealousy of Epigenes (5.50.7) led him to bribe one of Epigenes' slaves to plant a forged letter from the pretender Molon, then challenging Antiochus III, among Epigenes' papers (50.11). An official search then led to the discovery of the letter—and to Epigenes' execution (50.12–14). Hermeias's maneuver was completely successful politically; he now became Antiochus's chief counselor (cf. 51.5). Nevertheless, Polybius is harshly condemnatory: Hermeias worked by means of lies (5.49.4) and "evil machinations" (κακοήθειαι, 50.5).

The breadth of Polybius's view here, and the sincerity of his concern, becomes even clearer when one considers his attitude toward the conduct of the Romans themselves. When the Romans engage in conduct that Polybius considers deceitful or in violation of good faith, he does not hesitate to point this out, with negative judgmental emphasis.

The most famous example is Polybius's assessment of the Roman seizure of Sardinia in 238/237. Under the terms of the peace treaty of 241, which ended the First Punic War, the island remained under Carthaginian control. But during the war that immediately developed between Carthage and the mercenaries, the mercenary garrison on Sardinia ap-

---

55. Livy 45.31.1–2 even includes criticism of L. Aemilius Paullus for not pursuing an objective investigation of this incident. On Polybian derivation of the passage, see above, Chap. I.

pealed for Roman protection, and eventually the Romans occupied it. When the Carthaginians protested, the Senate threatened war; and the Carthaginians were forced not only to cede Sardinia formally to Rome, but also to pay a large supplement to the war indemnity imposed in 241.[56]

Polybius consistently presents the Roman action as a violation of good faith—and condemns it. Thus in his direct narration of the Sardinia crisis, he indicates that the Romans falsely accused Carthage of preparing for war against Rome, and then used this false accusation as a pretext for declaring war themselves, forcing Carthage into a humiliating diplomatic surrender (1.88.8–12); this conduct is contrasted with previous Roman behavior, when "they are justly abiding by the treaty" (83.5). The affair reappears in Book 3, for Polybius considers it one of the main causes of the Second Punic War; and the resultant discussions are even more explicitly condemnatory of Rome. At 3.10.1 Polybius says that during the original Sardinia crisis the Carthaginians were confident of the justice of their position (τοῖς δικαίοις)—but the Romans refused even to negotiate (10.3). A bit later Polybius criticizes Hannibal for not revealing the true causes of his hostility to Rome: instead of complaining about Saguntum, he should have demanded back Sardinia and the extra war indemnity so unjustly demanded by the Romans (ἀδίκως, 3.15.10). Then, in discussing the series of treaties struck between Rome and Carthage, Polybius indicates that the Sardinian and monetary "additions" forced upon Carthage by the Romans during the Sardinia crisis were "contrary to sworn oaths" (παρὰ τοὺς ὅρκους, 3.28.1), and "completely unjust" (παρὰ πάντα τὰ δίκαια, 28.2).[57] Finally, when Polybius gives his summarizing judgment as to who ultimately was to blame for the new war, he indicates that he considers the Roman conduct regarding Sardinia and the extra war indemnity to have been "robbery" (ἀφαίρεσις, 3.30.4), and concludes that from this perspective the Carthaginians therefore had good reason for entering upon a second war (εὐλόγως, ibid.).[58]

It is hardly likely that Polybius was expressing here a pro-Punic politi-

---

56. For a convenient summary of the Sardinia crisis of 238/237, see Errington, *Dawn of Empire*, 30–34. Roman seizure of Corsica was at issue as well (Errington, 33).

57. Pédech, *Méthode*, 191–92, believes this passage to be almost completely legalistic in tone. But when Polybius indicates that the Roman seizure of Sardinia was "contrary to sworn oaths" (3.28.1) as well as παρὰ πάντα τὰ δίκαια (28.2), there is surely a strong moralizing element present.

58. The word ἀφαίρεσις occurs only here in the extant Polybian text. Mauersberger translates it merely as "Wegnahme," i.e., "seizure" or "confiscation" (*Polybios-Lexikon* I:1, col. 297). But in view of Polybius's stress on the injustice and illegality of Roman actions (3.28.1–2), and his opinion at 3.30.4 that the Carthaginians had good reason to go to war (where ἀφαίρεσις makes its appearance), the darker term "robbery" seems a reasonable rendition. Cf. Schweighauser, *Lexicon Polybianum*, col. 77: "adimere, tollere, eripere"; and the remarks of Walbank, *Commentary* I: 358.

cal bias; as far as is known, he had no personal ties to Carthage or to individual Carthaginians. Instead, these early volumes of *The Histories* were written in Rome, where he was a politically vulnerable detainee, and had established close personal associations within the Roman elite. One might therefore have expected a defense of Roman conduct in the Sardinia affair—not an attack. Indeed, the Romans had evolved just such a defense, based on the Punic imprisonment of Italian merchants who had been trafficking with the rebel mercenaries about 240. Polybius rejects this (see 3.28.3; cf. 1.83.7–11).[59]

On the Sardinia affair, then, Polybius appears to be exercising firm independence of judgment.[60] His stress on Roman bad conduct in 238/237 perhaps originates partly in his austerely intellectual interest in the nature of historical causation, that is, his sincere belief in the causative impact of events in the far past, as opposed to the surface events immediately preceding an outbreak of fighting.[61] Probably Polybius also wished to demonstrate his own original thinking and research on the topic of this particular war—including thinking regarding the impact of Sardinia.[62] But finally, another important element behind Polybius's stress on Roman bad conduct in 238/237 seems simply to have been his distaste for the sort of behavior he thought the Romans had displayed.[63]

The lack of good faith shown by Rome in 238/237 resulted, in Polybius's opinion, in negative military-political consequences: a devastating new war with Carthage. But it is important to note that Polybius is equally censorious of Roman bad faith when it has *no* negative consequences— and even when it strengthens Roman power. Polybius's presentation of three episodes from the 160s and 150s—when Rome already held undisputed hegemony over the Mediterranean world—demonstrates this aspect of the historian's thought.

59. Pédech suggests that the "merchant" tradition comes from Fabius Pictor (*Méthode*, 192); Walbank suggests that it derives from contemporary polemics in the late 150s (*Commentary* I: 356).

60. Polybius's highly negative depiction of Roman behavior in the Sardinia affair is more evidence showing the incorrectness of recent assertions that because of Polybius's position as a political detainee, and/or as a "client" of the Aemilii, he had little choice but to paint every Roman action in as positive a light as possible: so now esp. Reiter, *Aemilius Paullus*, 20–21 and 32; Green, *Alexander to Actium*, 278.

61. Polybius's description of the origins of the Second Punic War was one of his prominent didactic examples of the distinction between true αἰτίαι (causes) and mere ἀρχαί (events precipitating hostilities): 3.6–7. Cf. the remarks of Pédech, *Méthode*, 191–94.

62. Note his delight in being able to bring into the debate over the causes of the war Hannibal's story of the oath against Rome that he took before his father, Hamilcar (3.8–12); this was new. Cf. Pédech, *Méthode*, 193.

63. It may be that Rome's association with mercenaries in the Sardinia crisis (Polyb. 1.88.8) is another reason why Polybius instinctively viewed Roman conduct in the affair as disreputable: cf. Musti, *Polibio e l'imperialismo romano*, 54.

First: another example of Roman interaction with Carthage. In 162 or 161 the Senate effected the resolution of a dispute going back to around 167 between Carthage and King Massinissa of Numidia, over the prosperous Lesser Syrtis region.[64] Polybius describes the final Roman act of arbitration—and every previous Roman involvement in this matter—as a cheat. Massinissa's claims on the Lesser Syrtis, Polybius says, were unjust (31.21.7). Nevertheless, the Carthaginians always came off second best in the arbitrations of the dispute, not because of the rights of the situation (οὐ τοῖς δικαίοις, 21.6), but because the Roman arbitrators were convinced that it was in Rome's best interest to decide against Carthage (συμφέρειν, ibid.).[65] Thus in the end, Polybius says, the Carthaginians not only lost the Lesser Syrtis and its wealthy towns, but were also forced to pay Massinissa the large sum of five hundred talents as "recompense" for the revenues allegedly lost from the region during the dispute (31.21.8). In Polybius's view, the decision of 162/161 strengthened Roman power (cf. 21.6). Yet it is equally clear from Polybius's language that his intention in 31.21 was to criticize the Romans' lack of good faith as arbitrators, and to evoke in the reader sympathy for the Carthaginians.[66]

Next: Polybius's presentation of a Roman interaction with the Ptolemaic kingdom. In 163 Ptolemy VIII (nicknamed Physcon, "Big Gut") came to Rome to complain about the division of the kingdom that had just been negotiated, in which he had received only Cyrene, whereas his elder brother, Ptolemy VI, had gained Egypt itself, and Cyprus.[67] Ptolemy Physcon now begged the Senate to assign him Cyprus as well as Cyrene; even so, his share of the kingdom would remain much inferior (Polyb. 31.10.2–3). The two Roman envoys who had been present during the Ptolemaic negotiations—evidently L. Canuleius Dives (pr. 171) and Q. Marcius Philippus (son of the consul of 169)—strongly supported the original division of the kingdom, and the position of Menyllus, the ambassador of Ptolemy VI. They stressed Ptolemy Physcon's deep unpopu-

64. For the dates of the inception and final resolution of this quarrel, see Walbank, *Commentary* III: 489.

65. The Roman interest lay generally in restricting Punic wealth and power. Perhaps also the Senate was concerned about disturbed conditions in Cyrene in this period, and wished to interpose the friendly Massinissa between Cyrene and the Carthaginians: cf. Hoffman, "Römische Politik," 330 n. 54; Walbank, *Commentary* III: 492.

66. Polybius's concern for justice in the Carthaginian-Numidian affair is noted by Ferrary, *Philhellénisme et impérialisme*, 307–8.

67. The Roman role in this negotiation is not clear. Roman envoys were present in Alexandria at the time (see below), and scholars often assume that their intervention was crucial: see, e.g., Otto, *Zeit des 6. Ptolemaers*, 90–94. But perhaps the brothers simply worked out the agreement between themselves, in the face especially of Physcon's deep unpopularity in Alexandria: see Polyb. 31.10.4, with the comments of Gruen, *Hellenistic World and the Coming of Rome* II: 696–7. See also next note.

larity with the Alexandrians, and declared that he had been lucky to get away from the capital with his life, let alone with Cyrene; and they stressed that Physcon had already solemnly exchanged oaths with his brother to accept the agreement (31.10.4–5).[68] Yet the Senate decided in favor of Physcon, and ordered an embassy to reconcile the two brothers and to establish Physcon's rule on Cyprus (31.10.9–10). Polybius's explanation of this decision is a famous passage (31.10.7):

> For many decisions by the Romans are now of this type: availing themselves of the mistakes of others, they effectively build up their own power, yet at the same time appearing to be doing a favor and conferring a benefit on those who have made the mistake [τοὺς ἁμαρτάνοντας].

In this case, Polybius says, the Senate feared the power of an Egyptian monarchy mostly in the hands of a single capable ruler, and so decided on a move to split the kingdom more equally between the two quarreling brothers (10.8–10).[69]

The point here is not whether this Polybian analysis of senatorial motivation is correct; rather, it is the very existence of it in the Polybian text in the first place. The whole of 31.10 is in fact rhetorically constructed to emphasize the immorality of the senatorial decision. By describing the testimony of the two Roman envoys in detail, Polybius stresses the unpopularity of Physcon, the reasonableness of the original agreement, and the fact that it had been sealed by oath. He then presents the *Patres* as deciding to overturn this solemn and evidently just agreement, simply in order to strengthen Roman power—and he adds that such cynical behavior is increasingly the Roman way.[70]

It may well be that personal bias plays some role in this passage. Polybius obviously despised Ptolemy Physcon, and held a somewhat better opinion of Ptolemy VI. In addition, he became a friend of Menyllus, Ptolemy VI's envoy to Rome during this episode.[71] But even if one chooses

68. On the identity of the two Roman envoys, see Otto, *Zeit des 6. Ptolemaers,* 93–94. Their relatively junior status—Canuleius was only an ex-praetor; Philippus had not yet held curule office—tells in favor of Gruen's thesis (above, n. 67) that the Roman intervention in the Ptolemaic agreement was minimal.

69. For the translation of τοὺς ἁμαρτάνοντας as "those who have made a (political) mistake," see the persuasive argument of Ferrary, *Philhellénisme et impérialisme,* 309–10. The "mistake" is then Physcon's: in his desire for more territory, he divided Ptolemaic power.

70. If τοὺς ἁμαρτάνοντας at Polyb. 31.10.7 is to be translated as "the guilty party"—so, e.g., Walbank, *Polybius,* 170; and "Polybius between Greece and Rome," 12—then Polybius's point is even more negative: the Romans were consciously helping unscrupulous characters throughout the Mediterranean.

71. Polybius's dislike of Ptolemy Physcon: see not only 31.10.4–5 but esp. 31.18.4. His opinion of Ptolemy VI: see esp. 39.7.5–6. His friendship with Menyllus: see 31.12.8–13; cf. Diod. 31.18.1; and Gruen, *Hellenistic World and the Coming of Rome* II: 699.

to emphasize this aspect of 31.10, Polybius's bias toward Ptolemy VI is easily seen as based in good part on ethical standards: he thought Ptolemy Physcon a brute, Ptolemy VI a mild and fairly capable ruler. Hence one should view his negative assessment of the senatorial decision to back the repulsive Physcon as rooted in ethical disapproval, too: it was contrary to justice, a fact not to be outweighed by Roman self-interest.[72]

Finally: the Roman actions involving Demetrius of Syria. Demetrius had been sent to Rome when a child, as a hostage for the behavior of his father, Seleucus IV. But in 175 Seleucus had been assassinated, succeeded eventually on the throne by his brother, Antiochus IV; then in 163 Antiochus had been succeeded by his own son, Antiochus V.[73] Polybius says that it had long been thought that Demetrius's detention in Rome was unjust (παρὰ τὸ δίκαιον), and even more so now, when the Seleucid throne was held by only distant relations (31.2.1). In addition, Polybius says, Demetrius actually had a more just claim to the Seleucid throne itself than did the sons of Antiochus IV (καθῆκειν γὰρ αὐτῷ μᾶλλον, 2.4). In 163 Demetrius therefore launched an appeal to the Senate to allow him to return home (2.5). The *Patres*, however, required him to remain a hostage (2.6). In Polybius's opinion, this decision was reached because the Senate thought it would serve Rome's interests better (συμφέρειν) to have a weak Seleucid regime with a child on the throne, rather than allow Demetrius, a vigorous young man of twenty-three, to take charge of Seleucid affairs (2.7). Hence the Senate now even sent out an embassy to Syria to order the destruction of the Seleucid fleet and war elephants (2.11).

The Roman embassy to demilitarize Syria ended disastrously, with the assassination of the senior envoy, Cn. Octavius (consul 165), by an outraged Greek.[74] The government of Antiochus V apologized profusely (Polyb. 31.11.2), but Demetrius thought it possible that the *Patres*, angry with Antiochus's regime, would now allow him to return home (summer 162). Polybius says that he advised Demetrius not to try the Senate again, because the *Patres* had not changed their goals (31.11.2 and 11–12); instead, he urged him simply to escape (11.5). But Demetrius was persuaded by his friend Apollonius—a young and naive person, Polybius comments (ἄκακος, 11.7)—to approach the Senate once more, on grounds of the obvious injustice of the situation (ibid.). Polybius, in his own voice, agrees with Apollonius's view that the Senate's policy toward Demetrius was unjust (contrary to τὰ δίκαια; cf. 11.11). But Demetrius's

---

72. Cf., rightly, Musti, *Polibio e l'imperialismo romano*, 81. By contrast, Walbank, "Polybius between Greece and Rome," 12, sees Polybius's view of Roman action in this affair as detached, or even approving on utilitarian grounds.

73. For the politics involved here, cf. Mørkholm, *Antiochus IV,* 36–37.

74. Sources: cf. Broughton, *Magistrates* I: 443.

second appeal to the Senate also failed, as Polybius had predicted—because the *Patres* saw their unjust policy as benefiting Rome (τὸ συμφέ-ρειν, ibid.).

Demetrius eventually did escape from Rome (late summer 162), and was able to establish himself as ruler of Syria. His propaganda, however, stressed his ties to the Romans—and he made sure to turn over to the Senate the assassin of Cn. Octavius, as well as the prominent anti-Roman orator Isocrates (Polyb. 32.2). Rome acquiesced in the coup: in 161/160 Demetrius was recognized as king by the envoy Ti. Sempronius Gracchus (31.33.3–4), and Polybius indicates that the Senate itself formally recognized Demetrius as king in spring 159 (32.2.3 and 14).[75] In 154 Demetrius again showed his desire for good relations with Rome by sending to the Senate Andriscus, the dangerous pretender to the throne of Macedon (he later escaped). Andriscus was a central figure in the last volumes of *The Histories,* so Polybius will surely have described this incident in detail.[76] Then in 153 Demetrius sent his young son to Rome, to be presented to the Senate. The senatorial reception was diplomatically correct, though perhaps not too enthusiastic (μετρίας ἀποδεχῆς, Polyb. 33.10.5). That seems a fair description of Roman relations with Demetrius's regime down to 153.[77]

This is the background that Polybius must have sketched in preparation for his discussion of the senatorial reception in 153 of the Seleucid pretender Alexander Balas. It is clear that though Alexander was backed both by Pergamum and Egypt, Polybius viewed him as a total fraud.[78] According to the historian, as a preliminary to Alexander's appearance before the Senate, Heracleides—a former high official of Antiochus IV—engaged in much "baseness and intrigue" (33.15.2); this must mean bribery (cf. Diod. 31.27a). When Alexander and Heracleides finally did appear before the Senate, they appealed for Roman help in regaining Syria for this "son" of Antiochus IV; at the least, they wanted explicit senatorial permission to attack Demetrius with their own resources (Polyb. 33.18.7–9). Polybius sneeringly describes the scene in the Senate as "artfully constructed theater" (18.10), and "complete trickery" (18.11).[79] He says that the more sober-minded men (οἱ μέτριοι, 18.11) found the whole affair

75. See, rightly, Gruen, *Hellenistic World and the Coming of Rome* II: 664–65; against Walbank, *Commentary* III: 517.

76. On Demetrius's turning-over of Andriscus to Rome, see Diod. 31.40a (in a Polybian context: cf. 31.40), and 31.15; Zon. 9.28; with Walbank, *Commentary* III: 560. Polybius's interest in Andriscus: see 36.10 *passim,* and 36.17.13–15.

77. Cf. de Sanctis, *Storia dei Romani* IV: 3, 163.

78. See the remarks of Walbank, *Commentary* III: 557. Note esp. Diod. 31.32a (in a Polybian context).

79. Heracleides' trick was helped by the appearance of Antiochus IV's real daughter Laodice at the side of Alexander (cf. Polyb. 33.18.6 and 9).

displeasing; and clearly he expects his audience to take the same contemptuous attitude. Yet the majority of the *Patres* voted for a *senatus consultum* authorizing the attack on Demetrius, and containing vague promises of Roman help for the project (18.12–13). This allowed Alexander to prepare a serious expedition against Demetrius (18.14)—one that would ultimately be successful.[80]

The conduct of the Senate in this sequence of incidents with Demetrius is obviously subjected by Polybius to heavy criticism. In 31.2 the historian draws the conflict between justice and expediency (the δίκαιον and the συμφέρον) in stark terms, and the Senate chooses the latter. The conflict between justice and expediency (δίκαιον and συμφέρον again) is repeated in 31.11, with a bitter remark indicating that only the innocent would expect the Senate to treat Demetrius with justice (11.5; cf. 12.1). And it looks as if Demetrius's friendly gesture in turning over to the Senate a dangerous pretender to the throne of Macedon is followed in Polybius by the Senate's disreputable decision to back a fraudulent pretender to Demetrius's own throne—a decision, Polybius says, repulsive to all moderate men (33.18.11).

Of course, Polybius was a personal friend of Demetrius, advising him closely on how to deal with the Senate and even helping him to escape from Rome in 162. But this does not mean that Polybius has consciously distorted the content and tone of senatorial policy for personal or political reasons. For what better evidence could there be that the historian sincerely felt Demetrius to be the victim of senatorial injustice than his personal participation in Demetrius's escape? This was a highly dangerous action for Polybius to take.[81] And on the other hand, the historian is clearly able to maintain a significant degree of objectivity and distance regarding Demetrius: he presents Demetrius as having a serious drinking problem while living in Rome (cf. 31.13.9); he presents him as a disgraceful drunk later on in Syria (33.19); and he views Demetrius's Cappadocian policy as unjust and deceitful (cf. 32.10.4–8).[82] The conclusion would seem to be that if Polybius depicted Demetrius as a victim of senatorial violation of justice and good faith in Books 31 and 33, it was because he sincerely believed that this was the correct interpretation.[83]

F. W. Walbank has argued, of course, that Polybius's perspective on

---

80. For the details of Alexander's successful campaign against Demetrius, which led to the latter's defeat and death in 150, see Walbank, *Commentary* III: 561 (with sources).

81. For detailed discussion, see Chap. I, above.

82. For detailed discussion of Polyb. 32.10, see Chap. I, above.

83. Cf. the comments of Musti, *Polibio e l'imperialismo romano*, 82—who, drawing on Polyb. 15.20, notes how well Polybius's negative portrayal of the Senate's relations with Demetrius in Book 31 fits into Polybius's general concern that young rulers not be taken advantage of by the more powerful. On this facet of his thought, cf. also 30.26.9 (discussed below).

Roman policy in Books 30–33 is "cynical and detached."[84] In other words: Polybius accepted the "Machiavellianism" of Rome's "new diplomacy" of the mid-second century; it was the legitimate instrument of an imperially minded state.[85] And this is because the historian in general did not pay much regard to "sentiment" where politics was concerned—"a pretty ruthless approach, but Polybius was ruthless."[86]

Walbank's view has certainly been influential. And to be sure, there are passages in Books 30–33 where Polybius recounts "Machiavellian" actions by Rome without much comment: the refusal of the Senate to allow Eumenes II of Pergamum an interview in 167 (30.19); the refusal of the Senate to hear the cases of the Achaean detainees in Italy, or to let them return home for trial in Achaea itself (30.32); a senatorial attempt around 160 to divide Eumenes from his brother, Attalus (32.1.7).[87] Furthermore, the fragmentary condition of Books 30–33 mandates a certain degree of caution in attempting to reconstruct any overall Polybian judgment of Roman policy in these volumes.[88] Yet the quantity of surviving material concerning Roman foreign relations is quite large, and given the interest of the Byzantine excerptor in the conduct of embassies, it may well be that little vital material has been lost on this particular subject.[89] Hence the evidence of the episodes collected above—concerning Carthage, the Ptolemies, the Seleucids—is surely enough to demonstrate that Polybius's attitude in Books 30–33 was often *not* emotionally "detached," or accepting of Roman "Machiavellianism." On the contrary: he often explicitly condemns such policies on moral grounds, as violations of justice (παρὰ τὸ δίκαιον), and he condemns them even when he is also explicit that such policies had great utilitarian value in maintaining or increasing the power of the Roman state.

Indeed, that attitude had apparently already been prefigured in Polybius's discussion, somewhat earlier, of a major event of 172/171. It was

84. See "Political Morality," 11; "Polybius between Greece and Rome," 11–12 (where cynical aloofness is in fact presented as congenial to Polybius's temperament in general); "Polybius's Last Ten Books," 147. Cf. also Gabba, "Aspetti culturali dell'imperialismo romano," 71.

85. Walbank, "Political Morality," 8 and 10; *Polybius,* 173; and, in general, "Il giudizio de Polibio su Roma," 1–20.

86. See Walbank, "Political Morality," 7 and 11; *Polybius,* 171 and 178.

87. Possibly one should add the Senate's refusal to punish the Syrian assassin of Cn. Octavius, in order always to have a grievance against the Seleucid state; but Walbank makes the point that Diodorus's description of senatorial statements on this issue as "devious and obscure" (31.30)—hardly complimentary—may well derive from Polybius himself (*Commentary* III: 521). As for the Senate and the Attalids of Pergamum, note that Polybius describes an earlier Roman attempt to split the family as "mad" (30.2.4), and praises the Pergamene diplomat who prevented the Roman scheme from succeeding (30.2 *passim*).

88. Cf. Ferrary, *Philhellénisme et impérialisme,* 306–7.

89. Persuasively argued by Walbank, "Polybius between Greece and Rome," 33.

here that Polybius (in a lost part of Book 27) first responded to what he viewed as a disturbing new stance of the Senate toward international political maneuvering. The *Patres* at that time approved the policy of Q. Marcius Philippus, who held out to King Perseus the prospect of a negotiated end to the current crisis between Rome and Macedon, although in reality Marcius was only playing for time while completing Roman preparations for war (Livy [P] 42.39–43). To judge from Livy, Polybius depicted this consciously deceptive policy as being approved of by the majority of the Senate, although not by the older men, and those who were mindful of the ancient ways (42.47.4). These men argued against Marcius's policy on moral grounds (47.5–8); they did not like—in a famous phrase—"this new and excessively clever 'wisdom'" (47.9); "but the day was won by that part of the Senate for whom pragmatic advantage was more important than honor" (ibid.).[90] Walbank vigorously denies that the Polybian judgment on senatorial policy that forms the base of Livy's depiction of the *Patres* in 42.47 carries any moral implications, or is an indication that Polybius disapproved of the ruthless and self-interested policies carried out by the Romans henceforth.[91] I simply do not see how this idea can be maintained if one accepts (as even Walbank does) that Livy 42.47 derives from Polybian material. On the contrary: what is apparent here is, precisely, a sternly negative Polybian reaction to senatorial "Machiavellianism." It is the same negative reaction often seen in Books 30–33.

Polybius's mood in Books 30–33—not "detached and cynical," then, but often ready to approve or disapprove of actions on moral grounds—can also be seen in the historian's descriptions of the various Greek embassies that come to Rome in the course of these volumes. If the Senate in 30–33 often acts for "Machiavellian" reasons, committing injustice in Polybius's eyes, so too the Greeks often act with deceit toward the Senate, and are condemned by Polybius for that—even when such conduct is politically successful.

A whole range of Greek actions belongs here. The charlatanry and bribery of Heracleides and the fraudulent Alexander Balas in 153 (Polyb. 33.15 and 18) has been discussed above, as has the picture of "shameless lying" regarding the dispute over Cappadocia in 158/157 (32.10). Ptol-

90. For Livy 42.47 as Polybian in derivation, see Nissen, *Kritische Untersuchungen*, 250; Walbank, "Polybius between Greece and Rome," 10–11 and 23; and Briscoe, "Q. Marcius Philippus and *Nova Sapientia*," 68 and n. 22. Note the opposition here between the cynical mass of the Senate and the older men, who are still motivated by antique Roman morality; the wisdom and moral superiority of the old is a strong Polybian motif (see Chap. V, below). Note, too, the explicit conflict in Livy 42.47 between honor and pragmatic advantage. That, too, is of course a persistent Polybian theme: for the conflict between the καλόν and the συμφέρον, see esp. 21.32c.1 (the explicit theory: above, p. 84); also: 15.24.4–5; 24.12.2.
91. "Polybius between Greece and Rome," 23–24.

emy Physcon attempts to mislead the Senate concerning the circumstances of the arrangement made with his elder brother, Ptolemy VI
(31.10.4–6); Ptolemy VI himself misleads senatorial envoys concerning
his willingness to abide by the new division of the kingdom decided upon
in Rome (31.18.1–2; cf. 19.1).[92] The *Patres* are consistently misled by the
accusations of aggression brought by Prusias II of Bithynia, and the Galatians, against Eumenes of Pergamum.[93] No wonder that the Senate eventually comes to view Greek accusations against one another with deep
suspicion—even when those accusations turn out to be true (32.16).[94]

Of course, Polybius's Greeks are busy deceiving each other in this period, too—not just the Romans—and receive Polybius's condemnation
for it. The Cydonians of Crete seize the city of Apollonia by surprise attack, though the Apollonians were united to them by sworn treaty of joint
citizenship (28.14.3); Polybius's comment is that this was an act "universally seen as terrible and treacherous" (14.1; cf. 14.4).[95] Antiochus IV renews his attack on Egypt in 169/168 in (it seems) direct contravention
of an agreement made the previous year with Ptolemy VI (29.26).[96] To
Polybius, this proves Simonides' maxim "It is hard to be good" (χαλεπὸν
ἐσθλὸν ἔμμεναι, 26.1). And he continues, in his own voice (26.2):

> For it is indeed easy to be *disposed* toward honorable behavior [τὰ καλὰ],
> and to strive for it, but to maintain such a policy consistently under every
> circumstance, holding nothing to be more important than honor and jus
> tice [τοῦ καλοῦ καὶ τοῦ δικαίου]—this is difficult.

Walbank dismisses Polybius's remark here as "banal."[97] But the moral
tenor of 29.26.2 should not be underestimated in this fashion. As with
Polybius's employment of Homer in the passage describing the death of
Cleomenes III (5.39), Polybius here is using a text familiar to his audience

---

92. Similarly, Polybius is probably the source for the story that Ptolemaic envoys appeared before the Senate in 169 tricked out in rags, in order to dramatize the plight of
Egypt in the face of aggression from Antiochus IV, and the story that Ptolemy VI successfully manipulated the *Patres* in 164 by appearing before them tricked out in rags, in order
to dramatize his plight after being expelled from Egypt by Ptolemy Physcon. See Gruen,
Hellenistic World and the Coming of Rome II: 657 and 694–95.

93. Hence Polybius's continual use of the term διαβολαί ("false accusations") to describe
these communications from the East: 30.30.5; 31.1.3, 8.2, 32.3; 32.1.5–6. Cf. Ferrary, *Philhellénisme et impérialisme*, 315.

94. On Polybius's disapproval of Greek diplomatic tactics in Books 30–33 as violations
of the καλόν, see esp. Petzold, *Methode des Polybios*, 60–61. By contrast, both Walbank (*Polybius*, 169–70) and now Ferrary (*Philhellénisme et impérialisme*, 315–17) use this material merely
to show that in Polybius's pragmatic judgment, the Romans could be careless in their diplomatic interactions.

95. For detailed discussion of this incident, see Chap. I, above.

96. For discussion of this agreement, see Walbank, *Commentary* III: 357–58.

97. *Commentary* III: 403.

in order to underline to them the seriousness of his comment.[98] And the
sincerity of Polybius's disgust with Antiochus's action is shown by the fact
that he criticizes it again a volume later: the luxury on display at Antiochus's festival at Daphne in 167, he says, had been stolen from Egypt
when Antiochus had treacherously attacked Ptolemy Philometor, who was
still a child (30.26.9).[99]

Polybius can therefore be shown often to have been disapproving in
The Histories of deceit and violations of good faith, no matter who had
committed them—a theme that is apparent even in those later books that
have been held up as the most cynical volumes in the work. It follows,
then, that adherence to honesty and good faith should win Polybius's
applause. And examples of just such approval can be found throughout
the Polybian narrative.

Hence Polybius wishes Roman conduct in 238, when the Senate refused to take Sardinia and Tunis under Roman protection against Carthage, to be seen in a positive light: at that time, he says—clearly as opposed to the later time when Rome in fact seized Sardinia—the Romans
"were holding loyally to their treaty engagements" (1.83.11).[100] Similarly,
Polybius praises his own Megalopolitans—along with the Stymphalians
and Cleitorians—for maintaining their loyalty to the Achaean League
(2.55.8–9); he praises the Acarnanians for maintaining their loyalty to the
Hellenic Symmachy (4.30.1–7); the Gazans for their loyalty to the Ptolemies (16.22a); the Seleucid commander at Perge for doing his duty toward Antiochus III (21.42.1–5); and the Prienians for their good faith in
dealings with Orophernes of Cappadocia (33.6). In all these latter incidents, those who kept loyally to their agreements ran terrible risks; and
the Megalopolitans, Gazans, and Prienians in fact suffered severely. But
clearly this is of little importance in Polybius's positive assessment of
their actions.[101]

And Polybius is concerned that individuals, as well as communities,
show good faith. This makes sense in view of his audience—aristocratic
men of affairs, who would be taking responsibility for important events.[102]

98. On Polybius's use of the *Iliad* in his portrayal of the last actions of Cleomenes, see
Chap. II, above. On the ideological importance that the Simonides quotation had for Polybius, see, rightly, Wunderer, *Psychologische Anschauungen*, 29; and Chap. VIII, below.

99. For Polybius's general concern about young rulers' being taken advantage of by the
stronger, see Musti, *Polibio e l'imperialismo romano*, 81 (cf. above, n. 83). To judge from Diod.
30.18, it is likely that Polyb. 29.26 is only one part of a much longer Polybian attack on
Antiochus in 169/168 on moral grounds. On the Polybian derivation of Diod. 30.18, see
Walbank, *Commentary* I: 478.

100. On Polybius's highly negative judgment of Rome's later actions in Sardinia, see
above, pp. 100–102.

101. For detailed discussion of all these episodes, see above, Chap. III.

102. On the nature of Polybius's audience, see above, Chap. I.

Thus Polybius tells his readers that it would be more agreeable and profitable to reflect upon the loyal conduct of Gelo of Syracuse than upon his disreputable son, Hieronymus, for Gelo sought to achieve the most noble of deeds in life (κάλλιστον)—not to esteem wealth or royal power or anything else above affection and loyalty to his family (7.8.9). Again, Polybius praises the loyalty of Achaeus toward his young kinsman Antiochus III: this was to act with nobility of spirit (μεγαλοψύχως, 4.48.9). But then Achaeus, puffed up by his military successes in Asia Minor, decided to declare himself king: Polybius calls this "running aground" (48.11). Similarly, he praises the mutual good faith and loyalty characteristic of the Attalid family of Pergamum, for this was indeed noble (λαμπρόν, 22.20.7).

Loyalty to family connects naturally to loyalty to the community. A particularly striking example of Polybius's ideology here is his discussion of the behavior of P. Cornelius Scipio. After his great victory at Baecula in 208, he refused the title of king offered him by the Spanish chiefs (10.40). Polybius presents the refusal as a great example of Scipio's nobility of spirit (μεγαλοψυχία, twice: 40.6 and 7). And later, Polybius says, Scipio could have obtained kingship in any part of the world he chose, for his conquests in Spain, Africa, and Asia were on such a scale that not only a man but even a god might have become overweening (40.7–8); but Scipio so far excelled others in nobility of spirit (μεγαλοψυχία again, 40.9) that when kingship was often offered him by Fortune he refused it, putting a higher value on loyalty to his country than on the monarchical power that is the object of universal admiration and envy (ibid.).

Polybius's praise of Scipio here could hardly be stronger, and it is especially significant that he is well aware of Scipio's ultimate fate: political defeat and disgrace in the 180s, followed by death in exile (cf. Polyb. 23.14). Utilitarianism is thus not Polybius's guiding star as he makes his assessment of Scipio in 10.40. Rather, honor is—in the form of good faith (πίστις, 40.9) toward one's community even in the face of unusual success, power, and temptation.[103]

Of course, in the above passages (as so often in this study) it is possible to find ways of questioning Polybius's sincerity, on grounds either of political bias or even sheer momentary rhetorical flourish. Thus the praise of Gelo's family loyalty (7.8.9) is part of a larger polemic aimed at historians

---

103. For discussion of the Scipionic political catastrophe of the mid-180s, see Astin, *Cato the Censor,* 59–73; and Scullard, *Roman Politics,* 290–303. The political career of L. Aemilius Paullus himself may have suffered in the 180s because he was an in-law of Africanus (cf. Scullard, 170). This cannot be proven (see Reiter, *Aemilius Paullus,* 113); but in any case the fall of Scipio must have made a great impression on Paullus and his family. Hence Polybius would have had access to much information—and it would surely have been presented to him as a tragedy of great proportions.

whom Polybius criticizes for their melodramatic descriptions of the reign of Gelo's evil son, Hieronymus (7.7 *passim*); and melodrama is one of Polybius's favorite accusations against literary rivals.[104] As for Polybius's praise of Scipio Africanus's loyalty to Rome (10.40), it is easy to suspect the working of personal bias here, since Polybius's friend Scipio Aemilianus had been adopted into Africanus's own family. And the passage certainly contains rhetorical exaggerations of Africanus's achievements.[105] Similar considerations of political bias might be advanced regarding Polybius's praise of the Pergamene royal family in 22.20: Polybius as a rising young politician in Achaea clearly had good relations with the Attalids, passing a pro-Pergamene measure through the Achaean assembly in 170/169 (Polyb. 28.7).

Such elucidation of the possible biases in the Polybian text is a necessary part of scholarship. But the possibility of such biases should not be allowed to obscure the likelihood of a strong element of sincerity in these passages. Thus while appeals to the virtues of family loyalty and solidarity may seem obvious enough, the world of the Hellenistic monarchies was in fact riven by destructive intrafamily feuds, which could sometimes degenerate into outright civil war. Polybius during his lifetime could observe this ruinous process within all three of the great dynasties—Ptolemies, Seleucids, Antigonids. Hence his praise and then his condemnation of the Seleucid Achaeus (for which no political bias has ever been adduced). The historian here is not merely mouthing clichés; this was an important contemporary issue.[106] And if he holds up the royal family of Pergamum as an especially positive example of mutual loyalty, he is equally comfortable criticizing Attalid policy when he thinks such criticism is deserved: witness the long and bitter discussion of the greed of Eumenes II in his relations with Perseus of Macedon (29.5–9).[107] As for Polybius's praise of Scipio Africanus's loyalty to Rome, it has already been noted in this study how much evidence exists to show that Polybius did not adopt a sycophantic attitude toward the family of L. Aemilius Paullus and Scipio Aemilianus. He can be critical when necessary. It was not the

104. Compare Polybius's similar criticism of Phylarchus (2.56–63).

105. Cf. Walbank, *Commentary* II: 253.

106. The Ptolemies: see esp. Polybius's remarks at 31.10.7. The Seleucids: Polybius's depiction of the career of his friend Demetrius I demonstrated the perils of family factionalism. The Antigonids: see the speech Polybius gives Philip V in 23.11, warning his sons of the dangers and immorality of family division (and the speech fails).

107. On Polyb. 29.5–9, see Chap. III, above. Note that Polybius's approving depiction of the virtuous harmony of Queen Apollonis and her sons (22.20) finds confirmation in several contemporary inscriptions, most famously *OGIS* 308 (the Hieropolis Dedication). These are, of course, official pronouncements; but the theme is most unusual, and it is difficult to believe that it is made up out of whole cloth. For discussion, see, rightly, van Looy, "Apollonis, reine de Pergame," 157–59.

family connections of Africanus but the man's personal qualities—as Polybius understood them—that played the greatest role in endearing Africanus to the historian.[108]

One final example serves to demonstrate the sincerity with which Polybius approached the issue of good faith in the conduct of politics. In 22.19 he records a dispute between the two Achaean statesmen Philopoemen and Archon. Because of the fragmentary condition of the text, neither the date of the dispute nor its topic—which was evidently of some importance—is clear.[109] But Polybius personally witnessed the colloquy, and he passes a moral judgment on the behavior he witnessed. At some point during the dispute Philopoemen changed his tactics and began agreeing with Archon, praising him warmly for having acted in a clever and adroit fashion (22.19.1). But, Polybius says (19.2), "I myself, being present, did not then approve of what was said—attempting to inflict injury upon a man while appearing to praise him—nor do I approve of it now, when I am farther along in years."

Polybius goes on to draw a sharp distinction (22.19.3) between the principles of the man who possesses great ability in practical affairs (ὁ πραγματικὸς ἀνήρ) and the man who merely aims at success by unscrupulous methods (ὁ κακοπράγμων). And then he draws an even sharper distinction (ibid.) between what he calls true skill (ἐντρεχῆ) and mere low cunning (κακεντρεχῆ): the one quality is the noblest to possess (κάλλιστα), but the other is the opposite; and we should not fail to distinguish carefully between them, although they share many points in common (19.4). Yet many people give both qualities equal admiration—because of the prevailing lack of good judgment (ibid.).

Walbank insists that the latter part of 22.19 cannot be aimed at Philopoemen, since Polybius would hardly have used such severe language in describing a man he regarded as a hero. The reference to "lack of scruples" and "low cunning" must therefore have been aimed at the conduct of Archon (whatever it was)—the conduct then under dispute.[110] This in itself would be a most interesting finding, however—since Archon had been the closest political ally of Polybius during Polybius's crucial hipparchy of 170/169.[111] Yet evidently Polybius felt free in *The Histories* to criticize even as close a political ally as Archon, when he felt the man

---

108. Modern scholars sometimes argue that Polybius's representation of Africanus makes him too rational a personage (see above, n. 4). But Polybius's favorable depiction at 10.40.9 of Scipio's adherence to good faith toward Rome grants Scipio a position based on ethics alone, without regard to narrow, rational utilitarianism.

109. On the possible historical background to the dispute in Polyb. 22.19, see Walbank, *Commentary* III: 209.

110. *Commentary* III: 210.

111. For discussion, see Chap. I, above.

had engaged in "low cunning" and "lack of scruples"—that is, immoral trickery—in political affairs.

Indeed, if Walbank is correct that Archon is the target of the latter part of 22.19, what is striking is that Polybius here is then attacking both his close ally, Archon, *and* his old hero, Philopoemen, on grounds of their employment of trickery in politics. For the Polybian attack on Archon is a hypothesis; Polybius's attack in Philopoemen is a fact. The historian describes the nature of Philopoemen's deceit—the false (or ironic) praise of Archon—and condemns it, twice (22.19.2).[112] One could hardly have a better example both of the distance Polybius sought to maintain in *The Histories* regarding all the personages he wrote about, and also of the importance to him of condemning evil-intentioned deceit in political life.

Unless, of course, *all* of 22.19 is actually an attack on Philopoemen and his deceit—which is also a possibility. Note that as the passage now stands, Philopoemen is the only figure explicitly engaging in such deceitful conduct, and Polybius explicitly attacks him for it (19.2). And despite Walbank, the appearance of such a negative commentary on Philopoemen here would not be completely surprising. Polybius had warned his readers early on in *The Histories* that he would praise or blame the same person depending on circumstances and conduct; he was comfortable with the complexities and contradictions of human behavior.[113] And in introducing Philopoemen himself in *The Histories,* he implies that both praise and blame (ἐπαίνου καὶ ψόγου) would be employed even in the depiction of this heroic personage (10.21.8, twice). Thus Polybius could criticize Philopoemen very heavily in 22.19 without shocking his audience—or departing from his generally very positive depiction of the man. On the above hypothesis, Polybius's point in 22.19 is simply that Philopoemen in the dispute with Archon had acted badly.[114]

Whether or not a condemnation of Archon accompanied the condemnation of Philopoemen in 22.19, it is therefore fitting to end the discussion of deceit and good faith in Polybius where this chapter began—with

112. That Philopoemen's remark in 22.19.1 is meant to be ironic is suggested by Pédech (*Méthode,* 226), and more strongly by Walbank (*Commentary* III: 210). But despite Walbank (ibid.), the sharpness of Polybius's language in 22.19.2–3 militates against the hypothesis that the passage is intended merely as a critique of the use of irony in political speeches. Something more substantial is involved: at the least, Philopoemen's conscious failure to maintain before an audience the crucial distinction between skill and low cunning, thus contributing to the degeneration of political life (19.3–4—assuming that this refers to conduct of Archon misleadingly described by Philopoemen; but see below).

113. See Polyb. 1.14.5–9, 4.8.7, and 16.28.4–9; with the remarks of Pédech, *Méthode,* 204–16.

114. On the criticism of Philopoemen in 22.19 as evidence for Polybius's attempt to maintain objectivity about the actions even of a man whom he considered overall to be a hero, see Lehmann, *Glaubwürdigkeit des Polybios,* 194–95.

Polybius's childhood idol. In Polybius's view, and using the terminology of 21.32c with which our discussion opened, Philopoemen may have done the politically efficacious thing in employing deceit in his dispute with Archon (τὸ συμφέρον), but it was certainly not a noble thing (an example of τὸ καλόν). Philopoemen is therefore subjected, despite whatever personal liking and respect Polybius felt for him, to the historian's moralizing criticism. If in 21.32c Polybius praises the skill with which Philopoemen in regard to Spartan policy had managed to combine both the συμφέρον and the καλόν, here in 22.19 he thus makes it clear that between the two, it is the καλόν that should be seen as superior.

CONCLUSION

It is typical of traditional aristocratic societies that they produce codes of behavior that emphasize honesty in interaction with others as part of the general ideology of honor. Conversely, deceit is seen as "low"—ignoble in every sense, including (ideally) restriction of such "low" behavior to those of low social status.[115] Hence in ancient Mediterranean culture one important reason why merchants, slaves, and the poor were all despised by the aristocracy was allegedly because their circumstances prevented them from engaging in honest speech, and prevailed upon them to lie— something that no honorable man could bring himself to do.[116] Polybius grew up within the aristocratic landowning culture of the central Peloponnese, and it is now clear that he fully partook of these ideas.

To be sure, there are passages in *The Histories* where Polybius seems to accept (or even praise) double-dealing or misrepresentation. But I have argued that much of this evidence has been wrongly interpreted, and that the rest of it must be viewed (for various reasons) as highly ambiguous. Thus this material does not in itself present a strong case that Polybius was in general a "Machiavellian" when it came to deceit and good faith.

Moreover, these episodes must be balanced by the very much larger number of cases where Polybius unambiguously condemns the employment of deceit and betrayal in public life, and explicitly praises specific acts of good faith. Examples run the gamut from condemnation of

---

115. Kautsky in his useful survey of the ideology of aristocratic cultures worldwide, emphasizes honesty (esp. the keeping of one's word) as an important element in such aristocratic ideology: *Politics of Aristocratic Empires*, 169–71. Furtiveness and cunning conceived of as "low" by such ideologies: ibid., 203.

116. For traders, see the references collected by MacMullen, *Roman Social Relations*, 115 and n. 88. For slaves, see especially Cic. *pro Sulla* 88. In antiquity, "the rich frankly confessed that only they themselves could afford to be honest" (MacMullen, 116, with manifold examples in n. 90 to the conceptual connection between poverty and deceitful behavior).

Rome's seizure of Sardinia from Carthage in 238/237, via condemnation
of Philip V in 215–200, to condemnation of Astymedes of Rhodes in the
160s; from praise of the Acarnanians for abiding by their word in 220,
via praise of Scipio Africanus's loyalty to Rome and its republican system,
to praise of the Prienians for maintaining good faith under very difficult
circumstances in the 150s.

In some of the cases discussed above, unethical conduct certainly led
to negative consequences for the perpetrator, either immediately or in
the long term (as with the Carthaginians' reaction to Rome after 238/
237). Sheer pragmatism thus plays a role in Polybius's urging his audience to avoid deceitful behavior. But in many other cases the perpetrator
suffered no ill effects, or even profited from breaking good faith—yet
Polybius still condemns him. This strongly suggests that Polybius was sincerely concerned with the καλόν. This is why, although to Polybius
the dividing line between skillful political manipulation and downright
double dealing was narrow and perhaps ill defined (cf. 22.19), it was also
crucial (ibid.). The historian viewed the political maneuvers of Scipio Africanus or T. Quinctius Flamininus as skillful. But when his hero, Philopoemen, crossed over the line here, Polybius was quite ready to criticize even
him—on moral grounds.

Of course, Polybius's moral judgment was not modern, nor was it
based solely on an ideal of humaneness. Deceit was literally ignoble (ἀγεν-
νής, 4.30.7); as such, it was unworthy of the aristocratic men for whom
Polybius was composing *The Histories*. To engage in such ignoble behavior
was, to Polybius, a betrayal of oneself (cf. 15.23.5).

But there was another negative aspect as well. Emphasis on the maintenance of correctly honorable behavior among his aristocratic audience
was all the more important to Polybius because in fact he saw society as
powerfully threatened by amoral and violently irrational forces, both
from within and from without. Correct and sternly honorable conduct
by the elite had to be the major bulwark against this threatening chaos;
conversely, "low" behavior by the aristocracy could contribute powerfully
to it. It is the deep social anxiety at the heart of Polybius's obdurate advocacy of the καλόν—an anxiety that has rarely been noted by scholars—
that forms the subject of the next chapter.

FIVE

Threats to the Social Order in
The Histories, and the Polybian Response

*What precisely is the machinery which in any society guarantees authority?
The fundamental answer . . . lies in the usage of language itself,
the way it is weighted in favour of approving one set of assumptions
and disapproving another.*
—ERIC HAVELOCK

INTRODUCTION

So far in this study, we have established Polybius's ideal of the politically responsible individual. He was a personally courageous man, willing to risk his life (or even die) for his community—and for the sake of honor (Chapter II). He was willing to take action—even go to war—not merely for narrowly pragmatic goals, but also (again) for honor's sake (Chapter III). He was resistant as well to sordid methods of financial gain; and even if well off, he maintained a style of life marked by profound moderation (Chapter III). Finally, in politics his conduct was marked by a firm rejection of deceit and treachery even if it promised utilitarian success, and by staunch adherence instead to ideals of good faith (Chapter IV).[1]

The common denominator in all this seems to be Polybius's advocacy of an ideology of self-discipline and steadfast duty, based upon a perception that such conduct was, in and of itself, worthwhile—and a sign of nobility of spirit (μεγαλοψυχία). Here one must also remember that Polybius's aristocratic audience was in fact continually confronted by the temptations to which ancient social and political power was heir: pride, luxury, indolence, brutality. He warned against this, as had a whole array of historical writers before him (notably Herodotus, and Hieronymus of Cardia). These warnings appear to address a continuing sociopsychological problem, and are not mere literary conventions.[2]

But beyond the threat to self that the possession of power entailed,

1. Polybius's ideal figure is, of course, male; such was the society in which he lived. For Polybius's attitudes toward females, see below.
2. On Herodotus, note the tone set against overreaching and "hubristic" behavior right from the beginning of *The Histories* by means of the stories of Candaules, Croesus, and

Polybius also believed that the men for whom he wrote were responsible for protecting society from the forces of disorder and chaos that threatened it everywhere. It was up to mature aristocratic males to fend off all these threats—by means of courageous and rational conduct.

The purpose of the present chapter is to outline the various threats that Polybius thought menaced orderly society, and to outline the human behaviors he saw as common to those threats. Polybius in fact saw civilization as threatened by several concentric circles of menace. First there were the true "wild men," the uncivilized barbarians from beyond the physical frontiers of the Mediterranean world. Then there were the mercenaries: these, too, were uncivilized people, whom the civilized actually *invited* into their communities (often with dire results). Third, there were the masses: the disorderly populace who—unfortunately—formed a large and integral part of the city communities themselves. Finally, there were the forces of chaos found not only within the city community but within the aristocratic household itself: the aristocratic young, and women.

Polybius viewed each of these groups as highly suspect because of their supposed innate tendencies toward passion, violence, and lack of self-control. Against such a background of menacing disruption and chaos, it becomes understandable why the historian would insist upon the maintenance of a firm code of behavior on the part of that element within civilized society—mature aristocratic men—who formed the leadership of that society, the primary bulwark against the forces that threatened it, and the bulk of his own audience.

BARBARIANS

Students of the ancient world are, of course, familiar with the threat that the peoples of northern Europe posed to the Roman Empire, especially from the third century A.D. onward. What needs emphasizing is that the urbanized cultures of the Mediterranean actually began facing serious problems with the northern peoples half a millennium earlier. From the 280s B.C., severe Celtic raids became a constant source of anxiety to the Greeks. In Europe, the Celtic threat was joined to that posed by the Thracians, Dardanians, and Illyrians. Meanwhile, the same population movements that had brought the Celts to the frontiers of Greece also brought them in large numbers across the Aegean into central and western Asia Minor. From the 270s onward, the raiding and plundering of these Gala-

---

Cyrus—on which, see above all Stahl, "Learning through Suffering?" 1–36. On Hieronymus's emphasis on φιλαρχία and πλεονεξία, see Hornblower, *Hieronymus of Cardia*, esp. 170.

tian peoples posed a constant threat to the life of the Greek cities of Ionia.[3]

The barbarian threat to the Greek cities of the northern Mediterranean would in fact be terminated only by the arrival of Roman power. The Romans tamed the Galatians in Asia Minor, and in Europe kept the wild tribes at bay—not without substantial cost—beyond the Macedonian frontier. But much of this occurred only late in Polybius's lifetime. The menace of the northern peoples was therefore a significant element in Polybius's world; and his remarks in 2.35 indicate that he expected the threat to remain all too real for the foreseeable future.[4]

As Polybius presents them, the barbarians his world had to confront had several outstanding characteristics, all of them disturbing.

First: the barbarians' overwhelming numbers when compared to the armies of the civilized peoples. This was already a severe problem for the Greeks of Europe in the third century (cf. Polyb. 2.35.8). And it was a severe problem even for the Romans, who lived in constant dread of the devastating power of Celtic raids from the Po Valley (2.18.6–7 and 22.6–8). Hannibal intended to take advantage of the great numbers of Celtic warriors he would find available to him along the Po (3.43.2; cf. 68.8).[5]

In Spain, and in Gaul itself (modern France), the story was the same. Even Hannibal had a difficult time against the Spanish *barbaroi*, because of their huge numbers (armies of up to 100,000: Polyb. 3.14.3–7).[6] Naturally, then, Polybius depicts Hannibal as having been seriously worried about his march from Spain to Italy because of the enormous numbers and savage character of the peoples along the way (9.24.4). This was precisely why many people thought the march on Italy unfeasible (3.49.2).

Farther east, the situation was similar. The Gauls of Asia Minor, Polybius says, were the most numerically formidable people in the region

---

3. On the northern population movements of the 280s and 270s (which threatened Italy as well), see, conveniently, de Navarro, in *The Cambridge Ancient History* VII¹ (Cambridge, 1928), chap. 2. For the threat posed by the Galatians, see McShane, *Foreign Policy of the Attalids*, 35–37, 60–63. For the continual barbarian threat to European Greece, note Polyb. 9.35.1–4 (where Macedon—fairly enough—is presented as shielding the Greeks from the *barbaroi*).

4. The Romans had constant problems along the Macedonian frontier once they undertook the responsibility for defending it (which Cato the Censor had opposed for that very reason: cf. *SHA* "Hadrian" 5.3). The scale and persistence of the fighting, including many Roman defeats, is discussed now by Kallet-Marx, *Hegemony to Empire*, chap. 1.

5. On the numerical strength of the Gauls of northern Italy, see also Polyb. 2.23.1, 29.6, and 32.7. Celtic warriors eventually made up half of Hannibal's army at Lake Trasimene and Cannae; for discussion, see Eckstein, *Senate and General*, 29–30.

6. For detailed discussion of Hannibal's Spanish campaign of 221, see now Dominguez-Monedero, "La campania de Anibal contra los Vaccaeos," 241–48.

(18.41.7). To judge from the Livian narrative of Cn. Manlius Vulso's war against the Gauls of Asia Minor in 189—which is in good part drawn from Polybius—the theme of Gallic numbers was once again prominent in Polybius's account of this campaign.[7] And even after Manlius had damaged Galatian power, Polybius evidently indicated that the tribes remained a serious danger. This was proven by the devastating Gallic raids on Ionia in the 180s, repeated in the 160s.[8]

In a discussion of the city of Byzantium, Polybius presents his audience with a classic example of the perilous life of those Greek cities that had numerous barbarian tribes as neighbors. Byzantium was surrounded by *barbaroi* (in this case, primarily Thracians with an admixture of Celts), and victory over one tribe only resulted in three more powerful ones invading its territory (4.45.3): such was the barbarian numerical superiority (διὰ τὸ πλῆθος, 45.2).[9] Nor did the payment of tribute relieve the situation, for a concession to one tribe only raised up enemies five times more numerous (4.45.4). Thus the Byzantines were involved in a war that was both hazardous and never-ending: the torments of Tantalus (45.4–5).

But it was not numbers alone that made the barbarians such a menace. Polybius also underlines their ferocity, their treachery, their uncontrolled greed.

Thus the Celts of Asia Minor were "the most warlike of peoples" (Polyb. 18.41.7). The Celts of Gaul were not only extremely numerous but also very ferocious, savage (9.24.4). Nothing could be more terrible (δεινότερον) than the charges of the Celts of northern Italy (2.20.8), though the Celtiberians of Spain were fearsome indeed (cf. 14.8.9). The Thracian auxiliaries of Perseus fought the Romans with the ferocity of wild beasts (Livy [P] 42.59.2).[10]

It is typical of Polybius's barbarians, however, that their battle courage is undisciplined, and tends to degenerate into mere frenzy. Hence his

7. The theme of great Gallic numbers: cf. Livy 38.12.4 and 12.6 ("Gallorum opes"), 16.1 (the population movement of the 270s), 16.13 (the great natural increase of the Celts once they were settled in Asia Minor), 16.15, 18.15, 22.7, 26.3 (the 50,000 warriors of the Tectosages and Trocmi). The parallels between Livy's account of Vulso's campaign and the surviving fragments of Polybius's Book 21 are very numerous and striking, showing the great extent of Livy's use of Polybius here. For discussion, see Nissen, *Kritische Untersuchungen,* 203–4. Livy also used Valerius Antias and Claudius Quadrigarius (cf. 38.23.8).

8. Polybius is likely to have covered the Galatian war of the 180s in some detail. He was interested in Ortiagon, the paramount chief of the Tectosages (see the character sketch in 22.21), and Ortiagon was a central figure in this war (see Segre, "Duo novi testi storici," 446–52, on the Telmessus inscription). On the devastating Galatian raids a generation later, see Polyb. 29.22.4 and 30.1.2, with McShane, *Foreign Policy of the Attalids,* 183 and n. 24.

9. For discussion, see Walbank, *Commentary* I: 498–99.

10. For this theme, see also Polyb. 5.44.7 and 10.31.2–3 (the primitive peoples of the Iranian mountains), and Livy [P] 37.18.7 (Galatians again; for the Polybian derivation of this passage, see Briscoe, *Commentary* II: 318).

description of the Ligurians in 154: they fought the Romans like maniacs, with madness and desperate courage (παραλόγῳ . . . θυμῷ); but they were defeated by the cool skill of Q. Opimius and his troops (33.10.5–6). Similarly, the anger and battle frenzy of the Ilergetes in Spain in 206 (παροξυν-θέντες . . . ἀλογίστως) were insufficient against the prudent calculation of Scipio Africanus (11.32.5–7). At Telamon in 225, the Celts were driven into self-destructive rage (θυμός, ἀλογιστία) by Roman tactics, dashing themselves insanely against the ordered Roman ranks (2.30.4); and the same phenomenon occurred during Cn. Manlius Vulso's campaign of 189 (Livy [P] 38.21.8–9).[11]

Polybius believed the behavior of the *barbaroi* had a tendency to degenerate even farther, into actions that contravened every human and divine law: what the historian calls παρανομία (21.40.2; cf. 3.3.5). One central component of *paranomia* was horrific, mindless violence. Polybius emphasizes that this was a prominent trait of all Gauls.[12] But the *barbaroi* whom the Greeks faced in the East were similar: the Hyrcanians destroyed innocent cities, murdering the innocent Greek civilians within them (10.31.10–11).[13] Another central component of barbarian *paranomia* was treachery; Polybius believed that barbarian promises—and even sworn oaths—were worthless. Thus the plan of the Iberian Abylix to betray Saguntum was "typical of a barbarian" (βαρβαρικόν) in its complete disregard of considerations of good faith (3.98.3; cf. 98.6). The Galatians planned to capture Cn. Manlius Vulso at a peace conference they themselves had asked for (21.39; cf. Livy [P] 38.25), and the Pergamene government was in constant fear of their treachery.[14] In fact, Polybius believed that the Celts were so inherently untrustworthy that for him, "Gallic treachery" (Γαλατικὴ ἀθεσία) was proverbial (2.32.8).[15]

Equally proverbial to Polybius was uncontrollable Gallic greed (2.7.6). The Celts were so greedy for loot that they even attacked one another when they were supposed to be allies (2.19.3). And of course, Celtic at-

---

11. This parallel in incident is another argument strongly suggesting that Livy's account of Vulso's war is primarily Polybian in derivation (see above, n. 7).

12. See Polyb. 3.3.5; 5.111.2; 18.37.9; 21.40.2.

13. On the behavior of the peoples of the East, see also Polyb. 9.34.3.

14. Polyb. 5.78.4; 15.24.7; 24.14.6–7.

15. On "Gallic treachery," see also Polyb. 3.70.4 and 78.2. Other *barbaroi:* 3.52.2–3 and 7 (Alpine tribes); 23.8.7 (Thracians). Yet Polybius's vision of pervasive "Gallic treachery" was not self-evident to everyone: a follower of Caesar could describe Caesar's opponents in Transalpine Gaul as having been "homines apertos minimeque insidiosos, qui per virtutem, non per dolum dimicare consuerunt" (*BAfr.* 73). To some extent, then, we are dealing with a Polybian cultural construct. And the close association in Polybius's mind between treachery and the βαρβαρικόν is yet another strong argument against the idea that he took a "Machiavellian" approach to the employment of such treachery in political life (see Chap. IV, above).

tacks on civilized communities—often sudden and unexpected (2.35.6)—were in large part caused by greed (2.22.2; 3.78.5).[16]

Barbarian numbers, ferocity, violence, treachery, greed, "insane" behavior: all these traits combined in *The Histories* to produce a picture of horrific disorder. Indeed, the term "barbarian" signified for Polybius disorder in general, because the *barbaroi* seemed to lead such undisciplined lives.

Polybius is explicit, of course, that the *barbaroi* were people in chaos. The unstructured, complicated, and constantly shifting politics of the barbarian tribes was an important factor in the great difficulties that civilized states had in establishing stable relations with them (cf. 4.45.4). It was symptomatic of Celtic behavior, for instance, that tribes putatively allied with each other could end up in bloody battle because of simple misunderstandings or mutual suspicions (2.18.4 and 21.4–5)—or that warriors could, in a fit of anger, murder their own chiefs (2.21.5). The problems here were exacerbated by the Celtic tendency toward anarchic drunkenness (2.19.4). Chaotic in their politics, the *barbaroi* were naturally disorderly in battle itself (ἀτάκτως, ἀταξία, 3.43.5, 12). It was precisely this close connection between the barbarian and disorder that allowed Polybius to describe the clash of cavalry at Cannae as degenerating into "true barbaric battle" (μάχην . . . βαρβαρικήν, 3.115.2)—by which he meant a battle where there was no orderly wheeling of military units, but only the struggle of every man for himself (ibid.). Indeed, Polybius's general judgment of the Celts in their war with Rome in the 220s can stand for his assessment of the character of barbarians as a whole: they always acted out of blind passion, rather than reason (θυμῷ μᾶλλον ἢ λογισμῷ, 2.35.3).[17]

When Polybius wishes to sum up his attack on the character of King Prusias II of Bithynia, he states that Prusias was entirely a stranger to literature, philosophy, and knowledge of the καλόν, but lived instead a feverish life of unrestrained sensual appetite (36.15.4)—"a barbarous life" (βάρβαρον βίον, 15.6). The link in Polybius's mind between disorder, lack of control, and the barbarian—and the contrast with civilized living (literature, learning, knowledge of the noble)—could not be clearer. And Polybius's emphasis on Prusias's lack of education is especially noteworthy, for this theme appears also in his description of the Celts of the

---

16. Polyb. 2.22.2 deals with the Gallic war of the 220s; other Celtic motives for this war, besides greed, include natural ferocity, and confidence in huge numbers (2.21.1–3). Some scholars stress Celtic fear of Roman aggression as the major cause of this war: Harris, *War and Imperialism,* 197–99; Dyson, *Creation of the Roman Frontier,* 28–29. One Polybian passage, connected to a condemnation of the "demagogic" tribune C. Flaminius, does emphasize this (2.21.8–9). But it is certainly not the primary element in the depiction Polybius presents.

17. Cf. also frg. 119 B-W, referring to ταῖς τῶν βαρβάρων ὁρμαῖς.

Po Valley. Polybius underlines the primitive physical conditions in which they lived: unwalled villages, beds of leaves, a lust for meat, a semi-nomadic life (2.17.9–11). But in addition, he is explicit about the Celts' total lack of exposure to higher thought: living merely for agriculture and war, they were ignorant of all the arts of civilization (17.9), and were without the slightest acquaintance of any knowledge or science (17.10).

This emphasis on intellectual barrenness is as close as Polybius comes to offering a deep explanation for the barbarous behavior of the barbarians: like Prusias, they lacked any exposure to a better life, which comes through education.[18] This is an explanation of barbarous behavior that Polybius, as we will see, applies to other categories of "disorderly" people.

Given the frightening depiction of the barbarian in *The Histories*, it will come as no surprise that in Polybius the typical reaction of civilized people to the barbarian is fear. The Gauls had struck paralyzing fear into almost all the Greeks during the great invasion of the 270s (cf. 9.39.4). The Greek cities of Ionia lived in great fear (μεγάλου . . . φόβου) of Galatian violence and *paranomia*—until the arrival of the Romans ameliorated conditions.[19] Even Hannibal feared the great numerical strength, ferocity, and treachery of the barbarians (9.24.4; cf. 3.78.2). And the Gauls of the Po Valley were a terror to all their neighbors (2.18.1)—including the Romans.

Polybius in 2.35 directly addresses such fears. He says that he has recounted the story of the failure of the Gallic attack on Italy in the 220s so that future generations should not be completely terrified by sudden and unexpected barbarian invasions (ἵνα μὴ τελέως . . . ἐκπλήττωνται, 2.35.6). The implication is that the barbarian threat is by no means resolved, but a continuing concern for civilized society; indeed, in this very passage Polybius says that even in his own generation the Greeks have often been terrorized by the prospect of barbarian attack (ἐξέπληξε, 2.35.9; cf. 25.6 *passim*). But he bids his audience (including the future) to remain steady in the face of this danger: for against the vast numbers and great resources of the barbarian tribes can be counterposed the power of determined courage and cool intelligence (2.35.8).[20]

Yet it is striking that Polybius at this point also finds it necessary to hold out the hope of the unexpected: after all, the great Gallic invasion of Greece in the 270s had failed because of unforeseen and strange events (2.35.7–8). This statement in fact suggests the depths of the morale prob-

---

18. See esp. Walbank, *Commentary* I: 184 (for the correct interpretation of 2.17.9–11). Polybius is in fact exaggerating the primitiveness of the Celts of the Po Valley (ibid.)—which only serves to underline the ideology involved in the passage.

19. Polyb. 5.111.7; cf. 3.3.5 and 21.40.2.

20. A persistent Polybian theme: see 3.14.3–7 (Hannibal's successes in Spain); 11.32–33 (Scipio Africanus's similar success); 33.10.5–6 (Opimius's success against the Ligurians).

lem among the Greeks of Polybius's age as they looked toward the barbarian frontier. The sense of living in a civilization threatened by great forces
of mindless chaos from the outside is a significant element in the mood
of *The Histories*.

MERCENARIES

To Polybius, mercenaries (μισθοφόροι) share many of the negative traits
of the hordes of *barbaroi* gathering outside the gates of Mediterranean
civilization. But there was one important difference: *misthophoroi* are a
force for chaos that has already been invited inside the gates. It is because
mercenaries represent such a direct threat to Polybius's vision of orderly
society that he dislikes and fears them so intensely.[21]

Mercenaries, to begin with, were redoubtable warriors. No one could
dispute this: it was the reason why communities hired them. Polybius
is clear about their martial abilities. Carthage, Massilia, Cleomenes III,
Antigonus Doson, Hannibal—all found mercenaries extremely valuable
in battle.[22]

Mercenaries were particularly formidable when well trained and under strict discipline (Polyb. 5.65.5; 11.13.3)—but Polybius repeatedly emphasizes the necessity that such troops be kept under strict control.[23] The
task required special skill on the part of their officers, and those officers
who could achieve it receive Polybius's approbation: most notably Hannibal (11.19.3–5).[24] The problem, however, was that mercenaries were by
nature very turbulent. Their sheer impulsiveness in battle could itself
have highly negative consequences.[25] In addition, they were easily disaffected from their officers and those who had hired them.[26] Officers perceived as weak were treated with overt contempt (5.30.1); indeed, Polyb-

21. This characteristic of *The Histories* was immediately recognized once Polybius became
available in the West during the Renaissance: see Momigliano, "Polybius's Reappearance,"
91–92. For Polybius, the problem was intensified by the fact that in his age, it was Thracians
and Gauls—*barbaroi*—who were coming to constitute the majority of mercenary troops (see
Griffith, *Mercenaries of the Hellenistic World,* 252–54).

22. See Polyb. 1.30.11, 48.3; 2.69.4; 3.45.2; 14.8.9; 15.13.1.

23. See Polyb. 1.66.10, 67.4–6, 68.1; 2.7.8.

24. See also Polybius's approbation of Xanthippus of Sparta (1.32; with the comments
of Griffith, *Mercenaries of the Hellenistic World,* 213), and the mercenary generals of Ptolemy
IV (Polyb. 5.63.11–65.7). Polybius's hero Philopoemen did a long stint as a commander of
mercenaries on Crete (Plut. *Phil.* 13). And Polybius himself, along with his father, Lycortas,
were requested by the Egyptian government in 169/168 to serve as generals against Antiochus IV (Polyb. 29.25.7). Presumably Polybius did not see mercenary service at this high
a level as dishonorable.

25. See Polyb. 1.30.11–12, 75.4; 16.37.6–7.

26. See Polyb. 1.9.3, 9.6, 67.4–6; 15.25.20.

ius believed that mercenaries were likely to be insufferably arrogant in the face of *any* perceived weakness (1.68.6–10; cf. 34.14.2).

This strong tendency toward total indiscipline—a trait they shared with the *barbaroi*—could easily lead mercenaries into wild and destructive rampages. And in such situations, their martial abilities could become dangerous in the extreme.

The classic case of such a rampage is, of course, the revolt of the *misthophoroi* at Carthage after the First Punic War. The Punic government lost control when it allowed mercenaries discharged from Sicily to gather in overlarge numbers, with their wives and children under their own control. The mercenaries, suspecting that the Punic government intended to cheat them of their full pay, became enraged (1.65.7, 67.6)—an anger fueled by confidence in their own power (1.66.6, 68.6–10). They murdered their Carthaginian officers, and thereupon degenerated into a wild mob. They began, Polybius says, to commit acts contrary to every human and divine law: they descended into παρανομία (1.70.5). They bound themselves with "impious oaths contrary to all human usage" (70.6), and soon were committing "hideous crimes" (ἀσέβεια, 79.8). A parallel rebellion of the mercenary garrison in Punic Sardinia resulted, Polybius says, in the torturing to death of every Carthaginian on the island (70.1–7). In sum, according to the historian, the rebellious mercenaries were not satisfied with merely human crimes, but "became like wild beasts, and madmen" (67.6).

Not men but beasts: this is a view of mercenaries, once they are released from externally imposed discipline, to which Polybius repeatedly returns. They "become like wild beasts" (ἀποθηριοῦσαν, 1.67.6; cf. 70.1)—a problem exacerbated by perpetual drunkenness (69.12). They became an "animallike" mob (ἀποθηριώσειαν, 1.79.8). They committed "animallike" crimes (ἀποθηριοῦσθαι, 1.81.5; cf. 81.9)—or, reversing the metaphor, "crimes worse than the cruelty of animals" (ὠμότερον . . . τῶν ζῴων, 81.7). For a civilized man, it was a terrifying prospect.[27]

Further, Polybius makes it plain that he is not referring here merely to the mercenaries of Carthage in 241–238: degeneration such as this was a problem typical of *misthophoroi* in general. Thus 1.67.4–7, where the "wild beast" theme first appears, is a general statement about mercenaries; the "animallike" behavior of the mercenaries of 241–238 is explicitly said to be just one example of it. Similarly, in 1.81.5–11, the "wild beast" theme occurs in the context of a Polybian attempt to frame a *general* psychological explanation for such explosions of mercenary savagery.

Nor is the war of 241–238 the only account of mercenary destructive-

27. On Polybius's depiction of the mercenaries during the war against Carthage, see in general Roveri, *Studi su Polibio*, 122–24.

ness in *The Histories*. Agrigentum was pillaged (2.7.7); Lilybaeum almost betrayed (1.43.7–9); Syracuse threatened (1.9.3, 9.6); Amphipolis almost pillaged and betrayed (Livy [P] 44.44.4–6); Phoenice in Epirus betrayed (Polyb. 2.7.6–11, in great detail); the Ptolemaic regime at Alexandria seriously threatened at least twice within a single generation.[28] At Messana in the 280s, mercenaries received into the city in friendship promptly seized it, murdering or exiling the men and taking the women and children for themselves (1.7.3–4). It was a famous incident; an example, Polybius says, of *paranomia* (1.7.2, 7.4)—the first to be recorded in *The Histories*. Polybius in fact considered such *paranomia* to be typical of the behavior of mercenaries.[29]

Messana was seized, Polybius says, because of the mercenaries' greed for the property of others (1.7.2). As with the *barbaroi*, so with the *misthophoroi*, the theme of ruthless greed is an important element in Polybius's picture. Gallic mercenaries pillaged cities and even temples they had been set to guard (2.7.7, 7.9); Thracian mercenaries threatened to do so at the slightest sign of governmental weakness (Livy [P] 44.44.4). The citizens of Tarentum knew that the Carthaginians had captured their city when they saw Hannibal's mercenaries systematically pillaging the Roman dead (Polyb. 8.30.12). The passionate avarice of mercenaries (ἡ πρὸς τὸ λυσιτελὲς ὁρμή) is, in fact, another of Polybius's general rules of politics (15.25.11).[30]

Polybius's analysis of why the *misthophoroi* possessed all these dangerous and destructive traits is that in origin, they were the uncivilized and uneducated outcasts of society. Gauls were often prominently represented in mercenary units, and from Gauls, of course, Polybius did not expect much: they were completely ignorant of the arts of civilization.[31] Polybius also believed that many mercenaries were in origin criminals. That was true of the Celtic unit that betrayed Phoenice (2.7.6), and of the mercenaries hired by Nabis of Sparta as well: murderers, robbers, burglars, highwaymen (13.6.3), men from all over the world who were guilty of the worst impieties and *paranomia* (6.4).[32] The mercenaries at Alexan-

28. See Polyb. 5.36.1–5 (the attempted coup of Cleomenes of Sparta) and 18.53–55 (Scopas the Aetolian). Note also Polybius's sour remarks on the power and arrogance of the mercenaries at Alexandria in his own day (34.13.3); and the comments of Griffith, *Mercenaries of the Hellenistic World*, 127–30. On Livy 44.44 (the story of the Thracians at Amphipolis) as deriving from Polybian material, see Nissen, *Kritische Untersuchungen*, 264.

29. On the incessant παρανομία of mercenaries, see 1.70.5, 84.10; 13.6.4; cf. 16.13.2 (ἀσέβεια καὶ πονηρία).

30. Cf. Polyb. 3.13.8, 17.7, 63.4, 86.10, 90.7, 111.8–9; 15.25.15, 25.20.

31. On the mental barrenness of the *barbaroi* as Polybius saw them, see above, p. 124.

32. This description of Nabis's mercenaries is accepted as basically accurate by Mendels, "Polybius, Nabis and Equality," 315; cf. also 318–23. By contrast, Texier, *Nabis*, 36 (cf. 27), presents Nabis's mercenaries as not real criminals but merely oppressed "social

dria—often feared by the Ptolemaic government itself (cf. 5.36.3)—were brutal and uneducated (βαρὺ . . . καὶ ἀνάγωγον, 34.14.2).[33] The idea that lack of exposure to any higher thought or civilization was the general explanation for the brutal behavior of mercenaries is central to Polybius's discussion of the origins of their often-bestial violence (1.81.5–6). Some men's souls, Polybius says, become animallike in an incurable way (81.5): their brutal, subhuman behavior is impervious either to kindness or to salutary discipline (81.8–9). The cause of this terrible phenomenon does not lie so much in natural or inborn traits but in bad, uncivilized upbringing (81.10):

> It is necessary to ascribe the original and most powerful cause of such a condition to the impact of uncivilized customs [ἔθη μοχθηρά] and bad up-bringing [τροφὴν . . . κακήν] from the time these men are children.

The effects of brutal customs and bad childhood training are then exacerbated by a life of habitual violence (81.11). This theme is prefigured at 1.67.8, where Polybius informs his audience that one of the lessons to be learned from the Mercenary War is the difference between "a barbarous, confused herd" and men raised with an education (παιδεία), under law and civilization.[34]

Under the conditions described by Polybius, the fundamental relationship between mercenaries and civilized communities—despite compacts of convenience—had to be mutual suspicion and potential violence. The treachery of mercenaries to their employers was, of course, a persistent Polybian theme.[35] But the historian does not hide the fact that there could be a lack of good faith on the employers' side as well. *Misthophoroi* were sometimes cheated of the full pay promised them.[36] A government might even find its mercenaries so much a threat that they were gotten rid of intentionally in battle. Hiero II removed his turbulent mercenary troops that way—to Polybius's approval (1.9.6). And the tone of satisfaction in that passage is matched by the satisfaction with which he later describes the annihilation of the Gallic Aegosagae (5.111.6–7): the tribe had been hired by Pergamum, and then had gone on a rampage in the Hellespont

---

bandits" (to use the terminology of E. J. Hobsbawm, *Primitive Rebels* [New York, 1959], chap. 2).

33. Note that a century later, Caesar could describe the social origins of the mercenary forces at Alexandria in words similar to Polybius's description of the social origins of the mercenaries of his own age: pirates, bandits, condemned criminals, exiles, fugitive slaves (*BC* 3.110).

34. Parallel comments on mercenary upbringing: cf. Polyb. 3.79.6, 89.5.

35. See above, pp. 126–27.

36. See Polyb. 1.66.5, with 68.4–11, on the Punic attempt to cheat the mercenaries in 241 (cf. Diod. 25.1); and Polyb. 4.60.2 (cf. 5–6) on a similar attempt by Polybius's own Achaeans.

(5.77–78, 111.2). But then, it was a Hellenistic commonplace that the person who rid a civilized community of "wild beasts" was doing humankind a favor (cf. Diod. 27.18.2).[37]

Polybius's depiction of the fearsome nature of mercenaries, and the fearsome threat they posed to a civilized community, was consciously meant as a warning to his audience. Even a city as powerful as Carthage had been in danger of destruction (1.65.4), and the story of the Mercenary War is narrated partly so that the audience can foresee and guard against the perils of using mercenary forces (65.7). That is also the explicit moral Polybius draws from the story of the betrayal of Phoenice in Epirus (2.7.2, 11–12).

Polybius's ideal is, in fact, a community that depends upon its own citizen soldiers for survival and freedom—not upon mercenaries. This emerges from his favorable comparison of Rome's military institutions (her citizen army) to those of Carthage: the best and noblest protection for a city was the martial courage of its citizen body, led by the local elite (cf. 6.52.4–7). Indeed, Renaissance and early modern political theorists found in Polybius an inspiration to get rid of their own mercenaries and to depend instead upon the valor of citizens.[38]

Polybius was well aware, however, that this was only an ideal. Not even Philopoemen, for instance, who worked so diligently to mold the citizen army of the Achaean League into an effective fighting force, had been able to put a total end to Achaean reliance upon mercenaries.[39] Therefore, although Polybius greatly preferred citizen armies (both on moral and practical grounds), the main thrust of his advice to his audience here is that since mercenaries will in all likelihood be employed, every effort must be made at least to control them carefully (cf. 2.7.12).

THE MASSES

Whereas mercenaries might be excluded from the civilized community, or at least their numbers and baneful influence kept to a minimum, the lower classes formed a large and permanent part of every city—and yet Polybius ascribed to them traits strikingly similar to those he attributed to *misthophoroi* and barbarians. No wonder, then, that he mistrusted "the mob," and viewed it as a frightening threat to orderly community life.[40]

Polybius viewed every *polis* as divided into a small elite (the ἀγαθοί, the

37. On this passage, see the important comments of Volkmann, "Griechische Rhetorik oder römische Politik?" 465.

38. Cf. Momigliano, "Polybius's Reappearance," 91–92.

39. For discussion, see Griffith, *Mercenaries of the Hellenistic World,* 103–6.

40. Wunderer, *Polybios,* 26, briefly (but correctly) notes the similarity between the Polybian depiction of the traits of the *misthophoroi* and the Polybian depiction of "the mob."

ἄριστοι, the προέστατοι) who were confronted by—and sought to control—the large and powerful force constituting the masses (called the πλῆθος, the πολλοί, or most pejoratively the ὄχλος, the mob).[41] The relationship between these two unequal parts of the city was an uneasy one. To be sure, in a certain mood Polybius is willing to compare the masses to a basically calm ocean—calm, so long as no wind stirs them up (11.29.9–11; 21.31.9–16). This must have been a comforting metaphor: the implication was that there was nothing fundamentally threatening in the socioeconomic structure of society, and hence the mass of the population was, when in its "natural" state, calm and harmless (ἀβλαβής, 11.29.10). But even the metaphor of the calm ocean indicated the peril the elite faced: those who sail upon the ocean have to beware of storms that can suddenly arise and overwhelm them (ibid.).[42]

The best order of affairs within a city, Polybius clearly believed, was one where the *plēthos* was obedient to the *aristoi*, who in turn earned this obedience by leading lives of self-restraint and wisdom.[43] The problem here for Polybius was that he saw the process of moral decay within an aristocracy as natural and in the long run inevitable.[44] And when decay had proceeded to a certain point, the elite lost control of itself, and soon after lost control of the masses.[45]

K.-W. Welwei has argued that the problem Polybius saw here resided in the striving of individual aristocrats for the favor of the masses—and not in any excess of freedom for the masses *per se*.[46] But this misses a central Polybian point about the *plēthos*. The misuse of influence and power by competitive aristocrats to corrupt the masses was indeed an issue of great concern to Polybius; it parallels his metaphor of the masses as basically a calm ocean, harmless unless stirred by the winds. But Polybius also believed that the masses themselves were all too easily corrupt-

41. The other term Polybius uses to indicate the general populace of a city—the δῆμος—seems to imply more respect: used mostly in regard to Rome and Rhodes, it is never used to describe, e.g., the "degenerate" masses at Alexandria or in Boeotia. See Mauersberger, *Polybios-Lexikon* I:2, cols. 454–56.

42. The metaphor of the "calm ocean" appears in two speeches Polybius attributes to historical figures. But there need be no doubt that Polybius approved this formulation: one speech belongs to his hero Scipio Africanus (11.29), and the other speech wins his explicit approval (21.31.6).

43. On this specific aspect of Polybian ideology, see Welwei, "Demokratie und Masse," 299. The idea adhered to by Polybius would endure in the Greek world far into the age of the Antonines: see the brilliant evocation of the political culture of the elites of the Greek cities in Brown, *Body and Society*, 9–13.

44. For discussion, see esp. Walbank, *Polybius*, 130–56.

45. See esp. Polyb. 6.44.5 and 57.7–9.

46. "Demokratie und Masse," 290; cf. 291 and 300.

ible, and that the more freedom they were granted within the political life of a community, the faster their corruption grew. That is: Polybius believed that the masses themselves could be an independent and very negative force in politics.

This belief comes through, for instance, in the general theoretical description of "the cycle of constitutions" (ἀνακύκλωσις) in Book 6. At the beginning of that discussion, it is the masses themselves, by their own violence, who establish a "democratic" regime—a regime that in turn contains the seeds of further degeneration into mob rule (6.4.9–10).[47] And at the end of the discussion, the populace once again—"aggrieved" and/or "puffed up"—is made responsible for the degeneration of the "mixed" constitution (6.57.7–9).[48] Equally important is that the collapse of moderate regimes and the rise of mob rule reveals to Polybius the terrible character of the *plēthos* once it has gained full freedom: the inevitable result is the emergence of "the regime of violence" (χειροκρατία, 6.9.8).[49]

Polybius believes that the reason a civilized community faces disaster once the mob has gained full power is because the masses possess little intellectual or moral capacity of their own. It is true that his picture here is not totally simplistic; for instance, occasionally in *The Histories* the masses behave rationally, or are persuaded to right action by rational arguments.[50] However, these are exceptional cases; Polybius did not view rationality as the normal basis of mass behavior. Instead, uncontrolled emotion was to him the most prevalent—and dangerous—characteristic of the masses and their conduct.

Not even the most benign of emotions—for instance, joy—can appear in the Polybian *plēthos* without threatening disorder and destruction. Thus in 196, the joy of the assembled Greek populace at T. Quinctius Flamininus's proclamation of "the freedom of the Greeks" resulted, according to Polybius, in a near-riot that threatened the life even of Flamininus himself (18.46.6–12).[51] The compassion of the mob, too, while often commendable,[52] has its dangers (see 27.9–10). And often, because of

47. τοῦ δὲ πλήθους ὀργῇ . . . γεννᾶται δῆμος. ἐκ δὲ τῆς τούτου . . . ὀχλοκρατία.

48. λήψεται δὲ τὴν ἐπιγραφὴν τῆς μεταβολῆς ὁ δῆμος. On this phrase, see Walbank, *Commentary* I: 745.

49. This "regime of violence" is brought about by the mutual interaction between aristocratic demagogues and the powerful passions of the masses (here esp. greed: 6.9.6–9). See further below, p. 137.

50. See 4.31.2 (Messene); 16.26.6 (Athens); 22.9.10 (Achaea).

51. The disorder depicted in this incident is emphasized by Wunderer, *Psychologische Anschauungen*, 41; *Polybios*, 26.

52. See 4.14.7–8 (Achaea); 31.6.6 (popular reaction to Roman oppression of Eumenes II of Pergamum); 38.18.4 (Achaea).

sheer lack of foresight, the joy of the *plēthos* at certain events is in fact utterly misguided.[53]

Usually, however, the emotions Polybius ascribes to the masses are dark to begin with. In contrast to their penchant for excessive joy, for instance, the masses in a crisis were highly susceptible to panic. Popular panic could be a threat to the rational management of a crisis at the very moment when a calmer assessment was both necessary and possible—as occurred at Rome after the defeat at Lake Trasimene (Polyb. 3.85.8–9), and during the Cannae crisis (3.112.7; cf. 118.7). Indeed, it is Polybius's considered opinion that if the *polloi* at Rome had been as powerful a force in decision making in 216 as they were at Carthage, then Rome would not have survived (6.51.5–8).[54]

But a far more prevalent theme than panic—and one that must have been even more disturbing to an author who wished to believe that the masses in their "natural" state were calm and harmless—is the theme of passionate popular anger. Sometimes such anger directly impinged on what Polybius describes as the prudent management of crucial military campaigns—and Polybius praises statesmen who have the moral fortitude simply to ignore it.[55]

It is not surprising, then, that Polybius deemed the *success* of an angry *plēthos* in interfering with the running of the state to be the gateway to catastrophe. The anger of the Alexandrian mob in 200 leads to scenes of horror as the government of Agathocles is bloodily overthrown.[56] The "anger and ingratitude" of the masses in Boeotia against their pro-Roman government (Polyb. 18.43.8) sets in motion in 197 a series of violent acts that eventually lead to Roman military intervention and the threatened destruction of the Boeotian state.[57] Fifty years later, an angry lower-class mob at Corinth, by insanely attacking a conciliatory Roman embassy, sets in motion the disastrous Achaean War (38.12.4–5). Examples could be multiplied.[58]

Polybius's depiction of popular anger as a powerful and destructive force in politics becomes even darker when it is linked with another per-

53. See 3.103.1–5 (Rome, in 216); 8.41.4 (Tarentum, in 213).

54. Low popular morale could also be a terrible problem in Achaea (2.47.8). Note that Polybius's *barbaroi* are subject to similar undisciplined panics: cf. 3.70.9 (Celts); 10.31.4 and 12 (Hyrcanians); Livy [P] 38.23.1–2 (Galatians).

55. Cf. 2.64.6 (Antigonus III Doson); 3.94.8 (Fabius Maximus). For this theme, note also 4.14.2 (Achaea); 29.1.1–3 (Rome during the Third Macedonian War).

56. Popular anger: 15.25.24(17), 26(19), 36(27); 15.27.1 and 3, 28.8, 32.6 and 7, 33.3. The ultimate result is a beastlike massacre: 15.33.5–9.

57. On the background to T. Quinctius Flamininus's invasion of Boeotia in winter 197/196, see, conveniently, Eckstein, *Senate and General*, 297–98.

58. On the riot at Corinth in spring 146, see esp. Gruen, "Origins of the Achaean War," 64. Cf. also 6.4.9–10 (a generalizing statement); 21.6.2 and 6.6 (Phocaea).

sistent Polybian motif—the inherent greed of the *polloi* for the property of others. Although in one passage Polybius does indicate an understanding that social tensions between rich and poor had their roots in local economic problems (5.93.4),[59] the general focus of his depiction of social strife lies in quite another direction: on the moral and intellectual failings of the *polloi* themselves.[60]

It was, for instance, inherent Aetolian extravagance (leading to debt), as well as sheer love of innovation, that led to popular calls for debt reform in Aetolia in 205 (Polyb. 13.1–1a)—and when, thirty years later, there was renewed debt agitation in Aetolia that led to murder, massacre, and the threat of civil war, Polybius's analysis apparently restricted itself to calling such agitation a "disease."[61] C. Flaminius's land-distribution proposal of 232 was, to Polybius, the first step in "the moral degeneration of the Roman people" (2.21.8)—for who knew what they would be demanding next?[62] In Sparta, the tyrant Nabis won popular favor not only by sharing out the land of the rich, but even their wives and daughters (13.6.2; cf. 16.13.1–2).[63] In Boeotia in the 190s, the *plēthos* was eager for the distribution of public funds, and agitated as well for the cancellation of debts, because (20.6.3):

> The masses thus learned to support and give political power to those men who would help them escape the legal consequences of debt and crime, and even in addition to be enriched occasionally from public funds by official favor.[64]

59. Interestingly enough, this passage concerns strife at Megalopolis, Polybius's own city.

60. Mendels, "Polybius and the Socio-Economic Revolution in Greece," 109, chastises Polybius for ignoring the causes of social strife despite the proclaimed emphasis in *The Histories* on the study of causation. This is too harsh: it is simply that Polybius's preferred *mode* of analyzing the causes of *stasis* is moral-political, rather than socioeconomic. Cf. also Welwei, "Demokratie und Masse," 300–301.

61. This Aetolian agitation is known only from Livy 41.25 and 42.5. But it derives from Polybian material: see Nissen, *Kritische Untersuchungen*, 241 and 243–44; Mendels, "Polybius and the Socio-Economic Revolution in Greece," 105. Livy's terms for the agitation: *furor* (41.25.7); *velut tabes* (42.5.7).

62. The criticism of Flaminius and the Roman *dēmos* here may well derive ultimately from Q. Fabius Pictor. Yet if it is included in *The Histories*, it is because of an act of volition on Polybius's part; i.e., it answered to a deep prejudice of his own. Cf. Walbank, *Commentary* I: 193.

63. For discussion, cf. Mendels, "Polybius, Nabis and Equality," 318–23. The sharing-out of the wives and daughters of the rich is downplayed by Texier, *Nabis*, 34–35.

64. The social agitation in Boeotia had a leader: the demagogic politician Opheltas (Polyb. 20.6.4). And Pédech, *Méthode*, 209, argues that for Polybius it is Opheltas who is the main factor behind Boeotian "degeneration"—a position similar to the general argument advanced by Welwei, "Democratie und Masse." But it is clear from the above passage that Polybius considered the Boeotian masses themselves, and their appetites, to be a crucial factor here.

The historian takes this social agitation in Boeotia not as evidence of so-cioeconomic distress, but merely as a sign of serious Boeotian mental dis-integration (καχεκτοῦντες . . . ταῖς ψυχαῖς: 20.7.4). Not surprisingly, with Boeotia in the hands of the mob, public policy was soon being decided on the basis of anger (20.6.10), followed by panic (6.12). The result, Po-lybius says, was final ruin for everyone (20.6.4, 7.1–2).

The classic example of Polybian political-moral analysis of social revo-lution, however, is his discussion of the disorder that rocked the city of Cius about 203/202, and that eventually led to its conquest by Philip V (Polyb. 15.21). The dominant figure in the Cian revolution was Molpa-goras, described by Polybius as a morally corrupt demagogue, greedy for power (21.1). Nevertheless, Polybius clearly did not conceived of the masses at Cius as mere passive instruments of Molpagoras. On the con-trary: the historian presents the masses as major culprits in the Cian tragedy.

The masses, Polybius says, were attracted to Molpagoras because he "flattered" them—and because he put the richer citizens in their power (15.21.2). It was thus with widespread popular *support* that Molpagoras murdered or exiled the Cian aristocracy, distributed their property among the *ochlos,* and won for himself tyrannical power (ibid.).

This description of the Cian revolution prompts Polybius to another of his long personal interjections into the narrative (15.21.3–8). The people of Cius met disaster, he says, chiefly owing to their own stupidity and perverse policy (21.3). For they advanced the worst men to power, and punished those who opposed them, "in order to plunder the for-tunes of their fellow citizens" (21.5). They thus walked open-eyed into a trap that had ensnared many others, showing themselves worse than the unreasoning beasts (τῶν ἀλόγων ζῴων, ibid.)—for animals at least do not readily approach those traps that have often caught others (21.6). Polyb-ius continues this bitter contrast (21.7–8):

> Men, on the other hand, although they have heard of cities having been utterly destroyed in the aforesaid fashion, and can see others being de-stroyed before their very eyes, nevertheless whenever anyone for the sake of winning their support holds out to them the hope of repairing their fortunes by laying hands on the property of others, thoughtlessly they rush for the bait, although they well know that of those who have swallowed such a bait not one has survived, but that such acts of policy have brought destruction upon all those who have adopted them.

It is obvious that this caustic passage is a commentary not upon the dema-gogue Molpagoras himself, but upon the forces that supported and in an important sense created him: the Cian masses and their appetites (cf. 21.4 and 7).

The theme of popular greed is paired by Polybius in 15.21 with the failure to look ahead—to perceive the negative long-term consequences of actions that are momentarily gratifying. In Polybius's view, the outcome in the case of the Cians was the tyranny of Molpagoras.[65] The same theme makes its appearance in Polybius's account of Boeotia (20.6–7), where the long-range consequence of popularly supported social agitation was the ruin of the entire state (20.6.4, 7.1–2). Indeed, Polybius in his commentary on the *polloi* at Cius is consciously establishing that the shortsightedness of the masses is a general rule of politics (see 15.21.3 and 7–8).

The prevalence of this lack of foresight among the masses is yet another reason why Polybius fears their intervention in the management of the state. And in a striking passage (38.11.9–11), it emerges that not even the historian's own Achaeans are exempt from such shortsightedness—which, as at Cius, Polybius couples with greed, and which, as in Boeotia, he pairs with popular anger.[66]

Polybius says that as the crisis between Achaea and Rome intensified (winter 147/146), the destructive demagogue Critolaus inflamed the anger of "the mob" (*ochlos*) against the Romans (38.11.9). Moreover, to insure himself popular support, Critolaus also got the Achaean magistrates to declare a moratorium on the repayment of loans, and on imprisonment for debt (11.10).[67] Polybius now interjects another bitter personal comment on the behavior of the masses (38.11.11):

> As a result of such appeals to the rabble [i.e., the debt reforms], everything Critolaus said was accepted as trustworthy, and the masses were ready to do anything he ordered—incapable as they were of taking thought for the future, and enticed by the bait of indulgence and ease in the present.

The end result of this process was the "insane" popular riot against Roman envoys at Corinth in spring 146, which set the stage for the outbreak of the disastrous Achaean war with Rome (38.12–13).[68]

Welwei, in his discussion of Polybius's exposition of these events, chooses to emphasize a somewhat earlier Polybian remark, at 38.3.13. There Polybius does indeed place the primary responsibility for the tragedy of 147–146 on the demagogic agitators, for they were the ultimate

---

65. See Walbank, *Commentary* II: 475. That tyranny, in turn, led to the brutal intervention of Philip V of Macedon: see Polybius's harsh comments about his behavior at Cius in 15.22; and Mendels, "Polybius, Philip V, and the Socio-Economic Question in Greece," 166.

66. The connection is noted by Wunderer, *Psychologische Anschauungen*, 40.

67. On the interpretation of Polybius's references to Critolaus's socioeconomic measures in 38.11.10, see above all Walbank, *Commentary* III: 703–5.

68. On the irrational riot at Corinth, see also above, p. 132.

authors of the destructive policies that were adopted.[69] Yet even in 38.3.13, the masses—despite Welwei—are not passive, helpless victims of agitators.[70] Polybius in fact forces the *polloi* to shoulder a good part of the blame: they acted in an ignorant fashion, and fell away from their duty (ἠγνοηκέναι . . . καὶ παραπεπαικέναι [τοῦ καθήκοντος]). If anything, what Polybius formulates in 38.3.13 is a destructive *mutual* interaction between the actions of the demagogues and the negative characteristics of the masses.[71]

Given all those negative characteristics, it was natural for Polybius to view outright rule by the masses as the equivalent of anarchy. Thus he describes the Athenian *dēmos* as a confused and quarrelsome ship's crew without a captain (6.44). To outsiders, he says, the resulting spectacle is disagreeable to observe "because of the confusion and contentiousness"; but to those actually on board the ship, it constitutes a real danger (44.6; cf. 44.8). In fact, to Polybius popular assemblies are in general places of confusion and charlatanry, sites of uproar and irrationality.[72] This is because the emotions of the *polloi* are naturally like a raging fire (27.9.1), or like a rushing mountain torrent that sweeps all before it (38.16.2).

In the worst possible case, the eruption of the masses into the politics of the state results in convulsive civil violence. At Cynaetha in Arcadia in the 220s, social and factional strife led to "constant mutual massacres, to banishments, the robbery of people's goods, and even to redivision of lands" (4.17.4). Finally the city was betrayed to outsiders, despite solemn oaths sworn between the contending sides—another sign, to Polybius, of the total corruption of the polity (4.17.9–11).[73] At Messene in 215 the revolution led first to banishments and a redivision of property (7.10.1), and then to mutual massacre.[74] In Aetolia in 174, agitation over debt led

69. "Demokratie und Masse," 293–95.

70. Cf. Welwei's own brief remark, ibid., 295 n. 67.

71. Cf. Gruen, "Origins of the Achaean War," 64, who persuasively argues that by winter 147/146 Critolaus was as much the follower of public opinion as its creator.

72. For this theme, see 9.32.1 and 24.7.2 (Sparta); 15.30.9 and 32.7 (Alexandria); 21.13.3 (Aetolia); 27.1.9 (Thebes); 29.1.1–3 (Rome); 36.7.3–5 (Carthage); 38.12.4 (Corinth). In general, cf. also 12.25d.6 and 38.15.8.

73. On the events of Cynaetha as inextricably mixed with an attempted social revolution (and not merely the result of excessive factional infighting), cf. Urban, *Wachstum und Krise*, 175–80. Polybius calls the intentionally false pledging of good faith by solemn oaths "an impious project" (ἀσέβεια, 4.17.11), and is outraged at what he sees as a terrible betrayal of trust (ibid.); later he finds the Aetolian destruction of the perpetrators "most just" (4.18.7). Statements such as this have a bearing on Polybius's allegedly "Machiavellian" attitude toward trickery in politics. See above, Chap. IV.

74. Cf. Polyb. 7.13.5–7, a remark clarified by the narrative in Plut. *Arat.* 49–50. Mendels, "Messene," 246–50, has suggested that in fact the first stage of the revolution at Messene (the banishments and redivision of lands) occurred in 219, and was thus separated by several years from the massacre. But in Polyb. 7.10—the only Polybian narrative of the process

once more to murder and massacre—and once more, the killing occurred despite previous solemn oaths of reconciliation.[75]

Indeed, Polybius regarding the masses instinctively employs a terminology we have run across already in this chapter: namely, *paranomia* (total lawlessness). Thus in the theoretical discussion of politics in Book 6, the anger of the *plēthos* against the arrogance of the oligarchs leads ultimately to a regime of "violence and total lawlessness" (παρανομία, 6.10.4). And the reason for the emergence of this condition of lawlessness once the masses have taken charge of things is, to Polybius, quite clear: it is a characteristic inherent in the masses themselves. His general rule here is established in 6.56.11, where he explains why the effect of religion in restraining the masses is highly beneficial: "Every multitude is unstable in character, and filled with totally lawless desires [ἐπιθυμιῶν παρανόμων], unreasoning anger [ὀργῆς ἀλόγου], and violent passion [θυμοῦ βιαίου]."

This, of course, is quite a different image of the masses from the picture of the *plēthos* as basically a "calm ocean" (discussed above, p. 130). Moreover, as with mercenaries, the onset of *paranomia* in the masses is closely linked in Polybius's mind with the ultimate degradation, the loss of humanity itself. Hence Polybius's description of the degeneration of "moderate democracy" into true mob rule (6.9): the masses, grown "greedy and corrupt" with flattery, eventually combine with an unscrupulous leader from among the elite, and institute a "regime of violence"; the result is massacre, banishment, and redivision of land (6.9.8). And, Polybius says, by the end of this process men have become "like wild beasts" (ἀποτεθηριωμένον, 6.9.9).[76]

Not men but beasts: it happened, according to Polybius, in Aetolia (ἀπεθηριώθη τὸ πλῆθος 20.10.15). And it had happened at Cynaetha as well, in the historian's own Arcadia (ἀπεθηριώθησαν, 4.21.6).

At Cynaetha, Polybius offers a specific explanation for the total lawlessness that developed (παρανομία, 4.20.2). The cause, he says, was a failure of education. The Arcadian countryside was harsh and poverty-stricken, and the life of toil it imposed led to a natural harshness in the Arcadian population (4.21.1–2). Moreover, the Cynaethans lived in the harshest part of Arcadia, and were therefore the most in need of those educational practices that induce gentleness and mildness (21.3–4)—es-

---

of revolution at Messene—there is no indication of any substantial gap in time between these events.

75. The massacre: Livy 41.25.4; considered to be "madness" (*furor*): 25.7. On the Polybian derivation of this material, see above, n. 61.

76. Note Polybius's emphasis on the *mutual* interaction of demagogue and masses (συναθροιζόμενον, 6.9.9) in creating the social catastrophe. The masses are not passive here. *Contra:* Welwei, "Demokratie und Masse," 290–91.

pecially the study of music (21.5). But instead, the Cynaethans neglected their education completely (21.11)—and the result was social catastrophe. Polybius concludes that the only way the Cynaethans can return from their bestial level to the level of humans again is to turn their attention back to education: in *paideia*, and especially in music, lies their salvation (ibid.).[77]

Polybius here is advocating the employment of education as a whole—not just music.[78] But by concentrating on the beneficial aspects of music, he was also participating in a serious contemporary discussion concerning the role of music in the orderly and harmonious operation of society itself. Stoic philosophers were especially interested in this concept, and one of its leading exponents was (it seems) Diogenes of Babylon—a man whose ideas Polybius knew and admired (33.2.10).[79]

Failure in upbringing as an important causal factor in the destructiveness of the masses appears not only at Cynaetha but also at Thebes (Polyb. 6.44.9). The reason for the destructiveness of the *ochlos* in the latter city, Polybius says, is the bad upbringing to which the populace has in general been subjected—"for violence and passion constitute their sole education" (ibid).[80]

In sum, for Polybius the masses often possess their own independent force—and it is usually a virulently negative force. But this in turn means that the responsibility of the elite for maintaining the stability of the state is all the heavier. It is therefore not surprising that the historian consistently gives his aristocratic audience advice on how to handle the *plēthos*. This advice is usually implicit—deriving from the positive or negative assessments of conduct that he offers in discussion of various individual incidents. But sometimes it is explicit.

Thus Polybius consistently commends those men who attempt to control the fierce passions of the *polloi*, or to reason with them about the negative long-term consequences of momentarily attractive policies. Hence his positive depiction of Alexander of Isus as Alexander attempts to persuade the Aetolian assembly of the dangers of debt reform and relief (13.1a)—a position with which we know Polybius personally

77. For the Polybian conception that the deep basis of "animal-like" behavior among the masses lies in their lack of education, see, rightly but briefly, Wunderer, *Psychologische Anschauungen*, 39.

78. Rightly noted by Roveri, *Studi su Polibio*, 131.

79. The connection is made acutely by Pédech, *Méthode*, 307 n. 17. On Stoic advocacy of music as a way to create harmony in societies torn by civil strife, see now Erskine, *Hellenistic Stoa*, 139.

80. On Boeotian lack of education, cf. Mendels, "Polybius and the Socio-Economic Revolution," 98. Note the similarity between this passage (6.44.9) and Polybius's explanation for the violent character of mercenaries, also deeply connected with the brutality and primitiveness of their upbringing (1.81.10; discussed above, pp. 127–28).

agreed.[81] The historian is equally favorable to L. Aemilius Paullus as he reasons with the Roman People in 168 to restrain their ignorant and destructive criticism of the generals in Greece (29.1.1–3). Similarly, Philopoemen is strongly commended because, although he pursued a long political career in Achaea, he did not court the favor of the mob but instead always spoke his mind (23.12.8–9). And in this case Polybius explicitly says that he is holding up such conduct for emulation by his audience (23.14.2).[82]

By contrast, as is well known, members of the political elite who choose the "demagogic" path are treated by Polybius with savage contempt.[83] C. Flaminius is presented as a boastful incompetent (2.33.7; 3.80–83), the corruptor of the people (2.21.8). At Sparta, the revolutionary leader Cheilon was a murderer who aimed at tyranny (4.81.3 and 5); Nabis was vicious and fanatic, an assassin and torturer;[84] Chaeron was uneducated, a murderer, a thief (24.7). And in Achaea in the 140s, Critolaus and Diaeus are portrayed as "the worst men" (38.10.8), unable to listen to reason (13.8), reckless (15.5), fiendishly cruel (18.2–6), completely derelict in their duty (17.8): in sum, guilty of the worst sorts of impiety and *paranomia* (13.8). Many other examples could be cited.[85]

The Polybian appeal for proper behavior by the elite toward the *plēthos* can also be seen in his theoretical discussion of aristocracy in Book 6. Polybius seems intent there on warning his audience against using their power within the community to perpetrate injustice (6.4.9), or to pursue wealth unscrupulously (6.8.5), or to engage in licentiousness and rape (ibid.); perhaps most important, he warns them against unrestrained political rivalry (6.57.5–7). All such behavior will work in one of two ways to undermine the legitimacy of the rule of the elite over the *polloi:* the latter will either become enraged at aristocratic oppressiveness (6.4.9, 8.6), or be "corrupted" by aristocratic seeking of their favor (6.9.6–9; cf. 57.7). In both cases, the outcome will be the emergence of the *polloi* as a destructive force, and ultimately, the development of the worst of all political regimes—mob rule (6.9.9, 57.9).

---

81. Cf. Polybius's own comments on debt reform at 38.11.11.

82. See also 2.48–51; 4.14; and 5.93.9–10 (all passages praising the conduct of Aratus of Sicyon in controlling popular passion); and 15.32.7 (Sosibius in Alexandria in 200—he failed).

83. See the discussions of Welwei, "Demokratie und Masse," 290–92; and Mendels, "Polybius and the Socio-Economic Revolution," 106–8.

84. For discussion of Nabis's alleged atrocities, see Mendels, "Polybius, Nabis and Equality," 313–14.

85. See, e.g., Scopas and Dorimachus in Aetolia (unscrupulous and reckless: 13.1.1–3); Malpagoras at Cius (15.21.1–2); Agathocles at Alexandria (15.25.36); and the revolutionary factions in Aetolia in the 170s, whom Polybius evidently characterized simply as "bad" (Livy [P] 42.13.8).

Polybius believes that this degenerative process may well be inevitable: sharp decline in the behavior of the aristocracy seems to him inherent in the nature of aristocratic rule (κατὰ φύσιν, 6.4.9). Nevertheless, Polybius implies that the degenerative process can at least be delayed if an aristocracy practices careful self-restraint.[86]

Indeed, though the historian is a strong advocate of the "mixed" constitution, he is not totally opposed to democracy—so long as it is hedged about with strong constraints.[87] Yet he sees it as an inherently fragile system, dependent for its orderly working on good qualities within both the *dēmos* and the political elite as well; and it is unthinkable without binding norms of law, religion, custom, and behavior (6.4.4–5):

> It is not a true democracy when the masses have authority to do whatever they wish. . . . But where it is traditional and ingrained to worship the gods, honor one's parents, respect one's elders, and obey the laws—in such communities, if the will of the greater number prevails, this it is proper to call a democracy.

But if Polybius felt that it was the duty both of the elite and of the *dēmos* to preserve law and tradition as guarantors of orderly community life, it is nevertheless clear that he thought that the best warrant for the preservation of orderliness lay not in the masses but in the *agathoi*—the rule of the "good men," understood as a true political aristocracy, free from greed and the desire for immediate pleasures, bound to uphold tradition and law and to act justly, able to take the long view of the needs of the community.[88] In the last analysis, then, the stability of society rests on the existence (or nonexistence) of a strong ethical code among its aristocratic leaders—the men who constituted Polybius's audience. This is an analysis of social relations, and resultant social problems, that most modern scholars—interested as they are in the economic basis of societies—find superficial.[89] Yet it is an idea that is crucial to the moral framework of *The Histories*.

THE YOUNG

Self-discipline within the aristocracy was a necessity for orderly society to be preserved from the threat posed by the *plēthos;* but a special danger

---

86. See, rightly, Welwei, "Demokratie und Masse," 297.

87. Ibid., 283.

88. Thus, while much is usually made of 6.56.11, where Polybius extols the value of religious practice and religious awe as a restraint upon the dark impulses of the *plēthos,* one should not forget that immediately afterward Polybius also points out the high value of religion in maintaining honor and good faith among the Roman elite itself (6.56.13–15). See now Morgan, "Antiochus Epiphanes," 38.

89. Cf. Welwei, "Demokratie und Masse," 300–301 (a very harsh judgment); and Mendels, "Polybius and the Socio-Economic Revolution," 109.

existed within aristocratic ranks. Every aristocrat faced the problem of restraining his appetites and impulses as he exercised power within the community (cf. 6.4.9). But those least able to withstand the temptations of wealth and of social and political power were the aristocratic young (the νέοι). The special qualities of their stage of life made this problem almost unavoidable. In Polybius's view the aristocratic young thus constituted—at least in potential—a powerfully disruptive force within society. And beyond their threat to social stability and harmony, it was upsetting to Polybius that the behavior of the aristocratic young could so easily degenerate into "the shameful" (αἰσχρόν). It is no wonder, then, that Polybius's depiction of this group tends to be highly negative.[90]

To begin with, the *neoi* in general had a very difficult time controlling their impulses; and the result was often improper, unintelligent, or even destructive behavior. Even Scipio Aemilianus, who is usually presented to Polybius's audience as a paragon, was capable as a young man of an abandonment to momentary emotion that Polybius found embarrassing (31.24.11).[91]

Polybius's concern about the inability of young men to control themselves has, in fact, several different aspects. He expresses misgivings, for instance, about the hot sexuality of young males. The historian is no prude: sexuality has its place within his spectrum of generally acceptable behavior (cf. 10.19.4). But he thinks it an all-too-disruptive presence when young men are engaged in the serious business of politics and war (10.19.5), and it can lead them into conduct that Polybius considers shameful (cf. 5.34.10). The problem here, then, is simply one of rational self-control; and Polybius's attitude is in fact rather typical of his aristocratic milieu: "Like society, the body was there to be administered, not changed." Young men tended to be careless administrators—in both areas.[92]

Polybius's misgivings about the propensity of *neoi* toward excessive drinking are far more pronounced. This was a serious problem for Tlepolemus of Alexandria (15.25.3, cf. 16.21.6–7); for young Genthius, the ruler of Illyria (29.13); for Ptolemy IV of Egypt (5.34.10); and especially for Polybius's friend Demetrius of Syria (31.13.8 and 33.19). Polybius's

90. These are, of course, young *men:* aged approximately fifteen (Hieronymus of Syracuse: Livy [P] 24.5.9) to thirty (T. Quinctius Flamininus: Polyb. 18.12.5). For Polybius's attitude toward women, see the next section of this chapter.

91. On this passage, see the remarks of Walbank, *Commentary* III: 498–99.

92. The quote is from Brown, *Body and Society*, 31—very perceptive on the attitude of the Greek political elite toward the sexuality of males. On the destructive impact of sexual passion on commanders when on campaign, see also Polybius's general statement at 3.81.6. For more on Polyb. 10.19, see Chap. VI, below. Polybius's criticism of obsession with sexual pleasure extended to older men: see 20.8 on Antiochus III's behavior in Greece in 192/191, which Polybius found both incongruent with the prudent management of state affairs, and also shameful *per se* (see esp. 20.8.2).

concern in these cases is greatly heightened because the young men involved were in positions of special political responsibility. But he also believes that young aristocrats in general spend altogether too much time in carousing (cf. 8.27.4 and 16.21.7).[93]

Connected with these misgivings is Polybius's reproof of the young for their general shallowness, their unwillingness to engage in the hard work and serious attitudes of mature adults. They are too concerned with frivolous things: clothes, banquets, fencing matches.[94] And the passions of the young in literature, Polybius complains, are for the vain and the shallow as well, rather than for the serious study of ethics and politics (τῶν ἠϑικῶν καὶ πραγματικῶν λόγων, 12.26c.4).

Even at Rome, which Polybius considers the sturdiest of societies, he finds the young men of at least his own time singularly lacking in energy and substance. He agrees with Cato the Censor in excoriating what he sees as their luxurious and decadent style of life (31.25.4–5a). Moreover, he appears to draw a connection between this style of life and the subsequent refusal of young aristocrats to undertake military service in Spain during the crisis of the late 150s. Cowardice, he says, was rampant (35.4.3–4)—and shameful excuses (αἰσχρόν, ἀπρεπές, 4.6).[95]

Polybius's unease about the young, however, is not focused primarily on their degenerate laziness; rather, it has much more to do with the quality of their actions once initiated. Youthful inability to control impulses and emotions often leads to disorder; and there are several passages where the arrogance, angry passions, and impulsiveness of the young even lead to major wars. Thus in 220 the reckless actions of the Aetolian Dorimachus precipitated the Social War, which engulfed most of European Greece; Polybius explains that Dorimachus was "young [νέος ὤν, 4.3.5], and filled with the violent and aggressive passion of the Aetolian." Again, in the 230s and 220s it was the young warriors among the Celtic tribes, "filled with unreflecting passion, and without experience of suffering or peril," who launched a major series of wars against Rome (2.21.2)—the outcome being disastrous defeat (cf. 2.31.1 and 35.4). This theme appears even at what Polybius conceives to have been a crucial

93. For further discussion, see below, "Appendix: Polybius on Drinking and Drunkenness."

94. See 16.21.1–2 and 6–7 (Tlepolemus of Alexandria, and the *jeunesse dorée* of Alexandria as a whole); 16.22.1 (the young courtiers of Philip V); 26.1.4, cf. Diod. 29.32 (the young courtiers of Antiochus IV).

95. On the integral, and moralizing, connection between Polyb. 31.25 and 35.4, see esp. Gruen, *Hellenistic World and the Coming of Rome* I: 348. By contrast Walbank, *Commentary* III: 646, adopts his usual position, downplaying the possibility of sincere Polybian ethical concern: he argues that Polyb. 35.4 is merely a passage of political propaganda inserted into *The Histories* to highlight the virtues of Scipio Aemilianus by exaggerating the faults of his contemporaries.

turning point in the history of the entire world, for it is part of his explanation for why Philip V of Macedon adopted a new policy of expansion toward the west in 217, and confrontation with Rome. Polybius writes (5.102.1):

> It was, I think, to be expected, in a king who was so young [νέον], who had been successful in his previous campaigns, who seemed extremely daring, and besides this came from a family that had always sought universal dominion.

The consequences of Philip's decision, which was an impulsive decision (cf. 5.105.1 and 108.5), would ultimately be deep Roman involvement in Greece—and catastrophe for Macedon.[96]

A case that is similar, and in some ways even more striking, is that of the young Hieronymus, king of Syracuse for a brief time during the Second Punic War. He was only fifteen when, at the death of his grandfather Hiero, he came to the throne; and—in Polybius's judgment—he soon proved himself a disaster as a ruler. Polybius consistently refers to him, with contempt, as the "boy" (μειράκιον).[97] The new king was "highly unstable by nature" (7.4.6). He was drawn to the side of Carthage by misleadingly positive accounts of Hannibal's accomplishments in Italy (4.4). Highly susceptible to flattery, his ambitions grew bloated and irrational: he soon was demanding Syracusan control over all of Sicily as his price for an alliance with the Carthaginians (4.2–9). Meanwhile, he had taken to executing those who disagreed with him (2.1), while wantonly insulting Roman envoys who came to renew Hiero's old treaty of friendship (3.4–9). The Punic government indeed recognized "the boy's complete instability and mental derangement" (7.4.8)—but thought it in their immediate interests to get him on their side. When the new treaty of alliance with Carthage came up for discussion, those of Hieronymus's advisers who opposed it kept silent, fearing the young king's lack of self-control (5.3).

This image of an irresponsible adolescent placed in charge of the fate of Syracuse is a frightening one. Hieronymus in fact set Syracuse on a path that within a few years had led to the city's sack by M. Claudius Marcellus and its end as an independent community.[98]

96. For detailed discussion of Philip's decision of 217, see Walbank, *Philip V,* 64–67; on its world-historical importance in Polybius's eyes, see *id.,* "*Symplokē:* Its Role in Polybius' *Histories,*" 199–204. For Polybius's ideological presentation of the decision, see Eckstein, "The Power of Irrationality," 10–12.

97. See 7.2.3, 4.6, and 5.8; cf. παῖς ("child") at 7.7.3.

98. On Polybius's depiction of Hieronymus, see Eckstein, "Polybius, Syracuse, and the Politics of Accommodation," 273–76. On the disastrous course taken by Syracusan politics in this period, see the detailed discussion in Eckstein, *Senate and General,* 133–65.

Perhaps the most intriguing example of impulsive youth in Polybius, however, is Hannibal at New Carthage in 220. Roman envoys had come to see him about his increasing pressure on Rome's friend, the town of Saguntum.[99] Polybius has already emphasized that Hannibal had come to Spain with a hatred of the Romans engendered by his father, Hamilcar (3.12.2–4; cf. 2.36.4). Now he describes Hannibal's bitter rejection of the Roman complaints, his vague threats, his dispatch to Carthage claiming that the Saguntines were actually the aggressors (3.15.7–8). The road to the Second Punic War had been opened.

What was the explanation for this undiplomatic conduct? Hannibal behaved so harshly, Polybius says, "because he was young [νέος ὤν], filled with passion for war, successful in his previous campaigns, and long since spurred on by his hatred of the Romans" (3.15.6). He was, Polybius continues, "filled with unreasoning and violent anger," and therefore took refuge in nonsensical pretexts, "as men do who disregard their duty because of long-implanted passions" (15.9). It would have been much better (15.10) if Hannibal had revealed the true causes of his anger: the Romans' seizure of Sardinia and Corsica from Carthage in 238 and their unfair imposition of a heavy financial indemnity upon the Carthaginians.[100] But Hannibal at this point was, according to Polybius, a young man so out of control that he could not do this (3.15.11).

Obviously, Polybius's assessment of Hannibal's behavior in this crucial passage—which sets in train the war that will be Polybius's primary topic for the next twelve volumes—is a highly negative one. In fact, Polybius's portrait of Hannibal at New Carthage (νέος . . . πλήρης ἀλογίας καὶ θυμοῦ βιαίου, 3.15.9) bears a strong generic resemblance to Polybius's depiction of the wild young *barbaroi* at 2.21.2 (νέοι, θυμοῦ . . . ἀλογίστου πλήρεις), and to the historian's most pessimistic depiction of the uncontrolled "mob" (πλῆρες . . . ὀργῆς ἀλόγου, θυμοῦ βιαίου, 6.56.11).[101]

Moreover, Polybius's judgment is not merely that Hannibal, in his irrational outburst of anger in 220, fumbled badly in preparing a reasonable diplomatic justification for the war with Rome. The historian actually thinks that Hannibal's mistake was far more fundamental—that a successful war against Rome was indeed possible for Hannibal, but that it required the gathering of far more resources before launching it

99. On the details of the growing crisis over Saguntum, see Eckstein, "Rome, Saguntum and the Ebro Treaty," 54–68.

100. For Polybius's attitude toward Rome's behavior in the diplomatic crisis of 238/237, see Chap. IV, above.

101. Cf. Eckstein, "The Power of Irrationality," 11–12, for the deep structure in Polybian perceptions that this comparison reveals. For Polyb. 3.15 as an example of Polybius's concerns about the impact of angry emotion on politics, see the insightful comments of Wunderer, *Psychologische Anschauungen*, 16.

(11.10.6–7). That is: Hannibal acted precipitously in a vitally important matter, because he lost control; and the result, despite some brilliant achievements on the battlefield, was disaster for Carthage.[102] Polybius underscores this point in the dramatic scene he presents between Hannibal and Scipio Africanus just before the battle of Zama in 202. Here an older, sadder, and wiser Hannibal confronts in Scipio a young man in his own youthful, self-confident mold. But he now counsels caution, and a compromise peace—yet fears that Scipio, both because he is very young (νέον . . . κομιδῆ) and because he has been the beneficiary of unbroken success, will not be interested (15.7.1). Hannibal's perception of Scipio echoes here what Polybius himself had said of the young and self-confident Hannibal in 3.15. And Hannibal attempts to convince Scipio of the virtues of caution by pointing—precisely—to his own subsequent, difficult, career (15.7.3–4). "Consider this, I urge you, and be not overproud" (7.5).[103]

Clearly, young men in power needed to be carefully watched, in order to avoid impulsive, destructive actions. Polybius even indicates that in the worst cases, their behavior could verge on disregard of all laws human and divine: toward the *paranomia* that the historian so feared and condemned. Thus, once the tyrannical Charops had gained control of Epirus in the 160s, "there was no crime he did not commit" (32.5.8); Polybius's explanation is that Charops was very young (νεός . . . κομιδῆ)—and had gathered around him the worst and most unprincipled of men (ibid.).[104] Genthius, the young king of Illyria, was licentious and a drunkard, generally cruel to his people—and murdered his own brother in order to marry the latter's fiancée (29.13.2). One reason that Philip V committed the atrocity of sacking the temples of the gods at Thermum in 218 was because of his youthful lack of restraint (διὰ τὴν ἡλικίαν, 5.12.5). And it was the *neoi* who at Sparta during the factional infighting of 220 butchered the ephors as they engaged in solemn sacrifice within the temple of Athena of the Brazen House itself (4.35.3). Polybius's reaction is one of outrage (35.3–4): this was a savage and brutal deed (ὠμότητα), done in a temple whose sanctity normally protected even convicted murderers who had sought sanctuary there.

As prominent in *The Histories* as the tendency of the *neoi* toward ex-

102. On the important but often neglected 11.10.6–7, see Eckstein, "The Power of Irrationality," 13; also Chap. VII, below.
103. Walbank, *Commentary* III: 452, suggests that Hannibal may really have said something like this to Scipio; but in any case, the speech as we have it certainly fits neatly into Polybius's ideological framework.
104. On the unscrupulous behavior of the young Charops even before he attained power in Epirus, see Polybius's hostile comments at 27.15.5–6 and 8, discussed in Chap. IV, above.

treme violence, however, is their tendency toward sheer incompetence, mostly because of inexperience. Thus Antiochus III, young and inexperienced at the battle of Raphia in 217, seriously misjudged the course of the fighting and was defeated (5.85.11). The same thing happened to Aratus of Sicyon at Cynaetha in 241, because he was still young and inexperienced in generalship (νέον . . . ἄπειρον, 9.17.9).[105] Apollonius, the friend of Prince Demetrius of Syria, seriously misjudged the ruthlessness of the Senate, because he was "very young and naive" (ἄκακος ἦν καὶ κομιδῇ νέος, 31.11.7). Later, Polybius worried that Demetrius would be incapable of carrying out the complicated plan for his escape from Rome, not only because of his drinking problem, but also because of his extreme youth (31.13.8).[106]

When young men are, nevertheless, successful in political and military endeavors, Polybius's ideology becomes even more obvious—for he consistently asserts that they are successful *despite* their youth. Thus, although Hiero II of Syracuse was very young when he seize power (κομιδῇ νέος), his natural aptitude for political affairs made him qualified to be a king (1.8.3). Again, T. Quinctius Flamininus in 198/197 handled both his own projects and those of the Roman state in admirable fashion, "although he was very young" (νέος ἦν κομιδῇ, 18.12.5). And Scipio Africanus managed to keep his head when offered kingship by the Spanish chiefs after his victory at Baecula in 208, despite the fact that he was both very young (κομιδῇ νέος) and favored by success (10.40.6). Such self-control was in fact an example of Scipio's special nobility of mind (ibid).[107]

Polybius in fact believes that in general, young men are desperately in need of older advisers to help them make correct decisions. But because the characters of young men are very malleable, the character of their advisers becomes crucial in itself. This point is made with great emphasis in Polybius's discussion of the negative impact of Demetrius of Pharus on the young Philip V. Demetrius, Polybius says, was bold and courageous—but also totally lacking in reason and judgment (3.19.9, cf. 11). The result

105. On the date and context of the events in Polyb. 9.17, see Walbank, *Commentary* II: 142–43.

106. On Demetrius's escape from Rome, and Polybius's role in the affair, see Chap. I, above. Other passages on the theme of youth and inexperience, or youth and disastrous decisions: 5.75.4 (a general statement); 8.24.10, 28.13, 31.2 (Tarentum in 213); 29.3.5 (Genthius of Illyria). Given Polybius's views here, it is not surprising that mature men whom the historian judges to have acted "like adolescents" (μειρακιωδῶς) receive the harshest criticism: cf. 10.33.6 (M. Claudius Marcellus); 11.4.7 (Machanidas of Sparta); 2.68.2 (Alexander son of Admetus, the Antigonid cavalry commander at Sellasia in 222).

107. Scipio compares there very favorably to the young and successful Hannibal and Philip V, who were carried away by their successes and went on to make serious mistakes. Another Polybian figure who is successful "notwithstanding extreme youth" (8.10.8) is Alexander the Great.

of his growing influence over Philip was a fundamental change for the worse in the young king (7.11.1): impiety toward the gods, transgressions against men by violation of the laws of war, and the spoiling of his own projects by an implacable cruelty (7.14.5).[108] Polybius then appends a general comment (7.14.6):

> Of such decisive importance for young kings [νέοι], as leading either to misfortune or to firm establishment of their kingdom, is the judicious choice of the friends who counsel them—a matter to which most of them, however, by some unaccountable carelessness, pay not the slightest heed.[109]

Polybius makes it equally clear what kind of conduct he considers to be proper in an older adviser. It was such an adviser who recalled the overconfident Antiochus to reality at Raphia in 217, in an attempt to save the battle (5.85.11). And Aratus of Sicyon, Polybius insists, played this constructive and restraining role for Philip V—as long as the young king let him.[110]

Indeed, the proper function of older men as they appear in Polybius is to restrain the shortsighted and destructive passions that threaten the community—passions that often originate, precisely, with the young. It was older men (τῶν πρεσβυτέρων, 4.34.9) who at Sparta in 220 reminded the assembly of the benefits conferred upon the Spartans by Antigonus Doson, and therefore urged—against the young and violent (4.34.6)—the maintenance of the Spartan alliance with Macedon. This was a political position that Polybius clearly viewed as morally and pragmatically correct.[111] Similarly, it was older men among young King Philip's counselors (τῶν πρεσβυτέρων, 4.23.9) who prevented him from taking harsh measures against Sparta on grounds of the Spartans' suspect loyalty. Again, it was older men within the Aetolian council who prevailed upon the angry Aetolian masses in 191 to give Roman envoys at least a hearing before definitively breaking with Rome (Livy [P] 35.33.1).[112]

But beyond the counsel of intelligent and mature advisers, Polybius offers a second way to counter the socially destructive anarchy of young men. In regard to the *barbaroi*, the *misthophoroi*, and the *plēthos*, Polybius

---

108. On Demetrius of Pharus, see the comments of Pédech, *Méthode*, 401–2 and 416–17.

109. Other destructive older counselors to young rulers: Hermeias, the cruel and treacherous adviser of the young Antiochus III (Polyb. 5.41.1 and 3; cf. 42.7 and 49–50, discussed in Chap. IV, above); and Pantauchus, for the young Genthius (29.3.5–4.3). On Polybius's conception of the importance of advisers in the maturation process of young rulers, see, briefly, Welwei, *Könige und Königtum*, 138.

110. On Aratus's relations with the young Philip as portrayed by Polybius, see Polyb. 5.10–12 and 7.13; cf. Walbank, *Aratos*, 122–56.

111. See Polybius's own positive assessment of Antigonus's settlement of affairs with Sparta after the Sellasia victory of 2.70.1 and 5.9.8–10.

112. On the Polybian derivation of this passage, see Briscoe, *Commentary* II: 193.

indicates that the source of their destructive behavior lies in bad upbringing and their lack of education—but he does not offer much hope in that
direction.[113] By contrast, Polybius did think deeply about the education
of young men, and advocated a quite specific program of intellectual-
moral training that would teach them self-control, and turn their powerful energies to constructive and honorable paths.

Polybius was proud of the formal education he himself had received,[114]
so it was natural that his program of education for the *neoi* would focus
in good part on purely intellectual matters. He openly criticized Roman
aristocrats for their failure to provide a formal education for their children (Cic. *de Rep.* 4.3). And when he criticizes the *neoi* for reading vain
and shallow works instead of studying ethics and politics (12.26c.4), it is
clear that he is advocating to them the study of the latter.[115] Indeed, to
judge from Plutarch's *Life*, the formal philosophical and literary education received by Philopoemen was very prominent in Polybius's encomiastic biography—a biography that Polybius himself says was especially
devoted to a depiction of Philopoemen's early training (10.21.5). Polybius's hero, then, studied as a young man under the Platonist philosophers
Ecdemus and Demophanes (Plut. *Phil.* 1.2; cf. Polyb. 10.22.3–4)—who
later professed themselves well pleased with their product (*Phil.* 1.4).[116]
Philopoemen also applied himself to reading the works of many other
philosophers, "those whom he thought would be conducive to the
achievement of virtue" (πρὸς ἀρετήν, *Phil.* 4.3). In addition, he studied
Homeric poetry, in order to inspire himself to deeds of courage (πρὸς
ἀνδρείαν, 4.4). And he did not neglect practical textbooks on military
affairs, or the histories of Alexander, for he wished to be well informed
on military technique (ibid.).

Pédech may well be correct that Polybius's biography of Philopoemen
was intended to inspire the young Scipio Aemilianus; if so, then the emphasis on Philopoemen's intellectual education takes on even more
point.[117] Certainly Polybius personally applied himself to the intellectual
education of the young Scipio (cf. 31.23.9). And we know that Scipio ben-

113. For detailed discussions, see above, this chapter.
114. For detailed discussion, see Chap. I, above; and the comments of von Scala, *Studien,* 19.
115. Cf. Polybius's contempt for what he considered the shallowness and childish-
ness (μειρακιώδες, παιδαριωδέστερον) of much historical writing: 12.25a.5, 25i.5, 25k.9, and
esp. 26d.6.
116. On Ecdemus and Demophanes, and the Platonist influence in Megalopolis, see esp.
von Scala, *Studien,* 52–54. Note that Polybius's encomium of Philopoemen evidently stressed
that Ecdemus and Demophanes were especially concerned for the maintenance of order
within society (cf. Plut. *Phil.* 1.3).
117. Cf. Pédech, "Polybe et l'éloge," 94–96; and already Wunderer, *Psychologische Anschauungen,* 26, for the possible educational purpose Polybius intended for the biography.

efited also from the careful discussions of cultural issues and political theory later undertaken in his presence by Polybius and the Stoic philosopher Panaetius (Cic. *de Rep.* 4.3; Vell. Pat. 1.13.3).[118]

But Polybius's concern for the educational experience of young men goes well beyond intellectual training. There is a focus as well on moral training and the building of "character." Thus in a famous passage, the historian approves the elaborate rituals that surrounded the funerals of great Roman aristocrats because they inspire the young men of Rome to seek glory by service to their city (6.54.3).[119] In a closely related passage, Polybius praises the beneficial impact of the busts of the ancestors (the *imagines*) in inspiring young men at Rome not only to love of glory but to love of virtue (φιλαγαθῷ, 6.53.9).[120] The historian also approves of L. Aemilius Paullus's belief that hunting was the best training for young men (31.29.5), since hunting provided a training ground for deeds of courage (29.9). Here Polybius even draws an analogy between the training of young aristocrats and the training of well-bred dogs (29.7).[121] In the encomium, too, Polybius evidently emphasized the moral virtues of hunting (cf. *Phil.* 4.1)—as well as the strictness and simplicity of the young Philopoemen's style of life (*Phil.* 3.3–4; cf. Polyb. 10.22.4–5).

Polybius's account of the development of the young Scipio Aemilianus (31.25–30) amounts to another outline of the educational experience that the historian deemed most appropriate for adolescent aristocrats. Polybius praises young Scipio's desire to achieve the καλόν (31.25.2)—and Polybius's point in the subsequent narrative is not that Scipio merely earned a *reputation* for temperance, financial honesty and generosity, and physical courage. On the contrary: Scipio learned actually to live in a temperate fashion (cf. 31.25.8 and 28.12–13), truly learned to practice the virtues of honesty and generosity with money (cf. 31.25.9–10), and truly learned to perform real deeds of valor (31.29.11; cf. 29.8). All this is consonant with generalizing remarks on education evidently made by the historian while discussing the virtues of the early Romans (6.11a.11): "It is neces-

118. On Scipio, Polybius, and Panaetius, see the comments of Walbank, "Political Morality," 1–2. On Scipio and Panaetius, see Astin, *Scipio Aemilianus*, 294–99; and now Erskine, *Hellenistic Stoa*, 213–14. (Panaetius knew Latin: cf. Cic. *Tusc. Disp.* 4.4). For Polybius's views on the necessity of training young men for political responsibility, see Welwei, *Könige und Königtum*, 137–39.

119. On the moralizing tone of 6.54.3, see esp. Petzold, *Methode des Polybios*, 79.

120. Polybius's interpretation of the purpose of the *imagines* is strongly supported by Sall. *Jug.* 4.5; cf. Walbank, *Commentary* I: 739–40.

121. The point about hunting in 31.29 is all the more emphatic in view of Polybius's excoriation of the lazy and dissolute style of life of most young aristocrats at Rome (31.25.4–5a, discussed above, p. 142). In this respect, note that Polybius evidently approved even of gladiatorial spectacles as a way of accustoming young men to the display of courage: see Livy [P] 41.20.12, discussed in Chap. I, above.

sary that every branch of virtue be practiced by those who aim at a good education; and the training should be from childhood (but physical courage is the most important)."

Presumably if Polybius's biography of Philopoemen were extant, this theme of the education of the young would stand out even more prominently in his writings. But it would seem that Polybius hoped that by means of an education both moral and intellectual, the convulsive energy of young men—potentially so destructive—could be harnessed for the benefit of the social order. The historian is not completely sanguine about this—for he believes the process of education to be, in fact, a difficult and lengthy task.[122] Nevertheless, he has more hope for the *neoi* than he does for any other of the groups that he sees as constituting a threat to orderly and civilized life. Perhaps that is because Polybius at one time had been an aristocratic youth himself.

WOMEN

Females, in contrast to the *neoi,* constituted the quintessential Other in the eyes of Greek males. Here the polarity was not merely social or social-moral, as was the case with the barbarian, the mercenary, or the masses. The polarity was deeper: biological. Greek men throughout antiquity believed that their bodies were sharply differentiated from those of females by the balance of "humors." Only male bodies were thought to possess enough of the precious vital "heat" that made for true vitality and nobility of spirit (μεγαλοψυχία), that made males "strong to think and act." Women were said to be cooler, softer, clammier, more "liquid." And precisely because of this physiological incapacity, women were thought unlikely ever to be capable of achieving the καλόν.[123]

Offensive as such ideas are to moderns, it is clear that Polybius fully shared this ancient male perception.[124] One consequence was Polybius's

122. For detailed discussion of this aspect of Polybian educational ideology, see below, Chap. VIII.

123. On Greek male attitudes toward the female body and its "deficiencies," see now the highly useful discussion in Brown, *Body and Society,* 9–10 (with sources). But the attitudes described by Brown originated much earlier than the period on which he concentrates. Thus Empedocles in the Classical age believed that a "hot" womb gave birth to a male child and a "cold" womb to a female (cf. Ar. *Gen. An.* 765a), while Aristotle himself thought of women as "maimed men," and childlike (ibid., 737a; cf. 728).

124. See esp. Polybius's understanding of what "womanish" men are like (discussed below, pp. 155–56). It is a shocking fact that the basic study of Polybius's attitude toward women remains that of von Scala, *Studien,* 256–58 ("Polybios und die Frauen")—now a century old. Cf. also Wunderer, *Psychologische Anschauungen,* 56–57 (who accepts Polybius's hostile depiction as accurate!). Pédech, *Méthode,* 235 n. 144, still depends upon von Scala. Dixon, "Polybius on Roman Women and Property," is not concerned with Polybius's general gender attitudes.

tendency to view women as yet another force for disorder within society. This force was especially disturbing because Polybius's female subjects were for the most part aristocrats. That is, the women of most concern to him were—like the *neoi*—a force for disorder that dwelt not merely within the city, but within the aristocratic household itself.

Since Polybius deals almost exclusively with war and politics, and since in the ancient Mediterranean these were almost exclusively male domains, it is natural that females are marginalized figures in *The Histories*. Nevertheless, although women do not appear in Polybius with the frequency that they do in (say) Herodotus, there are almost three times as many references to women in the extant (fragmentary) Polybian text as there are in all of Thucydides. Moreover, Polybius provides fairly detailed depictions of some women's individual personalities—again, something unknown in Thucydides.[125]

In several cases, Polybius's depiction is in fact quite positive. Most striking is his comment on the wife of the semilegendary figure Demaratus of Corinth (6.11a.7): "Among other useful qualities, she was admirably suited by nature to assist in any political enterprise."[126] Similar is 5.36.1: Berenice the daughter of Magas (brother of Ptolemy IV) was feared by the prime minister Sosibius because of her daring (τόλμα)—and so was murdered along with her father. As we have seen in Chapter II, Polybius also praises the courage of the wife of Hasdrubal during the fall of Carthage (38.20). And another case that wins Polybius's approval is that of the Galatian princess Chiomara, who contrived the death of the Roman centurion who had raped her (21.38.1–6).[127] Polybius evidently had met Chiomara personally, and was impressed with "her dignified spirit and intelligence" (21.38.7).[128]

More conventional is Polybius's praise of Apollonis, the wife of Attalus I of Pergamum, for her restrained style of life amid the temptations of royal wealth, and for having preserved amity among her children (22.20). Perhaps there is a hint of politics in that latter remark, but basically these

125. Herodotus refers to women 373 times; Thucydides, less than 50, and—unlike Herodotus—never in any detail. For discussion, see Weidemann, "Thucydides, Women, and the Limits of Rational Analysis," 162–69. By contrast, there are more than 130 references to women in the extant text of Polybius's *Histories* (which constitutes only about a quarter of the original work). See Mauersberger, *Polybios-Lexikon* I:1, cols. 406–8.

126. On the traditions surrounding Demaratus of Corinth and his wife (alternatively called Tanaquil or Gaia Caecilia), see Walbank, *Commentary* I: 672–73.

127. Note that Polybius connects the brutality, greed, and lust of the centurion directly to his lack of education and culture (ἀμαϑὴς καὶ ἀκρατὴς ἄνϑρωπος, 21.38.3).

128. The account traditionally labeled Polyb. 21.28 is actually drawn from Plutarch (*Mul. Virt.* 22). But the theme of lack of education as an explanation for the centurion's brutal behavior (see last note) strongly suggests that Plutarch here was indeed very closely following the Polybian text.

are domestic virtues.[129] Polybius's sympathetic portrait of the elderly wife of the Ilergete chief Mandonius is similar (10.18.7–15): the focus is on chastity, dignity, and reticence before men—as opposed to courage and vigor.

All these women may be (in various ways) admirable to Polybius; but by and large his view of women focuses instead on their potentially negative impact upon society and politics. This emerges both in his general statements about women, and in his depictions of individual females. Such a negative attitude toward women is, of course, the usual attitude of Greek males in any period of antiquity.[130] What is important for this study is the nature of Polybius's criticism: women's primary characteristic is that they are the carriers of a disturbing irrationality.

Polybius believes that the emotions of women are, typically, "frenzied" (κορυβαντιώσαις γυναιξί, 12.12b.2). Their inherent hyperemotionality is especially revealed, the historian indicates, by their often hysterical religious behavior.[131] But this constitutes only one aspect of the more general phenomenon that women are easily overcome by emotion (cf. 10.4.7). This means that women often go out of control during a crisis, when calmness is all-important. It happened, for instance, at Mantineia in 223 (2.56.7), and at Carthage in 149 (36.5.7).[132]

Connected with the hyperemotionality of women is their basic shallowness. Women, like young men, are too much interested in finery.[133] They seek to manipulate men through sensuality (14.7.4–6; cf. 22.20.2). Like the masses, they are too fond of "chatter" (λαλιά, 31.26.10); and once started on a topic, they never have too much of it (ibid.).[134]

These generalizations about female behavior give a much more accurate picture of Polybius's thinking about women, unfortunately, than do his few positive descriptions of "exceptional" females. It follows that, for him, the direct involvement of such hyperemotional creatures in public life would lead to disturbance and even violence. Thus at Alexandria in

129. For discussion of Polybius's assessment of Apollonis, see also above, Chap. IV.

130. Two pioneering works on this subject are Slater, *The Glory of Hera: Greek Mythology and the Greek Family*, esp. chap. 1; and S. Pomeroy, *Goddesses, Whores, Wives and Slaves: Women in Classical Antiquity*, chaps. 4–7. See also the very grim—and perhaps somewhat exaggerated—picture in Keuls, *The Reign of the Phallus: Sexual Politics in Ancient Athens*. A more balanced view, which nevertheless does not whitewash Greek misogyny: Brown, *Body and Society*, chap. 1.

131. See 12.24.5; 15.29.9; cf. 9.6.3–4 and 32.15.7. On Polybius's view of women as excessively superstitious, see von Scala, *Studien*, 258.

132. Ibid. Note that in both their (alleged) susceptibility to superstition and in their (alleged) inability to deal calmly with a crisis, women as a gender in Polybius greatly resemble the masses as a social group.

133. See Polyb. 11.9.7; 38.15.6 and 11.

134. For the λαλιά of the masses, cf. Polyb. 3.20.5 and 29.1.3.

200 the involvement of women in the revolution against Agathocles made the hatred against him in the city twice as vehement, because of the women's rage (ἐκ τῶν γυναικῶν ὀργῆς, 15.30.1).[135] Such rage could result in specific acts of atrocity. At Alexandria it was young women who battered to death Agathocles' henchman Philammon, strangled Philammon's innocent young son, and dragged out his wife, stripped her naked, and slew her as well (15.33.11–12). The image here is of people totally out of control.[136] Similarly, after the assassination of the Seleucid prime minister Hermeias at Apamea in 220, the women of the city are found stoning Hermeias's wife to death (Polyb. 5.56.15).

As for individual women, in at least five prominent cases Polybius outlines a specific tendency toward fierce and mindless violence, and, ultimately, *paranomia.*

Thus Apega, the wife of the tyrant Nabis of Sparta, in fact "greatly surpassed him in cruelty" (Polyb. 18.17.3); as a result, she subjected the women of Argos "to every kind of outrage and violence" (17.4).[137] Philotis, the mother of the tyrannical politician Charops of Epirus, was another great expert at extorting wealth from her fellow women through violence (32.5.13–14). Orthobula, the wife of the Aetolian politician Proxenus, involved herself in the infighting in Aetolia over debt reform in the 170s, and ended up poisoning her own husband—a man Polybius respected (Livy [P] 41.25.6).[138]

Even more disturbing is Polybius's picture of Oenanthe, the mother of Agathocles of Alexandria (15.29). When the Alexandrian rebellion against Agathocles was nearing success, Oenanthe hysterically sought divine aid at the temple of Demeter and Persephone—or rather, Polybius says, she attempted to cast magic spells (29.9). When other women tried to console her, she called them "beasts" (θηρία). She threatened and cursed them ("I shall yet make you taste the flesh of your own children!" 29.12), and she ordered her bodyguards to beat them (29.13). Later, Polybius says, these women prayed to the goddesses that Oenanthe be cursed with the fate she had threatened to bring on others (29.14).

---

135. Cf. S. Pomeroy, *Women in Hellenistic Egypt,* 50.

136. Pomeroy, ibid., 51, implies that Polybius approves of the revenge taken on the family of Philammon by these young women, who had been companions of Philammon's victim, the princess Arsinoë (cf. 15.33.11). But Polybius's disapproval of their conduct here is patent in his stress on the fact that Philammon's son, murdered by them, was "hardly more than a child" (ἀντίπαιδα τὴν ἡλικίαν ὄντα, 33.12).

137. On Apega's depradations at Argos, see also Livy [P] 32.40.10. The story of Apega's brutal conduct at Argos is obviously intended by Polybius as part of his general presentation of the regime of Nabis as a horror. For a rationalizing explanation of Apega's behavior, see Texier, *Nabis,* 57.

138. On the Polybian derivation of Livy 41.25, see Nissen, *Kritische Untersuchungen,* 241; Mendels, "Polybius and the Socio-Economic Revolution," 105.

If even the peripheral involvement of women in politics could lead to scenes of primitive superstition and hysterical anger like this,[139] it follows that to Polybius a woman in actual power within a polity would be an unmitigated disaster—not just politically, but also in terms of the violation of accepted norms of conduct. Such is the case, of course, with his presentation of Queen Teuta, ruler of the Illyrian Ardiaei (2.4–11).

Teuta succeeded her husband, Agron (himself a drunkard; cf. 2.4.6), in 231. Polybius sneers that she ruled "by women's reasoning" (λογισμοὶ γυναικεῖοι, 2.4.8). Puffed up by the recent success of Illyrian raids into northwest Greece (ibid.), she allowed her privateers to run wild, ordering her commanders to treat all states as enemies (2.4.8–9; cf. 12.6). One result was a Roman embassy to Teuta complaining of Illyrian pirate raids on Italian merchant shipping in the southern Adriatic. The younger envoy, Polybius says, spoke to Teuta with tactless bluntness (2.8.9–10), and she responded in kind, answering "with the passionate and irrational rage of a woman" (γυναικωθύμως κὰλογίστως, 8.12). Indeed, Teuta's anger reached such a point that she ordered the envoy's murder (ibid.). Polybius stresses that the murder of an ambassador—even a young and tactless one—was an act "in defiance of the just customs of the human race" (ibid.); it was, in fact, an act of παρανομία (8.13). Later, Teuta once again sent her raiders into the Adriatic. Polybius attributes her motive to simple greed (2.8.4), and the Illyrians employed treachery to gain their aims (2.9.1–7). Meanwhile, at home, Teuta's regime was dissolving into destructive factional infighting (2.11.4).[140] In the end, an angry Rome (2.8.13) easily disposed of Teuta's pirate monarchy (2.11–12).

Much has been written about the possibility that the actions of Queen Teuta's government in this period were actually all quite rational.[141] But for the present study, what is important is the tone and content of Polybius's narrative. It has been plausibly suggested that at the heart of that narrative lies a hostile Roman account of Teuta, most probably the work of the early Roman annalist Q. Fabius Pictor, a contemporary of these events.[142] But Polybius was well aware of Fabius's prejudices (cf. 1.14, a famous passage), and was quite prepared to reject him in certain circumstances (cf. 3.8.1–9.5).[143] If the Greek historian nevertheless was willing to accept the hostile picture of Teuta that he found in the existing tradi-

139. For a different assessment of Oenanthe and her career, see, however, S. Pomeroy, *Women in Hellenistic Egypt*, 49–50.

140. Compare Syracuse under the regime of the adolescent Hieronymus (discussed above, p. 143).

141. For a convenient discussion, see Errington, *Dawn of Empire*, 34–40.

142. Cf. Walbank, *Commentary* I: 153.

143. For discussion, see esp. Meister, *Historische Kritik bei Polybios*, 127–49.

tions, it was mostly because that picture confirmed his own ingrained prejudices about how women tended to behave.[144]

Polybius's negative view of women also finds significant expression in his contempt for men he feels have acted in a "womanish" fashion.[145] The term "womanish" (γυναικώδης) is itself vague, but its constituent elements to the Greeks have now been well described by Peter Brown, and Polybius's usage seems to fit the pattern. Like most Greek aristocratic males, then, Polybius uses "womanish" to mean a deficiency in "heat" and decisiveness (yet calmness) in manner and behavior; a lack of high-spirited momentum but also of poise; a flagging in the firm self-restraint and elegance of conduct that made a mature man a man.[146] The classic Polybian example of such a "womanish" man is Prusias II, the king of Bithynia.

Polybius's use of the epithet first occurs in his excoriating description of Prusias's visit to Rome in 167. The historian introduces Prusias as "a man not at all worthy of the dignity of being a king" (30.18.2), and capable of "very ignoble" behavior (ἀγεννέστεραν, 18.4).[147] Now he prostrated himself before the *Patres,* and hailed them as savior gods (30.18.5). Polybius's comment is that "no one could surpass him in unmanliness or womanishness, or in servile flattery" (ἀνανδρίας . . . καὶ γυναικισμοῦ, ibid.). He adds that during later talks with the Senate, Prusias did things that it would be improper (ἀπρεπές) even to mention (18.6).

In 30.18, then, "womanishness" connotes cowardice, shameful servility, and, it seems, disgracefully overwrought behavior in general. Polybius uses the epithet again in discussing Prusias's campaign against Pergamum in 155, and yet again in his obituary of the king. The historian first describes Prusias's magnificent sacrifices and intense prayers in 155, especially to the god Asclepius: his emotional genuflections and prostrations were "like a woman" (γυναικιζόμενος, 32.15.7). Yet later Prusias looted a statue of Asclepius himself from the great temple complex at Nicephorium (15.6 and 8); and in the end, Polybius says, he "did nothing worthy of a man" in his war with Pergamum, but instead behaved "in an ignoble manner, with the irrational passion of a woman" (ἀγεννῶς καὶ γυναικο-

144. Cf. von Scala, *Studien,* 257.

145. This contempt parallels Polybius's contempt for mature men who act "like adolescents": see above, n. 106.

146. See Brown, *Body and Society,* 10–11. Brown (11) also rightly concludes that because of the ancient concept of "vital male heat" as the "humor" that divided males from females—a "heat" that could leak away—each and every male was constantly on the brink of *becoming* "womanish"; it did not take much of a false step. Hence, I think, Polybius's strong warnings to his readers about this phenomenon.

147. For detailed discussion of the incident behind Polybius's comments here, see Chap. VII, below.

θύμως, 15.9). Here "womanish passion" is linked with unstable, self-contradictory behavior, as well as with dishonorable loss of self-control. Finally, Polybius sums Prusias up (36.15): he possessed fair reasoning powers (15.1), but with respect to military affairs he was "ignoble and womanish" (ἀγεννῶς καὶ γυναικώδης, 15.2); for, Polybius explains, he was not only a coward, but was also incapable of putting up with any sort of hardship. In short, Prusias was "womanlike" (ἐκτεθηλυμμένος) both in mind and in body (ibid.). Not surprisingly, then, he had no control over his sensual appetites (15.4), and lived a barbarous and uncultured life (15.6). No wonder, Polybius concludes, that Prusias's subjects were ready to rebel against him at the slightest opportunity (15.7; cf. 15.3).

It therefore turns out that, according to Polybius, Queen Teuta early in *The Histories* and King Prusias toward their end share quite similar defects of character. Nor is the resemblance between the barbarous, "womanish," fickle and unpredictable Prusias and the unpredictable, greedy, and violent barbarian Teuta likely to be accidental. On the contrary: Polybius's idea of "womanish" behavior provides a lethal conceptual link between the two portraits, and helps explain (to himself and to his audience) their failure as rulers.[148]

If women represent a potentially disruptive force in society—and the more disruptive, the closer they are to the centers of power—what advice does Polybius then offer his aristocratic male audience on how to handle this problem? Since women were of only marginal concern to the historian overall, in the extant text there are only a few hints. But these hints suggest that Polybius believed women could and should be controlled, ideally through the regimen of a stable marriage that also imposed limits on the behavior of males.

That Polybius approved of the direct control of women by their menfolk is shown by his approving description of the Roman custom of daily inspection of women by their relatives to insure that they had not been drinking (6.11a.4). As for the historian's ideal of stable married life, this comes out in several passages in *The Histories*. The elderly and dignified wife of Mandonius showed what could result, in terms of decorum and self-restraint, from such a marriage (cf. 10.18).[149] Apollonis the wife of Attalus I of Pergamum lived a sedate life with her husband and sons, and wins Polybius's praise for it (22.20). But equally significant here is Polybius's praise of Attalus himself for having lived "a life of utmost virtue

148. The striking ideological implications of these passages on "womanish" Prusias are completely missed by Welwei (*Könige und Königtum*, 144), by Pédech (cf. *Méthode*, 225), and even by Walbank (cf. *Commentary* III: 441–42 and 674–75).

149. Note that Mandonius himself is presented by Polybius as deeply concerned for his wife; that seems the implication of the story of Edeco, Indibilis, and Mandonius in 10.34–35.

and goodness in regard to his wife" (18.41.8).[150] Polybius thinks it natural even for a mercenary, the lowest of the low, to desire to live in repose with his wife and children (cf. 1.66.8). Conversely, the historian finds it unusual and disconcerting that at Sparta the custom was for three or four men to share one woman (12.6b). Naturally, Polybius condemns the disruption of the stable home life of families caused by the sexual depredations of tyrannical rulers.[151]

Moreover, there is intriguing if indirect evidence that Polybius himself experienced the stable married life he advocated. No mention of wife or children occurs in *The Histories*. But at 12.25h.5–25i.1, Polybius asserts strongly that historical writers, if they are to be worthwhile commentators on the historical process, must partake in the most common experiences of human-kind—and among those experiences he specifically includes marriage and the raising of children (25h.6). As Walbank says, Polybius "would hardly make demands on a historian which he was personally unable to fulfill."[152] Similarly, some twenty volumes later Polybius again speaks out harshly against those men who do not marry and raise children. They are guilty of greed and indolence (36.17.7), and their cities, as a consequence of their conduct, grow weak from want of population (17.8). On these grounds (i.e., of personal morality and public utility), Polybius advocates the passage of laws making it compulsory to rear children (17.10). It is possible that the man who repeatedly expressed such opinions publicly, in his written work, was unmarried and childless himself; but in an intellectual world much given to ridicule, it seems highly unlikely.[153]

Insofar as Polybius thought that the problem posed to orderly society by the presence of women was solvable, it was therefore long years of married life that constituted the historian's program. And in the concept of a stable married life in which the male, himself voluntarily subject to a strict standard of self-discipline, also carefully controls the female, Polybius was participating in a vision of domesticity—evolved by Greek male intellectuals—that would have a history in ancient Greek society long after his own time.[154]

150. σωφρονέστατα μὲν ἐβίωσε καὶ σεμνότατα πρὸς γυναῖκα.

151. Cf. 10.26.3 (Philip V at Argos); 13.6.3 (Nabis at Sparta); 15.25.22 (Agathocles of Alexandria).

152. *Commentary* II: 397, agreeing with Ziegler, col. 1462. The implication of Polyb. 12.25h.6 was first pointed out by von Scala, *Studien*, 256.

153. Laws requiring the begetting and rearing of children were actually not uncommon among ancient city-states; this was often viewed as part of one's duty as a male citizen. For discussion, see, e.g., Brunt, *Italian Manpower, 225 B.C.–A.D. 14*, 566–88.

154. Compare Plutarch's description of the ideal marriage as "a school of orderly behavior" (*Praecept. Conjug.* 47); with the comments of Brown, *Body and Society*, 17–25. Plutarch,

CONCLUSION

The cultural ideals Polybius enshrined in his *Histories,* as set forth in Chapters II–IV above, mandated a regime of strict self-discipline in the aristocrats who formed Polybius's audience. The present chapter has offered a wider perspective in which those stern ideals can now be viewed. For it would appear that Polybius was a writer haunted by the specter of social chaos and—ultimately—destruction.

Polybius's world was one menaced with anarchy simultaneously from a multitude of directions. From beyond the boundaries of civilization itself, powerful barbarian peoples constantly threatened to bring savage violence into the *poleis* of the Mediterranean. Meanwhile, some states were tempted, for military or political reasons, to invite disorderly mercenary soldiers within their ambit—which could easily threaten disaster. And whereas mercenaries could be excluded from the *polis,* other forces for disorder dwelt permanently within it. Polybius deeply distrusted the masses, whom he often saw as a repository of profoundly anarchic and destructive impulses. He worried about the impact of undisciplined aristocratic youth on politics, and he saw women (and "womanish" men) as additional disruptive elements in public life.

All these categories of people were sources of highly destructive irrationality, dangerous passions, that menaced the orderly administration of society by a civilized and mature male elite. Indeed, to Polybius the behavior of all these groups threatened at its worst the transgression of all human and divine laws: the descent into that *paranomia* that meant the collapse of civilization itself.[155]

The causes underlying all these threats to society also seemed to Polybius remarkably similar. The *barbaroi* were uneducated; the *misthophoroi*— barbarians themselves, or sprung from the lowest social orders—were brought up in violence and without culture; the *plēthos,* equally the victims of poor upbringing, dwelt in ignorance; the *neoi* were dangerous precisely because they lacked correct training. Theoretically, a modicum of hope existed for all these groups, since their lack of exposure to *paideia* could (theoretically) be remedied. But Polybius seems to take this seriously as a solution only in the case of young aristocratic males—and even there, the road is hard.

The threats, then, will continue. Therefore, Polybius offers his audi-

---

though writing some 250 years later, was a man with a social background very similar to that of Polybius.

155. In his spectrum of increasingly negative phenomena, from mere obsession with sexual pleasure to outright παρανομία, Polybius seems to reflect the concerns and worries of Greek civic notables in general; for a similar exposition of the spectrum of concern among the educated Greek elite, see Brown, *Body and Society,* 30–31.

ence advice on how to combat each of them. Against the *barbaroi*, he can advocate only courage (a virtue dear to his heart). Against the *misthophoroi*, he advocates exclusion (ideally); but if mercenaries *are* required to supplement citizen troops, then their numbers and behavior must be strictly controlled. The *plēthos*, too, must be strictly controlled—ideally by a political elite that itself provides a good example to the masses by stern *self*-control. The *neoi* must be restrained as well; but above all, the *neoi* need training by the elite, until they are ready, as the next mature generation, to take over the responsible administration of the state. As for women, Polybius apparently recommends the discipline of a stable married life. But here, too, it is important to remember that Polybius's ideal of marriage includes *self*-discipline on the part of the mature male.

Indeed, the persistence of that latter theme throughout *The Histories* is striking, and provides a continuity with the earlier chapters of this study. Polybius's main response to the multiple threats to order in his world is to harden his expectations regarding the only category of people he thinks capable of administering the state: the men of the political elite. In a world menaced by instability from so many quarters, such men bore a heavy social responsibility.[156]

Hence Polybius reserves his harshest attacks for those men of the political elite who themselves give in to irrationality and violence: men such as Prusias of Bithynia or Charops in Epirus, Nabis of Sparta or Diaeus and Critolaus in Achaea. Polybius in *The Histories* seeks to distinguish the mature men of the political elite from the Others, who threaten society— but these men have in fact *become* the Other.

It must have been Polybius's deepest fear. If the mature men of the ruling stratum, in the face of the avalanche of savagery and irrationality that threatened society, abandoned their responsibilities out of cowardice or some other moral weakness—or worse, joined *with* the savages—then nothing was safe. But Polybius's very insistence throughout *The Histories* upon the maintenance of self-discipline within the elite only serves to betray his anxiety—amply borne out in the narrative—that self-discipline was extremely difficult to maintain. The boundary between the civilized and the uncivilized was all too easily crossed. This was a threat Polybius felt called upon constantly to battle, as he urged his aristocratic audience to perform their duty (the καθῆκον) and therefore achieve moral nobility (the καλόν).[157]

---

156. Compare the comments of Brown, ibid., 22, on the response of the Greek civic gentry to the instability caused by the crisis of the third century A.D.: a hardening of their expectations regarding personal behavior.

157. The term τὸ καθῆκον (duty) and its cognates appear 133 times in just the extant text of *The Histories*, which is only about a quarter of the original work. See Mauersberger, *Polybios-Lexikon* I:3, cols. 1198–1201.

A particularly instructive example of this Polybian ideology is the image of generalship in *The Histories,* and it is to this topic that we turn next. To Polybius, the good general was the man who imposed order: upon the chaos of his own army, upon the chaos of campaign and battle—and upon himself.

SIX

The Art of Generalship
as the Imposition of Order

In war, with its enormous friction, even the mediocre is a
substantial achievement.
—VON MOLTKE THE ELDER

INTRODUCTION

To Polybius, the command of armies in war was "the grandest and most solemn" of all human endeavors.[1] Superlatives on this subject came naturally to all ancient men. The responsibilities shouldered by an ancient general were enormous: wars could be lost in a single battle, in a few hours (or minutes); the fate of thousands of men, of cities and whole states, rested directly upon the commander. This opened the way for "brilliance," for personal achievement of the highest order (τὰ κάλλιστα).[2] But equal to the personal responsibility was the difficulty. Polybius stressed that inattention to the smallest of details of generalship could lead ultimately to disaster, while correct management of every single aspect of the enormous endeavor of war was still barely sufficient to achieve success (9.12.9–10).

In *The Histories*, Polybius therefore often gives his audience technical advice on battle management—and even includes within the work a special digression on the art of generalship itself (9.12–20).[3] But in view of the nature of his audience as he conceived it, it is perhaps no surprise by now that Polybius's advice is not limited to matters of technique. On the contrary. Throughout *The Histories* Polybius makes it clear to his readers that the task of a general is, above all, to exercise control over the great

1. τὰ κάλλιστα καὶ σεμνότατα, 9.20.9.
2. Examples: Xanthippus the Spartan, whom Polybius believed single-handedly saved Carthage in 256/255 (see 1.34–37); cf. Philopoemen's enormous personal impact upon the fortunes of Achaea and its army (discussed below, pp. 163–64), or the presentation of Hannibal's personal impact upon the Second Punic War (see esp. 9.22.1).
3. Polybius also wrote a separate monograph on tactics (cf. 9.20.4, and p. 162 below), now almost totally lost; see Walbank, *Commentary* II: 148.

chaos inherent in military endeavors—and that this means, first and foremost, control over oneself.[4]

This conception of generalship comes out in detail in an extraordinary
passage in Book 3. Injecting himself personally into the narrative of Hannibal's campaign of 217, Polybius explains that a commander should always study the personality of his opponent (3.81.1–3). The historian then
lists what he perceives as the typical weaknesses to which commanders
are heir (3.81.4–9); strikingly, it is a list of moral—not intellectual—deficiencies. There are laziness and lack of energy, which have ruined not
merely private endeavors, but whole states (81.4). Then there is drunkenness—a widespread problem (81.5). There is also obsession with sexual
pleasure: some men have ruined not only themselves but their communities by overindulgence here, bringing their lives to an end in disgrace
(μετ᾽ αἰσχύνης, 81.6). Cowardice, too, is a disgrace (ὄνειδος), and in a
commander-in-chief it can lead to calamity (81.7). But, Polybius says,
there are even worse vices: recklessness, irrational anger (θυμὸς ἄλογος),
excessive vanity and conceit. These latter are the defects of character
most easily taken advantage of by the enemy, and hence the most dangerous to one's own side (81.9).

What is clear from this list of character defects is the common theme
of loss of self-control (a theme we have come across before, of course). A
commander's self-control must be maintained for reasons of broad social
utility—the safety of the army and the state (cf. 3.81.4, 6, 8, 9). But it
must be maintained as well because not to impose order upon oneself is,
in and of itself, disgraceful (cf. 3.81.6, 7).[5]

The second duty of a commander is to impose some sort of order upon
his army. Indeed, the imposition of order and a sense of mission upon
thousands of men—the reforming of attitudes and morale—was to Polybius one of the *essences* of generalship. This is shown by a surviving
fragment of Polybius's *Treatise on Tactics*. According to Aelian (3.4), Polybius in that work defined generalship as the imposition of useful order,
through purposeful training, on what was at the beginning merely "a
disorganized mob" (πλῆθος ἄτακτον).

---

4. Such advice makes good sense down through Book 15, i.e., about 150 B.C. Even after
the Greek military and political disasters of the 140s, following which Polybius no longer
believed that the Greek civic elite would have the power or responsibility for engaging in
important military operations (see the late insertion at 3.59.4), Polybius continued to offer
such advice in a general way: see, e.g., 39.6.

5. Polybius's special concern about irrational anger in 3.81 both mirrors a worry typical
of the Greek civic elite (see Brown, *Body and Society*, 30–31), and has particular relevance to
the character defect of Hannibal's opponent in this section of *The Histories*, the Roman C.
Flaminius (see 3.80.3–5 and 81.12–82.7, very emphatic).

Since the *Tactics* antedated the writing of *The Histories*,[6] it is no surprise to find a specific historical example of the Polybian theoretical model being presented in the later work: Philopoemen's reform of the citizen army of the Achaean League.

Polybius emphasizes that Philopoemen himself always lived a life of hard work and strict moderation, as a result of correct training in youth (10.22.1–5).[7] As hipparch (cavalry commander) of the League in 210/209, he found his forces totally disorganized and dispirited (10.22.6). But by dint of constant and strenuous personal effort, putting the men—and their officers—through a long and rigorous course of training, he managed to turn the Achaean cavalry, man by man and unit by unit, into a superb body of troops (10.22.6–7; cf. 24.7). Then, as general of the League in 208/207, Philopoemen repeated the process with the entire army—and it is clear that Polybius delighted in describing it in detail.[8] Philopoemen took the worthless Achaean infantry and made them use heavier weapons and shields; and he reorganized them carefully—as he had the cavalry—unit by unit.[9] But beyond improved technique, Philopoemen also imposed a moral revolution, urging the leaders of the phalanx to live a more "manly" and restrained style of life (11.9.7).[10] It took eight months of such intensive training before the reorganized Achaean army was ready for battle (11.10.7–9). But the result was the smashing Achaean victory over Sparta at Mantineia in 207. And Mantineia was a victory not only of improved battle technique but of the moral regeneration Philopoemen had engineered: it was visible in the heroic Achaean shout and countercharge against the Spartan phalanx, which decided the battle (11.17.2). As the historian remarks in commenting approvingly on one of Philopoemen's speeches that urged both military and moral reform upon the Achaeans (11.10.1–2): "So true is it that one word spoken at the right time not only deters listeners from what is worst, but urges them on to what is best [τὰ κάλλιστα]."

The task confronting Philopoemen in 210–208 was the imposition of

6. See Polyb. 9.20.4 (where it is apparently referred to as an earlier work), with Walbank, *Commentary* II: 148.

7. For detailed discussion of Polybius's presentation of Philopoemen's upbringing and education, see Chap. V, above.

8. See Polyb. 8.11.8–10 (clearly only a fragment of the original discussion), and Plut. *Phil.* 9.2. The latter is fuller, and probably based on Polybius's biography of Philopoemen: see Pédech, "Polybe et l'éloge," 82–85.

9. The rearming and retraining of the Achaean phalanx: Polyb. 11.8–10. The reorganization of the phalanx: not in the extant text of *The Histories*, which is highly fragmentary, but see Plut. *Phil.* 9.2. In general, cf. Anderson, "Philopoemen's Reform," 104–5.

10. This moralizing theme was evidently stressed even more strongly in Polybius's biography of Philopoemen: see Plut. *Phil.* 9.3–7.

order upon a lackadaisical citizen army; other generals in *The Histories* face somewhat different tasks in terms of transforming the inchoate mass of their soldiery into a purposeful instrument of war. And all these generals face still another terrible problem: mastering the chaos inherent in actual campaigning and battle. In this chapter, after examining the general character of the soldiery as portrayed by Polybius in *The Histories*, we will turn to three specific case studies of generalship. These are case studies in which the Polybian ideology of command in war as the imposition of order and control—upon oneself, upon others, upon battle—is particularly striking.

THE CHARACTER OF THE SOLDIERY

Polybius's views concerning the soldiery of the Hellenistic armies have never been studied as a discrete topic. Yet it is impossible to appreciate Polybius's depiction of Hellenistic generals without taking into account his understanding of the human raw materials with which they had to work.

To Polybius, the soldiery of his age possessed, in their "natural" state, three outstanding characteristics. They had a strong tendency toward self-indulgence; they were greedy for loot, sometimes to the point of self-destruction; and they often suffered from fragile morale when faced with actual battle. Self-indulgence, greed, fear: these were the waves of "irrationality" among his troops that a general was called upon to control if he wished to be successful.

First, self-indulgence. With shocking regularity, the common soldiery in *The Histories* tend to collapse into unrestrained eating and drinking, followed by heavy sleeping and dangerous negligence, once discipline has been at all loosened. This phenomenon occurred in the army of the lax Punic general Hanno in 240: with Hanno himself off at the baths in Utica, the Carthaginian soldiery—scattered, idle, and negligent—were heavily defeated in a counterattack by the rebel mercenaries (Polyb. 1.74.7–12). It occurred as well in the army of the overconfident Seleucid general Xenoetas in 222. Having captured the camp of the pretender Molon, Xenoetas allowed his troops a period of relaxation, during which they went utterly wild; when Molon suddenly counterattacked, Xenoetas's army was not merely defeated but totally destroyed, with most of his men slaughtered in their drunken sleep, unable even to defend themselves (5.46.5–48.5).

In these two cases, Polybius strongly blames the generals for allowing the laxness that led to ultimate defeat. Hanno was an incompetent (1.74.13); Xenoetas was inexperienced in command, and wrongly contemptuous of his opponent, Molon (5.46.6). But neither Hanno's faults nor those of Xenoetas would have been so disastrous if not for the self-indulgent, even primitive character of their troops—which Polybius emphasizes is a general phenomenon (5.48.1).[11]

A classic case of military deterioration was evidently presented by Polybius in his account of the Seleucid expedition to Greece in winter 192/191. The commander—Antiochus III—set the tone by spending all his time in feasting, drunkenness, sexual dalliance with his new wife, and sleeping (Polyb. 20.8; cf. Livy [P] 36.11.2). These habits of life were then adopted by Antiochus's officers (36.11.3). And as outside discipline relaxed, the soldiers themselves soon reverted to their "natural" state of total indolence; not even minimum sentry duty was kept (11.3–4). By the spring of 191, Polybius indicated, Antiochus barely had an army left (11.5).[12]

Polybius's picture of the army of Antiochus's son Seleucus in summer 190 apparently kept this theme of laziness and indiscipline before the reader. Because his forces met no opposition while ravaging the countryside around Pergamum, Seleucus's army soon developed a contempt for the enemy (Livy [P] 37.20.4). Thus negligence quickly spread (37.20.5):

> A large part of the cavalry kept no saddles or bridles on their horses; a few men were left in arms at their posts, but the rest were scattered here and there over the whole plain, some engaged in youthful games and drinking, some picnicking in the shade, and some even stretched out asleep.

It is a classic Polybian scene; and the result was a heavy defeat administered by a small but highly disciplined force of Achaeans, led by the League *stratēgos* Diophanes (37.20.13–14)—a commander, Polybius evidently said, in the mold of Philopoemen (20.2).[13]

Many other instances of this Polybian theme could be cited.[14] Even

11. Bar-Kochva suspects political bias in the presentation of Xenoetas, since Polybius's sources here were hostile to Hermeias, the chief adviser of the young Antiochus III, and Xenoetas was one of Hermeias's allies (*Seleucid Army*, 98). But Polybius does not follow his sources blindly (see Badian, "Review of La Bua," 208). And here Polybius's point is not so much about Hermeias and his allies as about generalship and armies; that is shown by the generalizing statement about self-indulgent soldiery at 5.48.1. Polybius does not hide the fact that Xenoetas was an Achaean (45.6).

12. For Livy 36.11 as deriving from Polybian material, see Briscoe, *Commentary* II: 2 (cf. 235); confirmed by Polyb. 20.8.

13. For Livy 37.19–20 as an especially close paraphrase of Polybius, see Briscoe, *Commentary* II: 319 and 321.

14. For negligent, sleepy, and/or drunken troops, often leading to catastrophic results, see also Polyb. 8.37 (Syracusans in 211); 11.3.1 (Gauls in 207); Livy [P] 31.23.1–4 (Macedonians in 200); Livy [P] 31.24.5–6 (Athenians in 200); Livy [P] 31.41 (Aetolians in 199); Livy [P] 35.37.2 (Spartans in 192); Polyb. 29.15.1–2 (mercenaries and Macedonians in 168). Cf. also frg. 40 B-W: another reference to drunken and disorderly soldiers unable to hear a word of command or take thought for the future. The context is unclear (but see Walbank,

Scipio Africanus made the mistake of relaxing discipline too far. After the great victories over the Carthaginians in Spain, Polybius indicates that Scipio's troops became "demoralized" because he allowed them too much leisure, and even (as with Xenoetas's troops) too much food (11.25.7). This relaxation in discipline soon led to a widespread mutiny over pay, with order restored only by means of public execution of the ringleaders (11.25–30). And it is this incident that provides Polybius with the opportunity for proclaiming another of his general rules: never allow the soldiery too much rest or idleness, or too much luxury (11.25.7).[15]

Indeed, what is striking here is that the soldiers of Rome are presented by Polybius as being similar in their weaknesses to those of any other polity. Roman soldiers, too, have a strong tendency to fall asleep at their posts; the only thing that keeps *Roman* sentries awake at night is a stern system of inspection, and the threat of severe punishment (6.36–37). The same severe punishment is also meted out—to Polybius's obvious approval—to those officers who fall asleep themselves, failing to make their nightly rounds of the sentry posts (37.6).

It is not surprising, then, that Polybius also heartily approved of the constant and severe drilling that Greek mercenary captains around 220 were imposing upon the lackadaisical troops of Ptolemaic Egypt, previously totally worthless (5.63.11–65.10). These captains, Polybius says, were men who had some notion of the reality of war (63.13). And similar is Polybius's evidently hearty approval of the stern discipline (including strict sentry watch) that the consul L. Aemilius Paullus imposed upon the slovenly and resentful Roman army in Greece in 168.[16]

If to Polybius a major trait of Hellenistic soldiery was a strong tendency toward sleeping, eating, drinking, and general self-indulgence if given the least opportunity, it was natural that such men would find in looting a particularly irresistible temptation. As Polybius depicts it, not an army of his age escapes this temptation—or the dangers attendant upon it.

For obvious reasons, mercenaries were especially eager to loot. For modern analysts, the reasons seem socioeconomic; to Polybius the reasons were moral: the brutal character and upbringing of these men.[17] But the behavior of Aetolian citizen-soldiers was similar—for similar reasons.[18] Seleucid armies suffered from the same problem (cf. 5.57.7–8).

Commentary III: 746). On the Polybian derivation of the various Livian passages cited here, cf. Briscoe, *Commentary* I: 1–2 (cf. 115 and 121), and *Commentary* II: 2 (cf. 181).

15. For discussion of the great Sucro mutiny, see Scullard, *Scipio Africanus,* 100–101.

16. See Livy [P] 44.33.5–9, and Plut. *Aem.* 13.5. Polybian derivation: see Nissen, *Kritische Untersuchungen,* 264.

17. For detailed discussion, see above, Chap. V.

18. See Polyb. 4.6.10 and 12; Livy [P] 35.36.6–10 (Polybian derivation: cf. Briscoe, *Commentary* II: 2, cf. 181). Aetolian moral weakness: see Polyb. 13.1–1a.

And the soldiery of Antigonid Macedon constituted another formidable looting machine.[19]

Roman troops, as Polybius depicts them, were just as greedy. One way to improve *their* morale was to promise them good looting.[20] At Astapa in Spain in 206, Roman soldiers were so eager for the gold and silver (which the Astapans were attempting to burn) that they rushed right into the enormous pyre of burning metal, and thus many were burned to death (11.24.11).[21] Polybius's general view of Roman soldiers as primitive and uncouth comes through also in his account of the Roman sack of Corinth in 146 (39.2).[22]

Yet if Polybius sees ordinary Roman soldiers as no different from any others in this respect, another *system* developed by the Romans helps preserve their armies from the most deleterious effects of the lust for loot. The historian explains this in a commentary he appends to the Roman sack of New Carthage in Spain in 209 (10.16–17).

Polybius's general rule is that it is almost impossible to keep Greek soldiers from anarchic looting, for the Greek custom is for each soldier to keep whatever he can personally steal and conceal. Thus Greek commanders lose control of their men as soon as the pillaging of a captured camp or town begins (10.17.2–4), and disasters can occur if the enemy unexpectedly counterattacks the now-disorganized troops (17.4, cf. 16.8–9). The problem is incorrigible, Polybius says, because most men will not pass up a chance to engage in looting, no matter what the risk (17.1).

But the Romans are more organized. They never employ more than half their available men in looting, reserving the others to stand guard against counterattacks (10.16.2–4 and 8–9). The looters bring their booty to their officers, who then sell it and divide the proceeds equally among the men (16.5). And no one secretly appropriates plunder for himself, because the Romans maintain the good faith (πίστις) of their oaths, and so no one fears being cheated (16.6 and 8–9).

The Roman system was not infallible, as the example of Astapa showed (see above). What made it work as well as it did was, of course, the good behavior of the officers—who had sole control over the proceeds from the sale of the booty. But Roman aristocrats felt as bound by their oaths

---

19. On Macedonian looting, see Polyb. 4.65.1 (Oeniadae); 4.72.1 (Psophis); 4.84.5, cf. 73.5 (Elis); 5.19 (Laconia); 5.8.6–9 (Thermum, the capital of Aetolia, where the loot included 15,000 beautifully decorated suits of armor dedicated to the gods).

20. See Polyb. 2.31.4 and 3.76.13; and Livy [P] 36.24.7 (Polybian derivation: see Briscoe, *Commentary* II: 2; cf. 226 and 241).

21. For detailed discussion of Astapa, see Chap. II, above.

22. Similar is Livy [P] 37.32.8–14, the looting of the city of Phocaea, despite a promise from the praetor L. Aemilius Regillus that such conduct would not occur; but he was helpless to prevent it. On Polybian derivation, see Briscoe, *Commentary* II: 2.

as any other Roman, a fact already underlined by Polybius (see 6.56.13–15); the same could not be said of the Greek elite (ibid.). The officers had sworn not to steal from the camp (see 6.33.1–2).[23] Polybius wishes that his Greek audience would imitate the Roman system (10.17.5), but it depends not only on carefulness, but on good faith.

The lust for loot is only the most glaring aspect of the atmosphere of "greed" in which Polybius believes the soldiery existed. Hellenistic armies also had trouble when the men fell behind in their pay: Polybius presents serious incidents of this with the Seleucids, with the Achaean League—and with the Roman army.[24] Soldiers certainly deserve their pay. But by constant remarks on the desire of troops for more money, Polybius reinforces the image of armies made up of lazy, greedy men. It is, of course, a quintessentially aristocratic perspective.

Finally, modern scholars often assert that Hellenistic armies were better fighting forces than the amateur citizen levies of the Classical age, because of the intensification of drill and the presence in most armies of true professionals.[25] One could not tell that from Polybius. On the contrary: what is striking in *The Histories* is the tremendous fragility of soldiers' morale, especially when faced with actual battle. Perhaps this phenomenon should not be so surprising, given the hideous realities of ancient army life and of ancient battle itself.[26] But the resulting picture in *The Histories* only serves to underline the dimensions of the task Polybius believed commanders faced in seeking to impose order and purpose—and hence, success—upon their armies.

One particularly interesting example here is Hannibal, because his army—though involved in an especially risky enterprise—was also composed of veteran mercenaries who should have had a tougher attitude than ordinary citizen-soldiers.[27] Yet the morale even of these hard-bitten men was very easily cracked: it happened at the Rhone (Polyb. 3.44.10–13); in the Alpine foothills (3.49.13); in the high mountains, where the soldiery was on the verge of total moral collapse (54.1–2 and 7); in 217, when confronted by the marshes of the Arno (78.8 and 79.4–6); even after the great victory at Lake Trasimene (87.1–3). Indeed, even on the

23. For the connection between Polyb. 10.16.6 and 6.33.1–2, see Walbank, *Commentary* II: 217.

24. Cf. Polyb. 5.50.1 and 9, 57.7–9, 60.3 (Seleucids); 5.30.5 and 94.9 (Achaea); 11.25.9 (Scipio Africanus's troops).

25. See, most recently, Culham, "Chance, Command and Chaos in Ancient Military Engagements," 192.

26. See now the excellent study by Hansen, *The Western Way of War: Infantry Battle in Classical Greece.*

27. On the tough background of Hannibal's troops, see Polybius's remarks at 3.79.6 and 89.5.

eve of Cannae, Hannibal's troops could be demoralized by the slightest military setback (111.1). The result is that Polybius portrays Hannibal as, time and again, the sole person responsible for the success—and even the bare survival—of his army.[28] And this depiction was intentional. When in Book 11 Polybius offers a retrospective on Hannibal's achievements during the Second Punic War, he naturally mentions Hannibal's excellent generalship and unusual courage (11.19.1). But the aspect of his career that most impresses Polybius is Hannibal's ability to hold his army together at all, and to compel it—under the most difficult circumstances—to do his will (19.3–5).[29]

Given the nature of the struggle experienced even by Hannibal in maintaining the cohesion and morale of an army of seasoned veterans, it will come as no surprise that *The Histories* are rife with other instances of poor performance by the ordinary soldiery.

One may begin with Polybius's own Achaeans—for the historian by no means hides their poor record of battle performance. The *stratēgos* Timoxenus feared it in 221 (Polyb. 4.7.6–7), and so did Aratus of Sicyon (cf. 2.47.8); rightly so, for under his command the Achaean levy broke and ran at Caphyae (4.12.8–12)—only the latest in a string of Achaean military disasters in the 220s. A decade later it took Philopoemen years of hard work (210–207) before the Achaean army was battle-worthy (see above). In the 190s, while some elite Achaean units fought well (see above), other units were doubted by their commanders (cf. Livy [P] 33.14.6), and still others fought very poorly indeed—even under Philopoemen's personal command.[30] And the uneven record continued throughout Polybius's own adulthood. In the 180s the Achaean army was strong enough to overawe the Messenians and Spartans.[31] But the Achaeans fled shamefully before Roman forces in the war of 146; and it must have been particularly painful to Polybius—the former hipparch—that at Corinth the flight was led by the panicky League cavalry.[32]

Polybius evidently blamed the Achaean military failure of the 140s on the poor leadership of the *stratēgoi* Critolaus and Diaeus; Critolaus in par-

28. See 3.44.10–13, 54.2, 55 *passim,* 87.1–3, 111.1.

29. Polybius here uses the metaphor of the general as ship's captain; note also 10.33.5 (also in a Hannibalic context); the soldiers are helpless without such a person.

30. On the Polybian derivation of Livy 33.14, see Briscoe, *Commentary* I: 275. On the Polybian derivation of Livy 35.26.9 (the Achaean panic of 192, despite Philopoemen's presence), see Briscoe, *Commentary* II: 181.

31. For detailed discussions, see Errington, *Philopoemen,* 133–94.

32. On the generally shameful performance of Achaean troops against the Romans in 146, see Paus. 7.15.2–4 and 10, and 7.16.3, based apparently on Polybian material. For detailed discussion of the fighting and our sources, see Gruen, "Origins of the Achaean War," 65–69.

ticular was depicted as a coward.[33] Polybius deeply disapproved of the policies of these two men, but more than politics is involved here. Much earlier, he had launched a rather similar attack on Eperatus, the Achaean *stratēgos* of 218/217, for his sloth, incompetence, and failure to impose order and purpose on the army (5.30.1, 91.4); and he made the same bitter points against Euryleon, the *stratēgos* of 211/210 (10.21.1). At least part of the issue in these passages, then, has to do with Polybius's basic concept of generalship and its duties.[34]

But in fact in Polybius fragile morale is characteristic of the soldiery of almost all the Hellenistic armies. After the poor performance of his troops at Raphia in 217, Antiochus III—who was personally a formidable warrior (see Polyb. 10.49)—considered his entire army to be made up of cowards (5.85.13; cf. 87.2). He did not trust his army to meet the Romans in the open field in Greece in 191, nor at Magnesia in 189—and he was correct to hesitate.[35] Ptolemaic troops were generally considered worthless.[36] In 217, Acarnanian troops fled from the prospect of battle: a shameful act (αἰσχρῶς, 5.96.3). The army of Elis twice fled from battle without a blow being struck against it (5.69.4–8, 95.8–9). Most of the Aetolian army shirked the Thermopylae campaign of 191: the generals were simply unable to get their men to take the field (Livy [P] 36.15.4–5).[37] The Carthaginian citizen cavalry panicked shamefully at the battle of the Great Plains in 203 (Polyb. 14.8.8), as did the citizen infantry at Zama the next year (15.13.3 and 5)—as Hannibal had feared it would (15.16.3).

Polybius, of course, thought the Romans to be good soldiers in general (6.52.6–10), and he recorded outstanding instances of Roman bravery.[38] Yet if Polybius considered the Romans good soldiers, that only reveals the nature of his standards—for often enough he depicts Roman troops

33. See esp. Paus. 7.15.2–4. Diaeus comes off somewhat better, but even Diaeus is depicted as giving up too quickly at Corinth, fleeing his army while the fighting is still going on (7.16.3–4).

34. On Euryleon, wee Walbank, *Commentary* II: 220. In attacking Eperatus, Polybius may have relied on Aratus's memoirs, for Eperatus was one of Aratus's political opponents (see Walbank, *Aratos*, 136). But if so, it is clear that Polybius found Aratus's criticisms of Eperatus congenial on deep ideological grounds. As for Critolaus and Diaeus, Polybius profoundly despised physical cowardice (see above, Chap. II).

35. See Livy [P] 36.15.5–16.3 and 37.39.6, on Antiochus's doubts about his troops. Polybian derivation: see Briscoe, *Commentary* II: 241 and 303. A significant portion of Antiochus's army did panic at Magnesia; for detailed discussion of the fighting, see Bar-Kochva, *Seleucid Army*, 163–73.

36. See Polyb. 5.62.7, 66.7, 69.9–10, 107.1–3. They could be improved—with stringent training (5.63.8–65.7).

37. For Livy 36.15 as deriving from Polybian material, see Briscoe, *Commentary* II: 241.

38. See, e.g., the spirited Roman assault on the walls of New Carthage (10.13.6–10); or, from the legendary period, the description of Horatius at the bridge (6.55).

as wavering or even panicking. Roman armies suffered from low morale after Lake Trasimene (3.90.3–4), and before the battle of Cannae (3.107.4–5). In 199 there was a serious mutiny at Apollonia in Greece, caused by war-weariness (Livy [P] 32.3).[39] If part of Antiochus's forces panicked at Magnesia in 189 (see above), so did the Roman left wing; their flight was stopped by the military tribune M. Aemilius Lepidus (Livy [P] 37.43.1–3).[40] During the Third Macedonian War, Roman army morale plummeted after Perseus's victory at Callinice (Livy [P] 42.61.6; cf. 60.6)—and later there were at least three important cases of outright panic.[41] At Pydna in 168, the consul L. Aemilius Paullus demonstrated confidence to his soldiers in the face of Perseus's grimly advancing phalanx by riding along the Roman lines without helmet or breastplate: a magnificent gesture of personal courage, and perhaps a necessary one.[42]

Interestingly, there is only one army in Polybius that is free from disgraceful panic in combat, one army whose energy and courage consistently impressed him: not the army of Rome but the army of Macedon. The Macedonians, Polybius tells his audience, are like the sons of Aeacus in Hesiod: they enjoy war as if it were a banquet (5.2.6).[43] Their reputation for ferocity was enough, in itself, to make their enemies run away (4.60.4–8). Their sterling martial qualities were demonstrated in their splendid assaults on Phthiotic Thebes in 217 (5.100.6), on Lissus in 212 (8.14.9)—and on Lamia in 191 (Livy [P] 36.25).[44] As marines, they greatly distinguished themselves in the naval battle off Chios in 201, often fighting to the death.[45] In defense of fortified positions the Macedonians were as formidable as in assault: they defeated T. Quinctius Flamininus's attack on Atrax in 198, and forced him to rethink his entire plan of campaign (Livy [P] 32.17.4–17). Flamininus thought his men inferior in quality to

39. On the Polybian derivation of this passage, see Briscoe, *Commentary* I: 172, arguing strongly against Nissen, *Kritische Untersuchungen,* 132 (who thinks it annalistic in origin).

40. For Livy 37.43 as deriving from Polybian material, cf. Briscoe, *Commentary* II: 303.

41. For the Roman panic at Phalanna in 171, see Livy [P] 42.65.6 (L. Pompeius rallied the troops); for the Roman panic at Cassandreia in 169, and again at Meliboea, see Livy [P] 44.12.3 and 13.6. For the Polybian derivation of these passages, see Nissen, *Kritische Untersuchungen,* 250 and 254–55.

42. Plut. *Aem.* 19.1–2; Polybian derivation: see Walbank, *Commentary* III: 388–89. The Roman evaluation of themselves on the issue of military courage was, of course, somewhat different from Polybius's cautious assessment; see e.g., Enn. *Ann.* 470: "Fortes Romani sunt tanquam caelus profundus."

43. Polybius's reference to Hesiod here makes the point most emphatic. On Polybius's use of poets as a way to reach out to his audience and underline a sentiment or idea, see Chap. II, above; this is not merely a frigid display of erudition.

44. For Livy 36.25 as deriving from Polybian material, see Briscoe, *Commentary* II: and 225–26.

45. See Polyb. 16.3.8, 3.11, and 4.13.

the Macedonians, and found their phalanx truly dangerous (32.18.1).[46]
And that same energy was still evident a generation later, during the
Third Macedonian War—at Callinice and then at Mylae in 171, at Uscana
in 170.[47] Even after the terrible omen of the eclipse of the moon before
Pydna, the Macedonian army was eager for battle (Livy [P] 44.37.9–10).
And it fought bravely: that is shown by the twenty thousand dead it left
on the battlefield (44.42.7).[48]

It makes sense that the formidable nature of the Macedonian army was
a theme that ran deeply in *The Histories*. Polybius, working from Achaean
experience, saw the power of Macedon as having posed as large a problem to Greece as did the power of Rome.[49]

And Polybius also evidently offered at least a partial explanation for
the Macedonian fierceness in war. He emphasized the harshness and poverty of upland Macedon, which was exposed, in addition, to the destructive raids (and bad cultural influence) of barbarian neighbors (Livy [P]
45.30.7). The passage strikingly resembles Polybius's discussion of the
harsh physical environment of his own native Arcadia, and the effect this
had on Arcadian culture and character (4.20–21).[50] A good portion of the
Macedonian population, then, was simply more ferocious than ordinary
men (*ferociores,* Livy [P] 45.30.7).

Yet the Romans beat them—and the Romans were much more like
ordinary men. To Polybius, there were several crucial factors involved in
the destruction of Macedon: Tyche (Fortune) on the one hand; the personal deficiencies of Philip V, and then Perseus, on the other.[51] But as
far as the strictly military aspect of the problem went, Polybius's answer
concentrated once again on the *systems* (including the legion) that the Romans had evolved to make their soldiers more orderly and effective.[52] Of

46. On the crucial strategic importance of the defeat of Flamininus at Atrax for the campaign of 198, see Eckstein, "Flamininus and the Campaign against Philip in 198 B.C.," 131–
36. On the Polybian derivation of Livy 32.17, see Briscoe, *Commentary* I: 2.

47. See Livy [P] 42.54 and 59–61, and 43.18. Polybian derivation: see Nissen, *Kritische
Untersuchungen,* 254 and 258.

48. For the Polybian derivation of Livy 44.37 and 44.42, see Nissen, *Kritische Untersuchungen,* 264.

49. On Polybius's views of the Macedonian army, see, cogently, Walbank, "Polybius and
Macedonia," 306 and nn. 91–92; cf. 296–97 (on the general threat posed by Macedon to
Greece).

50. But the crucial difference is that the Arcadians have taken steps to mitigate the harsh
effects of their environment by means of education (Polyb. 4.21; see Chap. V, above)—
and the Macedonians have not. On the Polybian derivation of 45.30, cf. Nissen, *Kritische
Untersuchungen,* 276.

51. These aspects of Polybius's thinking on the defeat of Macedon are discussed in detail
in Chaps. VII and VIII, below.

52. On the legion, see esp. Polyb. 18.30.4–33.7.

direct concern for the present topic are the systems of punishment and reward meted out to ordinary Roman soldiers.

The various Greek systems of military punishment were very lax by Roman standards; commanders had little power of punishment, especially over citizen troops.[53] Similarly, the Greek systems of military reward were all more rudimentary and haphazard than the Roman system—as Polybius well knew (cf. 6.39.11).[54] The historian underlines the resulting problems when, for instance, he notes how difficult it was for Achaean commanders to impose military discipline upon their fellow citizens.[55]

Polybius's discussion and praise of the Roman systems here is long (6.35–39) and illuminating. The Romans provided their soldiers with an extensive list of specific military delicts, such as laxity in sentry duty (6.35.8–37.7), or throwing away one's weapons in battle (evidence of fear: 37.11). The penalties were all assigned immediately, by courts-martial in camp (37.1). And for many offenses, the penalty amounted to death—the running of a gauntlet of cudgels and stones, which it was theoretically possible to survive, but which few men did (37.2–3).[56] If whole units were guilty of dereliction of duty in battle, they suffered decimation—even though citizens (cf. 6.38.1). This stern regimen of punishment was certainly no guarantee of Roman behavior in battle as Polybius presented it (see above). But to the historian it seemed admirably designed to minimize "unmanly and shameful behavior" (6.37.10).[57]

Similarly, the Romans had an extensive list of public commendations and rewards for specific acts of valor: for example, for being the first to mount the wall of an enemy city, or saving the life of a comrade (6.39.5–6). And the recipients of such rewards were continually honored throughout the rest of their lives, especially in religious processions (39.9). As with the heavy Roman punishments, so Polybius finds the elaborate Roman system of rewards "an admirable method of encouraging soldiers to face danger on the battlefield" (39.1). And he concludes that this careful system of rewards and punishments for ordinary soldiers is a crucial factor in Rome's military success (39.11).

53. For discussion of discipline in Greek armies, see Pritchett, *Greek State at War* II: 232–45, who concludes that steadfastness in battle depended in Greek armies not on formally imposed discipline but on the informal desire to maintain one's personal good repute.

54. On Greek military rewards, see the comments of Pritchett, *Greek State at War* II: 290.

55. Thus the men who made up the Achaean cavalry were often politically powerful, and could cause trouble for any Achaean hipparch attempting to impose discipline on them: see the remarks of Walbank, *Commentary* II: 225 (on 10.23.9).

56. For discussion, see Walbank, *Commentary* I: 720.

57. Polybius's word usage here (ἀνανδρία, αἰσχύνη) shows that the issue of military discipline is being presented not merely in utilitarian but in moralizing terms. Cf. 6.38.4, 37.12–13.

Such praise makes sense in view of Polybius's belief that the ordinary soldiers' lack of self-discipline constituted a significant and permanent threat to any military endeavor. But in general, like Aeneas Tacticus before him, Polybius thought that the driving force and discipline in any military enterprise could come only from the commander himself; because of their psychological weaknesses, he could not put much trust in his own troops.[58] This prevailing lack of self-discipline among the troops is what made it all the more imperative that the commander impose strict standards upon himself (cf. Polyb. 3.81). Indeed, Polybius sees the successful imposition of order and discipline upon their armies by such figures as Philopoemen and L. Aemilius Paullus as merely one expression of the moral discipline already prevalent in these men's own lives.[59]

But the heavy burden of command did not end with the imposition of order and discipline upon oneself and upon one's unruly soldiers. War itself was, as Polybius knew, a matter of confusion and contingent events.[60] And ancient battle was a process of entropy: the decay of organization under the impact of violence. The commander somehow had to handle this threat as well.[61] In the following sections three examples of Polybian generalship will be examined in detail. Here all the themes discussed above take their place in the structure and ideology of Polybius's narrative of crucial events.

HAMILCAR BARCA AND THE MERCENARY WAR

Polybius's main purpose in providing a detailed account of the mercenary rebellion against Carthage in 241–238 is to explain the origins of the Hannibalic War in the Roman seizure of Sardinia attendant upon the rebellion.[62] But an important subsidiary purpose is to show "the great difference between a confused barbaric horde and the customs of men brought up in education, under law, in civilization" (1.65.7). It is an ideologically revealing statement: chaos and order are placed in direct opposition. And in Polybius's narrative of the rebellion, the representative of order and civilization is Hamilcar Barca, the father of Hannibal.

---

58. On the treatise of the fourth-century Peloponnesian writer Aeneas, and the ideology of generalship implicit in it, see Pritchett, *Greek State at War* II: 237.

59. On Philopoemen, see above, pp. 163–64. On L. Aemilius Paullus's imposition of discipline upon the unruly Roman army in Macedon in 168, see above, n. 16; on Paullus's personal self-discipline, see Polybius's encomium at 31.22.

60. See, e.g., Polyb. 10.32.12; 15.15.15; 18.31.2.

61. See esp. Culham, "Chance, Command and Chaos in Ancient Military Engagements," *passim*.

62. For Polybius's highly negative view of this Roman action, see Chap. IV, above.

Polybius introduces Hamilcar first as an extremely skillful general against the Romans in Sicily (1.56–58). But at the end of the First Punic War, what is stressed above all is his rational self-control. After the Punic defeat at the Aegates Islands, Polybius says, the Carthaginians would still have continued the struggle if guided merely by their passions (1.62.1)— passions, Polybius emphasizes, that Hamilcar deeply shared (3.9.6–7).[63] But the Carthaginians were now at a loss as to how the war was to be fought, so they left the decision up to Hamilcar himself—and he chose to sue for peace (1.62.2–3). Polybius's comments are approving. Hamilcar here "performed the act of a gallant and wise leader" (62.3). He had left no strategem untried while there was still a reasonable chance for success (62.4), but now he very wisely yielded to circumstances (62.5). This was as it should be, "for a general should know both when he is victorious and when he is defeated" (62.6). In this passage, then, Hamilcar personifies the Polybian ideal of the self-controlled aristocratic leader.

By contrast, the mercenaries are the personification of disorder. Arriving from Sicily, they were so unruly and lawless (1.66.6) that the Punic government persuaded them to leave Carthage altogether. They set up their own separate camp, where they lived a life of relaxed discipline, idleness, and luxury—"the usual causes of mutiny," Polybius says (1.66.10).[64] As a result of disputes over back pay, there soon emerged a spirit of rebelliousness (1.67.2). The camp became "a scene filled with confusion, tumult, and turbulence" (67.3), a place of disorder (69.6, 70.1)—the opposite of the orderly military encampment, representative of the orderly society, that should have existed.[65] There were increasingly savage outbursts of anger.[66] And in the end, in their developing turbulence and rage, the mercenaries sank to the level of madmen, even of beasts (67.3). Now in open revolt, they threatened the destruction of Carthage itself (65.4).[67]

The initial Punic response to this threat was itself a descent into disor-

---

63. The latter passage, of course, introduces the theme of the "Wrath of the Barcids" as the origin of the Second Punic War. On the origins of this tradition, see the debate between Errington, "Rome and Spain before the Second Punic War," 26–32; and Sumner, "Rome, Spain and the Outbreak of the Second Punic War: Some Clarifications," 469–80.

64. Compare Polybius's comments on the origins of the great mutiny in Scipio Africanus's army in Spain in 206 (11.25.6–7, discussed above, p. 166). Mercenaries, however, were especially dangerous when undisciplined: see 1.65.6–7, with the discussion in Chap. V.

65. Note Polybius's use of heavily weighted terminology to describe the mercenaries' camp: ἀμιξίας, θόρυβος, τύρβης (1.67.3), ταραχάς (69.6), and ἀκαταστασίαν καὶ ταραχήν (70.1).

66. Polyb. 1.67.5; cf. 67.6 and 68.4.

67. For the theme of mercenaries as "beasts," see the detailed discussion in Chap. V, above.

der, desperation, and despair (1.68.6, 71.2).[68] The Carthaginians' first choice as general against the rebels was Hanno, previously a brutal governor (1.71.3) and soon revealed as a military incompetent, who failed to impose discipline upon the Carthaginian army—or upon himself (1.74, discussed above).

So the Carthaginians turned to Hamilcar (1.75.1)—who was immediately successful. He broke out of blockaded Utica by taking advantage of a wind that reduced the depth of water at the mouth of the Bagradas River—a phenomenon he carefully investigated (1.75.5–8). The result was a crossing of the river at night—and the enemy taken totally by surprise (75.10). In the battle that followed, Hamilcar feigned retreat, so that the mercenaries pursued rashly and in disorder (76.4–5)—whereupon he successfully wheeled his disciplined army and counterattacked. The mercenaries were taken by surprise, and panicked; they fled in the same "loose and confused" formation in which they had been advancing (76.7). In the confusion, they collided with more mercenaries advancing behind them, with disastrous effect; many were trampled to death by their own elephants (76.8).

The deep ideological structure of this narrative could hardly be clearer. On the one side, careful planning followed by orderly tactics; on the other side, indiscipline, disorder, and rashness, followed by disaster.[69]

A siege of Carthage by the mercenaries eventually failed, and this led to a new stage of fighting in the open. Here, according to Polybius, the mercenaries proved themselves the equal of Hamilcar in daring, but were worsted because of their lack of tactical skill (1.84.5). The historian explains that this was because Hamilcar possessed the experience and scientific technique of a true general (ἐμπειρία μεθοδικὴ καὶ στρατηγική), whereas the mercenary leaders had at their disposal "the inexperience and mere unreasoning routine of the common soldier" (ἀπειρίας καὶ τριβῆς ἀλόγου στρατιωτικῆς, 84.6). It is an ideological polarity similar to the one established in the account of the battle of the Bagradas.[70]

As the war in the open continues, Polybius presents Hamilcar as the careful general making his considered moves "like a good draughts player" (1.84.7)—and the mercenaries as his helpless counters. Hamilcar's maneuvers often cut off and surrounded large numbers of the enemy, destroying them in detail almost without a fight (ibid.). In clashes of

68. Again, note Polybius's heavily weighted terminology: κατάπληξις, πτοία, δυσθυμία, δυσελπιστία.

69. On this battle, see now Thompson, "Battle of the Bagradas," 111–17. As Walbank points out (*Commentary* I: 142), the words Polybius uses to describe Hamilcar's maneuvers here (ἐπιστροφή, περισπασμός, 1.76.5) are terms of specific military drill.

70. This same polarity between the στρατηγική and the merely στρατιωτική also appears at 3.105.9 and 9.14.1–4 (see Walbank, *Commentary* I: 146).

more importance, Hamilcar enticed the mercenaries into ambushes, or threw them into a panic through sudden and unexpected attacks by day or night (84.8). This is the "scientific generalship" of 1.84.6. Eventually Hamilcar trapped the major mercenary army in a valley where his own defensive position was impregnable. Soon out of supply, the mercenaries were reduced to cannibalism (84.9–85.1). Polybius's commentary is highly moralizing: "this was a fitting retribution . . . for their violation of every human and divine law" (ἀσέβεια, παρανομία, 84.10 and 12).[71]

Hamilcar and his colleague Hannibal then besieged Tunis, where the remnants of the mercenaries held out. But the negligence and overconfidence of Hannibal led to a severe Punic defeat as the mercenaries—in what should now be clear is a classic Polybian motif—attacked his carelessly guarded camp (1.86.5). Polybius implicitly absolves Hamilcar of the disaster: the mercenaries did not attack *him* (presumably because his encampment was not characterized by negligence). Nevertheless, the upset of the Punic government (1.87.1) led to the reemergence of Hamilcar's bitter political rival Hanno, with an army and powers equal to his own.[72] The Punic government worked hard—and successfully—to effect a reconciliation between the two men, for the good of the state. Both generals exercised self-control, and because of their mutual cooperation, the mercenaries were defeated in a crucial final battle (1.87.5–10).

Thus was order restored to North Africa, and Carthaginian civilization saved. The architect of that restoration of order was Hamilcar Barca; *he*, clearly, is the primary exponent of "men brought up in education, under law, in civilization," with whom Polybius contrasts the anarchic and irrational mercenaries (1.65.7).[73] Thus Pédech is surely correct to catalogue Hamilcar here among the "Polybian rational heroes."[74]

SCIPIO AT NEW CARTHAGE

In Polybius's account of P. Cornelius Scipio's campaign against New Carthage in 210/209, the polarity between orderliness and victory, as op-

71. On the heavily moralizing tone of this passage, see Roveri, *Studi su Polibio*, 124; cf. even Walbank, *Commentary* I: 147.

72. Polybius's account of the Punic failure at Tunis may well be slanted in Hamilcar's favor: the reemergence of Hanno as a coequal of Hamilcar suggests that Hamilcar was held at least partially responsible for what happened (cf. Walbank, *Commentary* I: 149). But it is precisely Polybius's *presentation* here—the ideological polarity between orderly generalship and disorderly disaster—that is our concern.

73. Thus the Carthaginians themselves, as Polybius portrays them during this crisis, are continually susceptible to disreputable emotion (see 1.68.6, 71.2, 81.1, 88.7).

74. *Méthode*, 217. But on the quite different picture of Hamilcar drawn by Polybius in connection with the origins of the Second Punic War, see Eckstein, "The Power of Irrationality," 5–8.

posed to disorder and defeat, is once more strongly apparent. Moreover, Polybius is all the more impressed with the calm and rational Scipio because the future Africanus was still at this point a very young man.[75]

Scipio arrived in Spain in autumn 210 in the wake of the disaster suffered by his father and his uncle, in which a good part of the Roman army was destroyed, and its two commanders killed.[76] But Polybius has Scipio carefully considering the strategic situation in Spain, and rationally analyzing the causes of Roman defeat, even before he left Rome. The young man ascribed the defeat to specific mistakes made by his father and uncle: they had rashly trusted their Celtiberian auxiliaries (who had betrayed them), and had unwisely separated their Roman forces (10.7.1). Moreover, Polybius stresses, Scipio soon perceived the disorderly condition of the Carthaginians after their victory. The armies of the Punic commanders were widely separated from one another (the same mistake Scipio's father and uncle had made)—and the Punic commanders were quarreling among themselves, and with their Spanish subjects (10.7.3–5). Polybius intended his audience to understand that Scipio's perceptions of Punic disarray were perfectly correct (cf. 9.11.1 and 4). He concludes that, "unlike most people," Scipio was therefore not downhearted or terrified of the Carthaginians (7.2).

The Polybian picture of the calm aristocratic general is clear here. And the picture is reinforced by Scipio's next actions in the narrative. Once in command of the remnants of the Roman army in Spain (which he bids be of good cheer: 10.6.1–6), Scipio is presented as a diligent researcher and planner. He learned that New Carthage—the main Punic base in Spain—was lightly garrisoned, because given the current military situation, no one could conceive of a Roman attack (10.8.1–5). In fact, the Carthaginians were so overconfident that none of their armies was as close to New Carthage as was the Roman army north of the Ebro (10.7.5). From interviewing fishermen, Scipio also learned that the lagoon just north of New Carthage was for the most part fordable, and also subject to ebb of its water level late in the day (10.8.6–7). On this basis he devised both a general strategic operation (a surprise attack on New Carthage), and a specific tactic (a flanking maneuver across the lagoon, in conjunction with the more usual frontal attack on the city walls).[77]

Scipio's discovery of the ebb of the lagoon at New Carthage bears a

75. On Polybius's image of Scipio Africanus, see esp. Pédech, *Méthode*, 219 (although the New Carthage campaign is not discussed in detail).

76. For discussion of this campaign, see, conveniently, Eckstein, *Senate and General*, 205–6.

77. On the geostrategic situation facing Scipio upon his arrival in Spain, see, conveniently, Eckstein, *Senate and General*, 205–10. Note that Polybius's criticism of the Punic generals in 211–209 is made both on pragmatic and on moral grounds (9.11 and 10.36 *passim*).

striking resemblance to Hamilcar's discovery through diligent inquiry that the lower Bagradas could be crossed (Polyb. 1.75.5–8), and to Hannibal's discovery through diligent inquiry that the Arno swamps could be crossed (3.78.8–79.1). But the resemblance is not merely tactical: all these tactical secrets were discovered through hard work, careful gathering of information. Love of hard work—that is, self-discipline—is in fact a trait that Scipio in Polybius shares with these other great generals (see 10.5.9, explicitly: φιλοπονία).[78]

Several other aspects of Polybius's depiction of Scipio's planning for New Carthage are worthy of comment. First, in his digression on generalship (9.12–20), Polybius has already explained that the good general keeps his most important plans strictly to himself (9.13.2–3): he is publicly unmoved either by hope or fear, or even by the natural garrulousness of humans when among friends, and reveals his ideas only to those without whom they cannot be executed. This is the image—already present, as we have seen, in Aeneas Tacticus—of the commander as the sole and lonely source of the drive behind his army.[79] It is an ideal that, obviously, required great self-discipline—and Scipio fulfilled this stern ideal. His plan to attack New Carthage was a complete surprise to all—his own troops as well as the Carthaginians—because, Polybius says, throughout the whole long stage of careful study and preparation, Scipio revealed his idea only to his chief lieutenant, C. Laelius (10.9.1).

Moreover, Laelius was told the plan for a specific reason: Scipio had made him commander of the Roman fleet in Spanish waters, and Scipio had decided that the fleet should arrive off New Carthage at the moment the land army arrived before the city walls (Polyb. 10.9.4). The attack was to be a carefully coordinated land and sea operation. And beyond the intended psychological impact, Scipio planned this, too, for a specific reason. Polybius emphasized to his audience that even the best-conceived plans, and the most carefully conducted operations, might fail.[80] Scipio in

78. There is a certain artistic coherence here, since Hamilcar at the Bagradas and Hannibal at the Arno each produce a spectacular Punic success, whereas Scipio's conduct indicates the growth of Rome's strength after the disaster at Cannae. Polybius was not immune to the lure of literary artistry (see his depiction of the battle of Cynoscephalae, discussed below). But there is no reason to think that he has distorted matters here for the sake of a satisfying literary parallel: he stresses that he had available Scipio's own written version of the New Carthage campaign, as well as oral testimony from Scipio's chief lieutenant, C. Laelius (10.9.2–3). As for love of hard work, Polybius's point seems to be that if one is simply lucky and favored by the gods (as many people thought was the case with Scipio), then no stern human effort was particularly necessary to achieve success—an idea to which he strongly objects (see 10.5.9).

79. On Aeneas Tacticus, see above, pp. 174 and n. 58.

80. See his comments at 9.9.1–10 and 12.9–10; 15.1.12; and the generalizing statement at 11.2.4–7, on the necessity of confronting the possibility of defeat—which most men prefer not to do.

Polybius is himself *prepared* for failure—both emotionally and in practical terms. If the initial surprise assault on New Carthage by the Romans went awry, and the Punic armies began to react and close in on the city, Scipio was prepared to use the fleet to evacuate his forces (10.8.9).[81] Young Scipio was a daring commander, but he was not overconfident or careless, like his opponents (cf. 10.8.4). To Polybius, it was a question of character (cf. 11.2.4–7).

The polarity of order and organization on the one side, and disorder, chaos, and defeat on the other, then, reappears continually in Polybius's narrative of the actual New Carthage attack. Scipio's assault was well conceived, well prepared, and enjoyed an enormous local superiority in numbers (cf. 10.9.6), and the city was surrounded by land and sea (10.12.1). By contrast, the Punic commander, Mago, is depicted as an impetuous man taken by surprise, suddenly far outnumbered, who had to improvise a defense force drawn mostly from the civilian population (10.12.3).

Mago actually began by attacking the Romans as they approached the eastern wall of the city. The sortie was vigorous but, Polybius indicates, badly planned, for it could be reinforced through only one gate in the city wall (10.12.6). In fact, Polybius says, Scipio had intentionally arranged his own forces so as to entice the Carthaginians out from their fortifications; Mago had played into Scipio's hands (12.7). Thus when the Carthaginians finally gave way before Scipio's larger numbers (12.8), their retreat turned into a rout as men panicked in their efforts to get back through the one available gate into the city; many soldiers were trampled to death (12.9). Mago's rash sortie ended catastrophically (12.10–11).

But the Roman assault on the eastern wall of the city was itself a difficult operation, because of the great height of the fortifications (Polyb. 10.13.6–10). Polybius emphasizes Scipio's nearby presence during the assault: he watched from a viewpoint so close to the battle line that he had to be protected from missile weapons by bodyguards with large shields (10.13.1–2). Scipio's visible presence encouraged the soldiery to great efforts (13.4). But his main purpose here was actually to keep tight control over the entire progress of the battle (13.3 and 5):

> Scipio contributed greatly to the success of the fighting, for he himself could see what was going on. . . . As a result, nothing was omitted that was necessary for the battle, but whenever circumstances suggested some step to him, he energetically set to work to do what was necessary.

It is the image of an ideal general in action.

Eventually, Scipio's buglers called off the attack (10.13.11). The order-

---

81. The problem Scipio would face if the initial assault failed was that the converging Punic armies would then far outnumber his own (Polyb. 10.7.6).

liness of what was merely a Roman maneuver (ibid.) is contrasted by Polybius with the emotionality of the Carthaginian defenders: "They were overjoyed—as if they had actually repelled the danger" (10.14.1). The very next sentence explains the trap the defenders had fallen into; Scipio was only waiting for the ebb of water in the lagoon (14.2–3).

At the right moment, the Romans then renewed their assault on the eastern wall. Polybius once more focuses attention on the defenders' emotions—this time on their confusion and despondency (10.14.4). Despite heavy losses, they did fight on (14.6). But just as the attack on the eastern wall was reaching its height, Polybius says, the water level in the lagoon receded—and the flanking attack was launched (14.7).

Scipio had guides ready to help the flanking force across the lagoon (10.14.9)—another example of his careful preparations for the battle. And he now appeared personally, to reassure his men that they would be in no danger of drowning (ibid.)—another example of his energetic leadership. Inspired by Scipio (10.14.10), the flanking force charged boldly across the lagoon. Reaching the northern wall, they found it undefended—for the Carthaginians had all been diverted to the east, against the new Roman attack, and had never thought that Scipio could come across the lagoon (14.13–14). Even after the northern wall was seized, there was no Punic response. Polybius explains why (14.15):

> There was such disorderly shouting [ἀτάκτου κραυγῆς] among the Carthaginians, and such crowding and confusion at the eastern wall, that they could neither hear nor see what was necessary to be done.

The contrast is enormous and intentional between the disorder of Mago's battle and the orderliness and perfect timing of Scipio.

The Romans now swept along the northern wall, catching the Carthaginians on the eastern wall in a classic pincer movement (10.15.1–2). The hapless Mago fled with a few troops to the citadel (15.7), but eventually surrendered. Even after the Punic surrender, however, Polybius emphasizes the calm and orderly fashion with which the pillaging of the city now went forward, with careful preparations taken against any sudden Carthaginian rising or counterattack (10.16.9–11).[82]

Polybius goes on to describe the carefully drawn and complex peace agreement that Scipio effected with the inhabitants of New Carthage: a case of clear thinking and hard work (10.17.6–16).[83] The theme of sober hard work even in the aftermath of great victory is then reiterated in the

82. For detailed discussion of the ideological aspects of 10.16, see above, pp. 167–68.

83. On Scipio's diplomatic success here, see Polyb. 10.17.16; with Eckstein, *Senate and General*, 210–11. Scipio was also engaged at this time in widespread and ultimately successful diplomacy with the Iberian tribes: see Polyb. 10.18; with Eckstein, *Senate and General*, 212–15.

story of the beautiful female captive offered to Scipio by his officers while he was working on the peace arrangements (10.19.2–5). Scipio refused her, on the grounds that for generals on active duty, sex was both a physical and a mental impediment (19.4–5). Polybius approves: Scipio's refusal of the beautiful captive was an example of the young man's self-restraint and moderation (ἐγκράτεια, μετριότης, 19.5).[84]

The Scipio of *The Histories* also believes in general that the hard work that is good for the victorious commander is good for his troops as well. Thus Polybius's narrative of the capture of New Carthage ends with a detailed description of the rigorous regimen of training that Scipio imposed on his army almost immediately after the taking of the city: three-mile marches at the double in full armor (10.20.2); the repair and polishing of armor and weapons (ibid.); individual combat practice (20.3); and the reequipping of soldiers, under Scipio's personal supervision (20.5). Laelius's fleet was also put through extensive practice in maneuvering and rowing (20.1 and 6). It was all done at a level of intensity that greatly impressed Polybius—and that he intended to impress his audience (20.6–7). Only after this period of retraining did Scipio march back to the Ebro, having secured New Carthage with a substantial garrison (20.8).

Polybius need not have interrupted his narrative of the Second Punic War in order to discuss at such approving length and detail how Scipio carefully refitted his army after the New Carthage victory. But Polybius was never a mere chronicler of events; his purposes were deeper. On the one hand, he was concerned to explain the reasons for Rome's rise to world power—and here the emphasis on the strict discipline Scipio imposed on his army makes sense. And on the other hand, Polybius was deeply concerned to point out to his audience the elements of proper aristocratic conduct—both in practical and in moral terms.

Certainly the main point for Polybius in the narrative of the New Carthage campaign is pragmatic success in the real world. The capture of New Carthage was a great Roman victory, and it also established Scipio's personal prestige; Scipio took care to see that it did (cf. Polyb. 10.19.8–9). But clearly, Polybius's account was also intended to leave the audience with the impression that Scipio's conduct here, from start to finish, partook of the noble (τὸ καλόν), in and of itself.[85]

84. Polybius stresses that Scipio was fond of women—and attracted to the captive (10.19.3–4). Pédech is thus incorrect to present Polybius's Scipio as a person so coldly rational as to be indifferent to sex (*Méthode*, 219); Polybius's point is, precisely, Scipio's self-restraint. That Polybius in 10.19.4 is stressing Scipio's special position of responsibility as the person in overall command (as opposed to an ordinary soldier in the army) is demonstrated by Walbank, *Commentary* II: 219 (cf. Polyb. 5.60.3), correcting earlier views.

85. One should stress once more that to Polybius, it is the quality of Scipio's conduct—not its total success—that is praiseworthy in terms of the καλόν. Hence Polybius's praise of energetic and organized generals who yet fail to achieve their goals: 9.9.6–9 (Hannibal and

THE BATTLE OF CYNOSCEPHALAE

The battle of Cynoscephalae (June 197) was the decisive battle of the Second Macedonian War. It ended the domination of European Greece by Philip V and established Rome as the arbiter of Greek affairs. The victorious Roman general was T. Quinctius Flamininus (consul 198, proconsul 197–194). Polybius had excellent sources for this battle, and there is no reason to doubt his outline of the course of the fighting—which has, in fact, been confirmed by recent archeology.[86] Yet it can also be argued that concerns about proper, self-controlled generalship powerfully shape the Polybian narrative of the battle—and the specific meanings Polybius draws from what occurred. This ideological thrust appears strongly in the contrast Polybius constructs between the careful and orderly management of the battle of Flamininus, and the rashness and lack of self-control of Philip.

This contrast stands out all the more clearly because it is missing from Livy—for whom desperation and desperate improvisation dominated the actions of *both* commanders during the battle. Yet Livy is also explicit that his account of Cynoscephalae is based directly on Polybius (33.10.10), so that one cannot seek the origin of the differences here in differing source traditions.[87] Rather, it lies in the differing ideological-literary purposes that inform the two narratives; Livy is less interested in drawing up models of good generalship for his audience than in impressing upon them the chaos and excitement of a crucial battle. But this conclusion only helps to clarify the ideology underlying and informing the narrative of Cynoscephalae presented by Polybius himself.

Of course, the Polybian contrast between Flamininus and King Philip must have been clear to readers of *The Histories* long before Cynoscephalae. The primary Polybian image of Philip in the period leading up to the Second Macedonian War is of a habitually cruel and treacherous, deeply

---

Epaminondas); 11.2 (Hasdrubal); 15.16 (Hannibal again). For detailed discussion, see Chap. I, above. Despite Polybius's emphasis on Scipio's self-discipline, in antiquity there existed a quite different tradition that underlined Scipio's attraction to the dissolute behavior of the Greeks (cf. Plut. *Cat. Mai.* 3.4–8). Cato the Censor was one of the originators of this tradition (ibid.), and Polybius knew Cato well (cf. Polyb. 31.25.5a and 35.6). But if Polybius was aware of this tradition on Scipio (as seems possible), the historian's ideological predilections therefore stand out all the more in the image of the sober and hardworking Scipio that Polybius chose to present to his audience.

86. Polybius had both Aetolian and Macedonian eyewitness sources for the battle: see Walbank, *Commentary* II: 575–581. The recent study by Hammond, "Campaign and Battle of Cynoscephalae," 60–76, demonstrates the exactitude of Polybius's geographical description of the site of the fighting—which suggests, *prima facie*, the exactitude of his description of the maneuvers that took place across this battlefield.

87. As does Carawan, "Flamininus in Livy," 221–24, who suggests that the differences here arise through Livy's extensive use of a Roman annalistic tradition that was, for some reason, hostile to Flamininus; Livy 33.10.10 seems to undercut that hypothesis completely.

irrational man.[88] If Philip retained some of his frenetic energy (cf. Polyb. 16.28.8), and could occasionally act with dignity (16.34.1–7), and was— as always—personally courageous in battle (Livy [P] 31.24.11–17), he was also a personage very susceptible to dangerous lapses in self-control (Polyb. 15.23.5 and 16.1.4, explicitly).[89] The primary image of Flamininus in Polybius, on the other hand, is of high intelligence combined with great prudence in managing affairs (18.12.2)—and this though he was still a young man, under thirty (12.5).[90]

From the beginning, Polybius's account of the Cynoscephalae campaign stresses the sober caution of Flamininus's generalship. He advanced into Thessaly slowly, preceded by scouts, making sure his soldiers were well supplied with equipment for defensive positions (18.18.1–19.9). The two armies clashed briefly at Pherae, but both commanders were dissatisfied with the ground (18.19.11–20.1). Philip then marched west toward Scotussa, north of the Cynoscephalae hills, hoping to find supplies and a suitable place to deploy his phalanx (20.2). Polybius says that Flamininus correctly deduced Philip's plan, and set his own army on a parallel course south of the hills, hoping to beat Philip to Scotussa (20.3). For two days the armies marched parallel to each other, separated by the hills, each unaware of the other (20.4).

On the second night there was a thunderstorm, and heavy fog the following morning (18.20.7). Polybius now focuses on the actions of Philip—which, in the fog, turn erratic. At first he started off rapidly toward Scotussa (20.8), but, hindered by the fog, he suddenly decided to entrench his forces instead (ibid.). He then allowed a significant portion of his troops to go out and forage (22.1)—but he also sent a force to seize the summit of Cynoscephalae ridge (20.9). He never expected a major engagement, because of the foggy weather (22.1).

Meanwhile, Flamininus had—cautiously (18.21.1)—pushed forward some of his own light troops toward the Cynoscephalae summit. The two scout forces encountered each other in the fog, and the Romans were soon pressed back (21.4). Flamininus sent reinforcements, including Aetolian cavalry; these reinforcements pressed Philip's men back to the crest (21.8).

Polybius emphasizes that the surprise encounter on the hills found Philip's forces in a highly disorganized state, with many of the men out foraging (18.22.1). Still, the king sent large reinforcements—mercenaries and Macedonian cavalry—up to the crest, and these troops drove the Romans back down the other side. Indeed, Polybius says that only the

88. Cf. Polyb. 13.3–5, 15.20–24, 16.1.2, and the retrospective in 25.3.9.

89. See also the negative description of Philip in Aristaenus's speech in Livy 32.21 (autumn 198), clearly based on Polybian material (on this, see below, Chap. VII).

90. On the Polybian image of Flamininus, see the detailed discussion in Chap. IV, above.

desperate bravery of the Aetolian cavalry now prevented a Roman rout. As it was, the Roman forces steadied themselves only low on the southern slope, and the whole Roman army was flustered (22.7). Flamininus now takes Polybius's center stage. He responded calmly to the disorderly retreat and the possibility of demoralization, leading the whole Roman army out of camp and deploying it in a careful line of battle at the base of the hills (18.22.7, cf. 23.1). This resolved the first crisis on the Roman side, as orderliness and confidence were quickly restored.

Polybius now switches the narrative back to Philip—who at this point acts very impulsively. This is the scene at Philip's camp (18.22.8):

> At the same time [as Flamininus was leading the Roman army out in battle array], one messenger after another came running to Philip, shouting "Sire, the enemy is fleeing; do not lose this opportunity; the Romans do not stand before our attack; the day is yours; this is the moment!"

Polybius says that Philip was dissatisfied with the prospective ground for the battle: the Cynoscephalae hills were high and rough, very poor terrain for the Macedonian phalanx (18.22.9). "Nevertheless," he comments, "Philip allowed himself to be provoked into battle" (ibid). Indeed, Polybius then *repeats* his negative assessment of Philip's decision (22.10): "Philip foresaw the difficulties of the hilly ground . . . but, fired up by the excessive optimism of the reports, he ordered his army out of camp."

Philip's hasty decision would lead to eventual disaster.[91] And the Polybian narrative has been constructed so that the audience already knows— as Philip does not—that the "glorious opportunity" presented to him by his messengers has already disappeared: Flamininus, across the hills to the south, has restored order in the Roman ranks (18.22.1–8; cf. 22.10). This is Polybian literary artistry.[92]

It is literary artistry, however, with a profound ideological point. Polybius's Philip is shown violating here one of the historian's fundamental rules of generalship: the *commander* chooses the time and place of battle, on grounds of strict calculation; he does not allow the time and place of battle to be chosen for him by mere circumstances. This is an important maxim of Polybius's Hannibal, Fabius Maximus, and L. Aemilius Paullus of Pydna.[93] Philip's decision is made to look even worse by the fact that he is carried away by emotion—as Polybius's terminology emphasizes.

---

91. Contrast Polybius's image of the impetuous Philip here with the historian's presentation of Scipio's calm and well-thought-out management of battle at New Carthage, discussed above.

92. A standard technique of Greek drama, of course, is to put the audience in the position of knowing more than the protagonist.

93. Hannibal, 3.69.12 (with Polybius's own firm assent); Fabius, 3.89.1–90.6 (cf. 3.104–5), Paullus, Livy [P] 44.36.9–14 (Polybian derivation: Nissen, *Kritische Untersuchungen*, 264).

The king was "provoked" into the battle, because he was "fired up" (ἐκ-κληϑῆναι, 22.9; παρορμηϑείς, 22.10), even though he well knew the rational reasons for not committing the phalanx on hilly ground (22.9 and 10). It is not so surprising, of course, that Polybius's Philip would lose control of himself at such a crucial moment; this is the image of Philip that Polybius has been presenting for the previous eleven volumes.[94]

How strongly Polybius's ideology of generalship informs this image of Cynoscephalae is shown by the fact that vital elements here are missing from Livy. The Roman historian has been writing in parallel with Polybius up to this point.[95] Yet there have already been subtle differences in emphasis. Livy's Flamininus is not quite the cautious general of Polybius: there is no mention in Livy of the carefulness of Flamininus's advance into Thessaly, no mention of Flamininus's orders to his light troops to proceed cautiously on the Cynoscephalae ridge. Instead, in Livy there is an emphasis on the *mutual* panic of the two scout forces when they clash in the fog on the heights ("pavore mutuo . . . primus terror," 33.7.5). This greatly exaggerates a brief remark at Polyb. 18.21.3, and is apparently added by Livy for the sake of drama. It is the first appearance of the "desperation" theme that will figure so strongly in Livy's account of the battle. The second appearance of that theme is Livy's depiction of Philip's decision to reinforce his light troops on the ridge: the king *sees* them being hardpressed, and fearing to lose them, sends up more men (33.7.9–10). Such a dramatic scene is missing from Polybius.[96]

This brings us to Livy's depiction of Philip as he makes the crucial decision for a general engagement. In Livy, the Macedonian reinforcements drive the Romans down the southern slope, but Flamininus's decisive response goes unmentioned (33.7.12–13). The Macedonian messengers report the success, and Livy does say that the reports were more encouraging than the battle warranted (33.8.1)—though he does not explain why. He continues (8.2): "This compelled Philip, though against his will, reluctant, claiming that it was a rash undertaking and that he liked neither the time nor the place, to commit to his entire force to battle." Livy's Philip is thus a much more cautious and reluctant figure than the Philip of Polybius, for what is missing here is exactly what Polybius underlined: Philip's own excitement and optimism. This in fact fits with Livy's strong emphasis on the idea that Cynoscephalae was a battle unwelcome to both sides. Indeed, rather than contrasting Philip's behavior with that of the calm Flamininus, as Polybius does, Livy instead *equates* them. "The

94. That is, ever since Polyb. 7.11–14 and Philip's "transformation for the worse" ca. 215, discussed above, Chap. IV, and below, Chap. VII.

95. Compare, for instance, Livy's discussion of the portable stakes employed for Roman marching camps (33.5), paraphrasing Polyb. 18.18. See Briscoe, *Commentary* I: 248 and 254.

96. Cf. Briscoe, *Commentary* I: 260.

Roman," he says, "did the same as Philip, committing his entire force from necessity, rather than to seize an opportunity in the fighting" (8.3).[97] Yet in Polybius, Philip acts impulsively precisely to seize such a (false) opportunity.

Polybius himself now returns from Philip to Flamininus—who, he repeats, was calmly drawing up his troops in battle order (18.23.1). The defeated advance forces are absorbed safely back into the main body (23.8, 24.5), and Flamininus is given a short speech by which he steadies his men as the victorious Macedonian cavalry and mercenaries approach (23.3–6). Leaving his right wing stationary, he then leads the left in a vigorous attack, driving the Macedonians back up the slope (23.7–8, cf. 24.4).

Meanwhile, the scene back on Philip's side is one of hasty improvisation. The foragers are recalled, but instead of waiting for them, Philip starts up the northern slope with only part of the phalanx, leaving his general Nicanor to follow as soon as the rest of the troops can be collected (18.24.1–2). The reader is then placed with the king as he arrives at the Cynoscephalae summit (another stroke of Polybian literary artistry). Polybius's Philip is at first overjoyed (περιχαρής) as he sees his forces advancing triumphantly down the southern slope; he is still, then, in the grip of high optimistic emotion. But his delight soon turns sour as Flamininus's counterattack causes the Macedonian advance forces to flee back up the slope with heavy losses (24.5–6).[98]

Philip is now led to his second impetuous decision: to rescue his cavalry and mercenaries, he determines to charge the Roman left with the men he has, even though the greater part of the phalanx has not yet come up (18.24.7). Polybius's comment is negative: Philip was "forced to decide the fate of the entire battle on the basis of a momentary circumstance" (ἐκ τοῦ καιροῦ, ibid.), rather than on the basis of calm calculation. It is another mistake.[99]

The ideological nature of Polybius's presentation of this scene is again underlined by a comparison with Livy. The Roman historian closely follows the outline of Polybius's account of the battle. He has the successful charge of the Macedonian cavalry and mercenaries down the southern

---

97. "idem et Romanus, magis necessitate quam occasione pugnare inductus, fecit."

98. Philip's premature and extreme joy on the crest (18.24.6) matches that of the defenders of New Carthage at the "repulse" of the first Roman attack on the eastern wall (περχαρεῖς, 10.14.1). It is an emotional condition that Polybius finds deeply suspect. See Chap. IX, below.

99. On the highly negative ideological implications of the phrase ἐκ τοῦ καιροῦ at 18.24.7, see Walbank, *Commentary* II: 582, citing Polyb. 11.16.4, where military action taken ἐκ τοῦ καιροῦ (and ending disastrously) is contrasted with action taken on the basis of sagacity (ἀγχινοία).

slope (33.7.12–13); if anything, the extent of the Macedonian success is exaggerated, apparently for the sake of drama.[100] Then comes Flamininus's response: the counterattack of the heavy infantry of the Roman left (Livy 33.8.1–8). But where Polybius twice refers to Flamininus's calmly drawing up his troops in battle order to face the Macedonian advance down the slope (18.22.10, 23.1), Livy instead has Flamininus acting unwillingly and in desperation (33.8.3).[101]

And just as Flamininus's rational management of the battle is missing from Livy, so is Polybius's impetuous Philip. Livy has Philip's arrival at the Cynoscephalae summit; at first (as in Polybius) he is delighted by what he sees (33.8.10), and then (as in Polybius) his delight turns sour in the face of Flamininus's counterattack (ibid.). Yet in Livy, Philip's second decision—to launch what he has of the phalanx down the southern slope— is determined not only by fear for his advance forces (as in Polybius) but also because his own safe retreat has been cut off ("ne ipsi quidem in tuto iam receptus erat," 8.11). This idea, which once more emphasizes the "desperation" theme, is missing from Polybius, and offers a totally new justification for Philip's decision: he had nothing to lose. Conversely, Polybius's negative assessment that Philip risked the whole battle on the spur of the moment (18.24.7) is missing from Livy. The Roman historian's account thus supplies plenty of drama for his audience—but no ideological lessons in generalship as the imposition of control.

In Polybius, Philip's charge at first actually goes well. The Macedonian phalanx (as usual) acquits itself splendidly (λαμπρῶς, 18.25.3), forcing Flamininus's left wing back down the slope. This causes a second crisis on the Roman side: Flamininus, Polybius says, saw that his left was not likely to withstand for long the weight of the Macedonian downhill advance. Still, "hope for saving the situation existed on the right wing" (25.4). This was because while Philip was charging down the slope with the part of the phalanx on hand, other sections of his army were simply standing around idly on the summit, while the rest of the phalanx itself was just arriving there in great disorder (25.4–5). Polybius emphasizes that Flamininus *saw* the disorder and confusion on the Macedonian left, and the opportunity it offered (συνθεασάμενος, 25.4). In Polybius's view, then, Flamininus acted at the crucial moment of the battle on the basis of correct personal observation combined with sagacious rational calculation.

Leaving his left to fight Philip's phalanx, Flamininus therefore rode over to the Roman right, and then personally led the legions up the slope against the Macedonian left (18.25.5). Polybius has already described the

---

100. See Briscoe, *Commentary* I: 260.
101. On the "desperation" theme, see (rightly) Carawan, "Flamininus in Livy," 221–24.

disorganization of the Macedonians here (25.5). Now he repeats and elaborates it: no one to give orders, the ground unsuitable for the phalanx, many soldiers still in marching order anyway, and unable to draw up into a proper battle line (25.6).[102]

It is into this mass of confusion that Flamininus in Polybius launches the fresh and orderly Roman right wing. Polybius indicates that Flamininus had intentionally kept the Roman right in reserve during the earlier stages of the battle (18.23.7; cf. 32.2–5)—another example of careful battle management, which now paid dividends. The disorganized Macedonian left immediately collapsed before the Roman charge, and fled (18.25.7). No doubt this is what actually happened in the battle;[103] yet Polybius must also have found it an ideologically satisfying event.

The ideological structure here is made all the clearer, again, by an examination of Livy. He, too, has the successful charge of Philip's phalanx against Flamininus's left, and Flamininus's switch to the Roman right and subsequent successful counterattack against the disorganized Macedonian left (33.9.1–8). But what Livy does *not* do is attribute to Flamininus the rational calculation upon which, in Polybius, this attack is based. Where Polybius has a long section of over fifty words giving the reasons for Flamininus's decision to attack the Macedonian left (18.25.4–5), Livy contents himself with the short and irrelevant remark that Flamininus "thought that the defeat of one part [of the Macedonian army] would entail the defeat of the rest" (39.9.5). What Livy is interested in is simply the drama of the attack itself.[104]

The Aetolians, too, had a version of Flamininus's conduct—contemporary to the battle, and highly unflattering. It apparently found vigorous expression in Polybius's account of the Aetolian diplomatic mission to Achaea in 192, in a speech of the Aetolian statesman Archidamus—who was no ordinary witness. He had been one of the Aetolian cavalry commanders at Cynoscephalae (Polyb. 18.21.5), that is, a leader of the force that Polybius had singled out to praise for outstanding bravery (22.4–6). Now, in a direct confrontation with Flamininus, Archidamus describes the battle for the Achaeans (Livy [P] 35.48.12–13):

102. It may even be that Polybius has exaggerated the confusion and chaos on the Macedonian left for his own ideological (and dramatic) purposes. Thus he says that the left was in a hapless condition because there was no one to give them orders (18.25.6); but he has previously indicated that this portion of Philip's army was under the command of Nicanor, one of the king's chief lieutenants (24.1). It is odd that Nicanor has suddenly disappeared: see Walbank, *Commentary* II: 583.

103. See esp. now the remarks of Hammond, "Campaign and Battle of Cynoscephalae," 72–76.

104. Carawan, "Flamininus in Livy," 223–24. Plut. *Flam.* 8.2 is similar in tone to Livy, but very unclear as to the situation in the battle (and esp. on the Macedonian left wing) when Flamininus launched his counterattack.

Not only the victory over Philip but even Quinctius's own safety had been gained by Aetolian bravery. For when had Quinctius ever performed the function of a commander? Taking auspices and sacrificing and performing vows like some priest—thus had he, Archidamus, seen Quinctius during the battle.

This picture of Flamininus helplessly imploring the gods is the opposite of the cool and calculating commander of Polybius's battle—yet it appears in a Polybian context.[105] Moreover, the theme of Aetolian accusations of panic or cowardice against Flamininus also occurs in Plutarch (*Comp. Phil. and Flam.* 2.3), which suggests that this was a significant tradition concerning Flamininus's behavior at Cynoscephalae. And Polybius relied on Aetolian sources for much about Cynoscephalae[106]—but obviously not here. Of course, he knew the Aetolians were likely to be biased against Flamininus, for he himself had recorded in detail the bitter feud that had developed after the battle (18.35–39).[107] But if Polybius intentionally rejected the derisive Aetolian version of Flamininus at Cynoscephalae, and substituted one in which Flamininus conducts and controls operations in the best tradition of Polybian generalship, this only underlines the idea that the version of Flamininus that appears in Polybius's account is the historian's conscious choice—from among several possible variants. Perhaps he felt that "this is how it must have been"; after all, Flamininus had won.[108]

Yet Flamininus's control over the fighting at Cynoscephalae is not perfect even in Polybius. First, while Flamininus's charge on the Macedonian left wins the battle, what turns it into total catastrophe for Philip is an action not by Flamininus but by one of the military tribunes on the Roman right. This man—unnamed—now took his troops across the Macedonian center and brought them in behind Philip's phalanx on the south-

105. For Livy 35.48 as deriving from Polybian material, see Briscoe, *Commentary* II: 206. Carawan argues that the Aetolian accusation here is not in fact Polybian ("Flamininus in Livy," 224 n. 27)—but he is forced to admit that everything else in Livy 35.48–49 *is* Polybian, including Flamininus's reply to the accusation! This can hardly be accepted.

106. See Walbank, *Commentary* II: 575.

107. On the development of the feud between the Aetolians and Flamininus, see, conveniently, Eckstein, *Senate and General*, 287–93.

108. Although Polybius was well aware of the "alternative" Aetolian tradition on Flamininus at Cynoscephalae (as is proven by Archidamus's speech in Achaea in 192), he does not mention it in his account of the battle—not even to reject it. It is, in fact, a typical Polybian rhetorical strategy to delay revealing an unacceptable "alternative" version of an event until later in the narrative. He does the same with the Aetolian accusation that territorial expansion had been a crucial factor in the Achaean decision in 198 to side with Rome against Philip: see Eckstein, "Polybius, Aristaenus, and the Fragment 'On Traitors,'" 147–50. Note that in Achaea in 192, Flamininus comes out the better in his colloquy with Archidamus (see Livy [P] 35.50.1)—although he never directly answers Archidamus's charges about his behavior in 197.

ern slope, attacking it from behind (18.26.1–5). The result was very heavy Macedonian losses, and the flight of Philip (who only now realized what had been occurring elsewhere on the battlefield: 26.6–7). Polybius provides no evidence that this Roman tribune had acted on orders from Flamininus—who was busy pursuing the Macedonian left (cf. 26.1 and 9).[109] And yet, second, even here on the Macedonian left Flamininus's control over the battle—and even over his own men—was insecure. The Macedonians being pursued by Flamininus raised their spears as a sign of surrender; on learning the significance of this gesture, the Roman tried to hold back his troops, but they had already begun to attack the Macedonians, instigating a massacre of which Polybius clearly disapproves (18.26.10–12).

Nevertheless, if in Polybius's version of events Flamininus's control over his own army is not perfect—if Flamininus is no Scipio Africanus— his control over his forces is still substantial, and substantially better than the control exercised by King Philip. The same holds true of Flamininus's *self*-control, his calm management of a complex and difficult battle—at least, as Polybius presents things.

The most recent study of Cynoscephalae, by N. G. L. Hammond, stresses that the Roman victory was in reality mostly the result of chance, and that insofar as Polybius presented T. Quinctius Flamininus as a brilliant general it was because the Greek historian could not afford to offend his Roman readers.[110] Polybius would certainly have found the first conclusion ironic. He says that he wrote up his discussion of Roman battle technique, appended to his account of Cynoscephalae, specifically to *combat* the idea that the Roman victory was the result of chance (18.28.5). In his view, the Cynoscephalae victory originated in the flexibility of the Roman legion and its subunits, and its adaptability to all types of terrain (18.32.9–10), as well as in the Roman custom of always keeping a significant portion of one's army in reserve (32.2–6). These techniques allowed Flamininus's successful uphill charge with his right-wing reserve against the disorganized Macedonian left, and the final encirclement of Philip's phalanx on the Macedonian right.[111]

109. But is may well be that Flamininus did order this maneuver: it involved almost a full legion. Walbank, *Commentary* II: 383–84, suggests that Polybius here may have been victimized by his Aetolian sources, in their consistent effort to downplay Flamininus's role in the Cynoscephalae victory.

110. "Campaign and Battle of Cynoscephalae," 76 (the role of chance), and 60 (Polybius's catering to his Roman audience).

111. Despite Polybius's efforts, a strong tradition persisted in antiquity ascribing Flamininus's victory to chance (rather than to Philip's impetuous mistakes and Flamininus's competent battle management): see App. *Mac.* 9.1; with the comments of Carawan, "Flamininus in Livy," 225. Here as elsewhere (see 10.5.9 and 36.17), Polybius knew he was fighting against the tide; indeed, it was hard to get people to read serious analysis at all (12.26c.4).

As for the hypothesis that Polybius must consciously have tailored his depiction of Flamininus at Cynoscephalae so as to please his Roman audience: this cynical or "Machiavellian" interpretation of Polybius's presentation of the battle ignores the fact that Polybius was quite comfortable in criticizing Roman generalship in many other cases. Nor is it clear why Flamininus—whose bitter feud with Polybius's hero Philopoemen was famous in antiquity—should have been the recipient of special political favor from the historian.[112] If Polybius's image of Flamininus at Cynoscephalae does have an artificial and ideological component, it lies, rather, in Polybius's deep concern that aristocratic commanding generals see the need to exercise control over their own emotions and behavior, and hence over both their own troops and over the chaotic course of battle. In this respect, Flamininus's conduct at Cynoscephalae is not different from the praiseworthy conduct of a Carthaginian commander such as Hamilcar Barca (as Polybius presented it)—and surely *that* portrait was not evolved by Polybius in order to gratify the Romans.

CONCLUSION

Polybius emphasizes the fact that the command of armies in war was the greatest honor an aristocrat could receive from his community—as well as the most difficult of tasks. There were three aspects to the difficulty; each involved the imposition of order upon disorderly phenomena. It is this element in generalship—the imposition of order and control, by an act of human will—that gives generalship, to Polybius, its *moral* stature.

First, the general needed to maintain strict discipline over his own emotions and actions, in the face of the manifold temptations that went with great personal power (drink, sex, idleness, rashness: Polyb. 3.81), and in the face of the psychologically disruptive vicissitudes of military campaigning (failure, success: 9.13.2). Nothing was possible, Polybius believed, without such self-discipline. But self-discipline alone was not enough. The commander also had to impose order upon his unruly

---

112. Polybius's criticism of Roman generals and generalship: Ser. Fulvius Nobilior and M. Aemilius Paullus, the consuls of 255 (1.36.10–37.6); C. Flaminius, as consul in 223 (2.33.6–7) and 217 (3.80–83); Ti. Sempronius Longus, the consul of 218 (3.70.7 and 75.1); M. Minucius Rufus, the dictator of 217 (3.105.9); C. Terentius Varro, the consul of 216 (3.110.3–5); P. and Cn. Cornelius Scipio, the commanders in Spain in 211 (10.6.2); M. Claudius Marcellus, as consul in 208 (10.32). Cf. also frg. 102 B-W (L. Postumius Albinus, the consul of 215?); frg. 110 B-W (M. Claudius Marcellus, the consul of 155). On the feud between Philopoemen and Flamininus, see Plut. *Phil.* 15.1, with Errington, *Philopoemen*, 122, 129–30.

troops, molding them into a purposeful tool for achieving his projects.[113] This, too, was no easy task, for the common soldiery were prone to laziness, drunkenness, negligence, greed (to the point where undisciplined looting constituted a major threat to military safety), and fear (especially in the face of actual combat). Third, a good commander had to have the ability to impose upon the terrible chaos and entropy of battle itself the orderliness of his own mind and character (often in the form of a plan). Only the best generals were completely successful at this last and most difficult task: men like Hamilcar, or Scipio Africanus. And because in 197 T. Quinctius Flamininus was better at all three aspects of generalship than was Philip V of Macedon (though not even Flamininus was completely successful), the Romans won the crucial battle of Cynoscephalae.

Polybius, as was shown in Chapter V, greatly feared any sort of chaos and disorder; and generalship gave an aristocrat the greatest of personal opportunities to demonstrate his mastery over these disturbing phenomena. It is in this way that generalship fits into the broader moral framework of *The Histories,* and into Polybius's emphasis on the duty of the aristocrat to perform "the noble" (τὸ καλόν).

But the duty of the leaders of the state—of Polybius's aristocratic audience—did not end with the military. In a broader perspective, these men had the heavy responsibility of guiding the state safely (and, it was hoped, with honor) through the dangers of international politics. In Polybius's age, this meant above all the careful management of relations with Rome. Polybius's attitude toward Rome and Roman power now becomes our subject.

113. Thus in Polybius armies tend to be reflections of their commanders, as were the undisciplined armies of Xenoetas and Hanno (above, pp. 164–65), and the highly disciplined armies of Hamilcar and of Scipio Africanus (above, pp. 175–76 and 178–82).

SEVEN

Politics: Greece and Rome

The art of politics consists of directing rationally the irrationalities of men.
—REINHOLD NIEBUHR

INTRODUCTION

A central factor in the widespread belief that Polybius's attitude toward politics was harshly "Machiavellian" has been modern scholars' understanding of his views on Greek relations with Rome. This was the overriding political issue for Greeks of Polybius's time, and many scholars believe that eventually he underwent a complete political, intellectual, and moral capitulation to the Romans.[1] The influence of F. W. Walbank has been very powerful here. He sees the Achaean historian's evolution as complex, but nevertheless tending in only one direction: Polybius while a politician in his native Achaea (prior to 167) was cautiously anti-Roman; during his subsequent exile in Italy (167–150) he became cynical and detached concerning Rome's policies, although traces of an anti-Roman attitude can still be found; finally, under the impact of the catastrophic events of 149–146, he became strongly pro-Roman.[2] Moreover, it is noteworthy that the most recent exposition of such a thesis—that of Peter

---

1. The pioneering study: Fustel de Coulanges, *Polybe*, 121, 130–31, 166–67, 196. See also, e.g., Momigliano, "Polibio, Posidonio e l'imperialismo romano," 698; and *Alien Wisdom*, 29; and now Dubuisson, "Vision polybienne de Rome," 243; and Green, *Alexander to Actium*, 279, 281–83, 285. See also next note.

2. See Walbank, *Polybius*, 166–83; "Polybius between Greece and Rome," *passim;* and "Polybius' Last Ten Books," 156–59. Walbank's thesis is accepted by, e.g., Momigliano (see "Historian's Skin," 78–79 and 88); by A. J. Pomeroy, "Polybius's Death Notices," 418; and by Green, *Alexander to Actium*, 283 and 285. Dubuisson, "Vision polybienne de Rome," 243, argues that Polybius's facility with Latin led eventually to an "unconscious Romanization" of his views on world politics.

Green—is also the most extreme: Polybius was a quisling, a hypocrite, a collaborator, a traitor, a Roman commisar.[3]

It is the question of Polybius's views on the proper relationship with Rome, and in particular the question of how far these were determined by purely pragmatic considerations and how far by the impact of morality on politics, that forms the focus of the present chapter. My argument here is that Polybius's attitude toward Roman power has been quite misunderstood.

Now, Polybius certainly did not have an idealistic view of the Hellenistic Mediterranean: he did not see it as a consensual community of states where the rule of "international law" held sway.[4] Rather, to Polybius international politics was a world where the rule of law was generally absent. The tone of *The Histories* on this point comes out best in 15.20, where Philip V and Antiochus III, as they prepare to descend upon the weakened Ptolemaic kingdom about 203, are compared to a pair of sharks.[5] And Polybius believed that the smaller polities differed from the great states merely in their more limited power. Hence he says of the Peloponnesian *poleis* that they were constantly at war with one another because they all sought supremacy in the Peloponnese, and none was prepared to cede primacy of place to a neighbor (5.106.5).

Polybius's explanation for the prevalence of *Faustrecht* in international relations was simple: there was no way and no one to enforce morality among the powers. Thus the dispute between the governments of Ptolemy IV and Antiochus III in 219/218 was impossible to resolve, despite long and intense negotiations, because of one basic fact (5.67.11): "There was no one to interpose between them [the two kings] with the power of restraining the side they might decide was morally in the wrong." The dispute between Antiochus III and Ptolemy IV could therefore be resolved only by war (5.68.1).

A true system of international law is possible only when there is a mechanism of enforcement; Polybius knew no such mechanism existed in his world.[6] Moreover, because Polybius's analysis of the lack of such an international enforcement mechanism occurs relatively early in *The*

3. *Alexander to Actium*, 279–81. Cf. also Reiter, *Aemilius Paullus*, 31 and 33.
4. As does, for instance, Klose, *Völkerrechtlichen Ordnung der hellenistischen Staatenwelt von der Zeit 280 bis 168*.
5. Scholars debate whether the plan and pact of Philip and Antiochus ever actually existed. But that is irrelevant here: Polybius believed it existed, and he believed it partly because of the prevailing tone of international relations. In favor of historicity, see Schmitt, *Geschichte Antiochos' des Grossen*, 218–20, 226–36, 242. Against: see Errington, "Alleged Syro-Macedonian Pact," 336–53.
6. On the absence of a true system of international law in antiquity, see esp. Badian, "Hegemony and Independence," 401–5 (who does not cite Polyb. 5.67.11). On the grim

Histories (in Book 5), we may assume that he came to the writing of his work with a conception of international politics as a jungle already firmly set in his mind.

But one should not mistake Polybius's tough-minded view of the nature of international relations for either approval or acceptance. On the contrary: as von Scala demonstrated long ago, Polybius urged upon his audience an entire system of constraints on international behavior. Among the ideas he advocated were the scrupulous observance of treaties (both in letter and spirit), the issuance of formal declarations of war (as opposed to surprise attacks), the sparing of innocent civilians and as much real property as possible, the general treatment of the weak with justice.[7] Yet because Polybius did not confuse these ideals with the grim realities of international politics as they were actually practiced, his view of the possibilities politics offered especially to the weaker states was bound to be limited.

On the one hand, Polybius was sympathetic to the predicaments weak states often faced. Thus after the Ptolemaic victory at Raphia in 217, all the towns of Coele Syria that had previously gone over to the Seleucids now went back over to Ptolemy IV. Polybius's comments are understanding: "Perhaps it is the way of all men at such times to accommodate themselves to the prevailing circumstances" (5.86.9). Confronted by overwhelming power, these towns did what they had to do in order to survive.

Yet Polybius immediately adds the remark that "it is especially the case with the inhabitants of that country [Coele Syria] that they have a natural tendency to worship success" (5.86.9). The comment is clearly pejorative, and it is followed by a sarcastic account of the extravagant honors that the towns heaped upon the victorious Ptolemy (86.11). For this sort of behavior, then, Polybius has no sympathy. In other words, there is a limit to yielding to circumstances beyond which honor forbids one to go.[8]

These are the twin themes that will be examined in the following discussion. The tension between them does much to inform Polybius's presentation of Greek relations with Rome.

It should also be stressed that in judging this issue, Polybius evidently attempted to carve out for himself a position of some political and intellectual independence. This emerges clearly in the "Second Introduction"

Polybian concept of international relations, see Wunderer, *Polybios,* 46 (based, in fact, on the comments in 5.67.11).

7. For a long list of such Polybian passages, see von Scala, *Studien,* 299–324. Sometimes Polybius's recommendations are presented on purely pragmatic grounds (as in 23.15); but often his recommendations are couched in highly moralizing language (as in 2.8, or 13.3).

8. In fact, these towns had always had better relations with the Ptolemies than with the Seleucids (Polyb. 5.86.10).

(3.4)—where he explains that the purpose of the new extension of *The Histories* (down to 146) is to show how the conquerors and the conquered conducted themselves under the new (post-168) conditions of total Roman hegemony brought about by the destruction of Antigonid Macedon. What had been the impact of this development (3.4.6)—politically, socially, and (by implication) morally—on both sides?[9] Polybius continues (3.4.7):

> For it will be evident from these topics whether those now living should shun Roman domination or do the reverse, and whether those in the future should consider the Romans' government worthy of praise and emulation, or of blame.

Because of the fragmentary nature of the last portion of *The Histories,* it is not clear how (or even whether) Polybius answered the questions set forth in 3.4; this will be an issue addressed below.[10] But it is worth noting that Polybius prefaced the above statement with the remark that those who have achieved great success often do not make proper use of it (3.4.5). That remark alone is enough to establish that Polybius intended the questions he raised to be taken very seriously: they were not *pro forma.* Nor were their answers immediately and obviously pro-Roman.[11]

POLYBIUS'S POLITICAL HERITAGE

Polybius's own life experiences, and in particular his long exile in Italy (167–150), obviously played a crucial role in shaping his understanding of the problem of Roman power.[12] But the hegemony of great states over weaker states was not a new phenomenon to the Hellenistic Greeks, arriving in the eastern Mediterranean with the armies of the Republic. On the contrary: the domination exercised by great *Greek* states over lesser states was as widespread a fact of life in the Hellenistic age as it had been in the Classical period.[13] No one knew this better than the statesmen of Polybius's own Achaean League. The League historically had always had to contend with greater powers (most prominently Macedon, before Rome)—or else find a way to accommodate itself to them. Since Polybius

---

9. The moral implications here appear in Polybius's assertion that he intended to discuss the transformations, both in public and private life (κατ᾿ ἰδίαν βίους), of both the conquerors and the conquered, that resulted from the new situation of Roman worldwide hegemony (3.4.6). For an example of the impact upon Roman private modes of life, see the harsh comments at 31.25.2–7.

10. See esp. pp. 225–36.

11. See Shimron, "Polybius on Rome," 105–6.

12. See esp. Fustel de Coulanges, *Polybe,* 182–87.

13. For discussion, see Heidemann, *Freiheitsparole,* 13, 20, 47–48; Walbank, "Monarchies and Monarchic Ideas," 62; and now esp. Austin, "Hellenistic Kings," 454–66.

himself came from a family that had long been important in League politics, one may assume that the lessons of Achaean political history were absorbed by him as a young man. They will have given him a unique perspective on the issue of power, including Roman power.

Nowhere was the dilemma faced by weak states demonstrated more clearly than in the career of Aratus of Sicyon, the man who may be called the true founder of the league. For twenty-five years from the mid-third century, Aratus had worked carefully and skillfully to rid the Peloponnese of the domination of Macedon. His success had been outstanding. By about 230 the free communities of the Achaean League encompassed the entire northern two-thirds of the Peloponnese—including Polybius's home town of Megalopolis.[14] Yet in the mid-220s Aratus's achievement fell apart when confronted by the sudden resurgence of the military power of Sparta, under its vigorous king Cleomenes III. By winter 225/224 Cleomenes had brought the League to the verge of destruction. In desperation, Aratus turned for support to the only power he believed capable of defeating Cleomenes: the Macedonians.[15]

Militarily, Aratus's maneuver was successful; the forces of King Antigonus III Doson of Macedon drove Cleomenes from the Peloponnese.[16] But the political price demanded for Macedonian intervention against Sparta was very high. Corinth and the Acrocorinth fortress—the greatest jewels in Achaea's crown—came under Macedonian occupation, giving them permanent access to the Peloponnese. In addition, the Achaean League became a premier member of "the Hellenic Alliance"—a new alliance system headed by Macedon. And under its terms, Achaean freedom of political action became more restricted than had been the case before Aratus's career began.[17] Aratus had managed to save the League from Sparta, but at the cost of reintroducing Macedonian power into the Peloponnese on a grand scale.[18]

The Achaean decision of 225/224 proved highly controversial: the contemporary historian Phylarchus, for instance, fiercely attacked Aratus as a traitor to Greece.[19] In *The Histories,* however, Polybius strongly defends Aratus. It is important to understand his reasoning.

Gruen has argued that Polybius makes Aratus the engineer of a grand

14. For discussion of the rise of Achaean power under Aratus, see Urban, *Wachstum und Krise,* chaps. 2–4.

15. On the military, political, and social crisis caused in Achaea by the war with Cleomenes of Sparta, see esp. Urban, *Wachstum und Krise,* 117–201.

16. Cleomenes fled to Egypt, where he eventually attempted a coup (see Polyb. 5.35–39, discussed in detail in Chap. II, above).

17. For detailed discussion of the position of Achaea under the "Hellenic Symmachy," see esp. Aymard, *Premiers rapports,* 54–61.

18. Cf. the comments of Aymard, ibid., 55.

19. For discussion, see Africa, *Phylarchus and the Spartan Revolution,* chap. 3.

scheme of honorable alliance with Antigonus Doson in order to save Greece from Cleomenes (and the Aetolians).[20] But this misses Polybius's main point. He asserts that it would have been "very noble" (κάλλιστον) if the Achaeans could have defended themselves without outside help (2.47.1), but in the end they were "compelled by circumstances" to appeal to Macedon (ἠνάγκαζε, 51.4). This justification—bitter necessity—was Aratus's own defense, as it appeared in the *Memoirs* (cf. Plut. *Arat.* 41.4). And Polybius's ideological stance emerges again in the praise he gives the Achaeans because even in their gravely weakened condition, and even after the Macedonian intervention, "they did not abandon self-reliance"; instead, they managed to recapture the important town of Argos on their own (2.53.1–2). Thus Polybius's account of the Achaean *volte-face* of the 220s has as its main themes the nobility of independence and independent action, combined with the necessity (not the nobility) of the Macedonian alliance.[21]

It is true that Polybius also portrays Antigonus Doson as an honorable man—at least as far as kings went.[22] But Polybius's point in praising Doson is that since one *had* to have Macedon as an ally in order to survive, Antigonus was an ally with whom it was not shameful to associate.[23] The main point—that Aratus's actions in the 220s were necessary to save the League from destruction—remains unchanged, and in fact is made repeatedly.[24]

Finally, Polybius well knew that the resulting Macedonian hegemony over the Peloponnese did not tighten over time, but rather had greatly moderated. This was the result, first, of Aratus's own initial steadfastness in asserting Achaean rights under the treaty he had engineered, and preventing the growth in Achaea of a sycophantic attitude toward Macedon; Polybius clearly approves (4.82.2–5). Second, it was the result of the Achaean military revival under Philopoemen after 210—a development, again, that Polybius heartily endorses.[25] And eventually, it was the result of Philip V's decision to withdraw his garrisons from Orchomenus and Heraea in 199, in an effort to maintain Achaean good will in the face of

20. "Aratus and the Achaean Alliance with Macedon," 622–23; cf. 619–20.

21. Note also Polybius's praise of his own Megalopolitans—along with the people of Stymphalia and Cleitor—for staunchly seeking to maintain their independence from Cleomenes under very adverse circumstances: 2.55.8–9 and 61.7–11.

22. One can accept the comments of Gruen, "Aratus and the Achaean Alliance with Macedon," 622–23, at least that far. Note the balanced judgment Polybius offers at 2.47.4–5.

23. Hence Polybius's praise of Antigonus's ability to withstand the pressure of the mob to take the field against Cleomenes when it would have been militarily unwise (2.64.6); this seems an assessment having to do with Polybius's ideology of good leadership (on which, see Chap. V, above).

24. See 2.47.3–4, 49.2, 51.1–4.

25. See above, Chap. VI.

Macedon's growing conflict with Rome.[26] In other words, the balance of power between states was continually shifting, and in the period especially after 210 it had shifted back toward Achaea. Thus Aratus's actions in 225/224 had not merely saved the League from immediate disaster, they had also left the Achaeans with some freedom of maneuver for the future—which would not have been the case if they had been conquered by Cleomenes. And Polybius knew—and recorded—that the Achaeans had eventually used that freedom of maneuver to their advantage.

The events of the 220s stood at the heart of Polybius's political heritage. Their lesson was that weak states often had limited options, and that it was the duty of the statesman to choose, in a rational and careful way, the option that was best within what was actually a circumscribed "arc of political possibility."[27] But what is also evident from the above discussion is that for Polybius, this did not mean that concern for ethics and the καλόν—specifically, the ethics of independence—was coldly shoved aside. Polybius would apply this same complex and modulated view to the problem posed by Rome.

Here a second event was central to Polybius's Achaean political heritage. In 198 the League suddenly reversed its policy of alliance with Macedon and became instead an ally of Rome against Philip V. Like the *volte-face* of 225/224, the reversal of 198 was highly controversial. King Philip publicly accused the Achaeans of treachery; the Aetolians described them as mercenaries who went to the highest bidder—in this case the Romans, who offered Achaea control of Corinth in exchange for support in the war.[28] Moreover, the decision of 198 was highly controversial within Achaea itself. Argos seceded from the League as a result; several other member states fiercely opposed the decision, including Megalopolis, Polybius's own home town (which had close ties to the Antigonids). Moreover, the man who engineered the decision was Aristaenus of Dyme, Achaean *stratēgos* for 199/198—a personal enemy of Polybius's father, Lycortas. And the men around Lycortas, including Polybius's political ally Archon as well as the great Philopoemen, were later all opposed to Aristaenus and his general policy toward Rome. It is therefore not hard to

26. See Livy [P] 32.5.4–6; with Eckstein "Polybius, Aristaenus, and the Fragment 'On Traitors,'" 140–42. Note also the presence of envoys from Rhodes—a state at war with Philip—already acting as mediators in disputes between Achaean cities in 200: *IG* IV².1.79; with the comments now of Ager, "Rhodes: The Rise and Fall of a Neutral Diplomat," 22 and n. 39. Philip could do nothing about it.

27. The phrase is that of Musti, *Polibio e l'imperialismo romano,* 73; cf. 78 and 87. On Polybius's political-strategic perspective as deriving from his background in a state that had never been a great power, see esp. Schmitt, "Polybios und die Gleichgewicht der Mächte," 80.

28. For detailed discussion of the Achaean reputation among the Greeks after 198, see Eckstein, "Polybius, Aristaenus, and the Fragment 'On Traitors,'" 146–49.

imagine the severe criticism leveled in Polybius's original *milieu* both against Aristaenus's policies and against Aristaenus himself.[29]

Yet in *The Histories* Polybius not only defends the *volte-face* of 198 and Aristaenus's role in it, but the policies of Aristaenus in general. By doing so, he was—as far as we can tell—making a sharp intellectual and political break with his Megalopolitan background, and even with the tradition of his own family. And the justification he offers for Aristaenus's actions is the same one he offers regarding Aratus's actions in the crisis of the 220s: necessity (ἀνάγκη).

This emerges clearly in the retrospective comments on 198 that appear in Polyb. 18.13–15. The context is a digression carefully defining treason. Polybius argues that Aristaenus, for one, was definitely not any sort of traitor (he evidently means to Achaea). Just the reverse: for by engineering the change of alliance from Macedon to Rome, he saved the League from destruction, and even increased its power (18.13.8–10). That is: Aristaenus realized that the Achaeans had no other choice but to support Rome, and wisely brought the majority of the Achaean assembly to the same conclusion. Polybius adds that statesmen who have to adapt to similar difficult circumstances deserve similar praise (13.11).

The theme of necessity, evident in these brief retrospective remarks, is likely to have appeared in detail in Polybius's account of the actual Achaean assembly meeting of autumn 198. Nothing of that account survives directly, for it appeared in Polybius's Book 17, which is totally lost. But Livy has a version of the assembly meeting, complete with a crucial speech by Aristaenus (32.21). There is every reason to believe that this speech is closely based on Polybian material: it displays a detailed knowledge of Peloponnesian history that only Polybius, of Livy's possible sources, would have possessed; it is rife with Polybian themes; and it even contains specific language that is echoed in an extant later portion of the Polybian text.[30] And the main thrust of that speech is fear of a devastating Roman attack (perhaps in conjunction with Sparta) if Rome's offer of an alliance is rejected. The image of sacked Achaean cities is repeatedly evoked. This, then, was the stark necessity under which Achaea labored in 198.[31]

Polybius's evident emphasis primarily on Achaean fears in 198 should not be viewed as merely an example of defensive local patriotism on the

29. For detailed discussion here, see Eckstein, ibid., 145–46.

30. Strong arguments in favor of the Polybian derivation of Aristaenus's speech: Aymard, *Premiers rapports*, 94; and now Eckstein, "Freedom of the Greeks," 54–58. Against: Carawan, "Flamininus in Livy," 214 (very strained).

31. For detailed discussion of the themes in Aristaenus's speech, see esp. Aymard, *Premiers rapports*, 91–94.

historian's part.[32] Polybius makes it clear that the Achaean decision was highly controversial among the Greeks, and that desire for Corinth played a role in the Achaean decision; ultimately he is the source of all our information on these two subjects.[33] And he explicitly says that Aristaenus's decision not only saved the League but increased its power (18.13.10). If the Achaean desire for territorial gain is nevertheless missing from Livy's account of the actual Achaean decision, it must be because Polybius honestly believed that fear—not greed—was the decisive Achaean motive in 198 (as it had been in 225/224), and shaped his narrative accordingly.[34]

Furthermore, at a point later in *The Histories* where defense of Aristaenus is no longer equivalent to defense of Achaea, Polybius still presents him as a respectable figure. It is a famous and somewhat controversial passage: the debate between Aristaenus and Philopoemen over policy toward Rome (24.11–13). Aristaenus argues that whereas great states should always act nobly (according to the καλόν: 24.12.2), this was not a luxury that weak states could always afford; sometimes they had to settle for practical advantage (the συμφέρον: ibid.). But worst of all was to achieve neither aim, because of foolishness (ibid.). In the particular case of Achaean relations with Rome, Aristaenus argues that since the Achaeans ultimately will always have to bend to Roman wishes and power, it is foolish to put up resistance that is both unavailing and eventually counterproductive to the Achaean state (because it increases Roman hostility); in fact, the Achaeans should strive even to anticipate Rome's wishes before they are expressed (11.4–5). By contrast, Philopoemen argues that it is best to resist the growth of Roman power in Achaea as much as possible, by sticking strictly to the letter of the Achaean treaty of alliance with Rome and not going beyond its terms except as a last resort (11.6–8). His stance is not unlike the policy adopted by Aratus in relation to the earlier Achaean alliance with Macedon (see above).

It is clear that Aristaenus is more prepared than Philopoemen to be immediately accommodating to most Roman wishes, for reasons of Achaean state interest. And it is equally clear that Polybius prefers Philopoemen's position to that of Aristaenus, since he characterizes it as both noble and prudent (καλήν, ἀσφαλεῖς, 24.13.8), and since for Polybius (as for Polybius's Aristaenus!) the "noble" is the highest category of praise.

32. Despite Edson, "Review of Walbank, *Philip V*," 827.

33. For discussion of this aspect of the problem, see Eckstein, "Polybius, Aristaenus, and the Fragment 'On Traitors,'" 148.

34. If the prospect of gaining Corinth had been a theme in Polybius's version of Aristaenus's speech, it is difficult not to believe that Livy would indeed have underlined (rather than suppressed) such an example of Roman generosity.

Yet Polybius characterizes the policy of Aristaenus here as itself both "respectable" and prudent (εὐσχήμονα, ἀσφαλεῖς, ibid.)—not as good as Philopoemen's policy, to be sure, but not completely lacking in moral stature either.

The key to understanding Polybius's judgment here is the term εὐσχήμων, which is used to describe Aristaenus's policy. Prominent scholars have detected in this word a negative connotation, taking it to mean "having a facade of honor," as opposed to being truly honorable.[35] But this is hard to accept—for in the ten other appearances of εὐσχήμων in the extant Polybian text, including in a speech that Polybius attributes to himself, the word clearly does mean, purely and simply, "honorable."[36] Hueltsch long ago realized the severe problem caused by general Polybian word usage, and proposed emending εὐσχήμων at 24.13.8 to ἀσχήμων ("undignified"). But this makes nonsense of Polybius's hearty praise of Aristaenus in the very next sentence, at 24.13.9 (see below)—praise that itself indicates that εὐσχήμων must be a positive epithet.[37]

Thus the description of Aristaenus's policy toward Rome in Polyb. 24.13.8 turns out to be another defense of it. And Polyb. 24.13.9 reveals the standards by which Polybius rendered positive judgment on Aristaenus's policy: he argues that both Philopoemen and Aristaenus equally staunchly protected the rights of Achaea against Rome under difficult conditions.[38] Thus the range of conduct and policy represented by Aristaenus and Philopoemen was all viewed by Polybius as honorable, honorable because it was patriotic, and patriotic because it specifically attempted to preserve some modicum of Achaean independence from Rome.[39]

But a quite different figure to Polybius is the Achaean politician Callicrates of Leontium—precisely because Callicrates adopted a consciously

35. Cf. Petzold, *Methode des Polybios*, 45–46; Musti, *Polibio e l'imperialismo romano*, 77; Walbank, *Commentary* III: 266–67; Green, *Alexander to Actium*, 274.

36. See, most recently, Ferrary, *Philhellénisme et impérialisme*, 297 and n. 102. Examples: "an honorable retreat" (Polyb. 3.40.13, 4.12.10, 5.110.11; cf. 4.19.8), an honorable means to deal with a situation (4.51.9), an honorable regulation (21.10.5 and 6). Polybius's speech: 28.7.12. Ferrary also notes that εὐσχήμων is a fairly honorific term on official decrees (cf. *Syll.*³ 608, 615, 667).

37. For the suggested emendation, see Mauersberger, *Polybios-Lexikon* I: 2, col. 1044 (who rejects it, on the basis of Polybius's praise of Aristaenus at 18.13.8–10).

38. ομως ἀμφότεροι διετήρησαν ἀκέραια τὰ δίκαια τοῖς Ἀχαιοῖς πρὸς᾽ Ρωμαίους.

39. One should note that at 22.10.14 Polybius quotes an Achaean suspicion that Aristaenus in the mid-180s twice sought to employ influential Roman senators in the factional disputes within Achaea. Polybius clearly thought this disreputable (ibid.)—but apparently not sufficiently disreputable to undermine his general assessment of Aristaenus as a patriot at 24.13.9.

sycophantic policy toward the Romans.[40] And if Aratus, Philopoemen, and Aristaenus were all clearly figures from Polybius's early political education, so, too, was Callicrates.

In 180, when Polybius was probably about twenty, Callicrates was sent to Rome as an envoy to defend the Achaean treatment of Sparta and Messene. The forcible inclusion of these states within the League had been Philopoemen's policy, furthered in the late 180s by Polybius's father, Lycortas. This Achaean expansion in the southern Peloponnese had caused tension with Rome, and the embassy of 180 was a response to the continuing problem.[41] But Callicrates, instead of defending Achaean policy, apparently told the Roman Senate that they had themselves to blame for the fact that their wishes were ignored in Greece, since they failed to support men (such as himself) who wholeheartedly believed that Roman wishes should always be obeyed; the *Patres* should change their policy and support such men (Polyb. 24.9 *passim*). The Senate agreed, immediately sending letters commending certain politicians to various Greek states, including Achaea itself (24.10.6). This was overt Roman intervention in Greek internal politics. Polybius says that from this point on, the Achaean League found it difficult to deal with Rome from a position approaching equality; and the Romans, while they gained many sycophants in Greece, came to have no true friends there (24.10.5 and 9). Especially from the Greek point of view, Callicrates' embassy was thus "the beginning of great evils" (10.8).[42]

It is likely that this highly negative judgment of Callicrates' embassy was part of Polybius's original political education. To be sure, Book 24 of *The Histories* was probably written after 145—almost three decades after the event. And by that time a personal grudge existed, since Callicrates was the man responsible for Polybius's own exile from Achaea in 167.[43] Nevertheless, Polybius was already a young adult in 180, and it was a policy closely associated with his father Lycortas that was at issue in Callicrates' embassy. The outcome of that embassy is hardly likely to have pleased Lycortas—nor Lycortas's son, who in 180 was just entering politics under his father's direct tutelage (Polyb. 24.6). Indeed, it seems that

40. For the contrasting Polybian categorization of Aristaenus and Philopoemen on the one side, and Callicrates on the other, see the remarks of Lehmann, *Glaubwürdigkeit des Polybios*, 249–50; and Walbank, *Commentary* III: 267.

41. For the background to the Achaean embassy of 180, see esp. Derow, "Embassy of Kallikrates," 13–15.

42. Callicrates' conduct is thus the opposite of Aratus's steadfast resolve to avoid sycophancy toward Macedon after 225/224: see Polybius's praise at 4.82.2–5 (and above, p. 199).

43. On Callicrates' role in Polybius's exile, see Polyb. 30.13.9–11, 32.1–2; cf. Paus. 7.10.11 and Livy 45.31.5. For the probable dates for the composition of *The Histories*, see Chap. I, above.

one immediate result of Callicrates' embassy was the temporary political eclipse of the men around Lycortas.[44]

For present purposes, what is important is the precise basis of Polybius's negative assessment of Callicrates' conduct. Thus Derow views Polybius's criticism of Callicrates as totally utilitarian in character: his advice to the Senate produced no real benefits either to the Greeks or even to the Romans themselves.[45] But while a good portion of Polybius's criticism of Callicrates is indeed utilitarian, that is not the whole story—nor is it likely to have been the whole story even in 180.

Much of Polybius's criticism of Callicrates' embassy is in fact couched in moralizing terminology. The *Patres*, taking Callicrates' advice, began to weaken those Greek politicians who worked for "the best" (τὸ βέλτιστον, 24.10.4), and to strengthen those men who always appealed to Rome "whether this was right [δικαίως] or contrary to right" (ibid.). Callicrates himself did the opposite of reminding the Senate of the claims of justice (τῶν δικαίων, 10.12). He returned to Greece overjoyed, not seeing that he had become the author of great evils (μεγάλων κακῶν, 10.8). Elected *stratēgos* by the Achaeans primarily out of fear (10.14), he then "began to take bribes—in addition to his other misconduct" (πρὸς τοῖς ἄλλοις κακοῖς, ibid.). And while Derow is correct that Polybius does not explicitly call Callicrates a traitor in any extant passage, the historian does quote others to that effect with no objection—indeed, with obvious great satisfaction (30.29 *passim*, esp. 29.7).

Thus the Polybian image of Callicrates in 180 is not merely of a politician who made errors of a utilitarian nature, but rather of a profoundly immoral man who betrayed Achaea, "the best," and "justice." Since the long-term utilitarian effects of Callicrates' policy could hardly have been known in 180 (especially regarding the negative impact even upon Rome's true interests in Greece), it is likely that the moral condemnation Polybius expresses in 24.10 is similar to the original feelings of the men around Lycortas at that time. After all, Callicrates had (1) gone against Achaean instructions, which were (2) as envoy to Rome to defend the policies of Lycortas.[46]

In terms of understanding the Polybian political agenda, it is also important to establish the exact nature of "the best policy" (24.10.4): the structure of Greek-Roman relations that was, in Polybius's view, severely

44. On political conditions in Achaea after Callicrates' embassy, see Gruen, *Hellenistic World and the Coming of Rome* II: 496–502, who corrects earlier views and argues cogently that Callicrates enjoyed only a temporary political ascendancy, 180–175, rather than throughout the 170s.
45. "Embassy of Kallikrates," 13.
46. Note that at 24.8.8–9 Callicrates is specifically attacked for having violated his position as an official ambassador.

undermined by Callicrates. And this is easily done, for it is obvious that
"the best policy" in 24.10.8–10 means the desire to deal with Rome "on
more or less equal terms" (κατὰ ποσὸν ἰσολογίαν, 10.9). Polybius makes
the same point in a slightly different fashion when he then offers his personal opinion that the method for Rome's allies to adopt in diplomacy
with the Republic is to be firm, sticking steadfastly to legitimate claims
based on justice (10.11).

There is—once more—every likelihood that this understanding of
"the best policy" in regard to Rome, and what a "change for the worse"
meant (24.10.10), was an integral part of Polybius's original political heritage. It is not only that independence as opposed to dependence was,
as a general concept, a basic and natural tradition among Greek aristocrats.[47] More specifically, both Polybius's childhood hero Philopoemen, and Lycortas as well, were outspoken advocates in the 180s of
maintaining an Achaean attitude of independence regarding the Romans. Philopoemen's position is clear from Polyb. 24.11–13 (discussed,
above).[48] As for Lycortas, Polybius himself proudly recorded the fact,
of his father's steadfast attitude toward the Romans, his stern opposition,
to any diminution of Achaea's independence.[49]

In fact, it can be shown that the Polybian definition of "the best policy"
as one that sought to maintain as much independence as possible in the
face of power is a constant in *The Histories*, appearing both early and late.
Thus in Book 27 Polybius praises the policy of the Epirote statesman
Cephalus as the Third Macedonian War was approaching (about 172).
Cephalus, Polybius says, was in general "a wise and steadfastly courageous man," and in this crisis he adopted "the best policy" (ἡ ἀρίστη
γνώμη, 27.15.10). This was first of all to hope that there would be no
war between Macedon and Rome—for a war would mean that a more
definitive hegemony over the Greeks would be established by one of the
two great powers (15.11). But if war came, then Cephalus was resolved
to act correctly toward Rome according to the terms of the Epirote alliance with the Republic, but "beyond this neither would he run and fawn
on the Romans, acting ignobly, nor would he be unduly subservient to
them" (15.12).[50]

47. See Arnheim, *Aristocracy in Greek Society*, esp. chap. 6.

48. See also Plut. *Phil.* 17.3, and Paus. 8.51.4; with the remarks of Walbank, *Commentary*
III: 266.

49. See esp. Polyb. 24.8.3–5, which in fact constitutes advice from Lycortas on how to
deal with the Romans that exactly parallels Polybius's own advice at 24.10.11. Also: Livy [P]
38.32.6–8 and 39.36–37, speeches by Lycortas strongly—even bitterly—asserting Achaean
independence from Rome; for Polybian derivation, cf. Nissen, *Kritische Untersuchungen*, 205
and 224.

50. Note the moralizing terminology in the passage: στάσιμος . . . ἀγεννῶς . . . παρὰ τὸ
δέον. Very similar in tone are two Livian passages clearly based on Polybian material: (1)

In contrast to Polybius's praise of Cephalus is his much earlier condemnation of the Athenians around 217, for taking precisely the opposite
political stance (5.106.7–8). The Athenians

> were profuse in their flattery of all the kings . . . continuing to pass every
> manner of decree and proclamation, and paying little heed to decency [τὸ
> καθῆκον] in this regard, because of the lack of judgment of their leaders.

The Athenian actions did not, according to Polybius, directly threaten
the political independence of the city, which at this time was fairly secure
(5.106.6). Their behavior was therefore not counterproductive; but it *was*,
in Polybius's opinion, disgusting. The Polybian attitude here is all the
more interesting since it is displayed so emphatically so shortly into *The
Histories*. It thus serves as an indication that Polybius's beliefs regarding
the proper relationship between small states and great ones arose early
on.[51]

If Polybius seems to have believed that there was a moral imperative
for weaker states to maintain what level of independence and dignity they
could—"the best policy"—he was nevertheless painfully aware that this
moral imperative often had to be balanced by the necessity of bending to
the facts of power. This was the crucial policy dilemma faced by the
weaker states, the fine line their leaders had to walk.[52] That dilemma in
fact also appears in the very earliest stratum of *The Histories*—not only in
Polybius's defense of Aratus of Sicyon (where one could perhaps argue
that the presentation is distorted by Achaean patriotism),[53] but also even

---

Livy 42.30.5–6, where "the best and wisest" of three categories of Greek politicians wishes
that neither Rome nor Macedon should emerge from the Third Macedonian War stronger,
so that the smaller states will retain freedom of maneuver; (2) Livy 45.31.4, where a category of Greek politicians in 167, opposed to two other categories that fawned upon the
Romans in order to gain wealth and power, is called the one that strove to guard "liberty
and constitutional government." For the Polybian derivation of these passages—which evidently represent original Polybian analyses of the political situation in Greece quite separate from, and additional to, Polyb. 30.6–9—see most recently Deininger, *Widerstand*,
161–64; Gruen, "Rome and Rhodes in the Second Century," 62–63; Walbank, *Commentary*
III: 428.

51. On the extravagant Athenian honors to kings in this period, esp. to the Ptolemies
and Attalids, see Walbank, *Commentary* I: 631. Polybius had good relations with both dynasties (see 24.6 and 28.7), but clearly he drew a line concerning what was acceptable behavior
toward them. Note his praise of the Achaeans for rejecting Attalid funding of the Achaean
Council: it might lead to a loss of independence of decision (22.7–8). Walbank (ibid.) sees
no reason to regard Polyb. 5.106.6–8 as a late insertion into the text.

52. Cf. the perceptive comments of von Fritz, *Mixed Constitution*, 11 (cf. 25); also: Musti,
Polibio e l'imperialismo romano, 79.

53. Cf. Gabba, "Studi su Filarco," 31–34; Africa, *Phylarchus and the Spartan Revolution*,
chap. 3.

earlier, with regard to the policy of Hiero II of Syracuse (a regime with which Polybius had no personal connections).

First, Polybius is profuse in his praise of King Hiero's decision in 263 to make peace with the Romans once large Roman armies had arrived in Sicily: this was the wise and rational thing to do (1.16.4 and 11). The result was prosperity for Syracuse and security for Hiero's own regime (16.10–11).[54] But Polybius's praise of Hiero's decision of 263 does not mean that in Book 1 of *The Histories* he was advocating that his audience take up a position of pro-Roman sycophancy. The contrary is proven by 1.83, where Polybius once more praises Hiero's foreign policy, but this time for a quite different reason. In describing Hiero's support of Carthage in the early years of the Mercenary War of 241–238, Polybius explains (1.83.3) that Hiero here acted "very wisely and intelligently": "For one should never contribute to the creation of a hegemony so complete that none dare dispute with it even on the basis of acknowledged treaty rights" (83.4).

Polybius's point is that by helping to preserve Carthage from destruction, Hiero sought to prevent his own polity from being completely dominated by Rome. Total independence may not be possible—indeed, Polybius does not think it was a reasonable aim for Syracuse even in the darkest days of Roman defeat early in the Hannibalic War.[55] But Polybius not only calls the policy of attempting to create some freedom of maneuver "wise and intelligent" (1.83.3), he advocates the attempted creation of such freedom of maneuver as a *general* rule to be followed by all small states: "It is necessary never to neglect such things" (ibid.). And it is precisely for violating the general rule of 1.83—for contributing to the creation of a Roman hegemony so complete that none dared to dispute with it even on the basis of acknowledged treaty rights—that Polybius chastises Callicrates in Book 24.[56]

The appearance so early in *The Histories* of Polybian advocacy of this complex stance regarding the necessities (and possibilities) faced by weak states suggests that the lessons of Achaean history, deeply absorbed by him, had come to form the framework of his political thinking even before *The Histories* were conceived as a project. And that hypothesis is con-

54. The Roman tradition emphasized not Hiero's rational calculations in 263 but his panic at the size and success of Rome's armies in Sicily (Oros. 4.7.3, *de Vir. Ill.* 37.5, Zon. 8.9). Polybius is thus clearly shaping his narrative here—among a choice of varying traditions—to conform to his understanding of what constitutes good political decision making.

55. See Polybius's highly negative description of the policies of Hiero's successor Hieronymus, at 7.3–8 (discussed below, p. 211, and in Chap. V, above).

56. For full discussion of Polyb. 1.83.3–4, see Eckstein, "Polybius, Syracuse, and the Politics of Accommodation," 272–73.

firmed by the policy we know Polybius adopted as hipparch of the Achaean League in 170/169—three years before his exile. The policy was discussed in detail in Chapter I, and need only be summarized here. On the one hand, Polybius supported an official Achaean policy of cooperation with Rome in the Roman war against Perseus of Macedon. On the other hand, Polybius did what he could to preserve specific Achaean interests, and he strove to stick to the strict letter of the Achaean treaty of alliance with Rome, and no more.[57]

In other words, Polybius in 170/169 acted in a manner similar to what Cephalus in Epirus had hoped to achieve (27.15), and to what Polybius in that latter passage calls "the best policy"—to abide by the Roman alliance, but not to fawn on the Romans.[58] This policy did not prevent Polybius from being deported to Italy after Pydna, along with many other Achaean politicians—thanks to the denunciations of Callicrates concerning their alleged anti-Roman views.[59] In pragmatic terms, then, Polybius's policy was a total failure—and the same was true of Cephalus.[60] Yet it is now also clear that more than the simple criterion of success or failure was at work here. Rather, what counted for Polybius was the stern resolve—while accepting the political necessity of cooperation with Rome—not to do anything "ignoble" (ἀγεννῶς, 27.15.12).

It is often the case in *The Histories* that states and leaders fail to maintain the delicate balance of policy that was Polybius's Achaean heritage and that he recommends under conditions of strategic inferiority—seeking to maintain as large a sphere of independence as possible (yet avoiding useless and destructive confrontation, especially of the military kind), while bending to power when necessary (yet also avoiding diplomatic servility and sycophancy). These studies in political failure now become our subject. But it should be emphasized at the outset that the nature of Polybius's criticisms of these political failures varies according to the two categories of error. In the one case (confrontation), he tends to stress the impact of unintelligent or irrational decision making, which misjudges the pragmatic situation. But in the other case (servility), he tends to stress that the decision making was immoral and "unworthy."

57. Polybius's policy of cooperation with the Romans: see 28.6 and 7, 28.13.7–9, 29.26.5. His attempts to preserve Achaean interests: 28.13.1–7 and 11–14.

58. The situation in 170/169 contained the additional complication that Polybius—like Cephalus—did not see it as a choice between the Romans and Greek freedom, but between Roman hegemony and the domination of Greece by Macedon: cf. 27.10.2 and 15.10. On this, see Walbank, "Polybius and Rome's Eastern Policy," 7–8; and *Commentary* III: 308; and Musti, *Polibio e l'imperialismo romano*, 79.

59. Sources: above, n. 43.

60. On Cephalus's fate, see Chap. II, above.

One cannot appreciate Polybius's political thought without taking into account *both* categories of error—and both criteria of political judgment.[61]

THE BEHAVIOR OF THE OPPONENTS OF ROME

Polybius, of course, tends to render a negative judgment against those states and leaders who chose to oppose Rome militarily. This theme first appears in the case of Queen Teuta of the Illyrians in 229/228 B.C. (see above, Chapter V), then in the case of the Illyrian dynast Demetrius of Pharus a decade later (Polyb. 3.16 *passim;* cf. 3.19.9). In both cases, reckless behavior on the part of the weaker power (2.8–9, 3.16.4: ἄγνοια, προπετεία) leads to political and military disaster. The theme then reappears with emphasis in the case of Hannibal at the outbreak of the Second Punic War, and gradually reaches a crescendo in the discussions of events after 150. But what disturbs Polybius here is not so much opposition to Rome *per se,* as poor-quality decision making: leaders who lose control of their emotions and act irrationally, thereby becoming derelict in their solemn duty to provide guidance to their polities during seasons of difficulty.

From the Illyrians perhaps Polybius did not expect much; but Hannibal was from a highly civilized society (cf. Polyb. 1.65.7). His destructive role in the diplomacy leading to the Second Punic War has already been discussed in detail in Chapter V, and it is enough now merely to reiterate that Polybius depicted Hannibal at the meeting with Roman envoys at New Carthage in 220 as a young man totally out of control of his passions, who abandoned his duty as a leader in order to satisfy ambition and hatred.[62] Moreover, Polybius also believed that if Hannibal had waited to attack the Romans until he had acquired much more power, then all his plans would have succeeded; as it was, his lack of self-control led him into war with resources too slender to win victory despite his battlefield brilliance (11.19.6–7). Hannibal's emotions blinded him to the realities of power as they existed in 220. Those realities might have shifted, however, if Hannibal had only been able to bide his time.[63]

The latter remark is hardly that of a man emotionally committed to the Roman cause; and even this is not the whole story. Two decades later, at the battle of Zama, Hannibal finally lost the war; yet now Polybius has only praise of the Carthaginian's actions. This is because in his opinion,

61. On Polybius's attempt at a "balanced" position, see esp. Musti, *Polibio e l'imperialismo romano,* 74 and 79: it was between the two extremes of military "rebellion" and total servility that the historian traced "the arc of political possibility" available to minor states.
62. See Polyb. 3.15.6, 9, and 12; with Eckstein, "The Power of Irrationality," esp. 8–15.
63. Ibid., 13; see also Chap. V, above.

Hannibal had conducted the battle with great skill, and according to reason (κατὰ λόγον); no one could have done better with the limited resources he had available (15.16.1–3). If, after having taken every possible
step to secure victory, Hannibal was still defeated, he was not to be
blamed (16.5); it sometimes happened that a great man was overpowered
by Fortune, or by a greater man yet (16.6).[64] Thus it would appear that
Polybius's criterion of judgment at the climax of the Second Punic War is
not mere pragmatic success or failure (let alone friendship or enmity toward Rome). Rather, what impresses Polybius here—as elsewhere—is the
sheer *quality* of conduct.[65]

Polybius seems to apply a similar criterion in the case of Hieronymus
of Syracuse. When Hieronymus sided with Carthage early in the Second
Punic War, he abandoned Hiero II's policy of cooperation with Rome,
which Polybius considers to have been a classic example of "balance" between realistic accommodation to a great power (1.16) and maneuvers
to retain as much independence as possible (1.83).[66] But what Polybius
condemns in Hieronymus is not antagonism to Rome *per se;* it is Hieronymus's fundamental misjudgment of the strategic situation facing Syracuse
in 215—his belief that Rome was finished. This misjudgment, in turn,
derived in Polybius's opinion from deep flaws within Hieronymus himself: youth, inexperience, bloated ambitions. The result was disaster for
Syracuse.[67]

A similar pattern appears in Polybius's discussion of the origins of the
First Macedonian War (212/211–205). This was the result of poor decision making by Macedon's young king, Philip V—stemming, in turn,
from *his* deeper character flaws. Polybius believes that Philip became an
ally of Hannibal because (like Hieronymus) he mistakenly thought Rome
was already beaten (5.101.3–10).[68] This mistake was exacerbated (as with
Hieronymus) by inexperience, by an inflated sense of his own power, and
by bloated ambition; indeed, Philip wanted to conquer the entire world
(Polyb. 5.101.8–10). It is not the anti-Roman aspect of these activities that
disturbs Polybius; rather, he sees them as just one aspect of an intensi-
fying lack of self-control in Philip's character. This was Philip's "change

64. The reference here is, of course, to P. Cornelius Scipio, the commander on the Roman side. Scipio is certainly a Polybian hero—but Hannibal is equally depicted, here and
in general (except for 3.15), in a heroic mold himself. On this, see Pédech, *Méthode,* 217–19.

65. For this aspect of Polybius's judgment of Hannibal at Zama, see (rightly) Pédech,
Méthode, 219.

66. On Hiero's policy, see above, pp. 207–8.

67. For detailed discussion of Polybius's depiction of Hieronymus, see Chap. V above;
and Eckstein, "Polybius, Syracuse, and the Politics of Accommodation," 273–75.

68. In this sense, the First Macedonian War grew "organically" out of conditions prevailing during the Hannibalic War: see Polyb. 3.32.7; with the comments of Pédech, *Méthode,*
101.

for the worse" (7.11.1), which began about 217/215, after his first few years as king. The most prominent feature of this change, Polybius says, was Philip's increasing habit of treachery and cruelty—against the Greeks.[69]

Polybius also sees the influence of Philip's adviser Demetrius of Pharus (now a refugee at Philip's court) behind Philip's decision to confront the Romans (5.101–2). But Demetrius was a bad adviser, reckless (3.16.4), a man "totally lacking in reason and judgment" (ἀλόγιστον . . . καὶ τέλεως ἄκριτον, 3.19.9).[70] Conversely, Philip's adoption of the anti-Roman policy marked to Polybius the decline in the influence over Philip previously exercised by the wise and cautious Aratus of Sicyon—who disapproved of the new policy specifically because he thought it involved "many difficulties" (7.13.1).[71]

Thus in the causal sequence leading to the First Macedonian War, Polybius links a growing irrationality on the Macedonian side with loss of royal self-control and the rise of evil advisers. The result, ultimately, is a poor quality of decision making (see 3.19.9: ἀκρισία).[72]

Polybius presents a similar story in regard to the origins of the Syrian-Aetolian War of 191–188. He explains that the fierce anger of the Aetolians (their ὀργή) was the cause of the war (3.3.3–4 and 3.7.1). It led them to urge Antiochus III to come to Greece and overturn the arrangements made by Rome after the Second Macedonian War (3.7.2).[73] Indeed, Polybius says that the fury of the Aetolians against Rome was so intense that they would have done or suffered anything to gain their ends (3.7.2).

The anger of the Aetolians derived from a perception that the Romans had shortchanged them in territorial rewards for their help against Philip in the Second Macedonian War (Polyb. 3.7.2). Modern scholars have often thought that there was substance to the Aetolian complaint; and some

69. See Polyb. 7.11.9, 13.3, and 13.5–7.
70. On Demetrius of Pharus and the Polybian depiction of his baneful influence on Philip, see esp. Pédech, *Méthode*, 102.
71. On Aratus's place in the story of Philip's decision to adopt an anti-Roman policy, see Eckstein, "The Power of Irrationality," 12.
72. On ἀκρισία, see also Polyb. 7.5.3 (Hieronymus); these are the issues of concern to the historian. Gelzer, "Achaia in Geschichtswerk des Polybios," 17–19, posits that Polybius's assessments of Philip's behavior (positive or negative) were based primarily on the impact (positive or negative) upon the interests of Achaea; so, too, Welwei, *Könige und Königtum,* 39–40. Note that this thesis results in a conundrum, since Polybius's harshest criticism of Philip in the earliest stage of his career concerns the king's sacking of Thermum, the capital of Aetolia (5.9–12)—and the Aetolians were the Achaeans' great rivals.
73. Polybius's views on the political origins of the Second Macedonian War itself (200–196 B.C.) are difficult to discern, because of the extremely fragmentary character of the text; so this subject is best left out of discussion. For contrasting positions here, see Derow, "Polybius, Rome and the East," 10–11; as opposed to Pédech, *Méthode,* 118–19.

suggest that Polybius thought so, too.[74] But Polybius already appears to be indicting the Aetolians for greedy behavior as far back as 196 (cf. 18.34.1–2), and indicates that at least some of the Aetolian postwar accusations against Rome were lies (18.45.8; cf. 3.7.3).[75] Moreover, no matter what Polybius may have thought of the legal validity of some of the Aetolian territorial claims, he certainly judged the quality of their decision making harshly. This is proven by his description of the Aetolians as driven by fierce ὀργή in the policy that led to war with Rome. Despite Sacks,[76] it is difficult to believe that ὀργή has no negative connotation here. In *The Histories,* overwhelming anger such as this is characteristic of the worst sorts of people, and it is an emotion overwhelmingly negative in its effects on those who surrender to it.[77] Moreover, it is obvious that Polybius in 3.7 is thoroughly hostile (not neutral) to Aetolian policy: he associates it both with lies (3.7.3) and with irrationality (ἀλόγως, ibid.).[78] The policy was a catastrophic mistake, prompted by emotions that were out of control; the result was not only a new war in Greece, but also (in 189) the emasculation of the Aetolian League itself by Rome. To Polybius, it seems to have been a classic example of a weaker state's failure to maintain the necessary balance when dealing—under difficult or even provocative circumstances—with a great power.

This need not mean, however, that Polybius instinctively took Rome's side in the Aetolian-Syrian War. It is true that, at an abstract level, Polybius thought Antiochus's war with Rome was the revenge upon him by Tyche for his immoral alliance with Philip against Ptolemy V (see 15.20.6); and it may be that at a political level, Polybius also criticized Antiochus for precipitous actions certain to provoke war with the very formidable Romans (cf. App. *Syr.* 37).[79] But once the war was actually under way, Polybius's criticism took an entirely different tack. He strongly censured Antiochus because in winter 192/191 the king spent his time relaxing with his new wife instead of pursuing the war actively (20.8), while allowing his army in Greece to fall apart (cf. Livy [P] 36.11.3–5).[80] Later, Polybius seems to have criticized Antiochus for giving up Thrace to the Romans without a fight (cf. App. *Syr.* 37), and he certainly censured

74. See Sacks, "Polybius' Other View of Aetolia," esp. 93–94 and 105; Derow, "Polybius, Rome, and the East," 11–12.
75. Noted by Mendels, "Did Polybius Have 'Another' View of the Aetolian League?" 64.
76. "Polybius' Other View of Aetolia," 93–94.
77. On the contexts of Polybius's use of the term ὀργή, see the detailed discussion in Eckstein, "The Power of Irrationality," 6–7. More briefly: Mendels, "Did Polybius Have 'Another' View of the Aetolian League?" 63 and n. 4.
78. See (rightly) Mendels, "Did Polybius Have 'Another' View of the Aetolian League?" 64–65 (replying to Sacks, 94–98).
79. On App. *Syr.* 37, see esp. Welwei, *Könige und Königtum,* 63.
80. For detailed discussion of this passage, see Chap. VI, above.

him for giving in to depression and lethargy after the battle of Teos in
190, thereby missing several important military opportunities (Polyb.
21.13.1–2). All this fits with Polybius's general assessment of Antiochus:
as the king grew older, he did not have the energy necessary to fulfill the
great tasks he had set for himself (15.37).[81]

In other words, Antiochus had not made war on Rome *effectively
enough*. This—once more—is hardly the historical judgment of a writer
who is a "collaborator." Indeed, politics does not appear to be involved at
all. Rather, Polybius's criticism of Antiochus's conduct of the war should
probably be seen as an expression of a broad and essentially apolitical
Polybian "philosophy of action," in which those men are chastised who
are lazy and halting in carrying out the large projects they initiate—no
matter what those large projects happen to be.[82]

In the war of 191–188, Philip V fought vigorously on the side of Rome,
to Macedon's territorial benefit.[83] Polybius viewed this policy as wise, part
of a new ("third") stage in the development of Philip's personality. The
king, Polybius thought, tended to lose self-control in periods of success,
but to respond well to situations of crisis and defeat.[84] Thus the disaster
at Cynoscephalae in 197 led to Philip's moral regeneration, demonstrated by his loyalty to his secret Greek supporters in burning their correspondence before it fell into the hands of the Romans (18.33.1–3)—as
well as by his rapid political accommodation to the hard fact of Roman
power (33.7). But even here, it is important to see what ultimate goal
Polybius postulated lay behind Philip's new policy toward Rome, and
that, moreover, Polybius approved of this goal (25.3.9–10): "When the
winds of fortune veered against him, Philip's moderation became conspicuous . . . and he tried by every possible means to rebuild the strength
of his kingdom."

The Achaeans had followed a similar policy of careful rebuilding after
about 210, while still acknowledging the hegemony of Macedon; that policy, too, won Polybius's approval.[85] In both cases, what gains that approval
is intelligent action taken in the interest of the power of one's polity—the
quality of political conduct.

This is the context in which to see Polybius's condemnation of Philip's

81. See the comments of Welwei, *Könige und Königtum*, 62–63.
82. Thus Polybius chastises both Philip V for failing to pursue his war aims vigorously
after the battle of Chios in 201 (16.10.2–4)—and shortly thereafter chastises the Rhodians
and Attalus (16.28.1–2) for failing to pursue vigorously their war against Philip!
83. For detailed discussion, see Walbank, *Philip V*, 186–221.
84. This aspect of Philip's personality is repeatedly emphasized by Polybius: see 16.28.3
and 8; 18.33.4–8; 25.3.9–10.
85. See above, pp. 199–200.

final ("fourth") stage of development. In the 180s, Polybius says, Philip became ever more provoked by Roman diplomatic pressure to give up some of his territorial gains from the Aetolian-Syrian War; so, like the Aetolians, he began to plan a war of revenge (22.18 *passim*). Philip was thus the origin of the Third Macedonian War, even though it began seven years after his death—for he conceived it and made every preparation for it before he died (22.18.10–11).[86] Polybius, however, did not blame Philip for the new war because it was an anti-Roman project. On the contrary: he blamed him because the new war led to the destruction of the House of Macedon itself (22.18.8, explicitly). And to Polybius such destruction was all too predictable, since Philip's new anti-Roman policy was not based on a rational calculation of strategic realities (as had been the case in his "third," successful period), but on sheer emotion—the king's fury (ὀργή, 22.13.2).[87] Indeed, Polybius sees Philip's war policy as just one part of a "heaven-sent madness" that characterized Philip's last years as a whole, and that found additional expression in his increasing oppression within Macedon itself (including the murder of his own son, Demetrius).[88]

Clearly, nothing good could be expected of a policy toward Rome designed by an enraged madman.[89] And indeed, Polybius viewed the new war (171–168) as a catastrophe for all the Greek states—for it fastened Roman domination upon the Hellenes in a much tighter fashion than before (cf. 27.15.10).

In addition, Polybius made sure to provide his readers with discussions of serious political errors made by the Greeks themselves during the war. The Boeotians, for instance, had their League broken up by Rome because "they rashly and irrationally chose to back Perseus, giving way to heedless and childish excitement" (27.2.10). It must be stressed that what disturbs Polybius here is *not* the fact that the Boeotians had backed the anti-Roman side. Thus he does not hesitate to praise the virtues of King Cotys of Thrace (moderation, sobriety, military skill)—although Cotys, too, had backed the anti-Roman side (27.12). Conversely, Polybius actually attacks Perseus for failing—like Antiochus before him—to conduct war against Rome with the requisite skill and vigor, thereby missing many

---

86. Modern scholars have persistently rejected Polybius's reconstruction of the origins of the Third Macedonian War: see, e.g., Gruen, "Last Years of Philip V," 221–46; and *Hellenistic World and the Coming of Rome* II: 399–419. But we are only concerned here with what *Polybius* believed about the war.

87. Philip was evidently most upset over his failure to retain the region of Orestis: see Walbank, *Philip V,* 163.

88. Cf. Pédech, *Méthode,* 125–28; Welwei, *Könige und Königtum,* 50.

89. See esp. the classic study of Walbank, "A Polybian Experiment," 55–68.

strategic opportunities.[90] But this, in turn, does not mean that Polybius
would have preferred a Macedonian victory; he did not, fearing the consequences for the freedom of the smaller Greek states (27.10.2–3; cf.
28.9.7). Rather, in all these cases it is (once again) the overall quality of
conduct that determines Polybius's assessment—not the politics involved.
Behavior he considers of poor quality is condemned (Philip, the Boeotians, Perseus); high-quality conduct (Cotys) receives praise.[91]

Roman hegemony over Polybius's Mediterranean was next shaken by
a major sequence of wars around 150. The focus for us is on Polybius's
depiction of the quality of conduct of Rome's enemies (Carthaginians,
Macedonians, Achaeans) during this final cataclysmic portion of *The Histories*.

In terms of formal analysis of causation, it is probable that aggressive
Roman motivation was seen by Polybius as the underlying cause (αἰτία)
of the Third Punic War. This is shown by his concentration on the development of sentiment for war at Rome (36.2; cf. 36.9)—the first occasion
in the extant text since the outbreak of the First Punic War where Polybius's analytical concentration is on Roman motivation and decision making, rather than on the motivation and decision making of Rome's rivals.[92] Yet this did not prevent Polybius from passing judgment on the
diplomatic and political decisions made at Carthage. That judgment was
negative.

This comes out in Polybius's discussion of the Punic *deditio* (absolute
surrender) to Rome in spring 149. The Carthaginians performed the *deditio* to avoid the war the Romans were threatening over Carthage's military confrontations with Massinissa of Numidia.[93] Polybius has emphasized to his audience (in 20.9–10), and reemphasizes now (in 36.4), that
the Romans viewed *deditio* as a true surrender of all rights, property, and
people, which left the surrendered totally at Rome's mercy.[94] But though

90. This criticism is made repeatedly: see (in chronological order) Livy [P] 42.44.3; Polyb. 28.9.4; Livy [P] 42.59.7–11 and 60.5–7; Polyb. 29.9.12 and 17–18. On Livy 42.44 and
59–60 as deriving from Polybian material, see Nissen, *Kritische Untersuchungen*, 250–254.

91. As Welwei remarks on Polybius's criticism of Perseus's unwillingness to spend money
on the war (28.9.4 and 29.9.12), Polybius would have criticized as irrational the excessive
frugality of *any* statesman in such a crisis as Perseus faced (*Könige und Königtum*, 58). For
another Polybian attack on the general attitude of the Greek populace during the war as
"childish and excitable," see 27.10.

92. Pédech, *Méthode*, 196–97, goes so far as to suggest that Polybius viewed the actions
of Cato the Elder (a man he knew well) as the specific αἰτίαι of the war.

93. The undertaking of such a war with Numidia, crossing the Punic frontier, was a
violation of the peace treaty of 201. For convenient discussion of the background to the
crisis of 150/149, see Errington, *Dawn of Empire*, 256–66.

94. For discussion, see esp. Freyburger, "*Fides* et *potestas*, πίστις et ἐπιτροπή," 177–85;
also: Gruen, "Greek Πίστις," 50–68. The actual political results of a *deditio*, of course, varied
widely, and could include the "reconstituting" of a city or people totally intact and "free."

the Punic government agreed to the *deditio*, and even gave Rome three hundred aristocratic hostages (and later, immense amounts of valuable war equipment) as a guarantee of its willingness to accept the full implications of the surrender, in the end the Carthaginians did not accept all the Roman demands—which included the harsh demand that their city be destroyed. Thus the Carthaginians went to war with Rome anyway (36.5–7).[95]

Much modern attention has been given to 36.9, where Polybius claims to present four Greek views of this unusual situation. Yet scholars remain divided about which (if any) of the four different views represents Polybius's own.[96] In terms of understanding Polybius's attitude toward the events of 149, however, it may be better to focus attention not on 36.9 but on 36.5—where Polybius's opinion about what the Carthaginians ought to have done is more explicit. Yet except for Pédech, this is a passage that most modern scholars have tended to ignore.[97]

In 36.5, Polybius presents the advice given the Carthaginian people by Mago the Bruttian after the *deditio*, and praises it as "manly and statesmanlike" (ἀνδρώδεσι καὶ πραγματικοῖς, 5.1). The Carthaginians were already worried by the Roman demand for three hundred hostages, and by the fact that no guarantee about their city had been given (36.4.6 and 9). Mago argues that the time to have questioned these things was before the surrender—not now (5.3). Having performed the *deditio*, they ought now to accept any Roman order "unless it is totally oppressive and beyond what could possibly be expected."[98] In the latter case, they must still consider whether they should lay their country open to war and its horrors, or—in fear of the enemy's attack—yield to every order (5.4). But in any case, this was the last moment when such a decision could still be made (cf. 5.1). Polybius says that the Carthaginians, confronted by Mago's two choices, feared war more than anything else, and so they reluctantly turned over the three hundred aristocratic hostages to Rome (5.6).

Pédech believes that Polybius presents Mago as advising the Carthaginians simply to submit to Rome, accepting all the possible conse-

---

See now Nörr, *Aspekte des römischen Völkerrechts: Die Bronzetafel von Alcantara*, 39–50 and 72–101.

95. On the sequence of events here, the Polybian fragments are supplemented by App. *Lib.* 74–93.

96. See the debate between Walbank, "Polybius between Greece and Rome," 14–18; and Musti, *Polibio e l'imperialismo romano*, 55–56.

97. Pédech, *Méthode*, 199–200. Walbank has little to say about 36.5 in *Commentary* III: 657. It is not discussed in his *Polybius*, nor in Petzold, *Methode des Polybios*, nor by any of the scholars in *Polybe*, Entretiens sur l'Antiquité Classique 20 (Geneva, 1974).

98. ἐὰν μὴ τελέως ὑπερήφανον <ἦ> καὶ παρὰ τὴν προδοκίαν (5.4).

quences—and that Polybius approved of that position.[99] But in fact what Mago is advocating in 36.5 is *either* a clear-eyed acceptance of complete submission, *or* an equally clear-eyed decision for war—before the three hundred aristocratic hostages are turned over to Rome and (in Mago's view) the last irrevocable step is taken (cf. 5.1 with 5.5). This is why Polybius considers Mago's advice not merely statesmanlike but "manly" (5.1).

But as Polybius sees it, what the Carthaginians actually ended up doing was highly irrational. Having indeed surrendered the cream of their young men, and having later practically disarmed themselves at Roman demand (36.5–7), they *then* suddenly found the Roman order to abandon the city—a demand they had long suspected was coming (cf. 36.4.9)—intolerable, and decided instead to go to war. Polybius emphasizes here the irrational, emotion-driven behavior of the Punic mob (36.7.3–5). The result, of course, was not merely the destruction of the city of Carthage, but the annihilation of the Carthaginian people as a whole.

Thus within an analytical framework in which the aggressive motivations of the Romans constituted the underlying cause of the Third Punic War, Polybius still found room to stress the deleterious impact of certain Punic policies—and politicians. These policies and politicians were criticized not for being anti-Roman but for having been criminally unintelligent. The Punic confrontation with Numidia provided the Romans with the pretext for war they had long wanted;[100] the Carthaginians then, having surrendered unconditionally and having given over their best resources to the Romans, decided for military resistance under absolutely impossible circumstances. If Mago the Bruttian had had more influence, either the Carthaginians would have maintained their *deditio* to Rome (in which case the Punic people would have survived), or at least they would have gone to war far better prepared. In the latter case they undoubtedly still would have lost, but—having done the very best they could—they would have gone down to defeat with far more honor.[101]

99. *Méthode,* 199–200.

100. Polybius is especially critical of the Carthaginian politician Hasdrubal—a tyrannical buffoon whose most prominent trait is lack of judgment (ἀκρισία, 38.7.2)—and since Hasdrubal had been the leader in the original Punic policy of confrontation with Numidia (cf. App. *Lib.* 70–74), it is likely that Polybius blamed him for providing Rome with the pretext for the war. See Pédech, *Méthode,* 200.

101. Note Polybius's hearty approval of the military capacity of the Punic cavalry general Himilco Phameas, who fought very well against the Romans (36.8; cf. also App. *Lib.* 97 for previous successes). Pédech argues that Polybius's praise of Himilco derives from the fact that Himilco eventually surrendered to Scipio Aemilianus (cf. App. *Lib.* 108), and is part of an ideological structure in Book 36 emphasizing that there was only one choice—submission to Rome (*Méthode,* 200; cf. his comments on Mago the Bruttian, ibid., discussed above). But in 36.8 what Polybius is praising is Himilco's highly effective *resistance* to Rome; nor is there any specific praise of Himilco in *Lib.* 108 for surrendering. Hasdrubal surrendered to Aemilianus, too—and Polybius excoriates him for it (see 38.20 *passim;* cf. 38.8.–10).

To Polybius, an even more powerful example of irrational behavior in this period was that of the Macedonians. Rome had broken up the Antigonid kingdom into four separate republics after the Third Macedonian War.[102] But in 150 a pretender to the throne appeared—Andriscus the Pseudo-Philip—and the Macedonians flocked to him, overturning the Roman arrangements that had endured for two decades. The result was a new war, total defeat, and the extinction of any sort of Macedonian independence.[103] And in a famous passage (36.17), Polybius concludes that in his opinion, the behavior of the Macedonians here is not subject to rational analysis. They had been freed from the tyranny of kings, and they were enjoying freedom and peace (17.13); Andriscus reimposed autocracy, arbitrary taxation, exile, torture, and murder (ibid.); yet the Macedonians fought more fiercely for this man than they had ever fought for the real Antigonids (17.14). Anyone would be at a loss to explain this (17.15), and unfortunately one must therefore fall back merely on the mysterious workings of Fortune (17.1–3), or perhaps "madness sent by the gods" (17.15, twice). The point here is the terrible and deeply irrational political misjudgments made by the Macedonian people.[104]

Polybius's assessment of the political behavior of his own Achaeans in this period is similar. There was room to pity the Carthaginians, he says (evidently because in an ultimate sense they were victims of Roman aggression), but the disasters that befell the Greeks in this period were the result simply of their own gross mistakes (38.1.5). He argues that none of the famous defeats or misfortunes previously suffered by Athens, Sparta, Mantineia, or Thebes were shameful (αἰσχρόν), since they resulted either from ineluctable historical circumstance or from the unjust behavior of a larger state—conduct that brought shame only to the larger state (38.2.4–3.8).[105] Only disaster brought about by one's own folly, Polybius concludes, can truly qualify as shameful (38.3.7). And this is precisely what

102. For detailed discussion of the Roman peace settlement in Macedon after the war with Perseus, see Gruen, "Macedonia and the Settlement of 167 B.C.," 157–67.

103. For detailed discussion of the Roman peace settlement in Macedon after the war with Andriscus, see now Kallet-Marx, *Hegemony to Empire*, chap. 1; against Gruen, *Hellenistic World and the Coming of Rome* II: 434–36.

104. Polyb. 36.17 is obviously highly rhetorical, but Polybius's general attitude toward the events in Macedon in this period is confirmed by his highly negative comments on Macedonian behavior in 36.10.

105. Polybius's use of shame words, but only to describe the oppressive behavior of the larger states: ἔγκλημα and ὠνείδιζον (against Sparta after 404: 38.2.7, 2.12), ἄδικα καὶ δεινὰ (against Alexander: 2.14). The specific assertion that the defeated and oppressed incurred neither shame nor disgrace: 38.2.4 (οὐ μὴν ὄνειδος οὐδ᾿ αἰσχύνην), a sentiment repeated at 2.9 (τί δὴ τοῦτ᾿ αἰσχρόν;). On the moralism of this passage, see, briefly, Petzold, *Methode des Polybios*, 49; downplayed by Walbank, "Polybius between Greece and Rome," 23–24; and *Commentary* III: 685–86.

happened with the Greek states in the 140s, especially Macedon and Achaea (3.9).

In the case of Achaea, both the populace and their leaders were responsible for the shameful mistakes (38.3.11–13 and 11.10–11). Polybius's picture here was discussed in detail in Chapter V, and needs only a summary. The demagogues Diaeus and Critolaus—criminally stupid, perhaps even insane, and physical cowards to boot—drove Achaea into a perhaps unnecessary and certainly hopeless war with Rome over Achaean control of Sparta. The Achaean populace, misled by demagogic promises of social reform put forth by their leaders, had their passions inflamed against Rome (38.11.1–11, cf. 12.4), until—utterly losing control of themselves (16.1–2)—they, too, were in the end driven mad (16.7–8). It is easy to see why Polybius believed that the picture he drew of Achaea in Book 38 was a shameful one.

Not everyone will agree with this analysis of the origins of the war.[106] But for the present study, what is important is the purpose of the Polybian analysis itself. Despite Walbank, the point is not to justify Rome's victory, nor does it show that Polybius's sympathies lay basically with the Romans.[107] The opposite is proven by the fact that Polybius was apparently as critical of Diaeus and Critolaus for failing to conduct the war against Rome with the requisite energy and courage as he was critical of them for having (in his view) provoked it.[108] Nor is it the case that the excoriating depiction of Achaean politics in Book 38 demonstrates Polybius's deeply ingrained "ruthlessness," his inherent lack of sympathy for any loser on the world stage.[109] The opposite is proven by the care Polybius takes at the beginning of Book 38 to list those states that had indeed suffered catastrophic defeats in the past, or severe political repression, but which were *not* subject to shame or disgrace, and gained instead pity and respect (38.2.4–3.8).[110]

It would seem, rather, that in Book 38 Polybius was seeking to drive home two ideas. First, he was attempting to provide some sort of political explanation for the Achaean War. He wished to discount the role of Tyche, or Chance, as much as possible—though some modern scholars have in fact found this a quite persuasive solution; instead he focused

106. See, e.g., Gruen, "Origins of the Achaean War," 56, 58.
107. "Polybius between Greece and Rome," 16–20.
108. For Polybius's criticism of the "cowardly" behavior of Diaeus and Critolaus in 146, see Chap. VI, above. Note also Polybius's reference at 38.3.10 to ἀνανδρία ("unmanliness," physical cowardice) among the Greeks opposing Rome in this period. Compare Polybius's remarks about the lack of energy displayed by Antiochus III and Perseus during their wars with Rome (above, pp. 213–14 and 215–16).
109. So Walbank, *Polybius*, 178–79; cf. also Green, *Alexander to Actium*, 283.
110. Note here as well the emphasis Polybius placed on Roman brutality at Corinth in 146 (39.2).

on the negative impact of power-hungry politicians, and on the negative impact of the increasingly irrational conduct of the Achaean masses themselves.[111] And that was Polybius's second goal in Book 38: to give his audience a general lesson in the horrific consequences of irrational, emotion-driven decision making on the part of a small state. His anger at the Achaeans may have been especially sharp because these were his own people, and they had somehow failed to draw the lessons in "balance" he had already stressed as crucial for small states in the first fifteen volumes of *The Histories*.[112] But his anger was also didactic: he does not hide the faults of the Greeks, he says, because he hopes his audience will find an unpleasant story at least a useful one, helping prevent them from falling into similar errors in the future (38.4.7–8). But the error of judgment here is (again) not merely war with Rome. It is something broader: what happens when the necessarily careful politics of small states are overwhelmed by "madness."[113]

The values Polybius is asserting are well summed up at 38.1.8. The Carthaginians did not physically survive the disasters of the 140s; the Greeks did. But, Polybius says, the Greeks—not only totally defeated but also deeply shamed by the origins and nature of their catastrophe—are *not* in the end better off than the annihilated Carthaginians, "unless we put out of our minds all thought of the decorous and the noble [τοῦ καθή-κοντος καὶ τοῦ καλοῦ], and consider only physical, material advantage [τὸ συμφέρον]." The passage is obviously highly rhetorical. Yet the standards of judgment that it sets up for conduct, though idealistic, are not less important for that reason. Clearly, Polybius did *not* expect his (aristo-cratic) audience to put aside considerations of "the decorous and the noble" as the ultimate criteria by which behavior is judged. And, equally clearly, the historian's claim at 38.1.8 is that he deeply shares this sentiment.

THE SERVILE

The adherent of such a point of view would not be likely to approve of acts of servility on the part of individuals or states. However effective in a strictly utilitarian sense, such behavior would—by its very nature—be indecorous and ignoble, and therefore liable to condemnation. And if

111. On all these aspects of Polybius's thinking, see the acute analysis of Gruen, "Origins of the Achaean War," 46–47, 56, 58.

112. Cf. Eckstein, "Polybius, Syracuse, and the Politics of Accommodation," 277.

113. Cf. Shimron, "Polybius on Rome," 108: what made the Achaean leaders of 146 so contemptible to Polybius was *not* their goal, nor their lack of success, but rather their terrible misreading of the situation they faced. For a similar Polybian judgment, from much earlier in *The Histories*, see 2.7.2.

one examines Polybius's depiction of those who adopted policies of servility toward Rome, disapproval is exactly what one finds. The uniformly harsh assessment of such conduct is not based on a perception that it is stupid or ineffective (as with the cases of confrontation with Rome discussed above). Rather, Polybius's evaluation is based solely on a perception that servile behavior is naturally "unworthy"—that is, immoral.

In general, of course, Polybius condemned those who willingly "enslaved" themselves to *any* power, or who cooperated in the enslavement of others. This idea lies at the heart of his view that the Macedonians must have been insane in 150 to have exchanged republican freedom (ἐλευθερία) for enslavement (δουλεία) to Andriscus's tyranny (36.17.13). Hence, too, his bitter condemnation of mercenaries because they often work with tyrants to enslave free citizens (11.13.6), and his denunciations of those men who betrayed free citizens to the violent Macedonian warlord Antipater (9.29.3–4), or who allowed themselves to be set up as tyrants over their own cities in Macedon's interest (9.29.6).[114] Moreover, as was shown above, Polybius adopted an attitude of contempt toward the cities of Coele Syria (5.86.9–11) and toward Athens (5.106.6–8), when he described what he took to be their servile behavior toward Greek kings.[115] This is parallel to his repeated expressions of detestation for courtiers, because of the servile attitude that they adopted toward kings.[116]

Roman power was overwhelming—as even Philopoemen in Polybius is willing to concede (24.13.1). This fact, however, does not alter Polybius's attitude toward those who would "enslave" themselves. Thus Polybius's Philopoemen goes on to argue that the best policy for the weaker state is to continue to struggle diplomatically with Rome, asserting its independence even though it is physically overmatched and knows it (24.13.2–3); conversely, the worst thing in such a situation is to behave as if one were already a slave (cf. 13.4). Polybius gives this attitude his highest accolade: noble (καλήν, 13.8). And Polybius's assessment here matches well with his famous judgment of an even more extreme situation. War, he says, is a terrible thing (4.31.4). But war is not so terrible that one should submit to anything in order to avoid it—and in particular, one should not submit to the destruction of political freedom (ἰσηγορία, παρρησία, ἐλευθερία, ibid.).[117]

114. These last two passages are from a speech (and an Aetolian speech at that: Chlaeneas at Sparta in 210). But the destruction of the Macedonian-backed system of tyrants had been a major goal of Polybius's hero Aratus of Sicyon, so that 9.29 is likely to reflect an authentic sentiment of Polybius himself.

115. See above, pp. 196 and 207.

116. On Polybius's detestation of the behavior of courtiers, see von Scala, *Studien*, 45, with a good collection of evidence (e.g., 4.87.1–2; 5.50.14).

117. For detailed discussion of 4.31.4, see Chap. III, above. One may then ask why Polybius so strongly condemns those states and leaders who opposed Rome in war, espe-

The sincerity of Polybius's hatred of servile conduct is easily shown by the historian's bitter portrayal of those he judged to have adopted such conduct—that is, too obsequious a policy—toward Rome.

Before the Third Macedonian War (171–168), the outstanding example of such sycophantic behavior is that of the Achaean politician Callicrates, in 180 (Polyb. 24.8–10), and Polybius's condemnation of Callicrates—both on pragmatic and moral grounds—has already been discussed in detail.[118] In the aftermath of the Roman victory over Perseus, it was natural that the "evil trend" originating with Callicrates (24.10.8) would now intensify.

The first postwar example of obsequiousness is that of Astymedes of Rhodes, whom Polybius presents as having sought to protect Rhodian interests at Rome by begging, by tears, and—worst of all—by denunciation of other Greeks for anti-Roman attitudes (30.4 *passim*). "Who can fail to disapprove?", Polybius remarks; it was unmanly (4.16–17).[119] Again, the pro-Roman Greek politicians who come flocking with effusive congratulations to L. Aemilius Paullus after Pydna are the very same men who denounce their political opponents to Paullus as anti-Romans (30.13); the picture, coming from one of the victims of this process, is hardly intended to be flattering.[120] Indeed, in the case of Callicrates and the other Achaeans who followed his policy of obsequiousness toward Rome, Polybius continually emphasizes the anger and hatred felt against them—delighting in the story that respectable people refused to use the baths after they had, and that children in the streets called them traitors (30.29 *passim;* cf. 30.32.2). Later, Polybius explicitly calls the passing-away of the postwar generation of violent pro-Roman politicians a "purification" of Greece (32.5.2)—hardly the sentiment of a collaborator, or a historian intent on pleasing his Roman readers at all costs.[121]

The most detailed surviving Polybian condemnation of servility toward

---

cially after 150. Part of the answer with regard to the Macedonians and Achaeans is that those wars were provoked not so much by the tyrannical actions of Rome as by the misjudgments and irrationality of the weaker state (see above, pp. 219–21). As for Carthage, Polybius seems prepared to approve a war with Rome at the point when the Carthaginians fear that Rome's actions and demands will lead to the destruction of Carthage itself (see the crucial 36.5, discussed above, pp. 217–18).

118. See above, 203–5.

119. For detailed discussion, see Chap. IV, above. In a later embassy, when Astymedes ceases to attack other Greeks in order to win Roman approval, Polybius calls his behavior "better" (30.31.2). But even here he does not absolve Astymedes completely of the charge of servility (ibid.).

120. Lyciscus the Aetolian and Callicrates were both prominent in these embassies—and in denunciations given to Paullus (30.13.11). On Lyciscus, see Polybius's attack in 32.4.

121. Most of Polybius's depictions of these men are lost; but for an example, see his excoriating picture of Charops of Epirus (32.5–6).

the Romans, however, is his depiction of the visit to Rome of King Prusias II of Bithynia in 167. Polybius says that Prusias had already shown by his behavior toward the Romans that he was in no way worthy to be a king (οὐδαμῶς . . . ἄξιος, 30.18.2). When Roman envoys had visited his court (ca. 172), Prusias had met them with shaven head and in the costume of a liberated slave, proclaiming himself a freedman of Rome who wished in every way to endear himself to the Romans and imitate them (30.18.3–4). Polybius comments (18.4): "It would not be easy to find a statement more ignoble [ἀγεννεστέραν]." But this was only the prelude. When Prusias came to Rome in 167, first he prostrated himself before the Senate, then he saluted the *Patres* as "savior gods"—acts that Polybius calls impossible to surpass "in unmanliness, in womanishness, in fawning servility" (18.5). Later, in his interview with the senators, Prusias "did things that it would be improper [ἀπρεπές] even to mention" (18.6). All in all, the king showed himself in his dealings with the Romans to be "utterly contemptible" (18.7).[122]

Polybius does not appear to have had any inherent political bias against Bithynia,[123] so 30.18 seems enough, standing alone, to establish that Polybius viewed Greek diplomatic obsequiousness toward Rome as inherently dishonorable, and therefore unacceptable. But (as has just been shown) Polyb. 30.18 is only one of a whole group of passages of similar outlook in *The Histories,* from at least Book 24 onward. Indeed, Prusias in 30.18 was violating maxims of dignified conduct in dealing with the Romans—even when dealing with them from a position of weakness—that Polybius attributes to his own father, Lycortas (24.8.3–5), and to his childhood hero, Philopoemen (24.13.3–4), and that the historian even proclaims directly in his own words (24.10.11–12).

Moreover, it should be stressed that in strictly utilitarian terms, Prusias's visit to Rome in 167 was a success: the Senate awarded him several diplomatic concessions.[124] Yet this has no impact on Polybius. On the contrary, Polybius argues that Prusias's success involved the Romans themselves in disgrace; for, he says, it was precisely because Prusias showed himself to be "utterly contemptible" that the Romans gave him a kind reception (30.18.7).

This last comment points up another aspect of Polybius's analysis. The relationship between a hegemonial power and a weaker state is a fluid one, even a dialectical one, and is affected not only by the actions of the hegemonial power but also by the actions of the weaker state itself. Digni-

122. Polyb. 30.18 is also discussed in detail (in terms of the misogynistic terminology of the passage) in Chap. V, above. On the incident in 172, see Walbank, *Commentary* III: 441.

123. Note his praise of Bithynian "manliness" (36.15.2–3).

124. For detailed discussion, see Eckstein, "Rome, the War with Perseus, and Third Party Mediation," 437–42.

fied and steadfast behavior on the one side will encourage restraint on the other; servile behavior on the one side will encourage tyrannical behavior on the other (cf. 24.13.1–4, explicitly). Thus Prusias's conduct was not only immoral (in the sense of being "unmanly"); it had the practical consequence of unnecessarily increasing Roman tyrannical tendencies. And to increase tyrannical tendencies within a hegemonial power was something that Polybius had been warning against as early as Book 1. But Polybius warned against such a development because—as one would expect in an aristocrat—his political analysis was itself predicated on a "morality of independence." That is: the historian naturally viewed the growth of tyranny (any tyranny, including the tyranny of Rome) as a highly negative development.[125]

THE BEHAVIOR OF THE ROMANS

Polybius's acerbic comment on the Senate's conduct in the Prusias affair naturally raises the question of Polybius's general attitude toward Rome's behavior once the Romans had achieved hegemony in the Mediterranean. If Polybius was aware that the nature of any hegemonic relationship was in part determined by the behavior of the weaker state (see above), he was obviously even more alert to the less subtle impact on the nature of hegemony made by the actions of the paramount state itself. And it appears that Polybius's criteria for evaluating political conduct— partly pragmatic, but also partly moralistic—did not change when it came time to pass judgment on the hegemonic power.

One major obstacle to such a hypothesis has been a theoretical discussion of empire by the first-century-B.C. historian Diodorus—an analysis that some scholars have taken to be Polybian in origin. In examining the empires forged by Philip and Alexander, and then by Rome, Diodorus formulates the following general rules for gaining and maintaining empires (32.2):

> Those who wish to attain hegemony over others employ courage and intelligence to gain it, moderation and acts of kindness to extend it widely, and paralyzing terror to secure it.

The case of the Romans, Diodorus says, bears out these maxims. They created their empire by courage in war, and then extended it widely through the kindest possible treatment of others (32.4.4). Once they held hegemony over the entire world, they then secured it through terror— the destruction of many famous cities, including Corinth, Carthage, and Numantia (4.5).

125. Cf. Musti, *Polibio e l'imperialismo romano*, 44, 84–85, 145.

It is clear from Diodorus's language that he viewed such conduct as legitimate.[126] If Polybian ideas really do stand behind Diodorus here, then Polybius, too, accepted a policy of amoral political manipulation, and a policy of terror, as the legitimate tools of an imperial state. Here would be "Machiavellianism" indeed—and it takes on an even more sinister aspect when one remembers that *The Histories* were written by Polybius as a handbook of decision making for statesmen.[127]

In fact, however, though much in Diodorus's Books 30–32 is drawn from Polybius, there is little reason to think this the case with 32.2 and 4; rather, the ideas here are far more likely to be Diodorus's own. Touloumakos pioneered this direction in interpretation, pointing out, for example, that whereas Diodorus uses the destruction of Thebes by Alexander as an example of efficacious terror (32.4.3), Polybius says the opposite about this incident (38.2.13–14).[128] Again, Diodorus presents the abolition of the Macedonian monarchy by Rome as an example of efficacious use of terror (32.4.5)—whereas in Polybius himself (36.17.13), it is presented as an example of Roman *benevolence* toward the Macedonian people.[129] Moreover, Diodorus's discussion of the development of empires comes in the proem to Book 32, and it is precisely in such introductory sections that he is most independent of his sources, and personally creative.[130]

This thesis can be greatly strengthened by stressing another contradiction: between the ideas in Diod. 32 and Polybius's own reflections on the developmental stages of empire. But it is also vitally important to establish the nature of Polybius's reflections here because Walbank, though now accepting the non-Polybian origin of Diod. 32, has gone on to argue that nevertheless, Polybius's actual attitude toward imperial power *was* very close to the ruthlessness displayed by Diodorus.[131]

Polybius's general ideas on proper behavior by a hegemonial state first find expression in 7.11–14, his discussion of the early years of Philip V of Macedon. Polybius says that Philip, so long as he pursued policies based on honor (7.11.9, cf. 14.4), was extremely popular (7.11.9)—"the darling of the Greeks" (11.8; cf. 14.5). Polybius acknowledges here Mace-

126. Cf. Walbank, *Commentary* II: 246, for argumentation.

127. For this interpretation of Diod. 32.2, see Gelzer, "Nasicas Widerspruch," 290; Astin, *Scipio Aemilianus*, 52 and n. 3; Petzold, *Methode*, 63; Gabba, "Storiografia greca e imperialismo romano," 638 n. 34.

128. Touloumakos, *Zum Geschichtsbewusstein der Griechen in der Zeit der römischen Herrschaft*, 28 n. 28.

129. Cf. Ferrary, *Philhellénisme et impérialisme*, 336.

130. Cf. Sacks, *Diodorus Siculus*, 45 (on Diod. 32.2 specifically), and, in general, chap 1.

131. "Polybius between Greece and Rome," 20. Note, too, that some scholars still see the cynical Diodorus passages as Polybian: see, e.g., Vogel-Weidemann, "*Carthago Delenda Est: Aitia* and *Prophasis*," 82–83.

donian political hegemony, but stresses both its beneficial impact (cf. 7.11.7 and 14.5), and also the voluntary nature of the Greeks' submission to Philip's leadership (11.1 and 9). This was evidently Polybius's idea of what a hegemony ought to be.[132] But soon Philip began to engage habitually in treachery and violence against the Greeks. As a result, Polybius says, there was a devastating change in the Greeks' opinion of him— and a consequent undermining of Philip's political position (7.14.5). And Polybius sees this as only natural (κατὰ λόγον, 11.10). He explains (11.10–11):

> Since he totally reversed his previous principles of conduct, it inevitably followed that he should also totally reverse men's opinion of him, and that he should meet with totally different results in his undertakings than before.

One must stress, of course, that this formulation is precisely the opposite of Diodorus's understanding of the (efficacious) impact of a policy of terror (see above). Moreover, as has been noted earlier, Polyb. 7.11–14 is strongly moralizing in tone: Polybius not only condemns Philip's terrorism because it was counterproductive, he also condemns it as immoral conduct *per se*. Thus, before Philip's "transformation for the worse" (7.11.1), the basis of his policies had been "honor and good faith" (11.9), "principles of nobility and dignity" (14.4). But now he began to commit "enormous impious crimes" (13.6), including mass murder (14.2). He was guilty of "impiety toward the gods" and "crimes against men," always acting unjustly (14.3–4). In the end he was a savage tyrant—if not, indeed, a werewolf thirsting for human blood (13.7–8). This is not the language of a Machiavelli.[133]

The theme of 7.11–14—that it was best, for both practical and moral reasons, for political hegemonies *not* to change from their original principles of benevolence to those of terror—receives even more emphasis in Polybius's comments on the Carthaginians in Spain once they believed their hegemony had been permanently established by victories over Rome in 211. The theme of moral degeneration appears first at 9.11.1, where Polybius remarks that "the Punic commanders, having mastered the enemy, proved unable to master themselves." In their success, they gave way to greed, and to sheer love of domination (πλεονεξία, φιλαρχία, 11.2); thus they alienated their Spanish subjects (11.4). A volume later the theme is reiterated. Describing again the alienation of the Spanish

132. Polybius's vision here fits well, of course, with the developed Hellenistic theories of "good" kingship: see Welwei, *Könige und Königtum*, 133–37; and now Walbank, "Monarchies and Monarchic Ideas," 81–84.

133. For detailed discussion of the Greek terminology and the moralizing implications of 7.11–14, see Chap. IV, above.

subjects by Punic oppression and haughtiness (10.35.6–8), Polybius remarks that the same thing has happened to many people; for while success in public affairs and victory over the enemy are great things, it requires much more caution and skill to use success well (καλῶς, 10.36.1,
cf. 36.2). Thus the Carthaginians in Spain, thinking they had achieved
victory, began to treat their subjects with arrogance (36.3), with the result
that their friends and allies became instead their enemies (36.4). And this
served the Carthaginians right, Polybius says (36.4–5):

> For they thought that there was one method to gain dominion, and another
> by which it is maintained; they had not learned that those preserve their
> supremacy best who best adhere to the principles by which they gained and
> established it.

Polybius continues that it is obvious that the best way to acquire power is
through beneficent action and the holding-out to others of the prospects
of further benefits (10.36.6). However (36.7):

> When, having attained their desire, men begin to act wickedly [κακῶς] and
> to treat their subjects tyrannically [δεσποτικῶς], it is only natural that with
> the change in character of the rulers, the attitude of the ruled should
> change as well.

In this passage, as in 7.11–14, Polybius is indicating what happens
when a hegemonial state changes its original principles of behavior. But
in 10.36 Polybius is arguing explicitly that a hegemonial state should *not*
change its principles of beneficent action once it has attained supreme
power, or it courts danger (as happened to the Carthaginians). The problem that Polybius saw, however, was that the degeneration of hegemony
into outright tyranny was a natural phenomenon attendant upon great
power. The idea appears not only very strongly here in Books 9–10, but
it is prefigured in 7.11–14, and appears again in 15.24 (with respect to
monarchies in general, though the focus is once more on Philip V), and
as late as 38.2 (with respect to Spartan behavior after the Peloponnesian
War). This pessimistic view of the corrupting effects of power was in line
with the thought of many other Greek historians.[134] What Polybius is urging in 10.36 is that his audience be aware of this corrupting trend, and
fight *against* it.

It should be clear that Polybius's expressed opinions in 7.11–14 and
10.36—though they have not appeared in recent discussions of Diod.
32—absolutely rule out Polybius as the source for Diodorus's ideas on
empire. They cannot be Diodorus's source, because the principles of political action and reaction in 7.11–14 and 10.36, and what amounts to
Polybius's explicit advice to rulers in 10.36, are in fact precisely the oppo-

134. Cf. Ferrary, *Philhellénisme et impérialisme*, 334.

site of what Diodorus says. Polybius's maxims are instead typically conservative in tone: he advocates caution in prosperity (10.36.1), steadfast *constancy* to original principles (36.5–6), self-restraint and the avoidance of oppression of one's subjects (9.11.1), and the avoidance of arrogance in success (10.35.8).[135]

The goal of such advice is certainly in great part pragmatic: avoiding oppression of one's subjects and remaining faithful to one's original principles of beneficent action is the best way to maintain one's hegemony (10.36.5 and 7). Erskine, in the most recent discussion of 10.36, asserts that the passage is in fact solely concerned with such political expediency, and has not the slightest element of moralizing.[136] Yet both Polyb. 10.36 and its precursor 9.11 (like Polyb. 7.11–14) contain much moralizing terminology—from the condemnation of the Punic generals for their failure to control themselves (9.11.1), right through to the advocacy of the avoidance of evil (κακῶς), in the form of tyranny, at 10.36.7. One may compare Polybius's disquisition in 15.24 on the behavior of kings: they begin by treating their adherents as friends and allies, but as they become accustomed to power they come to treat their adherents tyrannically (δεσποτικῶς, 24.4). By doing so, they perhaps gain some immediate practical advantage (τὸ συμφέρον), but they betray the standards of nobility of conduct (τὸ καλόν, 24.5).[137]

The maintenance of a reasonable hegemonic political situation, in Polybius's view, thus depends to a significant extent on the moral character evinced by the ruler, or by a hegemonic state and its people. The possession of empire produces not merely a political challenge, but a moral one.

What, then, is Polybius's view of the quality of Roman hegemonic behavior? The question is highly controversial, since much of the final portion of *The Histories*—where this issue would have been addressed extensively—has been lost. But it has already been argued in detail in Chapter IV above that Polybius's depiction of senatorial policy even in the highly fragmentary Books 30–33 shows strong signs of having been decidedly negative, on grounds of growing Roman immorality. To Polybius, the Senate in the post-Pydna period was consistently guilty of violating the canons of just behavior (τὸ δίκαιον) merely for the sake of political expediency. This is his judgment of Roman policy toward the Attalids (30.1–3), the Ptolemies (31.10), the Punic disputes with Numidia (31.21),

135. For the traditional moral conservatism embedded in the terminology here, see Edmunds, "Thucydides' Ethics as Reflected in the Description of Stasis," 75–88.
136. *Hellenistic Stoa*, 185.
137. For detailed discussion of this interpretation of Polyb. 15.24.4–5, see above, Chap. IV. Philip V, of course, is Polybius's specific subject in 15.24—and he was a man whom Polybius thought was morally incapable of withstanding the temptations of great success (evidence: see above, n. 84).

the Seleucids (32.1–2; cf. 33.18), and toward his personal friend Demetrius of Syria (31.2 and 11). These judgments conform perfectly to Polybius's acid comment on the Senate's positive reaction to the disgracefully
subservient behavior of Prusias II of Bithynia (30.18, discussed above).

In a certain mood, Polybius can trace the very beginnings of this Roman moral degeneration back as far as the Hannibalic War, and the ex-
propriation in 211 of the art treasures of Syracuse—an untoward example of greed (9.10).[138] Yet Polybius's view is that even into the 190s,
most Roman aristocrats were still honest and virtuous (18.35.1). The historian does claim that a new "evil trend" began in Rome in 180, with
the embassy of Callicrates (24.10.8; cf. 10.10). But it would seem that for
Polybius, the first important sign of a harsh and cynical new Roman attitude toward power was the decision of the Senate to approve the policy
of Q. Marcius Philippus in winter 172/171, which mandated deceiving
King Perseus about the possibility of a negotiated peace, while in reality
merely playing for time in order to complete Roman preparations for
war (Livy [P] 42.39–43). To judge from Livy, Polybius condemned the
policy as truly dishonorable—a radical departure from the old ways of
Rome (42.47.5–9).[139] It is this policy that then recurs in the politically
expedient but unjust actions Polybius listed in Books 30–33 (see above).
Moreover, the transformation, once begun, was unlikely to be reversed,
for Polybius's repeatedly expressed opinion of the younger generation of
Roman aristocrats of the 150s was that they were deeply corrupted by
Rome's success and new wealth (31.25 and 35.4).

A similar deep concern for deterioration already comes through in
Polybius's depiction of the reaction of L. Aemilius Paullus to the appearance of King Perseus before him as a prisoner (29.20: summer 168). In
Polybius's historical schema, of course, the destruction of the Macedonian
monarchy marks the definitive emergence of Rome as master of the
world (see 29.21).[140] But L. Aemilius Paullus's reaction to this epochal
event is—to Polybius's approval—one not of elation but of warning. He
tells his officers (and especially the younger ones) that they should learn
from what they are witnessing as Perseus surrenders (29.20.1). And the
lesson is: never to be improperly boastful in the hour of success, never to
be arrogant, or merciless toward anyone—never, in sum, to place confi-

---

138. Cf. Gruen, *Hellenistic World and the Coming of Rome* I: 348. Note that this first sign of
Roman degeneration comes just five years after 216, where Polybius places the acme of the
Roman state and culture. In fact, "corruption" of the Roman populace was detected by
Polybius as early as 232 and the land reform of C. Flaminius (see 2.21.7–9); i.e., its roots
existed even before Rome's acme was reached.

139. For detailed discussion of Livy [P] 42.47, see Chap. IV, above.

140. Cf. Polyb. 1.1.5 and 3.1.9–10.

dence in the permanence of present prosperity (ibid.). Paullus continues (20.2–3):[141]

> For it is especially in moments of personal or community success that we
> should reflect upon the opposite extremity of fortune; only thus—and then
> only with difficulty—can a man prove moderate [μέτριον] in the hour of
> good fortune.

No doubt L. Aemilius Paullus did say something like this to his officers
in summer 168.[142] Nevertheless, it was Polybius's choice to insert Paullus's
words here, in a highly dramatic context. Thus at the climax of Roman
success the historian has injected a stern warning against the arrogance
of power, and placed it in the mouth of one of his great heroes.[143]

Paullus was in fact given a second dramatic speech, at the close of Book
29, in counterpoint to the public celebration at Rome of his great victory.[144] The occasion was Paullus's public mourning of the deaths of his
two sons—deaths that had occurred, ironically, during the public celebra-
tions. Since Paullus had given away his other two sons in adoption, this
meant the end of the family: "No Paullus is left in my house, save one old
man" (Livy [P] 45.41.12). But Polybius evidently had Paullus consciously
accept this tragedy in front of the *Populus,* in the hope that in this way
the vengeance of Tyche for too much success might be diverted from the
Roman People onto himself (Livy [P] 45.41.9 and 12). He feared that
Tyche would never let the acme of Roman success last permanently
(41.8).[145]

The depiction of Paullus as tragically bereft at the very moment of his
greatest success must have been intended by Polybius as another literary
set piece and a moral lesson. For Polybius employed Paullus here—
against the background of the actual moment of the establishment of
Rome's world empire—both to indicate the correct demeanor for the

141. Similar Aemilian sentiments in Livy 45.8.6–7, Diod. 30.23.1–2, and Plut. *Aem.* 27.2–
4—where Aemilius urges especially his younger officers not to give in to "the empty pride
and insolence" attendant upon total victory.

142. Polybius knows Aemilius spoke in Latin (29.20.1), and it is likely that he got his
information here from Aemilius's son Scipio Aemilianus, who was present: see Walbank,
Commentary III: 392.

143. The theme of Aemilius's consciousness of the mutability of Fortune evidently also
occurred somewhat earlier, for when Aemilius saw Perseus's envoys appearing as suppliants
at his camp after Pydna, he himself "wept for the lot of man"—since not long before, Perseus had found even rule over Macedon insufficient for him (Livy [P] 45.4.3; on Polybian
origin, see Nissen, *Kritische Untersuchungen,* 272).

144. The original Polybian text has not survived, but versions of it are found in Livy
45.41, Plut. *Aem.* 36, and Diod. 31.11.

145. Cf. Plut. *Aem.* 36.3–6. On the Polybian origin of Livy 45.41, see Nissen, *Kritische
Untersuchungen,* 278.

wise and knowledgeable statesman, and to point out the ironies that Tyche always manages to inflict upon mortals.[146]

Diodorus appends to his version of Paullus's speech in Macedon the comment that so long as Rome's empire over the world was directed by men with attitudes similar to those of Paullus (i.e., modest, moderate, generous), Roman hegemony attracted no hatred (30.23.2). It is possible that this passage is based on a Polybian comment, since it is immediately preceded and immediately followed by Polybian material.[147] And one should be well aware of the pessimistic implications of such a remark—for Polybius had emphasized to his audience that Paullus, a man of old-fashioned virtues and simplicity, was already in his own time an increasingly anachronistic figure at Rome (18.35.4–5; 31.22).[148] In any case, Polybius certainly felt comfortable having at least some Greeks argue specifically, in the context of the Carthage crisis of 149, that the Romans had now departed from the original principles of conduct through which they had attained hegemony, and were becoming instead treacherous and tyrannical (36.9.5 and 9–10).[149] And as Carthage itself finally burned, Polybius would of course depict Paullus's son Scipio Aemilianus—who stood out anachronistically among *his* generation because he possessed virtue (31.25.3 and 9–10)—as warning of the impermanence of Roman success, and even envisaging the destruction of Rome itself (38.21–22). Polybius approved of Aemilianus's sentiments, as he had approved of the sentiments of Paullus after Pydna, finding them "statesmanlike" and "insightful" (νουνεχής, 38.21.1). But it would now appear that they really represent a *re*assertion of an important Polybian theme about Rome and Rome's possible future—a theme that takes on an even darker tone in view of the warnings and indications in the last ten books of *The Histories* that Roman deterioration was proceeding apace.[150]

146. That Polybius intended Paullus's speech to be a dramatic high point in *The Histories* is rightly noted by Reiter, *Aemilius Paullus*, 39 (who, however, finds the result to be a congeries of unimpressive platitudes).

147. Cf. Reiter, *Aemilius Paullus*, 57. Diod. 30.23.1–2 is Aemilius's speech to his officers in Macedon; 30.24 is an account of Rhodian diplomacy at Rome based on Polyb. 29.19.

148. On Polybius's depiction of Paullus as a man of old-fashioned virtue who was an increasing anachronism at Rome, see Reiter, *Aemilius Paullus*, chap. 1. But Reiter tends to dismiss this as simply Polybius's pro-Paullus propaganda. I would argue, rather, that the picture of Paullus is meant very seriously, and has broad implications for Polybius's thought.

149. Ferrary rightly urges caution in assuming that any of the four opinions in 36.9 is Polybius's own (*Philhellénisme et imperialisme*, 327–34); the passage may well be an attempt to express the complexity of the crisis of 150/149. For our purposes, what is interesting is that the theme of "departure from original principles" appears as a serious argument within the four arguments presented in 36.9.

150. See Astin, *Scipio Aemilianus* 286, for the idea that Scipio's emotions at the destruction of Carthage (which, after all, he had engineered) were necessarily mixed, and that Polybius has chosen—for his own purposes—to emphasize one of those emotions over all

If Polybius's verdict on Roman rule (the proclaimed major purpose of the last ten books) was to be rendered using L. Aemilius Paullus's character as the measure, then the passing of men like Paullus, and their increasing replacement at Rome by lesser men, confronted Polybius's audience with an uncomfortable image. The terribly fragmented condition of Books 30–39 may not permit us certainty concerning Polybius's final judgment on the nature of Roman rule in the Mediterranean. But at least it should now be clear, from the above discussion, what Polybius's standards of judgment were.

CONCLUSION

In 12.13.8–11, Polybius recounts the accusations made by the historian Demochares against Demetrius of Phalerum, who ruled Athens for the brutal Macedonian warlord Cassander between 317 and 307. Demochares charged that Demetrius prided himself on his statesmanship, as if its only purpose was to insure abundance in the marketplace and everything available cheaply; yet the very pomp and ingenuity of Demetrius's processions through the city were a symbol that all that was noble (καλόν) in Greece was under the tyranny of Cassander. Polybius thought Demochares' charges "not trivial" (13.9), and he implies that Demetrius ought to have been ashamed of his policy of tame submission to Cassander (αἰσχύνεσθαι, 13.11). It is a typical Polybian expression of the moral value he placed on independence.

The purpose of this chapter has been to show that remarks such as those in 12.13—where not even a polity's prosperity outweighs the moral cost of tame submission to power—were in fact typical of Polybius. For the historian was a man who believed that love of freedom was inherently noble (φιλελεύθερον καὶ γενναῖον, 2.55.9), that an attitude of servility was inherently base (ἀναισχύντως καὶ ἀνελευθέρως, 28.9.4), and that, in the last resort, the preservation of freedom was worth war, no matter what the odds (4.31.3–4).[151]

Yet Polybius also believed that the task of the statesman was to manage affairs so that the grim choice between slavery and war could be avoided—and this within an international system where only power

---

others: not joy or satisfaction at great accomplishment or the destruction of a great enemy of Rome, but fear that in the end something similar might well happen to Rome itself, at the hands of some unknown, powerful enemy.

151. On Polyb. 2.55.9 (praise of the Peloponnesian city of Cleitor), see Chap. IV, above. Polyb. 28.4.9 is from a speech by the Aetolian statesman Pantaleon against Lyciscus in 170, in a situation so closely resembling Polybius's condemnation of Callicrates' conduct in Book 24 that it is obvious that the historian approves of Pantaleon's sentiments. On Polyb. 4.31.3–4, see the detailed discussion in Chap. III (and above, p. 222 and n. 117).

ruled (cf. 5.67.11). In such a system—as Polybius well knew from the history of his own Achaean League—the hegemony of great states was natural, while the options open to weaker states were limited. The mature statesman realized this, and acted with care. It was the elite—not the masses—who knew what the real difference was between war and peace (12.25k.6–7), and their responsibility was consequently heavy.[152]

In Polybius's world, the primary diplomatic responsibility of the elite was management of relations with Rome. Yet what the historian found, and condemned, was that time after time, the leaders of weaker states had led them into unnecessary and disastrous wars with the Romans, acting from strategic misjudgment, and/or simple irrationality and passion. Polybius's condemnation of such politicians has, in turn, led to charges that he himself had capitulated intellectually to Roman power. But his own idea of "the best policy" toward Rome (24.10.4 and 11.12, 27.15.10) was one that, while acknowledging the hard fact of Roman power, was sternly resolved not to increase Roman hegemony by servility or sycophantic diplomacy. To stand up for one's legitimate rights with the Romans, wrestling with them diplomatically even while knowing that one was physically overmatched: this was "noble" (καλήν, 24.13.8, cf. 10.4). Conversely, he did not hesitate to condemn overly submissive conduct toward Rome—or toward *any* great power (cf. 5.106.7–8)—on grounds that, no matter what momentary advantages it brought in the real world, such behavior was morally disgusting and "unworthy." Prusias of Bithynia (30.18) is only the most obvious example here.

Polybius therefore applied both pragmatic and moralizing criteria in judging the conduct of weaker states. And he employed those same criteria in judging the conduct of the greater states—including Rome. He sharply criticized the moral decline he perceived among the Romans. The moral virtues that had helped Rome win her worldwide empire (and that the historian found very attractive: see especially 6.52–58) were in the process of being destroyed by the very power and wealth the Romans had achieved (31.25, 35.4); men of rectitude such as L. Aemilius Paullus were becoming anachronistic figures (cf. 18.35); the Senate was coming more and more to adopt policies that were cynical and unjust. It was, Polybius thought, the all-too-natural result of success (cf. 6.57 and 10.36).

Thus if relationships between great states and small were fluid and changeable, so too was the character of Rome itself. The specter was that Roman hegemony was becoming (and would continue to become) gradually more oppressive—helped along both by Rome's own increasing arro-

---

152. The maxim here is that of Timaeus; but Polybius clearly accepts it, and in fact views it as obvious (12.25k.9).

gance, and also by serious Greek mistakes (both of military confrontation and oversubmissiveness). Yet Polybius also knew from Achaean experience that relations between a weaker state and a stronger state could change in more than one direction. Circumstances altered, and with them the balance of power—not necessarily to the advantage of the stronger (as Philip V learned with regard to Achaea between 220 and 200). But if circumstances were always altering, then what was required above all from Greek politicians was patience and steadfastness. Hence Polybius's advocacy of "balance" as "the best policy." It avoided both direct military confrontation and diplomatic oversubmissiveness, both of which (by different routes) led only to intensified Roman domination; it was mature and cautious; it was moral; and it had the additional advantage of playing for time, as the weaker state fought its long rear-guard action to preserve its portion of *eleutheria*. And with time, anything might happen. Rome's policies were falling into the arrogant pattern of the Carthaginians in Spain (cf. 10.36), and Polybius believed that despite all the practical virtues of the structure of the Roman state, it was as tied as any other polity to the degenerative "wheel of constitutions" (see especially 6.57). Perhaps Aemilius Paullus and Scipio Aemilianus were right to have doubts.[153]

The basic dilemma produced by this doctrine, however, was that it required constant compromise with Roman demands; for while oversubmissiveness was disgusting, a certain willingness to give in to Rome (not without a diplomatic struggle) was often a practical necessity. How many compromises were possible before one was totally compromised—and *eleutheria* effectively lost? Polybius said that there were some things that could not be borne, and required war instead (4.31.3–4); but how was a statesman to know when that point had been reached? All one can say is that in the cases discussed in the last ten books of *The Histories,* Polybius did not believe that such a point had yet been reached—except perhaps with Carthage in 149. The problem here was unresolvable; one may doubt, at any rate, that Polybius ever resolved it. It lay not in some deep Polybian instinct for "collaboration," but simply in his desire to give his audience the best possible advice in a very difficult situation.

The resulting picture of the world and the political possibilities it offered was not a particularly happy one. Yet Polybius's deepest feelings

153. Note that Polyb. 6.57—like 9.11, on the Carthaginians in Spain—is especially focused on the weakening of a state or empire because of internal quarreling among an increasingly degenerate ruling elite. Shimron, "Polybius on Rome," 115, argues that Polybius viewed part of his (bitter) task as being to demonstrate to the Greeks that the Romans were there to stay. But this may be a retrojection of our own knowledge of the future of Polybius's world back anachronistically onto the views of the historian himself. He was a person who believed profoundly, as did so many Hellenistic Greeks, in vicissitude and change.

about moral duty were founded precisely on that perception—on the perception of the intractable difficulties and inescapable temptations with which human beings were constantly surrounded. The question of how Polybius's general sense of human limitations informed the general moral (as well as the political) perspective of *The Histories* now becomes the focus of the final section of this study.

EIGHT

Optimism and Pessimism

Videtur autem non minus philosophi quam historici personam induisse.
—BODIN (1566)

INTRODUCTION

Every historian, consciously or unconsciously, brings to the writing of history a view of human nature, and of human life and its possibilities. This view subtly informs almost every sentence a historical writer produces; it is the historian's deepest ideology. No ancient writer of history is richer in comments on human nature and on human life and its possibilities than is Polybius. He continually interrupts his narrative to comment personally on the general characteristics of human beings and on human possibilities—to comment, to advise, often to warn, often to criticize, occasionally to praise. Yet there have been few modern attempts—systematic or even merely impressionistic—to describe Polybius's general approach to life.

The lack of scholarly effort in this direction has probably resulted in good part from the fact that modern scholars, desperate for solid information about a crucial but ill-attested period in the development of European civilization (namely, the rise of Rome to world power), have concentrated their attention mostly on exploiting Polybius as a good source of facts. This is the heritage of nineteenth-century German historical *Wissenschaft;* and of course it is not a bad thing in itself. But the result is that a major element in *The Histories*—one crucial for understanding the work and for understanding Polybius's ultimate purposes in writing it—has been consistently slighted.

Among those few modern scholars who have attempted an overall evaluation of Polybius's view of life, there are clearly two schools of thought. One school sees Polybius as basically an optimistic person. Thus Wunderer asserts that Polybius, although well aware of human foibles and weaknesses, had a healthy and positive view of life ("ein starkes . . .

237

Lebensbejahung"), far removed from any weak impulse of despair over the world ("Weltangst").[1] Similarly, Pédech gives Polybius a powerful faith in human reason as the central motive force of the historical process— "an unlimited confidence in the intellectually superior portion of the human being to dominate reality." And, Pédech concludes, "un rationaliste est facilement optimiste."[2] On the other hand, von Scala presents a Polybius with a somewhat darker personality; he emphasizes Polybius's deep sternness as an observer of and commentator on human affairs.[3]

Though von Scala's work is in fact the oldest of the above studies, it is the thesis of this chapter that it has come closest to Polybius's true point of view. In particular, though Pédech's *Méthode historique de Polybe* is in many ways a magisterial work, one may reverse Pédech's formulation: Polybius's problem was that he had only a *limited* confidence in the power of human rationality, to dominate either the historical process or even the basic drives of human character.[4]

Moreover, although Polybius's outlook on human character and possibilities was never sunny at any time, it seems possible to trace a trend of growing pessimism in *The Histories*. Perhaps down as far as Book 15 and the end of the narrative of the Second Punic War, Polybius's world— though a terribly difficult and demanding place—remained for him a place where rationality and human heroism could still make an important impact. By the final volumes, however, the world of *The Histories* has become ever more dark and chaotic, increasingly populated by degenerate or even insane politicians, and dominated by their irrational policies—or by inexplicable events, and a capricious Fortune (Tyche). At this stage in his writing, Polybius himself seems often on the verge of abandoning his rigorous attempt to impose a framework of understanding upon the experience of his age.[5] Yet ultimately Polybius did not give way to complete despair; he labored on, motivated by a fierce desire to finish *The Histories* (39.8.2–3; cf. 3.5.7). Since one of his main goals in writing was the education of statesmen, and this idea occurs even in the final volumes (cf. 38.4.8), it is clear that Polybius even at the end continued to place some hope in the ameliorating impact of education. But given his perceptions of human weakness and the difficulties of the world, it can only have been a slim hope.

1. *Polybios*, 3, 14, 18, 19; cf. *Psychologische Anschauungen*, 28, 32.
2. *Méthode*, 600, 603; cf. "Idées religieuses de Polybe," 68. For the "rationalist-positivist" Polybius, see also, briefly, Mioni, *Polibio*, 75, 102; von Fritz, *Mixed Constitution*, 351. Most recently: Podes, "Handelserklärung bei Polybios," 226.
3. *Studien*, 62; cf. 39, 41, 45.
4. Cf. esp. Chaps. V, VI, and VII above.
5. On Polybius's growing pessimism, see the comments of Gruen, *Hellenistic World and the Coming of Rome* I: 348; cf. Petzold, *Methode des Polybios*, 60–63. This theme is explored in detail below.

HUMAN CHARACTER

Polybius's ambitions were large; that is shown by the very fact of his attempt to write a universal history encompassing the entire Mediterranean world. It is not surprising that such a writer would also offer his audience an evaluation of human character and its working within the historical process. And Polybius viewed human character as complex and malleable, but fundamentally weak.

One common ancient view of human psychology was that every human being had a fundamental nature that was unchangeable; if people acted differently at different times and under different circumstances, this was because the different times and circumstances revealed the "real" nature that previously had been hidden.[6] Polybius explicitly rejected this view (9.22.7−10). Instead, he thought human character was both complicated and malleable.

This emerges most strikingly in his discussion of Aratus of Sicyon at the beginning of Book 4. Aratus, of course, was one of Polybius's great heroes.[7] Nevertheless, in this discussion Polybius finds fault with him severely, because although Aratus possessed many political and even military virtues, in Polybius's opinion he came close to being a physical coward when confronted with set-piece battle (4.8.1−6). And the contradiction here is explained by the following assertion (8.7−8):

> There is something multiform [τι πολυειδές] about the human personality [ταῖς ψυχαῖς]. Nor is this a surprise: it is a fact familiar to all those willing to pay attention.

Hence, Polybius says, not only does the same man have talents in one thing but not in another, but even in very similar things the same man will have differing ability: intelligent in some, dull in others, audacious in some, cowardly in others (4.8.8). This complexity, Polybius continues, explains why he will be found making contrary pronouncements about the same man—a phenomenon, the historian admits, that may take some readers aback (4.8.12).[8]

This emphasis on human internal complexity seems a bit contradicted by a formulation in 9.22–26, based on Polybius's contemplation of the personality of Hannibal. Here Polybius argues that it is very difficult to detect the truth about the natures (φύσεις) of public men, because these men act under the complicated influence of complicated and changing circumstances and different friends and advisers. It is the complexity of

6. On the traditional view, see Walbank, *Commentary* II: 151; and *Polybius*, 93. It is most famously expressed in Tac. *Ann.* 6.51.6, on the emperor Tiberius.

7. For discussion, see Chap. VII, above.

8. See also 1.14.7–8, and 16.28.4–9.

these influences—and *not,* Polybius says, that one nature can be the source of such contradictory behavior—that explains, for instance, how Cleomenes III of Sparta could be an excellent king, a ferocious tyrant, and a charming and courteous personality, all at the same time (9.23.3–6). The same complexity of circumstances explains the complex behavior of Agathocles of Syracuse (23.1–3), and Phillip V as well (23.9).

Yet the difference between these passages and the one in Book 4 is not really as sharp as it appears. Polybius evidently thought that although the human personality often contained inherent contradictions, there was also a *limit* to the intensity of contradictions that could originate within a single individual. In Aratus's case that limit was not reached (a man good at surprise attacks was not good at withstanding set-piece battle). In Cleomenes' case, for instance, that limit *was* reached—and so a different explanation for his behavior had to be offered.[9]

Indeed, the influence of complex and changing circumstances, and of varied friends and advisers, could even change one's "nature." Thus the strategic difficulties Hannibal faced in Italy, along with the influence of evil advisers such as Monomachus, not only did violence to Hannibal's true nature, causing him to act cruelly (9.26.1); in the end these pressures actually changed his nature, hardening it (φύσιν . . . μετετίθετο, ibid.).

In short, Polybius believed that individual "nature" was not only many-sided, but was also only part of the total human personality that individuals eventually presented to the world; the total personality was also heavily the result of external pressures. Thus one fundamental and crucial characteristic of human beings for Polybius—in contrast to the views of many ancient thinkers—was their sheer malleability. As Walbank says, this is a quite sophisticated view of human character, not out of step with modern developmental psychology.[10]

The malleability or plasticity of complex human character has serious implications for Polybius's understanding of human possibilities (see below); but it is only one of the aspects of human personality that Polybius underlined. From his frequent generalizations about human beings, one can actually gain quite a detailed picture here. And it appears that while the historian does point to a few positive human qualities that are widespread, his negative generalizations about human character far outnumber such positive references.

Among positive qualities, Polybius seems to have been struck—to be-

9. For a good discussion of the contrast between 4.8.7 and 9.22–26, see Walbank, *Polybius,* 93–96.

10. *Polybius,* 96. Note also Wunderer's formulation: Polybius gives φύσις a very wide range of action, yet he does not see it as decisive, because natural disposition (whatever it may be, and however complex) can be brought to fruition only by circumstance and "practice" (*Psychologische Anschauungen,* 24–25; cf. 27).

gin with—by a perception that humans respond to kindness and tact, often with long-term loyalty. It is this human trait, he says, that explains the enduring loyalty of the Spartan populace to Cleomenes III, even after that king had been driven into hopeless exile (4.35.7). Similarly, at 31.26.9 Polybius implies that people naturally admire generosity, thinking it noble (καλόν).[11]

Second, the historian believes that human beings have a natural compassion toward people who are in great difficulties or who are suffering from oppression. This human tendency, he says (φύσει τῶν ἀνθρώπων), explains the popularity of Eumenes II of Pergamum among the Greeks after the Third Macedonian War—for the Greeks felt he was being unfairly treated by Rome (31.6.6). Similarly, it was natural sympathy for the underdog that led to Perseus's popularity in Greece when he began to defeat the Romans—like the sympathy of the crowd for the underdog at a wrestling match, Polybius says (27.9).[12]

Third, Polybius believes that those who have committed evil deeds are often tortured by bad consciences. Thus his comment on the fate of the Roman-Aetolian agent Zeuxippus, one of the murderers of the Theban politician Brachyllas (18.43.13): "For there is no more terrifying prosecution witness, no more fearsome an accuser, than the conscience that resides in each person's mind."[13] A similar point is made at 23.10.2–3, where Polybius describes the elderly Philip V as haunted by the Furies because of his past misdeeds.[14] Polybius's belief here seems related, in turn, to a belief—which, however, appears only once in the extant text—that people have a natural and very powerful sense of justice (31.16.1–2).[15]

The most important of the positive human qualities to Polybius, however, is the instinctive human openness to truth. The tone here is set in a famous passage at 13.5.4–6:

It seems to me that Nature has ordained that Truth should be a mighty goddess among men. . . . At least, when everything conspires to crush her, and every specious argument is arrayed against her, she somehow finds her way into men's souls [τὰς ψυχάς]. Sometimes she shows her power immedi-

11. The subject matter is the generosity of Polybius's friend Scipio Aemilianus; but the remarks made at 4.35.7, in such a different context (Cleomenes III, the enemy of the Achaean League), suggest that Polybius is sincere here.

12. A similar sentiment: frg. 192 B-W (context unknown). Cf. also 38.2.14, on the general pity evoked by the fate of the Thebans, unjustly destroyed (ἄδικα) by Alexander.

13. Walbank, *Commentary* II: 609, conclusively demonstrates the correct context of this passage (see Livy [P] 38.28.10). The moral implications are stressed by Wunderer, *Polybios,* 12 n. 18.

14. On this passage, see Walbank, "A Polybian Experiment," 59–62.

15. ἥ τε τοῦ δικαίου φύσις ἔχει μεγάλην δύναμιν.

ately; sometimes, after being obscured for a long period, she finally prevails, and crushes falsehood.

The context of this Polybian "hymn to Truth" is certainly polemical: it is part of an attack on Heracleides of Tarentum, a sinister secret agent of Philip V, whose misdeeds were eventually discovered.[16] But manifold other references indicate that Polybius did indeed believe in the natural power of truth to penetrate human consciousness. Thus Anthiochus III is presented as instinctively knowing that Hannibal speaks the truth when he recounts the story of the oath he took never to be a friend of the Romans (3.12.1); the troops of P. Cornelius Scipio (consul 218) instinctively recognize the truth of his remarks on the importance of the upcoming battle (3.64.11); the Achaean populace instinctively accepts the simple and truthful words of Philopoemen, rejecting the long and fancy speeches of his opponents (11.10.1–6). Indeed, Polybius says that because of Philopoemen's truthfulness, the affection felt for him by the Achaean people lasted long after his death (39.3.1).[17]

Finally, Polybius is certain that human greatness can be achieved— although only with great effort, and although the capacity of such greatness to affect the world remains limited both by Tyche (Fortune) and by physical circumstances. The most explicit surviving remark on this human capacity for greatness is—interestingly enough—Polybius's assessment of Hannibal at the height of the Second Punic War. Here was one man in charge of the entire Punic War effort, managing not only his own personal campaign in Italy, but also bringing his will to bear with great force (via lieutenants) simultaneously in Spain, Sicily, Greece, and Illyria as well (9.22.1–5). Polybius comments (22.6): "Such a great and wonderful product of Nature is a man with a mind duly fitted by its original constitution for the undertaking of any project within human power."[18]

But the achievement of human greatness such as this is by no means easy. It requires hard work: the acquisition of fortitude and temperance (ἀνδρεία καὶ σωφροσύνη, 6.48.4), presumably by strenuous early training (as we know Polybius emphasized in the case of Philopoemen). Only in

16. For the context, see Polyb. 13.5.6; with Walbank, *Commentary* II: 416. Walbank tends to dismiss the passage as mere rhetoric.

17. Note the parallel with the long-term Spartan affection for Cleomenes, stressed by Polybius (above, n. 6). Similar passages on human ability to recognize truth (or sincerity): Polyb. 3.108.2, 12.25h.4, 15.17.1–2.

18. Polybius's admiration for Hannibal's energy and skill as he goes about his attempt to destroy Rome is yet more evidence of the historian's broadly based and essentially apolitical standards for judging human conduct (see above, Chap. VII). It hardly fits with the image of Polybius as the "quisling and collaborator," most recently put forth by Green, *Alexander to Actium*, 279–81.

this way can an individual not be overmastered by evil tendencies originating within, or by forces pressuring him from without (ibid.).[19]

And the achievement of human greatness seems all the more difficult to Polybius because the historian believes strongly that most people are, if not actually evil in character, then fundamentally weak, and therefore subject precisely both to evil internal impulses and the powerful pressures of environment and circumstances. This dark view finds expression—once again—in the frequent generalizations about human beings that Polybius persistently inserts into *The Histories*.

Polybius provides a convenient catalogue of human weaknesses at 3.81.4–9, a passage already discussed in detail in Chapter VI. This list of weaknesses, which Polybius stresses are characteristic of many men (πολλοί, 3.81.4 and 5), includes indolence and lack of energy, uncontrollable drunkenness, uncontrollable sexual lust, cowardice, stupidity, rashness, uncontrollable anger, vanity and arrogance. These are faults that Polybius finds not only widespread, but deeply shameful.[20]

The common denominator in the above list is human psychological turbulence, and this is a theme to which Polybius returns repeatedly. Uncontrollable anger (ὀργή), for instance, has the power to determine even the most important of events, including the instigation of both the Hannibalic War and the Syrian-Aetolian War—the wars that led to Roman domination of the entire Mediterranean.[21] Again, *The Histories* are rife with instances of shameful or inexplicable panic. No one is immune: not soldiers or generals, not the civil populace or its leaders.[22] Sloth and inactivity are repeatedly underlined. Soldiers suffer from it constantly;[23] and Polybius sees it as a special temptation of the leadership class.[24] As for drunkenness, there is no ancient writer of history whose comments on heavy drinking are so frequent or so negative—or who provides so many examples of its negative effect.[25] The psychological weaknesses outlined

19. Passages expressing a similar opinion on fortitude, temperance, and the surmounting of difficulties: 3.4.5; 5.8.1–3.

20. 3.81.6 (μετ' αἰσχύνης), and 81.7 (ὄνειδος).

21. For detailed discussions, see Chaps. V and VII above.

22. On the behavior of the soldiery, see Chap. VI, above. Cowardice among generals: Aratus of Sicyon (Polyb. 4.8.5–6), Hasdrubal the leader of Carthage in the Third Punic War (38.20), Diaeus and Critolaus in the Achaean War (discussed in Chap. VI, above). Panic among civilian populations and/or leaders: 3.85.7–10 (Rome); 3.118.6–7 (Rome); 9.6.1 (Rome); 30.9 (Rhodian leaders); 36.7–8 (Carthage).

23. For detailed discussion, see Chap. VI, above.

24. See the comments on Ptolemy IV (5.87.3), Attalus I (18.41.5–9: he avoided the dangers here), and Antiochus III (20.8), and the general statement at 3.81.4.

25. For Polybius on drinking and drunkenness, see the detailed discussion in the Appendix, below.

in 3.81 (and proclaimed there to be very common) thus recur consistently in the later text. The resultant picture of human character is quite disturbing.

But there is more. Human psychological turbulence also finds expression in a tendency toward violent fluctuations from one emotion to another. This phenomenon, too, appears repeatedly throughout the Polybian text: among the populace of Punic cities (1.82.8–9), and among the populace of Carthage itself (1.87.1; cf. 36.7); among Romans (3.103.1), Rhodians (15.23.4–6), Boeotians (20.6.6–12), and, of course, Aetolians (20.10.9); among generals (C. Terentius Varro: compare 3.110.2–3 with 116.13), and among kings (Antiochus III, 8.20.9; Prusias II, 32.15).[26]

This tendency toward violent fluctuations in emotions is exacerbated by gullibility: for although Polybius had faith in an ultimate human openness to the truth (see above), in a certain mood he also insists that humans are easily and repeatedly deceived.[27] Related to this is the human propensity for superstition. Polybius attributes it to sheer impatience with rational explanations (cf. 33.17.1–2); impatience, indeed, is yet another psychological weakness common "in all men" (πᾶσιν ἀνθρώποις, 3.112.5). Thus Polybius stresses how common is the belief in miracles (16.12.2–11)—and superstitious fear of lunar eclipses (29.16; cf. 10.2.10). And his contempt for this human weakness comes out in a bitter statement about omens, prodigies, and miracle stories at 12.24.6: "Because of ignorance, inexperience, and poor judgment, many men [πολλούς] are, so to speak, absent when present, and blind with their eyes open."[28]

But some aspects of human character as portrayed by Polybius are not merely weak. Some aspects he finds positively evil, or insane.

First, greed: for money, for power. "Lust for wealth is the peg for every vice," Polybius says; "I ask myself, does it not make fools of us?" (29.8.10–9.1). Such avarice leads directly to self-destructive acts: stupid treachery (33.5.2–4), or unrestrained looting by soldiers who forget about the enemy (10.17.1–2)—and even plunge into fire, in order to retrieve gold (11.24.11). The king of Cappadocia loses his throne because of his rapacious extortion of money from his own subjects; he fell victim here to his

---

26. Cf., briefly, Wunderer, *Psychologische Anschauungen,* 17.

27. See 12.25d.6–7; 18.40; cf. 29.17.2.

28. A similar sentiment: 12.28a.10. On Polybius's views regarding superstition, see Pédech, "Idées religieuses de Polybe," 35–36; on miracles, 58. Polybius does view religious belief—when not carried to excess—as a positive force in society, tending to hold society together (6.56.6–15, 16.12.9); and he even praises leaders who can manipulate the religious feelings of the masses for benevolent purposes (10.2.8–12). Such manipulation may be necessary because, according to Polybius, "men are not all philosophers," but just the opposite (6.56.10).

passion for wealth, "as not a few men have" (32.11.1). Thieves, in their greed, fall out, Polybius says (4.29.4)—and his example is two monarchs (Philip V, and Scerdilaidas of Illyria). Indeed, at one point the historian indicates that humans are simply thieves by nature (12.4.13). And it is clear that Polybius considers such behavior not merely counterproductive in a pragmatic sense (cf. 32.11.1), but shameful, too: that is shown by his extreme reluctance to attribute avarice to a great man such as Hannibal (10.25–26).[29]

Greed for power is even worse. It threatens to tear apart royal families and whole kingdoms: the Attalids, the Ptolemies, the Seleucids, the Antigonids.[30] It threatens to tear apart republics as well, for greed for power (τὸ φιλαρχεῖν, 6.9.6) is the origin of tyranny, and it is the primary motivation for the treachery of citizens to their own polity (18.14.9). It often succeeds in destroying the stability of international relations as well—as Polybius explains in his harsh condemnation of the plot of Philip V and Antiochus III to dismember the Ptolemaic domains, now ruled by a child (15.20). In this passage Polybius indicates how the "unrestrained lust for power" can reduce human beings to acts of total dishonor, to the level of beasts (20.3–4). Moreover, he believes that such hunger for power only grows with success; it is a principle of human behavior (1.20.1 and 2.31.8).[31]

Conversely, Polybius also believes that wealth and power—or indeed, any great accomplishments at all—tend strongly to provoke jealousy and envy in others. Thus he praises the Spartan general Xanthippus for leaving Carthage in 255 immediately after his personal leadership had saved the city from Rome (1.36.2–3): "This was a prudent and sensible decision on his part; for brilliant and exceptional achievements tend to give birth to the deepest jealousy and venomous slander."[32] Again, Polybius praises Hiero II of Syracuse because his restrained style of life kept him clear, in fifty-four years of rule, "of that envy [φθόνος] that is wont to be provoked by greatness" (7.8.4). The Romans, by seizing the art treasures of Syracuse, attracted to themselves "that envy [φθόνος] that is wont to follow those who have great possessions" (9.10.6). Indeed, Polybius takes it as

29. Cf. also Polybius's comments on the greedy Cretans Bolis and Cambyses (8.36.9), and on Alexander of Isus (21.26.10).

30. The Attalids: cf. 18.41.10; 22.20; 30.2. The Ptolemies: see 31.10 and 17 (part of what was evidently a long and detailed discussion). The Seleucids: see Polybius's detailed account of the rebellion of Achaeus in Book 5. The Antigonids: see the highly dramatic—and ultimately unavailing—speed Polybius gives to Philip V, addressing his feuding sons.

31. On the implications of these two passages, see Walbank, *Commentary* I: 72–73.

32. Note that this highly negative comment on human character occurs extremely early in the text of *The Histories*.

natural that Greek kings should all be fiercely jealous of one another—
and that this should be a cause of great international turmoil (29.7.2).[33]

The ugliness of this image of human interaction is completed by Polybius's belief that those who *do* gain great wealth and power have a strong
tendency, for their part, to become arrogant, debauched, and cruel. The
general rule is established in 18.41.4: "Wealth is not only a great source
of jealousy [but] also contributes in the greatest way to the corruption of
both body and soul. For few are those spirits who can withstand its dangers."[34] The primary Polybian example of the dangers of debauchery
inherent in great wealth is the depraved Ptolemy IV (5.87.3). The primary Polybian example of the arrogance and cruelty of power is the career of Philip V of Macedon (as Polybius understands it). But in Polybius
the problem of arrogance and cruelty in success is hardly Philip's alone.
Thus the Tarentines suffer from "the arrogance caused by prosperity"
(8.24.1); the same holds true of the Punic commanders in Spain after
their great victories in 211 (10.36.3; cf. 9.11.1–3)—and here Polybius says
that "the same thing has happened to many people" (πολλούς, 10.36.1);
speakers consistently warn the Romans of this danger.[35] And this warning
makes sense, for Polybius has explicitly told his audience another general
rule: polities that achieve great success have a natural tendency to develop much *hubris* and arrogance (6.18.5).[36]

As an aristocrat, Polybius believes that fine ancestry can help guarantee
fine behavior (see, e.g., 11.2.3). Yet because he is also so aware of the
corrupting tendencies of power and wealth, Polybius sees the moral degeneration of an aristocracy into a depraved and oppressive oligarchy as
a natural human phenomenon (6.8.3–6)—just as he believes that those
born to wealth and power will tend to squander it (6.1.8 B-W).

The dark situation here is exacerbated by yet another human trait:
just as people react with loyalty to kind treatment from the powerful
(4.35.7), so they tend to react with hatred to the cruel and arrogant treatment of the powerful. The problem is that in Polybius, there are far more
examples of oppressive conduct by the powerful (with resulting hatred)
than of kind conduct (with resulting loyalty).

It is for these reasons (cruelty, arrogance, oppression) that the Libyans
hate the Carthaginians (1.72.1–5), and later the Spanish do (10.35.6–
36.7). It is for these reasons that the Greeks switch from love of Philip V
to hatred of him (7.11–14). This is why the Messenians hate Philip (8.8.1–

---

33. He was not wrong; on the social and economic reasons for the ferocity of Hellenistic
royal rivalries, see esp. Austin, "Hellenistic Kings," 454–65. On the theme of jealousy (φϑό-
νος) in Polybius, see in general Wunderer, *Psychologische Anschauungen*, 19.

34. On this passage, see Wunderer, ibid., 7.

35. On this latter point, see the detailed discussion in Chap. VII, above.

36. ὃ δὴ φιλεῖ γίνεσϑαι ("as is wont to happen").

2), and later hate the Achaeans (cf. 23.15.3). It is why the Alexandrian populace hates the Ptolemaic prime minister Agathocles (cf. 15.25.22–24: ὕβρεως, ὑπερηφανίας); and it is why the allies of the Spartans hated them after the Peloponnesian War (6.43.4). It is why the masses hate the elite when the aristocratic state has degenerated into an oppressive oligarchy (6.8.4–9.1). It may also be that Polybius indicated a growing hatred of Rome itself in the Mediterranean for these very reasons (cf. Diod. 30.23.2).[37]

And at its worst, Polybius says, human behavior descends to the level of beasts (ἀποθηριοῦν, θηριώδης). This is most prominently the case with mercenary troops—whom Polybius tends to view as bestial anyway, as a result of the harshness and cruelty he believes typical of their upbringing.[38] But cruelty and oppression can indeed drive all men to this level of savagery (see 6.6.9, 6.10.5, 23.15.3)—as can fear (32.3.7–8). This sort of behavior occurs not only among the Aetolians (4.3.1, 20.10.15), but among kings (Philip V and Antiochus III: 15.20.3), and major politicians (the vicious—and pro-Roman—Charops of Epirus: 30.12.3). It even occurs among Polybius's own Arcadians, when the latter are wracked with civil strife (4.21.6). Given the right circumstances, no one is exempt.

Indeed, at the height of his anger at the human race, Polybius can call humans even *worse* than animals. In two cases, this is merely a highly rhetorical expression of his exasperation at human stupidity (5.75.1–6, 15.21). But the third case is meant more seriously as a comment on general human character. Traitors persist in their treasonous behavior, Polybius says, although the usual fate of traitors is well known (18.15.14). Therefore, humans—who are supposed to be the most intelligent of animals—may with good reason be called the least intelligent (15.15), for animals are slaves merely to their immediate bodily wants, whereas humans get themselves into deep trouble not only from these, but from irrational desires as well (15.16). Here Polybius is offering a thoughtful reason (the impact of humans' greedy imaginations) for perceiving humans to be more uncontrolled and uncontrollable than animals, in a context where both destruction and self-destruction are emphasized. The fourth example is similar. In commenting on the irrational and savage actions of the anti-Punic mercenaries during the war of 241–238, Polybius exclaims that "no beast becomes at the end more wicked or cruel than a man" (1.81.7). And once more, a serious explanation is offered: the beasts do not have minds capable of being utterly twisted by the experience of harsh and brutal upbringing (81.10). Here human malleability leads to total corruption of the soul (81.9).

37. For discussion of the possible Polybian origins of Diod. 30.23.2, see Chap. VII, above.

38. For discussion of the many passages here, see Chap. V, above.

Greedy, grasping, jealous, arrogant, cruel, beastlike (or worse): this picture of humanity is grim indeed. And it is this picture that is the most widespread in *The Histories*.

The Polybius emerging from the above discussion seems almost the polar opposite of the optimistic thinker presented by Wunderer and Pédech.[39] But Polybius's view of human character was not totally bleak. There are at least a few glimpses in *The Histories* of a faith in natural human goodness (see above); and, because Polybius did believe deeply in human malleability, the human material (though inherently weak and potentially very irrational and savage) could nevertheless be trained in the right direction—through correct education (παιδεία). In this way the condition of the world could be alleviated. Perhaps the best example of Polybius's thinking here is the formal training in body, mind, and moral spirit that Philopoemen received as a young man, and that enabled him to accomplish so much that was noble.[40]

Obviously, the formal study of history could be only one part of such an all-encompassing and necessary *paideia*—a specialized part, aimed primarily at an elite of political leaders. This elite of soldiers and statesmen (primarily Greeks) was the main audience for whom *The Histories* was written. Indeed, Polybius states repeatedly that his main purpose is the education—and even the reform—of this elite of political men.[41]

But the nature of Polybius's educational project needs to be clear. To be sure, in many cases Polybius is intent merely upon offering pragmatic or technical advice to his audience: for example, on the value of cavalry in battle (3.117.5), on the value of a knowledge of astronomy and geometry for a general (9.14–20), on the value of Acarnanians as allies (4.30.5).[42] Yet one must stress that Polybius is intent as well on the inculcation of moral precepts, and standards of conduct. At 2.61.2–3 he is explicit: it is the historian's duty not merely to chastise criminal behavior (παρανομία), but—much more so—to call the audience's attention to noble and just behavior (τὰ καλὰ καὶ τὰ δίκαια). And although this comment does appear in a polemical context (an attack upon the historian Phylarchus), it cannot be explained away as mere momentary rhetoric, for the fact is

39. See above, pp. 237–38 and nn. 1–2.
40. For detailed discussion of Philopoemen's education, see Chap. V, above. On the Greek view of the powerful moral impact that it was possible to achieve with education, see, conveniently, Rahe, "Primacy of Politics in Classical Greece," 285 and n. 62 (with texts). On the importance of education according to Polybius, see von Scala, *Studien*, 18–19; Wunderer, *Psychologische Anschauungen*, 26–27; Welwei, *Könige und Königtum*, 137–39; and now esp. Meissner, "Polybios," 338–46.
41. On Polybius's intended audience, see the discussion in Chap. I.
42. Sacks, *Polybius on the Writing of History*, 132–34, argues that such pragmatic, political and technical advice is the only real "benefit" Polybius intended his audience to draw from his work. Cf., earlier, Siegfried, *Polybios*, 80–81.

that it does not stand alone. Rather, as this study has sought throughout to show, the moralizing theme is one to which Polybius returns again and again, in an attempt to inspire his audience to noble effort, and to teach them how to avoid shameful conduct.[43]

Indeed, the purely intellectual-technical purposes of *The Histories* are closely entwined with the moralizing purpose right from the opening statement of the work. Polybius says that he is seeking to inculcate the *paideia* necessary for an active political life (1.1.2). By this he means not only the important intellectual knowledge to be gained from the study of past events, but also a sort of moral fortitude as well (ibid.), for: "History is the truest and indeed the only method of learning how to endure the vicissitudes of fortune bravely and nobly [γενναίως]." That latter purpose cannot be achieved merely from cold inculcation of military science and political technique. This is why Nietzsche took Polybius as the paradigm of those history writers who seek to teach through moral exemplars.[44]

From this perspective, Polybius's belief that men can learn from the study of history takes on particular importance for the question of his optimism or pessimism about the human race and the historical process. One does not try to teach by reiteration of moral examples unless one thinks (or hopes) that the audience can in some way be reformed in their conduct in specific terms of ethics—to learn to seek "the noble" (τὸ καλόν).

Did Polybius actually believe that this goal could be accomplished? He certainly believed that lack of correct education and training—and/or improper general upbringing—was often responsible for savage behavior among humans.[45] Indeed, Polybius believed that even the reading of a "bad" book could cause the audience to adopt the faults of the book's author (12.26d.5: Timaeus). The logical corollary of such thinking is that, conversely, proper education—again, because of human malleability—could be morally beneficial. Thus he believes that the "beastlike" Cynaethans can be turned back into human beings through *paideia* (4.21.11). That is also his point in a passage concerned with "practicing" to tell the truth (6.11a.7). And that is his explanation for why he includes in *The Histories* a description of the character and early training of his hero Philopoemen (10.21.1–4). Many volumes later, it is his explanation for why

43. See esp. 9.9.9–10 and 16.22a.7 (discussed in Chap. I, above); there are, of course, many other such passages (see also below).

44. *Advantage and Disadvantage of History for Life*, 15; cf. Avenarius, *Lukians Schrift*, 23–24; and now esp. Meissner, "Polybios," 330–32, 337–38, 349–50. So also Wunderer, *Psychologische Anschauungen*, 32 and 38. Denied by Sacks, *Polybius on the Writing of History*, 132–34 (see n. 42, above). Polyb. 1.1.2 is one of the few passages in *The Histories* (like 2.61.2–3) where a moralizing statement by Polybius is taken seriously by Walbank (*Commentary* I: 16).

45. See 1.81.9–10; 4.20–21; 6.1.2; 7.14.6; frg. 112 B-W.

he has written the encomiastic epitaphs of Philopoemen, Hannibal, and
Scipio Africanus (a Greek, a Carthaginian, and a Roman—all presented
together); it was done to inspire all men "to attempt noble deeds": πρὸς
τὰ καλὰ τῶν ἔργων (23.14.6).⁴⁶

An impressive list of statements. Nevertheless, it also seems that Polybius believed that any such improvement (especially moral improvement)
through *paideia* (including the *paideia* offered by *The Histories*) could be
accomplished only by persistent, strenuous effort—and it was the sort of
effort of which he thought most people incapable. If the great avenue to
improvement of human conduct lay through education and the provision
of inspiring examples, the great obstacle to improvement was a pervasive
human weakness of will.

Thus Polybius thought that even the most technical self-improvement
through education—for instance, learning to read—could be achieved
only through great effort and determination, and that this was a prospect
that most humans found daunting. Many people, he says, find the very
concept of reading not merely difficult but impossible at the beginning
(10.47.4). The way to proceed is through persistence, and carefully chosen incremental steps, for things do become easier with practice (47.4–9;
the steps are outlined). The historian concludes the discussion with an
exhortation: "Thus one should never abandon anything useful simply
because of the difficulties that reveal themselves at the outset" (47.11).
But such an exhortation would hardly be necessary unless Polybius
thought that there was a great human tendency, when confronted with
the difficult task posed by *paideia*, to do exactly that.⁴⁷

If the acquisition of a mere technical skill presented such psychological
obstacles, then one would expect that reform of character in the direction
of the καλόν—a much more difficult and subtle task—would present
even greater psychological obstacles. And that is precisely what Polybius
indicates.

The theme of the difficulty of achieving excellence first appears in
Book 5. Polybius is attacking those writers who, like himself, claim to
write universal history, but who—unlike himself—produce works that
are extremely short and lacking in detail (5.33.1–5). He then appends a
generalizing comment (33.6–8):

46. Compare with 6.55.4, where the purpose of Roman funeral practices and heroic
stories is to inspire the young πρὸς τὰ καλά τῶν ἔργων. For the powerful impact of education,
see also 6.11a.13, with the comments of Wunderer, *Psychologische Anschauungen*, 24.

47. The disquisition on reading occurs in the context of Polybius's advocacy of his own
system of fire signaling, which (like reading) is very difficult at first, though in the end (he
asserts) very useful. Walbank, *Commentary* II: 261, speaks of Polybius's confidence in 10.47
in the virtues of practice. The confidence is there; but the problem is Polybius's doubt that
many people possess the steadfastness of will to maintain a program of practice in the first
place. See von Scala, *Studien*, 5; Wunderer, *Psychologische Anschauungen*, 22.

It is extremely easy to talk of engaging in the greatest enterprises, but by no means easy to achieve anything of excellence [τῶν καλῶν]. To promise is open to anyone possessing audacity; to achieve is rare, and falls to few in this life.

If this were the only passage where the difficulty of achieving the καλόν were emphasized, one might dismiss the sentiment here as mere polemical rhetoric. But the repeated appearance of this theme elsewhere suggests that the passage is meant seriously.

Thus at 8.8.3–9, Polybius, in discussing the panegyrics of Philip V produced by his court historians, acknowledges that there may be situations of such pressure that the difficulty of maintaining a principled and moral position is too great for many men—and here he is even willing to forgive them.[48] The theme of human weakness is reiterated in 11.8, where he chastises the Achaean officer class for being unwilling to engage in the intensive study and practice needed to become proficient in the military art. But he is not really surprised at their laziness. Most men, he says (οἱ πολλοί), do not even *attempt* to imitate the inner qualities of those who have achieved great things, but content themselves with imitating their outer trappings (in this case, fancy uniforms: 11.8.7).[49] This same theme reappears in 16.20, where Polybius holds out little hope that his own work will ever receive a large readership, because of its very seriousness; most people prefer the pretentious and showy instead of the truthful and useful (20.3–4).[50]

In Book 18, Polybius returns to the theme of how in humans the wish to be great often remains just that—a wish. In discussing the desperate military-political situation facing Scopas the Aetolian in Alexandria in 196, he remarks that Scopas gave way to sloth and indecision, whereas Cleomenes III, when faced with an even more desperate situation in Alexandria in 220, at least attempted glorious action (18.53.3). The historian attaches another generalizing comment to this comparison (53.1): "Many men [πολλοί] crave after bold and glorious deeds [καλῶν], but few dare actually to attempt them."

Scopas, of course, was an Aetolian—but 18.53 is no mere anti-Aetolian

---

48. A similar Polybian willingness to forgive the failure of achievement in historical writing, this time because of the difficulty in finding out the complete truth, occurs at 16.20.1–2. But note that there Polybius views the ability to *achieve* such mastery in historical writing, and over the truth, as καλόν (20.2). And of course there are passages where Polybius is by no means willing to grant pardon to inaccurate historians: 12.7.6, 12.12.4–7.

49. Compare Polybius's comments on the psychological obstacles humans confront at the mere thought of beginning the merely technical task of learning to read: 10.47.11, discussed above.

50. For human confusion of the real and the false, the good and the bad, see also 12.25d.6–7, 22.19.3–4.

polemic. That is shown by yet another Polybian exhortation against sloth, couched in very similar language, found at 27.20.3. The context is completely unknown, but the message is unmistakable:

> Many men [πολλοί], it would seem, are desirous of doing what is honorable [τῶν καλῶν), but it is only a few who venture to attempt it; and of those who do, rare indeed are those who persevere in their duty [τὸ καθῆκον] to the very end.

Even Walbank reluctantly admits that in view of the appearance of τὸ καθῆκον here, this passage must be taken to be a moralizing comment.[51] Indeed, the passage introduces a new complication into Polybius's thinking about the possibilities of human self-improvement; not only is the beginning of such a program difficult (so that for many people, there remains only the abortive wish), but perseverence in it is even more difficult.[52]

In 29.26, the moralizing theme found in 27.20 returns with great emphasis, and in exactly the same pattern. The passage has already been discussed above, in Chapter IV. It is yet another generalizing comment on human nature, based this time on Antiochus IV's decision to attack Egypt in 168 despite his recent formal agreement not to do so. The passage is a severe condemnation of Antiochus for his immorality. Polybius says that Antiochus's behavior demonstrates the correctness of the proverb of Simonides that "it is hard to be good" (29.26.1), and continues in his own voice, expanding Simonides' insight (26.2):

> For it is easy to have impulses toward noble behavior [τὰ καλά], and even to persist in those impulses up to a certain point; but to be steadfast in this under every circumstance, holding nothing to be more important than honor and justice [τοῦ καλοῦ καὶ τοῦ δικαίου]—that is difficult.

Thus the conclusion to draw is that Polybius took the psychological obstacles to the human pursuit of the καλόν and the δίκαιον very seriously, and that he believed those psychological obstacles were as difficult to surmount near the very end of the effort as they were at the beginning. Indeed, this theme persisted right through to the last volumes of *The Histories,* for in Book 38 Polybius contrasted the brave words of the Punic leader Hasdrubal (his vow to die with Carthage, a vow that was καλόν: 38.8.9) with his ultimate cowardice and surrender (8.10; cf. 38.20). As

---

51. *Commentary* III: 320.
52. The difficulty for humans in persevering in a task had already been underlined by Polybius at 16.10.3–4 (Philip V in his campaign of expansion in 201), and 16.28.1–2 and 9 (Attalus and the Rhodians, in their struggle against Philip).

always in Polybius, words are easy for humans, but deeds are extremely difficult to accomplish.[53]

"It is hard to be good." The picture of humanity drawn by Polybius is made even bleaker by his indications that when faced with actual failure to achieve, people tend to blame everyone but themselves. This was true of Perseus of Macedon, Polybius says (28.10), and he appends yet another generalizing comment:

> It seems to me that it is an easy thing to blame others and to detect their mistakes, but that it is the most difficult thing in the world to do everything that one can oneself, and to be thoroughly aware of one's own behavior.

A similar—and generalizing—comment appears in Polybius's description of the angry reaction of Orophernes of Cappadocia to his deteriorating political situation, for which he blamed his advisers, instead of his own savage greed, which had alienated his subjects (32.11.8–9).[54] And in fact the cases of Perseus and Orophernes are just two examples of a general rule about humans that Polybius had already laid down some twenty volumes earlier, in explaining that the source of the popularity of certain writers is the ferocity of their attacks on others (12.25c.1–3). Such savagery, Polybius says, plays directly on a major human weakness (25c.4–5): "And it seems to me that it is just the same in literature as in life as a whole; for there, too, it is very easy to find fault with others, but to behave without fault oneself is difficult."[55]

Several conclusions emerge from the above examination of Polybius's understanding of human character. First, it is clear that he thought deeply about human psychology, and thought he had much to tell his audience about it.[56] Polybius's observations reveal, second, that he possesses a sophisticated theory of human personality, which stresses its complexity, the multiplicity of forces that can influence it, and its great potential malleability. But third, it appears that Polybius's view of human character is quite dark; though he occasionally points to the existence of certain widespread human virtues, these seem overwhelmed within *The*

53. For detailed discussion of Polyb. 38.20, see Chap. II, above. Note that in Polybius's conception, Scipio Aemillianus—in contrast both to Hasdrubal and to his political rivals at Rome—is a man of deeds, not empty words (ἔργῳ πρὸς λόγον, 31.29.11).

54. For the historical context, see the discussion in Walbank, *Commentary* III: 533. The date is ca. 158/157.

55. The moralistic tone of this passage has rarely attracted the attention of scholars. Discussion of 12.25c.4–5 is missing from Walbank, *Commentary* II: 387, and in his *Polybius,* Sacks discusses it only in relation to the possible rearrangement of the fragments of Book 12 (*Polybius on the Writing of History,* 199–200); it is even missing from Petzold, *Methode des Polybios,* despite Petzold's interest in Polybian moralizing.

56. This, indeed, is precisely what Ziegler objects to, describing Polybius as "schoolmasterish"—and finding little of value in such comments (col. 1552; cf. also 1466).

Histories by an emphasis on human weaknesses and vice. Finally, Polybius does see education as offering hope of self-reform. But human weakness is so strong and pervasive, human willpower so flawed, and the process of education so difficult, that the human wish to be good can be transformed into reality only by immense effort. Most often the wish to be good therefore remains a mere wish.

POLYBIUS'S GROWING PESSIMISM

The approach taken so far has been to attempt a general and synchronic assessment of Polybius's understanding of human character and capabilities, because his general attitude here has itself been a matter of controversy. The general conclusion has been, of course, that Polybius's view of human character was not a sunny one. But a diachronic framework can also be imposed upon this material. Since the vast work of *The Histories* probably took several decades to compose, the text should give some evidence of intellectual and emotional evolution. That is certainly true of Polybius's changing goals in writing *The Histories*—and their changing subject matter (see Polyb. 3.4). The same should be true, then, of Polybius's view of human character, and the possibilities for positive human action within the historical process.

And that seems to be the case. Of course, some very negative comments on human character appear early on (e.g., Polyb. 1.36.2–3), whereas some very positive or confident comments appear rather late (e.g., 31.16, or 38.4.8); the situation is not simple. But a trend toward an increasingly pessimistic outlook can nevertheless be discerned. This in itself is not a new discovery;[57] but the precise nature of the trend remains to be carefully delineated. Polybius's view of humanity was never very optimistic; he always stressed how difficult it was for humans to achieve anything of magnitude; and how difficult it was to bring any sort of order out of the prevailing chaos of the world; the pessimism of the final sections of *The Histories* is merely an intensification of an attitude already evident in Polybius's writing from the first.

It is true that down to the end of the Second Punic War (i.e., the first 15 volumes), *The Histories* are dominated by titanic individual figures: Hamilcar Barca and his son Hannibal among the Carthaginians; Scipio Africanus among the Romans; Philopoemen among the Greeks. Polybius clearly considered these to be outstanding men, and their achievements, as presented by him, seem to indicate an early faith in the ability of individuals to have a crucial impact upon the world and upon the course of

57. See n. 5, above.

history.[58] The first volumes of *The Histories* thus seem to reflect the common Hellenistic belief—influenced so heavily by the Greek experience of Alexander—in the importance of "great men."[59]

An early Polybian confidence in the power of the human intellect seems apparent as well in the forceful dictum about the writing of history found at 2.38.4–5:

> It is clearly unbecoming and indeed lazy to speak of Chance or Fortune [in history], since neither those things that happen according to reason, nor those that seem to happen contrary to all reasonable expectation, can come without a cause.

This passage appears to contradict the much later and more famous statement about historical causation in 36.17, where a role in historical events is now left to the inexplicable, and Tyche.[60]

Yet "the rule of the titans" in the early volumes of *The Histories* was itself already deeply troubled by the forces of chaos. Polybius presents the great heroes of the first part of the work as having constantly to struggle against the inexorable pressures of circumstances, against the natural entropy of the tools of achievement available to them (their armies and their polities)—while sometimes finding themselves at the mercy of their own dark impulses. Thus Hamilcar, despite his personal brilliance, is in the end helpless against the vast resources of Rome—while it is Hamilcar's own troops, trained by him, who eventually form the core of the mercenary army that threatens the existence of Carthage itself (cf. 1.66.1–3 and 74.9). His management of the Mercenary War is constantly impeded by Carthage's own political disorder.[61] And later Hamilcar dies in Spain having set in motion, through the uncontrolled ferocity of his hatred of Rome, a second disastrous war for Carthage with the Romans (3.9.6–10.7).[62] As for Hannibal, his effort against Rome, brilliant as it is, is undermined from the beginning by the fact that his own destructive hatred of

---

58. Cf. 23.12–14, Polybius's tandem obituaries of these men. Philopoemen is obviously a much lesser figure on the world stage than the other two, but—obviously—his death in the same year as Hannibal's and Scipio's made the tandem obituaries too good an opportunity to pass up. It satisfied Polybius's Achaean patriotism, and gave the Greeks among his audience their own specific model to follow. One should add that Antiochus III, at least in the early stage of his career, was ranked by Polybius among the titans (see 11.34.15–16, and 15.13; with the comments of Welwei, *Könige und Königtum*, 61–62).

59. See esp. Pédech, *Méthode*, 204–9.

60. See the comments of von Fritz, *Mixed Constitution*, 390–91.

61. On the convoluted Punic politics of this period, see now Huss, *Geschichte der Karthager*, 252–68.

62. This strongly suggests that despite Pédech, *Méthode*, 216–17, Hamilcar is not a very good example of "the Polybian rational hero"; see in detail Eckstein, "The Power of Irrationality," 5–8.

the Romans leads him (in Polybius's judgment) to go to war prematurely, without sufficient resources (11.19.6–7; cf. 3.15.5–11).[63] All Hannibal's ingenuity and qualities of leadership are needed often just to keep his army together (cf. 3.54)—or to keep from being murdered by his own Celtic allies (3.78.1–4). And in the end all his efforts, too, are in vain, because Roman resources are simply overwhelming (9.26; cf. 11.19.6–7). Philopoemen's personal brilliance is unquestioned, but the Achaean troops he has to work with are deeply flawed.[64] And Achaean resources are barely sufficient to keep Sparta or Messenia in check, while as for Rome, Philopoemen knows all too well that any military struggle is hopeless (24.13.1–4).

Indeed, Scipio Africanus is the only personage among these four brilliant men to have left behind a truly permanent achievement—in the vast extension of Roman power in the Mediterranean. Similarly, the obstacles he faces in *The Histories* are not quite on the scale of those confronted by the other three—althought they are difficult enough. Thus Scipio's efforts in Spain are hampered by an army possessing shaky morale at first, and insufficient forces for his ambitious projects (10.6–7)—an army that could be mutinous even in victory (cf. 11.25). In Africa, too, Scipio was at first vastly outnumbered (cf. 14.1.5), and his efforts both before and after Zama to engineer a peace congenial to both his own political interests and those of Rome were hampered by the erratic character of Carthaginian internal politics (14.9.6–11; 15.1–3 and 19). In Asia a decade later, Polybius must have narrated the story of how a serious illness prevented Scipio's participation in the crucial battle against Antiochus III that he had done so much to prepare, and that won Rome hegemony over the Seleucid state.[65] In the surviving text, Polybius certainly emphasizes how Scipio's willpower and intelligence surmounted the various obstacles in his path;[66] but of course at the end even Scipio was brought down—politically destroyed by his enemies in the mid-180s. It was a story Polybius evidently told in detail, and with contempt for those who drove Scipio into exile (cf. 23.14.1–11). Yet it was those men, not Scipio, who won the final victory.

Polybius could speak with awe of Alexander the Great, who did rapidly accomplish enormous things in a career that was completely successful: he was a godlike personage (cf. 12.23.5). But in the period covered by *The Histories*, Polybius found no Alexanders—only men. Even the greatest of these men had his limitations, and each is depicted as having to strug-

63. See, in detail, Chap. V, above; cf. also Eckstein, "The Power of Irrationality," 5–8.
64. For discussion, see Chap. VI, above.
65. On Scipio's illness, see Livy [P] 37.37.6; for Polybian derivation, see Briscoe, *Commentary* II: 2 and 344.
66. Cf. 10.7–9; 11.25–30; 15.1–3.

gle valiantly against the formidable obstacles put in his way by Fortune and by circumstances (and sometimes by his own emotions as well). It is this struggle that stands out, and makes the successes of these early Polybian heroes, even though never complete, all the more moving.[67]

Indeed, already in Book 1 the Polybian theme of human limitation before Fortune is established with great force, in the story of M. Atilius Regulus. Regulus led the Roman invasion of Africa in 256/255, which drove Carthage to its knees. During the subsequent peace negotiations, Polybius depicts him as unpleasant and arrogant; he viewed the granting of any terms to Carthage as a favor (1.31.6). Negotiations failed—but then the Carthaginians utterly defeated Regulus's army, and captured Regulus himself. Polybius offers a personal comment (1.35.1–3):

> One who considers this incident correctly will find much in it to contribute to the better conduct of human life. For the idea that one should distrust Fortune [ἡ τύχη], and especially in times of success, is most clearly demonstrated to everyone by the disaster that befell Regulus. He who a short time ago had refused all pity or mercy to the defeated was now, almost immediately afterwards, led in chains to beg those very people for his own life.

Perhaps Polybius was working here from a passage in Philinus, one of his sources on the First Punic War; that is suggested by the content of Diod. 23.15.1–6, which is certainly drawn from Philinus.[68] But there is a notable—and sinister—difference between Tyche in Diodorus/Philinus and Tyche in Polyb. 1.35. In Diodorus τὸ δαιμόνιον punishes Regulus for his arrogance (23.15.2); but Polybius's point is Tyche's simple capriciousness—which can turn on a man in an instant.[69]

That same point is forcefully made again at the beginning of Book 2, in the story of the Aetolian siege of Medion (autumn 231). The Medionians were already in desperate straits when the time came for the election of a new Aetolian federal general (Polyb. 2.2.8). A dispute now arose between the old general and the new one as to who should have the right to distribute the upcoming booty, and to inscribe his name on shields to be dedicated in memory of the victory. After much bitter wrangling, it was decided that both men should share in these honors (2.2.9–11). But a large Illyrian army (working at the behest of Macedon) now suddenly descended upon the overconfident Aetolians, and utterly defeated them

67. By contrast, Pédech (*Méthode*, 231) argues that great men in Polybius find little to constrain them in the outside environment, since they are able to dominate and master it through their calculation and foresight. This is in line with Pédech's view that Polybius is essentially an optimist (see above, p. 238 and n. 2).

68. Cf. Walbank, *Commentary* I: 92–93.

69. On the crucial difference in outlook between Diod. 23.15 and Polyb. 1.35, see Pédech, "Sur les sources de Polybe," 255–56; nevertheless Pédech, as noted, sees Polybius as essentially optimistic about human affairs. Cf. also Walbank, *Commentary* I: 93.

(2.3). Amid the Aetolian booty captured by the Illyrians and Medionians were the very shields meant to be inscribed with the names of the victorious Aetolian generals—shields that now became symbols of Aetolian disaster (2.4.1–2). Polybius offers a long, personal, and generalizing comment (4.3–5):

> Tyche, by what happened to these people, was displaying her power to men in general [ἐνδεικνυμένης . . . δύναμιν]. For in the briefest interval of time, the very thing that these people were expecting to suffer from the enemy she allowed them instead to inflict upon the enemy.

Polybius concludes that the lesson here is that "we are but men" (ἀνθρώπους ὄντας), and that we therefore should allow for the unexpected in every matter (4.5).

Walbank sees this passage as either a banal philosophical trope, or else an expression of Polybius's enjoyment at a disaster inflicted upon the Aetolians, enemies of the Achaean League.[70] But as Walbank himself points out, Polybius uses very similar language about the power and capriciousness of Tyche in important passages elsewhere in *The Histories*.[71] In particular, the phrase ἐνδεικνυμένη . . . δύναμιν appears again at Polyb. 29.21.5, in a crucial discussion of Polybius's understanding of the flow of history, as exemplified in the fall of Macedon at Pydna in 168: "Tyche makes no compact with our lives, but always defeats our calculations through some novel stroke, demonstrating her power [δύναμιν . . . ἐνδεικνυμένη] by defeating our expectations."[72] Walbank also notes a striking parallel to 2.4.3–5 at Polyb. 30.10.1–2, where, again after Pydna, the victorious L. Aemilius Paullus appropriates for himself the very columns Perseus was constructing in his own honor at Delphi. Polybius once more cannot resist an edifying comment, and it is the same edifying comment as the one in 2.4.3–5: "From incidents such as this, one can clearly see both the capriciousness of Tyche and her abrupt changes of course."[73] Furthermore, the phrase "we are but men" (ἀνθρώπους ὄντας), used by Polybius at 2.4.5 to sum up the human condition—and a phrase by which Polybius, if anything, is *identifying* with the Aetolians in their unexpected failure—is another phrase that occurs repeatedly in *The Histories*. It is always employed to emphasize the stern limitations to which humans are subject when confronted with the complexities of circumstance—or with Tyche's decree.[74]

70. *Commentary* I: 154 and 155. Von Scala, *Studien*, 165 n. 2, is even stronger, seeing 2.4.4–5 as an example of Polybian "Philistinism."
71. *Commentary* I: 155. See Polyb. 11.5.8, 23.10.6, 29.19.2; cf. 1.4.5.
72. These words are actually a quote from Demetrius of Phalerum; but Polybius praises the sentiment highly (see 29.21.9).
73. Cf. Walbank, *Commentary* I: 155.
74. See Polyb. 2.7.1; 3.31.3; 8.21.11; 15.18; 21.14.4; 23.12.4; 24.10.11; 38.20.3.

On the basis of the above evidence, I would therefore conclude that the sentiment in Polyb. 2.4.3–5 was viewed by Polybius neither as a philosophical cliché nor as a mere enjoyable political swipe at the Aetolians. Rather, Polybius intended 2.4.3–5 to be taken with utter seriousness— the same seriousness he expected with the story of Regulus at 1.35.1–3. This does not mean that in Books 1 and 2 Polybius has already succumbed to deep and pervasive fatalism in the face of Tyche. Rather, the caution and pessimism of Polyb. 1.35 and 2.4 help put into perspective the intellectual confidence expressed in 2.38 (see above)—and vice versa. That is: to the writer of the earliest volumes of *The Histories*, human intelligence has its own great power, and great men could, with great effort, succeed in creating great—if incomplete—achievements. And yet the sense of a Polybian humility before intractable and mysterious processes is also already unmistakable.[75]

This tone of caution and pessimism about the possibilities open to humans can be shown to have grown stronger as the Polybian narrative passes beyond the age dominated by such heroic figures as Hannibal and Scipio Africanus. Because of the increasingly incomplete character of the text, it is not easy to discern the evolution of Polybius's attitude in any great detail. Still, it is instructive to examine the panorama of the Mediterranean that Polybius evidently created for his audience at the beginning of the Second Macedonian War (200 B.C.), and then at the beginning of the Third Macedonian War a generation later. What is clear is that Polybius's concern about the opportunities open even to great men is now joined by new concerns: the deteriorating quality of the human beings who are his major subject matter, and the power of Tyche to dominate crucial events.

The individual who is central to Polybius's narrative in 200 is Philip V of Macedon, and there is no doubt that for Polybius he is a lesser and more distasteful figure than Hannibal, that other great adversary of Rome. Polybius's Philip can act with commendable military energy in this period, and even with dignity (16.28.7–8, 34.1–7). But the overall picture is highly negative. Philip has ambitions for world empire (5.102.1, 15.24.6), but his project is undermined by his own cruelty, habitual treachery, and lack of self-control (cf. 15.20–24), which can sometimes descend into outright raving madness (cf. 16.1.1–2).

---

75. If Polyb. 2.70.2 is another example of Polybius's concept that Tyche decides things "contrary to reasonable expectation" (παρὰ λόγον), this would become another important passage indicating such early Polybian humility before the mysterious workings of Tyche. But the reading of the passage is hotly disputed. See Walbank, *Commentary* I: 289, who adopts Wunderer's attractive suggestion, made on the basis of the parallel passage in Plut. *Cleom.* 27.4, that the description of Tyche's action here should be παρ' ὀλίγον (she decides things "by a narrow margin"). Cf. also Siegfried, *Polybios*, 73, n. 140.

The ambitions of Antiochus III, the other predominant Greek ruler in this period, are—as with Philip—for universal empire (cf. Polyb. 11.34.16). Earlier, Antiochus had been presented in a heroic light (see 10.49.7–14), but by Book 15 he, too, has decayed. His greed for empire has—as with Philip—removed all moral boundaries from his behavior (15.20.1–4), and to Polybius he now appears unworthy of his former self (15.37, explicitly). As for the Ptolemaic kingdom, it is now in the hands of a child, various prime ministers of questionable character—and the mob (15.24a–36).

The situation among the smaller Greek states is little better. The regimes of Pergamum and Rhodes are lacking in energy (16.28.1–4). The Athenians are worthless (Livy [P] 31.15 and 44).[76] Sparta is being ruled by a bestial tyrant (Polyb. 13.6–8, 16.13). The Aetolians are moneygrubbers (18.34.7). In Achaea, the great Philopoemen is absent (away on Crete); political affairs are in the hands of competent but lesser men.[77] The one principle Polybius finds common in the Greeks of the period is that most of them can be bought, and few of them will do anything without a bribe (18.34.7).

In the western Mediterranean at this time, Carthage lies defeated—and it is likely that Polybius showed the city as riven by factional quarrels based on unjust jealousy of Hannibal.[78] As for Rome, the fact is that Polybius believed that the acme of the Roman *politeia* had in some sense already passed. It had occurred, in his opinion, in 216, at the time of the battle of Cannae (cf. 6.51.5–6); and the seeds of decay were already planted, among both the elite and the populace.[79] To be sure, the degeneration had not yet proceeded very far. Thus in the 190s most Romans, according to Polybius, were still honest men (18.34.7–35.1). But T. Quinctius Flamininus, the main Roman commander in the war against Philip, despite being a skillful young man (18.12), is nevertheless clearly a figure of lesser stature than Scipio Africanus.

Moreover, Polybius believes this entire rather gloomy panorama lay in the shadow of a vengeful Tyche, intent upon punishing Philip and Antiochus for their misdeeds by raising up the Romans against them—and eventually destroying their kingdoms as they had expected themselves to

---

76. For Livy 31.15 and 31.44 as derived from Polybian material, see Briscoe, *Commentary* I: 94 and 115.

77. For Philopoemen's activity on Crete, see Errington, *Philopoemen*, 27–48. On Achaean internal politics in his absence: Eckstein, "Polybius, Aristaenus, and the Fragment 'On Traitors,'" 140–42.

78. On Hannibal's flight from Carthage in the face of his political enemies, see Livy 33.45.6–49.7, drawn primarily from Polybian material; cf. Briscoe, *Commentary* I: 335–36.

79. On this, see Polyb. 2.21.7–9, and 9.10 *passim*, with discussion in Chap. VII, above.

destroy the Ptolemies (15.20.5–8). Thus in Books 15–18 Polybius is affirming the brooding power of Fortune (as he had already done, in one sense, in Books 1 and 2), while simultaneously dealing with men clearly inferior to the great heroes of the struggles of the third century. And yet here in Books 15–18 we are still less than halfway through the forty volumes of the completed work.

Whatever their grave faults, however, both Philip V and Antiochus III were at least striking figures—to their contemporaries and to Polybius. The Mediterranean world a generation later, at the beginning of the Third Macedonian War in 171, presents an even more unedifying Polybian spectacle than the world of 200, because of the almost total absence of such figures.

The new antagonist for Rome in this period is Philip V's son Perseus— not, like his father, a drunkard and a lecher, but a miser and a physical coward. Perseus is thus an altogether less vigorous figure than Philip.[80] Egypt is now about to be torn apart by civil war between the two brothers Ptolemy VI and Ptolemy VIII—neither a very outstanding personage, and in the case of Ptolemy VIII a repulsive one.[81] In Asia, the Seleucid domains are in the hands of the erratic Antiochus IV—a man with some good qualities (cf. 28.18), but whom Polybius perceives as in many ways immoral and even insane (26.1–1a, 29.26). Pergamum is ruled by Eumenes II, whose policies in this period are determined by his greed—a trait he shares with Perseus (29.5–9).[82] Rhodes, Epirus, and Aetolia are all riddled with factionalism, with at least one faction everywhere being cowardly or brutal.[83] In Achaea, the party once headed by Philopoemen is momentarily dominant, now led by Archon (and, not least, by Polybius himself); but the ruthless pro-Roman Callicrates is waiting in the wings (cf. 30.13).

But by this point in *The Histories*, the reader has perhaps become habituated to depictions of Greek mediocrity; what is new is the overt deterioration of the Romans. This has been discussed in detail in Chapter VII: prefigured by the advice to the Romans of Callicrates in 180, the Romans are now in the midst of a "transformation for the worse" as far as Greece

80. Perseus not a lecher or a drunkard, like his father: Polyb. 25.3.7; a skinflint: 28.8–9 and 29.8–9; a physical coward: 29.17–19 (scathing remarks, to which one should compare Polybius's praise of Philip's personal courage; see Chap. II, above).
81. Polybius's assessment of Ptolemy VI: see 28.21 and 39.7 (he had his good qualities) Polybius's assessment of Ptolemy VIII: 31.18.14–15.
82. For discussion of the greed of Eumenes as Polybius conceived it, see Chap. III, above; also Schleussner, "Pergamenisch-makedonischen Kontakte," 119–23.
83. Rhodes: Polyb. 30.8–9; cf. Gruen, "Rome and Rhodes in the Second Century," esp. 68–81; Berthold, *Rhodes in the Hellenistic Age*, 179–94. Epirus: Polyb. 27.15; Aetolia: 28.4, cf. 30.13.11.

is concerned (24.10.10),[84] and a degeneration in standards of conduct underlined by their conscious deception of Perseus regarding peace in winter 172/171 (Livy [P] 42.47).[85] The harsh new Roman attitude also found expression during the war with Perseus itself, in actions such as the brutal destruction of Haliartus—or the oppressive exactions imposed on Athens and Chalcis, even though these cities supported Rome in the war.[86] Nor was Roman generalship at all outstanding—until the arrival, that is, of L. Aemilius Paullus in 168. But Polybius believed that the self-disciplined and wise Paullus was already an anachronism within the increasingly degenerate society at Rome.[87]

And over this entire grim scene there presides an equally grim—and capricious—Tyche. The end of the Third Macedonian War calls forth a long sequence of comments informed by this vision. In 29.20, L. Aemilius Paullus himself is presented as warning his victorious officers never to trust in present prosperity, or to let success lead to arrogance—for Fortune can always turn.[88] Then in 29.21, Fortune (Tyche) is made directly responsible for the destruction of Macedon—and this is a Tyche who is abruptly mutable (21.2), cruel (χαλεπόν), powerful, and unpredictable (21.4–5). The assessment is that of Demetrius of Phalerum, who predicts (ca. 300 B.C.) that Tyche has only lent her present blessing to the Macedonians, until such time as she suddenly decides to deal differently with them (21.5). But it is a vision of Tyche and of human helplessness before incomprehensible and sudden events that Polybius explicitly endorses (21.7–9).

Walbank considers Polyb. 29.21 just another "monotonous, trite homily."[89] But the passage ends in a highly personal, awe-struck statement: "I saw the destruction of Macedon with my own eyes," just as Demetrius had predicted (29.21.8–9). And an equal warmth of feeling occurs almost immediately thereafter, at what is now 29.22.[90] Describing the shaky polit-

---

84. Note that this is precisely the same phrase (ἐπὶ τὸ χεῖρον . . . μεταβολή) used by Polybius at 7.11.1 to describe the crucial moment in the moral degeneration of Philip V.

85. On the Polybian derivation of this passage, see the detailed discussion in Chap. IV, above.

86. Polybius certainly recounted the Roman atrocity at Haliartus; that is shown by his several references to the *senatus consultum* that resulted from it (28.3.3, 13.11, 16.2; cf. also 30.20.1–4). The stories of Roman oppression at Athens and Chalcis (Livy 43.6.1–3 and 7.5–11) may derive, as we have them in Livy, from an annalistic source (so Nissen, *Kritische Untersuchungen*, 257–58), but it is difficult to believe that Polybius did not cover these incidents in detail too.

87. On this Polybian theme, see the detailed discussion in Chap. VII, above.

88. For discussion of Polyb. 29.20, see Chap. VII, above.

89. *Commentary* I: 19.

90. The current 29.22 should actually follow 29.23–25 in the narrative; see Walbank, *Commentary* III: 395.

ical situation of Eumenes II after the war, despite the strategic gain for Pergamum in the destruction of Macedon, Polybius offers yet another generalizing comment (22.3–4):

> For Fortune [ἡ τύχη] is able to confound human calculations with unexpected blows; and if she has favored someone, and thrown her weight into the balance for him, she will then, as if repenting it, throw her weight onto the opposite scale, immediately marring all his achievements.

All in all, I see no reason not to believe that these statements in Book 29 were meant very seriously indeed.

Polybius, of course, has referred earlier to the role of Tyche in the destruction of Macedon: at 15.20.5–8 he portrays Tyche as having acted to take revenge for the crimes perpetrated by Philip V.[91] The Tyche of Polyb. 15.20 is indeed a grim force, but at least her purposes and motivations are somewhat accessible to human understanding—and even provide a moral framework for the world. Yet fourteen volumes later, in these passages in Book 29, there is not humanly accessible motivation or purpose to Tyche's actions.

One must be cautious, however, about assuming that this shows a simple, linear, and increasingly pessimistic evolution in Polybius's thought.[92] For one thing, the whole concept of Tyche in Polybius is extraordinarily multifaceted and fluid.[93] In addition, the capricious and incomprehensible aspect of Tyche already appears with great emphasis in the earliest volumes of The Histories—as I have sought to show.[94] Conversely, the vision of Tyche as the punisher of wrongdoing occurs at least twice in Polybius at points well after the great vision of incomprehensible Tyche in Book 29.[95] Furthermore, even in the last volumes of The Histories, Polybius does not give up emphasizing that important phenomena that

---

91. On 15.20, see the detailed discussion in Chap. IV, above.

92. The hypothesis of Laqueur, Polybios, 249–60. Pédech, by contrast, argues that Polybius at heart always believed in a Tyche that was distributive justice, the righteous punisher of criminals: "Idées religieuses de Polybe," 57. But Pédech ignores too many passages that point in a much grimmer direction.

93. See esp. Walbank, Commentary I: 16. As Walbank further notes (I: 17), Tyche is also closely linked in Polybius's thinking with the equally vague concepts of τὸ δαιμόνιον and ταὐτόματον as sources of events that defy rational analysis. On this, cf. also Wunderer, Polybios, 4.

94. See above, pp. 257–59. For inexplicable and arbitrary Tyche as a theme deeply embedded in The Histories, cf. also Meissner, "Polybios," 321–22. Yet the passages he adduces to support this idea in fact cannot bear the weight he places on them: Polyb. 2.70.2 is undermined by a textual difficulty (see above, n. 75); Polyb. 8.2.3 can be translated quite differently (see Walbank, Commentary II: 69); and 21.16.3 does not specifically concern the arbitrary and inexplicable character of Tyche.

95. Polyb. 31.9.4 and 32.15.14; cf. Walbank, Commentary I: 21. Both cases involve punishment for despoiling the temples of the gods.

are widely attributed to Tyche actually have causes that are perfectly ame-
nable to rational analysis.[96]

Walbank has suggested that the answer to this riddle is that the motif of
a capricious and incomprehensible Tyche is not related to a chronological
evolution in Polybius's thought at all, but instinctively enters Polybius's
thinking whenever some event of great personal meaning is being discussed in *The Histories*—whether the discussion occurs early or late in
the text.[97] This hypothesis is quite persuasive, and it has two important
corollaries. First, with increasing frequency in Book 29 and after, events
come into discussion that are indeed of special emotional significance to
Polybius, since he is dealing increasingly with events of his own time, and
ones he says impressed him deeply (29.5.3; cf. 3.4.13). Second, it is striking that when Tyche is invoked by Polybius in connection with events that
call forth special emotional energy, invariably the Tyche that is invoked is
the most pessimistic vision of Fortune available. There could not be a
better indication of his deepest feelings about the difficult world he
thought humans, burdened already with their complement of natural
weaknesses and faults, had to face.[98]

Certainly in the last ten volumes of *The Histories,* which cover the period after the war with Perseus, the tone of pessimism about humanity
and human possibilities in the world is glaring. To begin with, the once-
virtuous Romans now appear to Polybius to be well on their way to corruption. The Senate now routinely pursues an amoral (if not downright
immoral) policy toward all other states, preferring pragmatic advantage
over considerations of justice.[99] Many of the individual leaders of the Roman state in this period are, in fact, presented as unattractive personalities.[100] Meanwhile, the younger generation of Roman aristocrats has

96. See 31.30.2 (on the achievements of Scipio Aemilianus), 32.8.4 (on the achievements
of Eumenes II), and parts of 36.17 (see below).

97. *Commentary* I: 16–26; cf. already von Fritz, *Mixed Constitution,* 387–92.

98. Walbank, however, tends to believe that Polybius always retained doubts about the
existence of an objectively active Tyche (*Commentary* I: 25). He notes that even in the late
passage 31.9.4 Polybius does not take personal responsibility for the opinion about the divine punishment inflicted on Antiochus IV, merely citing "what some people say," while at
32.15.14 he qualifies his account of the divine punishment inflicted on Prusias II with the
phrase "so it seemed" (ὥστε . . . δοκεῖν). But if Polybius does not take responsibility for the
opinion in 31.9.4, neither does he attack it. And 32.15.14 must be read with Polybius's
earlier statement that Prusias was insane for first supplicating the gods for help and then
despoiling their temples (32.15.7–9); nor does Polybius offer an alternative explanation for
what then happened to Prusias and his army.

99. For detailed discussion of this Polybian theme, see Chaps. IV and VII, above.

100. The tasteless and extravagant L. Anicius (30.22); the unfair C. Sulpicius Galus
(31.6.5); the treacherous and cowardly M. Claudius Marcellus (35.3.2 and 4.6); the stupid
L. Malleolus (36.14); the wordy, untalented, and cowardly A. Postumius Albinus (39.1); and,

abandoned itself to feasts, drunkenness, luxury, and amours with boys
and prostitutes (Polyb. 31.25.3–6). Many are physical cowards (35.4.1–6
and 8), though they are also destructively competitive with one another
(31.29.8–9). And the reason for this transformation for the worse in the
Roman polity (31.25.3, explicitly) is Rome's very success, which has
brought Rome wealth and arrogance (25.6).[101]

Yet the non-Roman peoples are in many respects even worse. This is
already apparent in Books 30–33. Egypt is now continually torn by ugly
dynastic strife—which Polybius covered in detail.[102] The Seleucid domains are ruled by Demetrius I: a personal friend of Polybius, whom he
nevertheless depicted in *The Histories* as a habitual drunkard (33.10; cf.
already 31.13.8). Demetrius's reign would end disastrously, a disaster Polybius described (cf. 3.5.3)—part of the complex civil wars that ended
Seleucid power forever.[103] In this same period Bithynia is in the hands of
Prusias II—a man whom Polybius portrays as totally repulsive.[104] In Aetolia, after factional fighting that Polybius calls "bestial" (30.11.5), the pro-
Roman Lyciscus is in control—a man whom Polybius calls "thoroughly
evil" (32.4.3). The situation is similar in Epirus, under the brutal pro-
Roman Charops (32.5–6), and in Boeotia and Acarnania (cf. 32.5.1–2).
And Achaea itself, as Polybius portrays it, is under the heel of the traitor-
ous, ruthless Callicrates (cf. 30.32.8).[105]

The degeneration continued after about 152 (Books 35–39). This was
"the time of disturbance and trouble" (ταραχὴ καὶ κίνησις, 3.4.12), much
of it incomprehensible (4.13). Here the central subjects, as so often, are
the Carthaginians, the Macedonians, and the Achaeans. The Carthaginians are now in the hands of Hasdrubal, a tyrannical and cowardly buffoon (38.8 and 20). The Macedonians have voluntarily given themselves
over to the brutal impostor Andriscus the Pseudo-Philip, who leads them
into what Polybius considers an insane and self-destructive war against
Rome (36.10 and 17). And the Achaeans are now led by the cowardly

---

of course, Ti. Sempronius Gracchus, son-in-law of Scipio Africanus, father-in-law of Scipio
Aemilianus, twice consul, censor—and a man castigated by Polybius for many different vices
(for discussion, see Chap. I, above).

101. On Polybius's belief in the general inability of polities to withstand the temptation
of wealth, see Chap. III, above.

102. See Polyb. 31.10 and 17 (fragments of what was clearly a very extensive narrative).

103. On the complicated Seleucid dynastic strife after 162, see Gruen, *Hellenistic World
and the Coming of Rome* II: 663–70.

104. See Polyb. 30.18; 32.15; 36.15; and Chaps. V and VII, above.

105. The picture here may be exaggerated: see Gruen, "Origins of the Achaean War,"
48–49; and *Hellenistic World and the Coming of Rome* II: 518. But that does not change the fact
that the picture of Achaea in the hands of the vile Callicrates is part of Polybius's general
presentation of a world in decline. Achaean hatred of Callicrates: see Polyb. 30.29.

blowhards Diaeus and Critolaus; they, too, provoke an insane and self-destructive war with Rome.[106]

Among the degenerate Romans of this period Polybius does find at least two outstanding personalities: one is his friend and student Scipio Aemilianus; the other is the aged M. Porcius Cato—a relic of another, better time.[107] What is striking, however, is that among the *non*-Romans there is not a single admirable figure in the surviving fragments of *The Histories*—except for the suicidal wife of the cowardly Hasdrubal.[108]

The mood of gloom here is added to by the reappearance of Tyche at her most capricious and incomprehensible.[109] The central passage is Polyb. 36.17, containing Polybius's reflections on the behavior of the people of Macedon. This passage was discussed in Chapter VII above, but now will be approached from a different angle.

In contrast to the theoretical discussion in 2.38, where Polybius asserted that every historical event had a rationally knowable cause, in 36.17 he now says that there are a significant proportion of events that are, in fact, simply beyond human understanding. In the latter category he first puts natural disasters such as storms, drought, and plague (36.17.2); that is not surprising. Moreover, he still says that the causes of many typical human actions are indeed rationally discernible, and thus subject to reform based upon such rational analysis.[110] But then Polybius admits that some human actions do *not* appear to him to be subject to rational analysis (36.17.2). And one of these is the behavior of the Macedonian people after 150; for the Romans had liberated them from the evils of monarchy, and yet they not only went to war against Rome for a brutal impostor (Andriscus) but fought more bravely for him than they

106. For detailed discussion, see Chap. VII, above.

107. Cato: Polyb. 31.25.5a. Aemilianus is explicitly described as having virtues otherwise missing in his generation: 31.25–30. L. Mummius, the Roman commander in Greece in 146, is praised by Polybius for his clemency and self-restraint (39.6.3), and L. Opimius is another competent commander (33.10). But obviously, neither of these two men is being presented as an outstanding hero.

108. On the wife of Hasdrubal, see the detailed discussion in Chap. II, above.

109. Again, one should resist the temptation to see this as a strictly chronological development; rather, it has to do with Polybius's confrontation here with subjects of great emotional importance to him (see above, pp. 263–64).

110. Polybius's test case here is the falling birth rate and consequent depopulation of Greece, which he ascribes not to Tyche but to the "extravagance, avarice, and sloth" of the Greeks themselves (36.17.7). This prevents them from having children, since they prefer to spend their money on themselves. Walbank discounts Polybius's moralizing analysis, stressing chaotic social-economic conditions in Greece as the real reason for the declining birth rate (*Commentary* III: 680–81). But this only serves to underline that Polybius's own approach to the depopulation problem is, in fact, moralizing (cf., briefly, Petzold, *Methode des Polybios*, 128 and n. 5). Polybius's projected reform in the test case of depopulation is the creation of laws making it compulsory for citizens to marry, and have children (36.17.10).

had ever fought for their legitimate kings (17.13–14). Polybius gives a personal comment (17.15):

How could anyone fail to be at a loss when confronted with these facts? For it is difficult indeed to discover a cause for them. Therefore, regarding phenomena like this, one may well say that the thing was an example of heaven-sent madness, and that the wrath of the gods had descended upon all the Macedonians.

Polybius's point is the totally incomprehensible nature of the Macedonian events. "Divine wrath" here (μῆνιν ἐκ θεῶν, 36.17.15) is just a synonym for madness (δαιμονοβλάβεια, ibid.)—and for incomprehensible Tyche.[111] But resort to "madness" and incomprehensible Tyche is a sign of Polybius's resignation to being unable to explain rationally the causes of the terrible process he is now recounting.[112]

Similar themes reappear two volumes later in Book 38, at the heart of Polybius's account of the Achaean War of 146. At one level, Polybius ascribes the war simply to Achaean stupidity, which led to horrific errors of policy.[113] But stupidity soon merges, in Polybius's account, into downright madness. In this period, the cities of Achaea are in a state of "frenzy" (38.12.5). The Achaean masses are all too ready to share in "the feverish fanaticism and madness" of the leaders Diaeus and Critolaus (12.7), in their "completely irrational" projects (10.13). After the first defeats, most of the Achaeans, "as if carried away by a mountain torrent," continued to support the "demented" plans of their leaders (16.2). Other people, meanwhile, were committing suicide senselessly (παραλόγως), or fleeing about aimlessly (16.5). Indeed, to Polybius all of Greece at this time "was under a strange and evil spell" (16.7).[114] Such a vocabulary of madness reveals Polybius's inability to arrive at a rational explanation for this war—any more than he could for the "mad" war of Andriscus in Macedon. It is true that no incomprehensible Tyche is involved here; but later Polybius does say that given the madness, insanity, and lack of judgment of the Achaeans (ἄνοια, μανία, ἀκρισία), it was only "some ingenious and resourceful Tyche" (τύχη τις) that prevented their total destruction (38.18.7–8). This phrase should not be dismissed as mere rhetoric.

---

111. Such conceptual vagueness is typically Hellenistic (see Pédech, Méthode, 336 and n. 27), as well as typically Polybian (see Walbank, Commentary I: 17).

112. Walbank (Commentary III: 682) takes Polybius 36.17 merely as an indication of Polybius's failure to understand the Macedonian point of view—the resurgence of national feeling under Andriscus. There is truth in this observation, but it does not take away from the fact that Polybius told his readers he was in fact unable to offer them a rational explanation for what had occurred.

113. Achaean stupidity: see Polyb. 38.1.5, 3.7, 10.13, 11.10–11.

114. On the correct translation of the phraseology in 38.16.7, see Walbank, Commentary III: 713.

It is, at the least, one more sign of Polybius's frustration at being unable to offer rational explanations for the cataclysmic events of the 140s.[115]

Given all of the above, it should come as no surprise that the image of a capricious Tyche should appear also, and prominently, in Polybius's account of the destruction of Carthage in 146. Polybius personally witnessed it—and was clearly moved by it. The result is one of the most famous passages in *The Histories*.

Polybius says that he was standing next to Scipio Aemilianus, watching as the city was burned at Aemilianus's order, when Scipio turned to him and said that it was a glorious moment (καλόν, 38.21.1), but that he had a fear and foreboding that someday someone would give a similar order regarding Rome itself (21.2). Polybius evidently added that Aemilianus produced a quotation from Homer as another indication of his fears for Rome's future: "A day will come when holy Troy will fall, / and Priam, and the people of Priam lord of spears" (*Il.* 6.448–49).[116] Polybius's comments on Scipio's reaction to the burning of Carthage are most approving. And the reason lies precisely in the mysteriousness and undependability of Tyche (38.21.2–3):

> It would not be easy to narrate an observation more statesmanlike or insightful. For in the moment of greatest triumph and of the enemy's total disaster, to reflect . . . on the possibility of a complete reversal of circumstances, and—in a word—to bear in mind in the midst of success the undependability of Fortune [τῆς τύχης ἐπισφάλειαν]: this is the mark of a great and indeed perfect man.

Polybius evidently also included at some point in his description of this scene the fact that Aemilianus wept as he watched Carthage burn.[117] The tears, too, are most likely to derive in Polybius's conception from Scipio's melancholy thoughts of how the destruction of Carthage illustrated the mutability of human fortune.[118]

In this passage, then—where the destruction of Rome's greatest enemy has brought Roman success to brand-new heights—Polybius's focus is not on triumph but on impermanence. Tyche had helped Rome to hegemony over the entire world; but for her own inscrutable reasons she could (and perhaps would) take such dominance away. It had happened to Macedon (cf. 29.21); Aemilianus fears it will happen to Rome; and

115. Polybius's reference to Tyche in 38.18.7–8 is taken seriously by Pédech, *Méthode*, 340 and 341; cf. also Gruen, "Origins of the Achaean War," 46–47.

116. On the Homer quotation, see Polyb. 38.22.2 (= App. *Lib.* 132), and Diod. 32.24; with Walbank, *Commentary* III: 723.

117. The story of Aemilianus's tears is in App. *Lib.* 132 and Diod. 32.24, but not in the fragmentary Polyb. 38.21. But there is no reason to doubt that Polybius is the source of both Appian and Diodorus here: cf. Walbank, *Commentary* III: 723.

118. Cf. Walbank, *Commentary* III: 724.

Polybius approves that fear. Partly he is approving Aemilianus's modesty. But we seem a long way here from the intellectual stance adopted at the opening of Book 1, where the course of Roman history was subject to rational analysis (1.1.5), and from the theme of Book 6, where the roots of Roman success—in political structure and moral attitudes—were rationally laid out for the audience.[119]

Finally, Polybius twice—in a highly personal way—indicates his own humility regarding Fortune's power over himself. First, in 3.5.7, having laid out the plan for extending *The Histories* down to the Greek catastrophe of 146/145, he remarks:

> Such, at any rate, is my plan. But yet it depends upon Tyche whether my life will last long enough to bring the plan to fruition.

Perhaps this passage was actually part of the first draft of *The Histories* (in which case it originally followed 3.3.9, and the "plan" referred to is the original plan of the work down to 168); perhaps the remark in 3.5.7 is actually a later insertion (and refers to the extension of the work down to 145).[120] But though Polybius's early intellectual stance is predominantly rationalizing, I have attempted to show above that an expression of humility before the forces of Tyche would not be out of character even for the Polybius who was writing the first volumes of *The Histories*.

A similar attitude is expressed at the very end of the work, in 39.8.1–3. Polybius has just finished describing his mission to the Senate (winter 145/144?), where he was successful in ameliorating the Roman conditions of peace originally imposed upon Achaea.[121] The historian continues:

> Therefore I pray to all the gods that the rest of my life may continue on the same course and on the same prosperous terms, well knowing as I do that Fortune [ἡ τύχη] is envious of the condition of mortals, and that she especially reveals her power when one believes one is most blessed and successful in life.

The passage ends with a properly demure remark: "And so it has happened to fall out" (8.3).[122]

---

119. Indeed, the emphases in the parallel passages in Appian and Diodorus (which draw on Polybian material: see n. 117, above) reinforce the impression that the focus of the Polybian account, taken as a whole, was precisely on the melancholy, helpless insecurity of the human condition—rather than on, say, the greatness of Scipio Aemilianus and his achievement.

120. For discussion of this problem, see Walbank, *Commentary* I: 304.

121. On the details of Polybius's diplomatic mission to Rome in 145/144, see Walbank, *Commentary* III: 741.

122. Lehmann, "Polybios," 191, contends that the subject of Polyb. 39.8.2–3 is the political status quo in Greece established (partly by Polybius's own effort) after 146. But if so, why would Polybius have limited his prayer merely to the extent of his own lifetime? The

There is no reason to question Polybius's sincerity in either of these two passages, for they stand in a very long line of similar remarks about human helplessness before capricious and inexplicable Tyche.[123] But what is striking about both passages is the strength of Polybius's acknowledgment that his own personal happiness and achievement are themselves dependent upon Tyche—a Tyche who can easily make all human effort meaningless.[124]

CONCLUSION

In the end, then, the possible meaninglessness of human effort, and of human history itself, looms as a threatening cloud over Polybius's *Histories*. Yet the primary task of history writing is to impose meaning upon the flow of events in time. And the imposition of meaning—of order—is the specific task that Polybius set for himself in the earliest volumes of the work, with their complex theories and categories of historical causation. What this chapter has shown, however, is that even in those earliest volumes, there are strong indications of a worry that the events of history are not subject to rational analysis, and that the efforts of deeply flawed human beings to impose their will upon the complex flow of historical events are often fruitless. One conclusion of this chapter—the first attempt in many years to offer a general assessment of Polybius's view of the character of human beings and on the possibility of human achievement in the world—is that his overall tone is pessimistic.

This is not to say that Polybius thought great human achievement was impossible. There were indeed a few individuals—sharply intelligent, sternly hardworking and careful, strong-willed and self-controlled—who were capable of enormous accomplishments. Polybius saw them as somehow touched by a greatness that was more than human (cf. 12.23.5, on Alexander). That is not surprising, given Polybius's gloomy opinion about the deeply flawed general run of humankind from which these men stood out—the stupid, the lazy, the weak-willed, the violent.

Yet it is another grim fact about *The Histories* that as the work progresses, great men become more and more rare. It is a phenomenon adding greatly to an atmosphere of increasing pessimism. The central

---

subject thus must be the conditions in his personal life that will enable him to complete *The Histories*. See Walbank, *Commentary* III: 741.

123. On Polybius's sincerity in 39.8, see esp. Wunderer, *Polybios,* 12 (though in general Wunderer plays down Polybius's submission to Tyche: ibid. 11–12). Cf. also Pédech, *Méthode,* 340–41 (despite a general position similar to that of Wunderer).

124. *Contra:* see esp. Pédech, "Idées religieuses de Polybe," 57 and 68, who argues that Polybius affirms the power of the human will as efficacious against both Tyche and even the gods.

figures of the first half of *The Histories* are true titans and world conquerors: Hamilcar, Hannibal, Scipio Africanus. In the last half of the work they are everywhere replaced by lesser figures (though a few men, like Scipio Aemilianus, stand out amid the pervasive corruption). Simultaneously, the arbitrary power of Tyche—which Polybius has acknowledged from the first (cf. 1.36 and 2.2–4)—comes ever more strongly to the fore as an explanation of events (cf. 29.21 and 36.17). This is a view in sharp contrast with the explanatory confidence (occasionally) expressed earlier (as at 2.38.4–5). But the world especially of the last ten volumes of *The Histories* is a world of darkness and inexplicable disaster—as Polybius himself well knows (cf. 3.4.12).

Polybius's hope that education could correct men's conduct and ameliorate conditions in the world was a hope that informed the entire work, and it could still find expression even in these last volumes (cf. 38.4.8). But given Polybius's perception of enormous human weaknesses of character, and thus the enormous difficulties involved in the process of education itself (a subject about which he had thought deeply), the hope here could only have been a slim one. But the slimmer this hope was, the more the very purpose of *The Histories* was itself undermined.

We have now arrived at a striking conundrum. If Polybius's view of human nature was so bleak, and his view of human possibilities in the world so limited or problematical, why did he labor fiercely on, decade after decade, in the face of increasing pessimism, to finish his great work? The answer to that question will bring a conclusion to this study of Polybius's moral vision.

NINE

Conclusion: The Duty to Act

The life pattern of the warrior has very little affinity with the notion of a beneficent Providence.
—MAX WEBER

The world depicted in Polybius's *Histories* was always, from the beginning, a world of difficulty and challenge; it was, in the end, grimly dark and chaotic. It was not quite a hopeless place, but it was a place where the prospect of rational and effective human action was problematic. The key to understanding Polybius's persistence in completing *The Histories* in the face of his own increasing pessimism lies precisely in the fact that the grimness of this view of the world did not undermine the aristocratic ethos of honorable conduct. On the contrary: the world's harshness and anarchy gave honorable behavior a moral seriousness—and even grandeur—that it would not otherwise have possessed.

Indeed, from Homer onward, the noble struggle of individuals against undependable circumstances and Fortune was a foundation of the view of life formed by Greek culture.[1] This was a view of life that Polybius deeply imbibed with the traditional literary education he had received as the scion of one of the great houses of Megalopolis, and it remained a powerful ideology in *The Histories:* the code of struggle, the code of the warrior.[2]

The Achaean statesman Philopoemen, Polybius's family friend, is as apt a symbol of this aspect of Polybian ideology—the nobility of action, even in the face of difficult circumstances and a capricious or cruel Tyche—as he was an apt symbol in Chapter II of Polybius's vision of the warrior aristocrat who nobly risked his life in the battle line. Philopoemen, the historian says, was second to none in excellent and manly quali-

---

1. Cf., for instance, Griffin, *Homer on Life and Death,* 81–102; Stahl, "Learning through Suffering?" 1–36 (on Herodotus); Knox, *Oedipus at Thebes,* 185–96.

2. On the old-fashioned character of Polybius's education and literary tastes, see Chap. I, above; cf. esp. Wunderer, *Citate,* 92–93.

ties (κατ' ἀρετήν); yet he was defeated by Tyche—captured by the Messenians and executed—although in his life previously he seemed always to have been favored by her (23.12.3). Polybius continues (12.3–7):

> But it seems to me that, as the common proverb says, it is possible for a man to be fortunate, but impossible for him to be fortunate always. Therefore we should call some of our predecessors fortunate, not because they were invariably so—for what is the point of foolishly flattering Tyche?—but because they were fortunate for most of their lives, and when Tyche did turn on them, they were met by only moderate misfortune.

Other ancient writers attributed Philopoemen's capture and death not to Fortune but to his own bad judgment and recklessness (Plut. *Comp. Phil. and Flam.* 1.3). But that fact serves only to underscore the character of the interpretation Polybius chooses to offer here. Nor is there any reason to believe that 23.12 is merely an attempt to hide Philopoemen's faults. Polybius does not distort the basic information; he is, after all, the source for all the information about Philopoemen's last campaign that could lead to the interpretation of recklessness. And the very length and detail of this Polybian disquisition on the power of Tyche—especially when combined with so many similar passages elsewhere in *The Histories*—also powerfully argues in favor of Polybius's sincerity here.[3]

But one should also emphasize that the helplessness before Tyche of even so formidable a figure as Philopoemen is only half the point Polybius wishes to make in 23.12. The whole of 23.12–14—the tandem obituaries of Philopoemen, Hannibal, and Scipio Africanus—has a quite different ideological goal. For Polybius wishes these obituaries to serve his audience as an inspiration to attempt the *achievement* of noble deeds (23.14.12). Mortals may be helpless before circumstances and the power of Tyche, but that does not relieve Polybius's aristocratic audience of the duty to act, in pursuit of the καλόν. It is the frequency of these exhortations to act that needs to be emphasized.[4]

Not surprisingly, the ideology of benevolent, honorable action appears repeatedly in Polybius's assessment of the Hellenistic monarchs. It was kings, of all mortals, who held in their hands the most concentrated personal power *to* act; in addition, the ideology of Hellenistic kingship asserted that the legitimacy of the monarch rested on his benefactions to

3. For detailed discussion of the variant traditions on Philopoemen's conduct in 183, see Chap. II, above.
4. Even Sacks, who normally is highly skeptical of the existence of any moralizing tendency in *The Histories*, sees 23.14.12 as more ethical than practical in intent (*Polybius on the Writing of History*, 136 n. 30). On the sincerity of 23.14.12, cf. also Wunderer, *Polybios*, 13 n. 20. By contrast, A. J. Pomeroy, "Polybius's Death Notices," 414–16, greatly downplays the moralizing aspects of the passage.

his own people (including especially the military defense of his realm), as well as his benevolent deeds throughout the wider world. Polybius clearly partakes of this ideology.[5]

Monarchs who receive Polybius's approval are, in fact, primarily men of benevolent action in the world. Thus Attalus I laid the foundation of the Pergamene kingdom by wise use of his personal wealth, defeated the Gauls of Asia Minor (who were a perennial threat to their Greek neighbors)—and, according to Polybius, died while fighting for the liberties of the Hellenes during the Second Macedonian War. He receives a powerful Polybian accolade (18.41). Eumenes II greatly expanded Pergamene power by his intelligence and indefatigable labor (φιλοπονία, 32.8.4). The same was true of the Seleucid Antiochus III; the early (good) part of his career was characterized not only by personal courage but by sheer love of hard work (φιλοπονία again, 11.34.14). Massinissa of Numidia transformed his domains economically—and possessed enormous personal energy well into old age (36.16). Hiero II of Syracuse was forced by circumstances to adopt more passive policies than other kings during his long reign; but he had originally gained rule over Syracuse through outstanding personal qualities, unaided by Tyche (7.8.1), and he conferred many benefactions upon both his own people and the Greeks as a whole (1.16.11, 7.8.6).[6]

Polybius in fact clearly *expected* monarchs to do their duty as he conceived it. Duty meant acting to defend their people—this was τὸ καθῆκον (28.21.3)—and not running away, even under difficult circumstances (ibid.; cf. 29.17–19). Duty meant acting to develop one's domains economically (see 7.8.4 and 36.16). Duty meant—in a word—to act energetically and with nobility (τολμᾶν τι βασιλείας ἄξιον: 31.11.5), and never to be discouraged by difficult circumstances or contrary Fortune (cf. 16.28.3).[7] Polybius thinks of both Alexander and his marshals as truly "kingly" men, not merely because of their great achievements, but precisely because of their willingness to undergo extraordinary dangers, hardship, and toil (πόνους, 8.10.9).[8]

Naturally, Polybius's advocacy of action hardly means that he approves of every vigorous act by a king. Royal power existed to be exercised with vigor, but not primarily for egotistical purposes.[9] Hence Polybius's savage

---

5. See esp. Welwei, *Könige und Königtum*, 123 and 129; cf. Walbank, "Monarchies and Monarchic Ideas," 82–83.

6. On the ideology behind Polybius's praise of these kings, see Welwei, *Könige und Königtum*, 123.

7. Ibid., 126.

8. Ibid.

9. Ibid., 129.

criticism of the aggressions of Philip V and Antiochus III in their "bad" periods (cf. 7.11–14 and 15.20), and of the aggressions of Antiochus IV (29.26).[10] But Polybius is equally contemptuous of those monarchs who take no glorious or socially useful action at all. This is most noticeable in his repeated criticism of Ptolemy IV; and even the glorious death of Ptolemy VI in battle does not absolve him completely of Polybian suspicion concerning his essential laziness.[11]

Polybius's advocacy of the ideology of benevolent action, however, is not limited to kings. It also informs Polybius's discussions of the conduct of statesmen of republics. A primary example is his overview of the impact upon Achaea of the career of Aratus of Sicyon. Before Aratus, Achaean ideas were good, but there were no great deeds (πρᾶξις ἀξιόλο-γος, 2.39.11). But eventually the Achaeans did find leaders who were capable of action: Aratus, and later Philopoemen and Lycortas (40.1). It was their deeds (πραξεῖς; cf. 40.2) that led to the unification of the Peloponnese, "the noblest of achievements" (ibid.)—noble, because Polybius tends to identify the expansion of Achaean power with the extension of liberty (cf. 2.42.3 and 6). Later, in the crisis of the 220s, Aratus's political skill enabled the Achaean League to survive the new threat posed by Cleomenes III of Sparta (at the cost, it is true, of a new Achaean dependence upon Macedon), and Polybius's judgment is that Aratus demonstrated here that "he was a man capable of meeting any emergency" (45.3).

Polybius's account of Aratus is certainly rife with Achaean patriotic motifs; but that only underscores how Aratus exemplifies for Polybius the statesman's duty to act vigorously in ways Polybius himself considers to be positive. Moreover, Polybius's praise of Aratus's efforts on behalf of Achaea is extended even though Aratus's ultimate goal—full Achaean independence from any great power—was never achieved, and was perhaps not achievable.[12]

The tandem obituaries of the republican statesmen Philopoemen, Scipio Africanus, and Hannibal (23.12–14) have relevance from this particular perspective too. Polybius hopes that study of the careers of these men (including the obstacles they overcame, placed in their paths by the very nature of the republican political systems in which they worked) will inspire his audience to attempt noble deeds (πρὸς τὰ καλὰ τῶν ἔργων,

10. For detailed discussion of these passages, see Chaps. IV, VII, and VIII, above.
11. Ptolemy IV: 5.34.4, 34.10, 87.3. Ptolemy VI: 39.7.7.
12. Welwei suggests that Aratus's political vigor and accomplishments led Polybius to view him as an inherently "kingly" man, even though he lived in a republic (*Könige und Königtum*, 129–30). This is certainly the case with Scipio Africanus (Polyb. 10.40.2–9, explicitly; cf. Welwei, 129–30). Both men, of course, faced serious failure late in their lives.

23.14.2). But it is the *attempt* to achieve the noble that weighs heaviest with Polybius (πρὸς τὰ καλά)—not pragmatic success.[13]

Of course, in the best of all possible worlds Polybius would prefer that men of energy and high moral qualities should succeed in their goals. This was mostly the case with Scipio Africanus, and somewhat the case with Philopoemen (but not at all the case with Hannibal). The ideal of hard work leading to just rewards comes out, for instance, in fragment 12 B-W (the context of which is unfortunately unknown):

> No darkness, no storm however violent, deterred him from his purpose. He forced his way through the obstacles confronting him, and overcame even illness by resolute labor [ἐκπονῶν], and was successful throughout his entire life.

Similarly, Polybius praises Scipio Africanus's love of hard work (φιλο- πονία, 10.5.9), and objects strongly to the idea that Scipio owed his successes to the favor of Tyche rather than to his own energy and personal effort (ibid.). And even in Hannibal's case, Polybius is contemptuous of those writers who attributed the Carthaginian's success in crossing the Alps to mere luck, and the favor of the gods; it was instead the result of hard work and careful preparation (3.47.6–48.12). The same was true of Philopoemen's great victory at Mantineia in 207 (cf. 11.8–10).

But Polybius also knew that in fact he was not living in the best of all possible worlds. Success was very difficult to achieve, fragile, often illusory. This is why so often in *The Histories* he depicts people as excessively joyful at momentary success (περιχαρεῖς)—only to have their hopes cruelly dashed.[14] The often terrible contradictions between hope and reality (at the extreme, between *hubris* and *nemesis*) were, to be sure, a Greek philosophical and historiographical commonplace. But this only means that Polybius's view of this issue (as of many other issues) fitted comfortably within the traditions of Greek ethical thinking.[15]

It is this Polybian awareness of the difficulties in achieving success that helps explain what has long gone unremarked in modern scholarship— his repeated praise for the energy and courage of people who yet meet

13. On the obstacles in the paths of Philopoemen, Hannibal, and Scipio, see 23.12.8–9 and 14.1–11; with the comments in Chap. VIII, above. On Polybius's approval of striving πρὸς τὰ καλά, cf. also 6.55.4.

14. For περιχαρεῖς as false consciousness, see Polyb. 1.20.1 (the Romans in 263); 1.23.3 (the Carthaginians in 260); 3.70.1 (Ti. Sempronius Longus, consul 218, before the Trebia); 10.14.1 (the defenders of New Carthage, in 209); 11.11.1 (the Spartan ruler Machanidas in 207, before the battle of Mantineia); 18.24.6 (Philip V in 197, at Cynoscephalae). Cf. also 1.41.1 and 44.7; 3.103.1; 24.8.10.

15. For comparison, see Lateiner, "No Laughing Matter: A Literary Tactic of Herodotus," 173–80.

with stalemate in the efforts to achieve their goals, or even with outright defeat. The substantial list of explicit and even emphatic statements to this effect was first laid out in Chapter I, and need not be repeated here in detail.[16]

Indeed, Polybius stresses that human beings must be *prepared* for failure. It is a Polybian maxim: found at 2.4.3–5, 11.2.4–7 (a very emphatic and generalizing statement), and also at fragment 102 B-W (with specific warning examples being given).[17] But the historian also asserts that the proper response to disaster is not panic, but to think and plan for the future (14.6.8–9, a generalizing statement). It may well have been a Hellenistic commonplace that defeat was the real test of nobility and greatness of spirit (cf. Plut. *Eum.* 9.1); but if so, Polybius believed it. The theme is stated emphatically at 6.2.5–6—at the beginning of a crucial explanation of how, even after the Cannae disaster, the Romans eventually rose to overlordship of the Mediterranean. Indeed, at 1.1.2, at the very beginning of the entire work, Polybius emphasizes that one of the great purposes of the study of history is to teach people how to react to adverse fortune "with courage and nobility" (γενναίως).

This is, in good part, an ethic of personal responsibility—the responsibility exercised by Scipio Africanus, by Philopoemen and Hannibal, or, as Polybius well knew, by Scipio Aemilianus at difficult moments during the siege of Carthage in the 140s (36.8.4–5).[18] It is not surprising that a man possessing such an intense ideology of personal responsibility could also write that Tyche often receives blame for disasters that are actually the result of carelessness on the part of those who are in charge of public affairs (frg. 83 B-W).[19] This is the same historian who writes that statesmen must maintain constant vigilance over the events occurring throughout the world; they must be like physicians with patients: eternally watchful (3.7.3–7). Similarly, Polybius argues that it is the statesman's personal duty (καθήκει) to inform himself energetically on important events of the past, so that he can be more effective in the politics of the present (3.21.9). This is in good part the ideological origin of Polybius's consistent demand that his own *Histories*—intended primarily for statesmen—should be read

---

16. But see, e.g., 9.8–9 (Epaminondas and Hannibal); 11.2.10–11 (Hasdrubal at the Metaurus); 15.16 (Hannibal at Zama); 36.8.1 (Homilco Phameas during the Third Punic War). Cf. also 1.31.8, 58.7–59.1, 62.1 (the Carthaginians during the First Punic War).

17. Cf. also Polybius's underlining of Scipio Africanus's preparations in this respect during his attack on New Carthage (10.8.8–9; with Chap. VI, above).

18. Polybius's ethic of personal responsibility is rightly stressed by A. J. Pomeroy, "Polybius's Death Notices," 410–12.

19. The context of the fragment is unknown: cf. Walbank, *Commentary* I: 22 n. 4; and III: 679 and 750.

with great care and diligence, including cross-referencing by the readers. This is an idea that Polybius not only underscores, but quite evidently enjoys repeating.[20] Let one more passage here stand for many others as expressive of the Polybian belief in personal responsibility. In the supreme crisis of Classical Greek history, during the Persian invasion of 480, Polybius recounts the Greek decision to fight the Persian invasion on their own, without becoming dependent upon the power of the tyrannical Gelo of Syracuse for their safety (12.26b.1–3). His praise of the Greeks for this decision is most warm (26b.3): "They relied upon themselves, and invited anyone who wished to do so to partake in the contest of valor and manliness [ἀνδρεία], and win the prize of excellence [ἀρετή]."[21]

It is congruent with such an ideology that Polybius also goes out of his way in *The Histories* to condemn laziness and indolence. The human fault of indolence (ῥᾳθυμία) in fact makes its first appearance within the first two hundred words of Polybius's work (condemned at 1.1.5). It is explicitly presented as one of those deep flaws that are common in the human personality (3.81.4). It is common to Greeks (2.5.6–7, 36.17.7) and non-Greeks: Carthaginians (1.74.10), Persians (3.6.12), Romans (3.76.9; cf. 1.19.12), Celts (3.79.4, where it is called φυγοπονία, "aversion to toil"). Polybius's own Achaeans are not exempt (4.7.6, 57.3, 58.12)—and that includes the Megalopolitans, the men of Polybius's own home town (2.55.2). And Polybius especially decries laziness and indolence when it occurs among the leadership of polities, whether the leaders are kings (Ptolemy IV and VI), generals (3.81.4)—or the republican elite of Achaea itself.[22]

And if Polybius expected the readers of his *Histories* to be very diligent (see above), naturally he extended such expectations to the writers of

20. Polybius's remonstrances that his work be read carefully and diligently, and his justifications for lengthy discussions: see 1.20.8, 64.1–2; 2.2.2, 71.1–2; 3.10.1–2, 31 *passim*, 34.3, 57.6–9; 4.38.11–13; 12.26c.4; 16.20.3–4. It is typical of the current cynical trend in Polybian studies that Vercruysse, "Fonction des passages méthodologiques chez Polybe," 34–35, now sees passages such as these as merely a Polybian rhetorical way of complimenting his readers for belonging to a select group—in order to win them over to accepting his versions of reality.

21. For the praise of self-reliance, cf. also Polyb. 2.47.1 (κάλλιστον), 50.11 (κάλλιον), 53.1; cf. the linkage of concepts at 2.55.9 (φιλελεύθερον καὶ γενναῖον), and 4.60.6–10 (with a generalizing comment).

22. Ptolemy IV and VI: see n. 11, above. The Achaean elite: see 10.21.1 and 11.8.1–6. Even Aratus can be criticized for this (in 219): 4.60.2 and 7. Cf. also the contemptuous description of A. Postumius Albinus, consul 151: φιλήδονος . . . καὶ φυγόπονος (39.1.10). Polybius had personal reasons for disliking Albinus, who had blocked the return of the Achaean exiles to their homeland in 155 (cf. 33.1.5). That does not change the importance of the terminology used to attack him, or its consistency with a Polybian ideology often and vividly expressed throughout the text.

history as well. To write history accurately and instructively was a duty (τοῦ καθῆκοντος, 16.14.3). But this task took effort. This is why Polybius can praise even the historian Timaeus, normally one of his *bêtes noires*, when Timaeus demonstrates diligence in research of documents—because the historian, Polybius explains, should be a very hard worker (φιλοπονώτερος, 12.26a.3; cf. φιλοπόνως at 26a.4).[23]

Usually, however, Polybius's advocacy of this form of hard work has to be deduced not from his praise of other historians but from his criticism of them. Thus he takes to task those writers who claim to be offering universal history when in reality they skim over important events, giving no substantial discussion (5.33). This is not mere polemic against rivals; Polybius presents the same theme—the absolute necessity of substantial discussion of important events—in nonpolemical contexts as well (cf. 2.2.2).[24] And if Polybius is stern concerning diligence in writing, he is equally stern in criticizing those who display insufficient diligence in research. Thus he savages those historians who write fancifully about the Alps, and Hannibal's crossing of them, without ever having gone to the trouble of crossing (or even viewing) the mountains themselves. These men have not done their research (οὐχ ἱστορήσαντες, 3.48.6). Similarly, while Polybius praises Timaeus for his searching-out and use of primary documents, in general (as is well known) Polybius attacks Timaeus repeatedly for laziness. He sat in a library and took "the more pleasant but the inferior road" (12.27.2), instead of exerting himself through travel and personal inspection of historical sites. He worked "without danger or hardship" (χωρὶς κινδύνου καὶ κακοπαθείας, 12.27.4), and so made careless and ridiculous errors (13.4.4). Acceptance of danger and hardship is, then, a duty even for historians, according to Polybius.[25] It is therefore not a surprise that Polybius also severely attacks those historians who dare to write about battle when they have never personally experienced it or risked their lives in it—as Polybius makes sure his readers know he has.[26]

23. For the emphasis on praiseworthy industriousness here, see also 12.25e.1, 25f.2, 26e.3, and 36.1.7 (the necessity for historians to possess πολυπραγμοσύνη). Cf. von Scala, *Studien*, 4.

24. For detailed discussion of Polyb. 5.33 and its ideology, see Chap. VIII, above.

25. For Polybius's attack on what he perceived as Timaeus's laziness, see also 12.26e.4–5, 27.4–6 and 10–11, and 28a *passim*. This attack is taken as sincere by Isnardi, "Τέχνη e ἦθος nella metodologia storiografia di Polibio," 102–10: without moral integrity (ἦθος), the historical writing itself (the τέχνη) is naturally bound to be deficient. In contrast, Schepens—in line with current scholarship—now sees Polybius in Book 12 as a hypocrite merely concerned to criticize Timaeus any way he can ("Polemic and Methodology in Polybius' Book XII," 39–61; cf. 68). Given all the information collected above (and see below), Isnardi seems correct to argue that the attack on laziness actually has a thought-out, philosophical basis.

26. See Polyb. 12.25h.5; cf. 28.13.1–2 and the important Amm. Marc. 24.2.16, with discussion in Chap. I.

Indeed, throughout *The Histories* Polybius emphasizes his own life of activity and risk taking in a dangerous world—a world that inflicted upon him both hardship and disaster. He indicates that he achieved a prominent political career in Achaea at an extraordinarily early age;[27] that he voluntarily partook in the dangers of Q. Marcius Philippus's mountain campaign against Perseus of Macedon in 169 (28.13.1–2); that he was not psychologically crushed by the political catastrophe of 168/167, which destroyed his brilliant political career and left him a deportee and exile in Italy. This was a real blow, administered by Tyche (cf. 1.1.2)—and by his political enemy Callicrates' unfair accusations to the Romans (cf. 30.13.9–11). Nevertheless, Polybius recovered, and was soon hard at work on a second career, as a historian (cf. 31.23.4).[28] And he presents himself as having energetically set about his research. He gained access to archives at Rome (cf. 3.26.1)—and found a way around the difficulty posed by the archaic Latin he found there (cf. 3.22.3: he persuaded experts to translate them for him). He is proud of having personally visited Lacinium in southern Italy, in order to take extensive notes on the military inscription left there by Hannibal, which provided detailed information on Hannibal's army (3.33.17–18). He is similarly proud of having discovered (evidently through interviews) the story of Hannibal's oath to Hamilcar, which seemed to put the origins of the Second Punic War in a new perspective (3.10–12).[29] Meanwhile, he acted as an adviser to the young Scipio Aemilianus (31.25–30); and not even serious illness kept him from participating in other politics, including some very dangerous activity on behalf of the Seleucid prince Demetrius of Syria (cf. 31.11–15). Other historians dared to write about Hannibal's crossing of the Alps without ever having seen them, but Polybius emphasized that he had both seen them and crossed them (3.48.12). He also recounted how he had personally explored the Atlantic coasts of Africa and Spain (cf. 34.15.7). Later, he helped engineer the return of the surviving Achaean exiles (including himself) to their homeland (35.6). He served as a military adviser to the Romans during the Third Punic War (cf. 36.11 and 38.19), and evidently depicted himself as fighting in the front line (cf. Amm. Marc. 24.2.16). Later still, he helped ameliorate the Roman political settlement after the disastrous Achaean War (39.5 and 8.1). In addi-

27. On Polybius's very rapid rise to political prominence in Achaea before 168/167 (cf., e.g., Polyb. 24.6.5), see now Eckstein, "Birth and Death of Polybius," 397–404.

28. The date of this reference to the borrowing of books from Scipio Aemilianus (and the confiscated Antigonid library) is evidently autumn 167: see Walbank, *Commentary* III: 495 and 497.

29. On Polybius's extensive use of interviews to gather information during his sojourn at Rome, see esp. Pédech, *Méthode,* 360–67.

THE DUTY TO ACT

tion, he now decided to recast his *Histories* on an even grander scale, to bring them down to the events of the 140s (3.4–5).

Evidently, Polybius closely identified with the Homeric hero Odysseus.[30] But what need to be underlined are the specific aspects of Odysseus that appealed to the historian's heart: not the trickster and storyteller, but Odysseus the diligent and careful general (*Il.* 10.251–53; cf. Polyb. 9.16.1), Odysseus the intelligent and widely experienced man of the world (*Od.* 1.1; cf. Polyb. 12.27.10), who suffered innumerable woes for the sake of higher goals (πολλὰ . . . παθεῖν, *Od.* 1.4; cf. Polyb. 12.27.11), who was seasoned by tempest and war (*Od.* 8.183; cf. Polyb. 12.27.11). "It seems to me," Polybius concludes in discussing Odysseus, "that the dignity of history writing requires such a man" (12.28.1). Yet, he adds, even for such men of action familiar with the world, the writing of history was not to be attempted carelessly (12.28.4). Rather, it was to be seen as a lifelong labor—labor in the most necessary and most noble of tasks (καλλίστων, ibid.).[31]

Thus the "Odyssean world" of Polybius was not a world of lighthearted adventure, but a dangerous and difficult place through which the Odysseus figure forged his way by means of his intelligence (*Od.* 1.1) and his ability to withstand toil and woe (*Il.* 10.251–53; *Od.* 1.4 and 8.183). Worldly success might be hoped for and, ideally, achieved. But intelligent and energetic activity was in any case a duty, and it guaranteed nothing, except perhaps honor. A warrior could expect no more—and no less.

Honor—the honor that comes from vigorous action (successful or not) aimed at accomplishing the καλόν: this, of course, has been the main theme of the present study. There is no doubt that Polybius sought to give his aristocratic audience good practical advice about politics, society, and war—advice that might lead to pragmatic success in the real world. This was certainly a major goal of *The Histories*.[32] But the modern fascination with Polybius's practical advice—a fascination that has endured since the Renaissance—has obscured the ethical purposes to which *The Histories* were also powerfully dedicated. The point has been reached where the

30. See, rightly, Walbank, *Polybius*, 51–52; cf. 25. Cato the Elder perhaps remarked on this as well (see next note).

31. Walbank, *Polybius*, 25, rightly notes that Polybius's references to Odysseus seem focused on the idea of a historian's being willing to undertake labor and hardship. Similarly, Cato the Elder's comparison of Polybius to Odysseus (Polyb. 35.6.3–4), though meant somewhat ironically, is based on Odysseus's willingness to undertake dangerous missions—in this case, Polybius's wish in 150 to ask the Senate not only to allow the Achaean exiles to go home, but to restore their public honors as well.

32. See the long list of practical Polybian advice now collected by Meissner, "Polybios," 324–28. Cf. also Sacks, *Polybius on the Writing of History*, 132–34.

scholarly *communis opinio* finds Polybius to be fundamentally a pragmatic, utilitarian, even "Machiavellian" writer.[33]

There is another element in the Polybian text that has allowed him to be read as cold, as an exponent of *Realpolitik,* and even as a "Machiavellian." That is Polybius's sense of blunt realism, his proclaimed awareness of the true nature of the world and of how people in power really act, his basic notion of a deeply flawed ἀνϑρώπεια φύσις. One is struck, similarly, by the historian's constant emphasis on self-control, and the repression of irrational emotion: modern scholars, for instance, would be more comfortable with Polybius if he actually evinced greater anger at the Romans for their behavior after 180. He does not—and hence has arisen the natural suspicion that he had a coldly "Machiavellian" approach to politics, or was even a man intent upon currying favor with the powerful.[34] But it is more likely that the reason Polybius does not evince greater anger at the Romans (though, I have argued, he certainly does direct substantial criticism at them) is simply because he is not surprised at their behavior. He sees their growing oppression and corruption (and is opposed to it), but he sees it as an all-too-natural process of politics and human nature. He is not afraid to criticize them, but one may doubt that he thought such criticism would do much good. It is a view of the world that goes back to Thucydides—and tragedy.[35]

Thus, the purpose of this study has been to rescue the moral seriousness of *The Histories*—a moral seriousness itself based upon a tragic view of the world—from its current obscurity. No claim is being made here that Polybius was a deeply original moral philosopher. On the contrary: the focus on his moral seriousness and its specific characteristics immediately establishes that he was a rather traditional writer. He was a writer who urged upon his (aristocratic) audience the traditional (aristocratic) virtues of personal courage, honorable behavior, simplicity and self-restraint (yet also generosity), honest dealings, the imposition of will under difficult circumstances, an attitude of determination in defeat, and of modesty and emotional caution in success. Nor should such a conclusion cause much surprise: the ancient historical writers whose works survive are *all* strongly moralizing figures. This was the basic literary-historiographical tradition available to Polybius. What is now clear is that it was a tradition with which he felt perfectly comfortable.

Moreover, not only are the ancient historical writers (including Polybius) all strongly moralizing figures, but it is striking that all of them (in-

---

33. Indeed, a strong moralizing element in Polybius's work is now once again denied by Walbank, "Motives of Hellenistic Historians," 263–66.

34. For such reactions, see esp. Walbank, *Polybius,* 178–79, and "Polybius between Greece and Rome," 16–20; and Green, *Alexander to Actium,* 279–81.

35. See esp. Macleod, "Thucydides and Tragedy," 140–58 (essential).

cluding Polybius) draw for their audience precisely the same moral. The attack on *hubris*, on arrogance, on self-indulgence, on uncontrolled violence (and on emotional turbulence in general) is consistent, and stretches in an unbroken chain from Herodotus to Tacitus and beyond.[36] The origin of this moralistic tradition among the ancient historical writers does not lie merely in the employment of moralizing motifs and terminology as convenient or expected literary tropes, nor merely in their employment as a convenient way of imposing an immediately intelligible (as well as esthetically satisfying) framework onto amorphous and complicated historical material. Rather, the main issue that confronted all the historical writers here was their knowledge of the real misbehavior of the powerful. Such misbehavior was made all too possible by the wealth and status enjoyed by the elites of ancient Mediterranean societies, and by the inability of ordinary people to bring aristocratic miscreants efficiently to justice. But ultimately such misbehavior could be terribly destructive to the legitimacy and stability of ordered society; and it was viewed by thoughtful people as ultimately self-destructive to the perpetrators of misdeeds themselves. Yet one does not have to point out persistently to one's audience the intimate connection between *hubris* and *nemesis* unless one knows (or fears) that the audience—the elite of society—tends strongly by its very nature toward the hubristic.[37]

The deep concern here of Polybius and other historical writers was certainly pragmatic at least in a broad sense: they themselves belonged to the elite stratum, and so had a powerful stake in the maintenance of the current social order. But there was also a true inability to see what could ever replace that social order except a horrible chaos destructive to all; and from that perspective the pragmatic concern for social stability need not be seen as merely self-interested. Also, since the flaws and crimes described by Polybius redounded often enough to the injury or

36. Herodotus: see, e.g., Stahl, "Learning through Suffering?" Thucydides: see, e.g., Edmunds, "Thucydides' Ethics as Reflected in the Description of Stasis." On Theopompus, see, e.g., Shrimpton, "Theopompus' Treatment of Philip in the *Philippica*," esp. 136–44. On Hieronymus, see, e.g., Hornblower, *Hieronymus of Cardia*, esp. 102–6. On Timaeus, see, e.g., Mitchell, "Historical and Historiographical Prominence of the Pyrrhic War," esp. 318–19. On Posidonius, see, e.g., Strasburger, "Posidonius on the Problems of the Roman Empire," 40–63. On Sallust, see, e.g., Earl, *Political Thought of Sallust*, chap. 4. On Diodorus, see now Sacks, *Diodorus Siculus and the First Century*, 21 and 25. On Dionysius of Halicarnassus, see, e.g., the comments of Fornara, *Nature of History in Greece and Rome*, 116. On Livy, see now Moore, *Artistry and Ideology: Livy's Vocabulary of Virtue*. On Tacitus, see now Plass, *Rhetoric of Historiography in Imperial Rome*, esp. 26–28, 56–57, 129–32. Cf. on Ammianus now Seager, *Ammianus Marcellinus: Seven Studies*, chaps. 1–5.

37. On the moralizing tendency in general, see the comments of Fornara, *Nature of History in Greece and Rome*, 111–19. On the sincerity of the motivations of the historical writers here, see esp. de Romilly, *Rise and Fall of States According to Greek Authors*, chap. 1.

even the destruction of their perpetrators, his warnings to his audience here take on a pragmatic tone in that sense. Yet even such a "broad" pragmatism had its limits in a world not only made up of societies that Polybius believed were in a state of inevitable degeneration anyway (tied to the wheel of the ἀνακύκλωσις), but in a world, as well, in which the human capacity to control personal destiny was itself terribly circumscribed.

This was a pessimism about historical circumstances and human possibilities from which Polybius had evidently never been free, but that grew increasingly more pronounced as, over the decades, the writing of *The Histories* continued. In such a grim and chaotic universe as Polybius posited, the call for ethical conduct took on a deeper meaning. It was not so much an attempt to preserve the social order; although Polybius believed this was vitally important, he seems to have doubted, in the end, that it could be permanently achieved. It was not so much an attempt to stave off personal disaster by means of personal reform of conduct; although Polybius believed it was important to attempt personal reform, he seems to have felt that Tyche and circumstances could inflict catastrophe on anyone, even the person who acted with self-restraint and disciplined intelligence. Indeed, Polybius himself had the best of reasons to know this.

Thus the value that lay at the heart of ethical conduct in the grim and chaotic world perceived by Polybius could only be not an instrumental value but an absolute one. In such a universe, the effort toward ethical and energetic conduct could guarantee only a sense of honor, a sense of having fulfilled one's duty, of having somehow accomplished the καλόν and rejected the αἰσχρόν. Ultimately, it was the superior quality inherent in the action itself that had to count. To Polybius, the long effort of writing *The Histories* was such an action.

APPENDIX:
POLYBIUS ON DRINKING
AND DRUNKENNESS

Polybius's attitude toward drinking and drunkenness has never received detailed examination from scholars. Yet even the surviving remnants of *The Histories* demonstrate that this was a work containing more negative depictions of drinking and drunkenness than is the case with any other extant historical writer from antiquity. Not even Herodotus or Tacitus—two writers well known for their interest in human foibles—approach the emphasis Polybius gives to this subject.[1] Such comparisons, of course, can be made only with extant works; and we know that among the works that have been lost, Theopompus (for instance) adopted a highly moralizing stance on the subject of heavy drinking.[2] The example of Theopompus shows that Polybius had available a highly moralizing historiographical

---

1. There are at least 16 references to drunkenness in Herodotus—a text somewhat shorter than the surviving parts of Polybius's *Histories:* see Powell, *A Lexicon of Herodotus*[2], cols. 188 and 218. But Herodotus's tone is usually objective and descriptive, not moralizing. To be sure, at 3.34 the Persians argue that their shah Cambyses has been driven mad by drink—but Herodotus gives Cambyses a powerful counterargument. And in 6.84 Herodotus records the Spartan belief that King Cleomenes I had been driven mad by drink—but it is an idea that Herodotus himself rejects. (In 3.22, healthful properties are attributed to wine.) In Tacitus's works—a text about the size of the surviving Polybian *Histories*—there are at least 14 references to drunkenness, and some of these references do convey negative implications; see Gerber and Greef, *Lexicon Taciteum* I: 344, and II: 1777. By contrast, in Polybius there are at least 37 references to drunkenness—more than twice the number in Tacitus—and they are almost all negative; see Mauersberger, *Polybios-Lexikon* I:4, cols. 1531–33 and 1699.

2. On Theopompus's moralizing, see Polyb. 8.9.4 and 9.7, with Shrimpton, "Theopompus's Treatment of Philip in the *Philippica*," esp. 136–44.

tradition to draw on, if he chose. What deserves underlining is that he chose to follow that tradition.

In *The Histories*, the widest variety of personages are depicted as indulging in heavy and destructive wine drinking. Drunkenness was clearly one of the major recreations—and temptations—in Polybius's world; his remarks on this problem are one aspect of his usefulness as a source on Hellenistic society and its tensions. Habitual drunkards in *The Histories* include important Greek kings (notably Ptolemy IV, Antiochus III, and Polybius's own friend Demetrius I), major Greek politicians (notably A-gathocles of Alexandria), Roman generals (notably M. Livius, commander of the Roman garrison at Tarentum)—as well as the more expected common soldiery (of all nationalities), disreputable mercenaries, and crude barbarians.[3]

Polybius's persistent and highly negative depiction of heavy drinking does not mean, however, that Polybius was a stern teetotaler; on the contrary, he was a connoisseur of fine wine (see 34.11.1; cf. 12.2.7). But as with sexuality (cf. 10.19.5), so with drinking, the key was moderation (25.3.7, explicitly).[4]

The problem here was that many of the people Polybius knew about—including key historical figures—had proven themselves unable to exercise such moderation. Furthermore, Polybius saw a failure to exercise moderation in drinking as symptomatic of a broader personality failure: in his mind, heavy drinking was closely associated both with lascivious sexuality (which he did consider disgraceful, especially in men who bore serious social responsibilities) and with irrational violence.

The close conceptual connection between drunkenness and shameful lasciviousness is borne out in several generalizing statements: about men tempted by power (3.81.5–6), about the signs of an aristocracy beginning to degenerate into a self-seeking oligarchy (6.8.5), about the degenerate younger generation at Rome (31.25.4). Specific portraits of drunkards are even more vivid. Thus Ptolemy IV "spent all his time in disgraceful amours and constant senseless drunkenness" (ἀπρεπεῖς ἔρωτας, ἀλόγους μέθας, 5.34.10), and even ordered that statues of his female cupbearer Cleino, scantily clad and carrying her wine pitcher, be set up in temples (14.11.2).[5] Heavy drinking led the Boeotian politician Bracchylas to asso-

---

3. Ptolemy IV: 5.34.10–11; cf. 14.11.2. Antiochus III: 20.8. Demetrius I: 31.13; 33.19. Also, Philip V: 25.3.7. Agathocles: 15.25.22 and 30.5. Livius: 8.25–30. Common soldiers: 4.57.3; 5.39.1, 48.1–9; 8.37. Mercenaries: 1.69.12. Barbarians: 2.4.6, 19.4; 11.3.1; 14.4.9; 29.13.

4. For detailed discussion of Polyb. 10.19, see Chap. V, above.

5. Walbank, *Commentary* II: 438, notes that Polybius may be drawing his account of Ptolemy IV's behavior from an eyewitness, Ptolemy of Megalopolis (cf. Athen. 10.425e–f). On the Greek association of the wine pitcher (and its bearer) with lasciviousness (as in Polyb.

ciate with "obscene degenerates" (Livy [P] 33.28.1–4).⁶ Agathocles of Alexandria, the prime minister of Ptolemy V, "spent the greater part of
each day in drinking, and in the sexual debaucheries that commonly ac-
company drunkenness" (15.25.22); he spared neither matron, nor bride,
nor virgin (ibid.).⁷

In the case of Agathocles, as also with the debased *aristoi*, it is clear that
one of the things repulsive to Polybius is that force is being used to gain
desired sexual goals.⁸ And Polybius elsewhere is explicit in connecting
drunkenness with unacceptable violence. The two important Antigonid
courtiers Megaleas and Leonteas disgraced themselves in 218 by physically attacking Aratus of Sicyon; they acted in this manner because they
were drunk (5.15.3–9). King Genthius of Illyria was driven by drunken
lust to murder his own brother, so that he could marry his brother's fiancée (29.13.1). This, Polybius says, was only one of the disgraceful acts
(ἀσελγῆ) caused by Genthius's heavy drinking (πολυποσίαν); in fact, he
was drunk day and night (13.2). Gallic barbarians often fell out among
themselves in mutual slaughter; violent quarrels were common among
these people, Polybius says, "chiefly caused by their inordinate drinking
and intemperate feasting" (οἰνοφλυγίας, 2.19.4).⁹

For Polybius, however, drinking could also have an opposite—though
equally reprehensible—effect: it could result in drunken sleepiness and
sloth. This phenomenon led to the fall of Tarentum to Hannibal in 213
(8.25–30), and to the fall of Syracuse to M. Claudius Marcellus in 212
(8.37.2–11). It led to the destruction of Xenoetas's Seleucid army at the
hands of the rebel Molon (5.48)—and to the destruction of Hasdrubal's
Gallic auxiliaries at the battle of the Metaurus in 207 (slaughtered in their
drunken sleep, by the victorious Romans: 11.3.1).¹⁰

Habitual overuse of wine could also result in a more general sloth-
fulness. Polybius chastises Ptolemy IV severely on these grounds
(5.34.10). And the historian offers a similar, generalizing comment at
20.4.6–7, when discussing the "degenerate" conduct of the Boeotians
after about 250:

14.11.2 and 15.25.32), see the collection of evidence in Goodenough, *Jewish Symbols in the
Graeco-Roman Period* VI: 25.
    6. For the derivation of Livy 33.28 from Polybian material, see Nissen, *Kritische Unter-
suchungen*, 144.
    7. On this theme, see also Polyb. 20.8.2 (Antiochus III), 23.5.9–13 (Deinocrates of
Messene).
    8. On the debased *aristoi*, cf. 6.8.5: ὕβρεις, ἁρπαγάς.
    9. On this theme, see also 1.69.12 (mercenaries), 15.25.31–32 (Tlepolemus), 18.55.2
(Chariomortus the ally of Scopas the Aetolian).
    10. On this theme, see also 4.57.3 (Ageira), 5.39.1 (Alexandria), 14.4.9 (the losing side
in the battle of the Camps in 203), and frg. 40 B-W (drunken, half-conscious, disobedient
soldiers; context unknown).

288   APPENDIX

They never again ventured to engage in noble activity [τῶν καλῶν] . . . but,
abandoning themselves to feasting and excessive drinking [μέθας], they
thus sapped the energy not only of their bodies but of their minds.

The reasons behind Polybius's consistent attack on heavy drinking—
his implied warnings to his audience that this was an activity to be
avoided—are undoubtedly in good part pragmatic: the negative pragmatic effect, in the competitive struggle of politics and war, of drinking
to excess. Thus M. Livius lost Tarentum to Hannibal (8.25–30), Antiochus
III wasted precious time while engaged in a crucial campaign against
Rome (20.8), Xenoetas's drunken soldiery were destroyed (5.48), Ptolemy IV soon faced serious challenges to his regime (5.34.10–11). Conversely, Polybius refuses to believe Theopompus's assertion that Philip II
of Macedon was a terrible drunkard (8.9.4 and 9.7), because Philip was a
successful ruler (8.10.5–11).

But one should also note the presence of a definite element of *moral*
opprobrium in Polybius's presentation of drunkenness—a moral opprobrium in which pragmatic success or failure is irrelevant. The Boeotians
carefully managed to avoid much political trouble between 250 and 172,
and were in that sense politically successful, but to Polybius they failed to
attempt achievement of τὰ καλά in this period—in good part because of
their addiction to drinking parties (20.4.6–7; cf. 20.6.5). The drunken
Ptolemy IV is associated in Polybius's mind with behavior that is shameful—not merely counterproductive—in a king (ἀπρεπεῖς, 5.34.10; cf. καχ-
εξία, 5.87.3). Conversely, Polybius compares King Perseus of Macedon
favorably to Perseus's father, Philip V; for Perseus, in his avoidance of
drunkenness and lascivious sexuality, kept clear of Philip's shameful behavior (ἀσέλγεια, 25.3.7), and acted in a manner worthy of a king (3.5).
The fact that Perseus would soon be destroyed by Rome has no effect on
the positive judgment rendered here on Perseus's restrained personal
style of life.[11]

In sum, Polybius saw drunkenness as a serious problem in his world,
and a serious temptation to his aristocratic audience, and went out of his
way in *The Histories* to condemn such behavior. He condemned it both as
destructive in itself and also for the lascivious sexuality, irrational violence, and sloth he associated with it. He condemned it both for its negative practical effect within the competitive struggle each man faced, and
also because, in a serious man of affairs, drunkenness was shameful *per
se*, "unworthy."[12] More broadly, it has already been shown in Chapter V

11. On Polybius's moralizing terminology on the subject of drinking, see also 6.8.5 (ἄδικον, ὕβρεις, ἁρπαγάς), 29.13 (ἀσελγῆ).
12. Polybius's concern here is not limited to males, however; he also approved of the
Roman aristocratic custom of inspecting their womenfolk each day to make sure they had
not been drinking (6.11a.4).

above that *The Histories* expresses—in a wide variety of ways—Polybius's intense anxieties about the stability and cohesion of his civilization. It was a civilization threatened from many directions, and perhaps threatened most when those in power acted in an irresponsible fashion. Polybius believed that only steadfast and self-controlled leadership could maintain the fragile social cohesion he valued so highly. This is why he rendered such an especially harsh judgment on those in power who succumbed to the temptations of wine—becoming degenerate, violent, indolent. Such men had deserted their aristocratic duty.

BIBLIOGRAPHY

Africa, T. *Phylarchus and the Spartan Revolution*. Berkeley and Los Angeles, 1961.

Ager, S. L. "Rhodes: The Rise and Fall of a Neutral Diplomat." *Historia* 40 (1992): 10–41.

Anderson, J. K. "Philopoemen's Reform of the Achaean Army." *CPh* 52 (1967): 104–5.

———. *Hunting in the Ancient World*. Berkeley and Los Angeles, 1985.

Arnheim, M. T. W. *Aristocracy in Greek Society*. Plymouth, 1977.

Astin, A. E. *Scipio Aemilianus*. Oxford, 1967.

———. *Cato the Censor*. Oxford, 1978.

Austin, M. M. "Hellenistic Kings, War and the Economy." *CQ* 36 (1986): 450–66.

Avenarius, G. *Lukians Schrift zur Geschichtsschreibung*. Meisenheim am Glan, 1956.

Aymard, A. *Les assemblées de la confédération achaienne*. Bordeaux, 1938.

———. *Les premiers rapports de Rome et de la confédération* achaïenne. Bordeaux, 1938.

———. "Le Fragment de Polybe 'Sur les traîtres' (xviii, 13–15)." *REA* 42 (1940): 9–19.

Badian, E. "The Treaty between Rome and the Achaean League." *JRS* 42 (1952): 76–80.

———. Review of *Filino-Polibio, Sileno-Diodoro*, by V. La Bua. *RFIC* 96 (1968): 203–10.

———. *Titus Quinctius Flamininus: Philhellenism and Realpolitik*. Cincinnati, 1970.

———. "Two Polybian Treaties." In *Miscellanea in onore di E. Manni* I (Rome, 1979): 161–69.

———. "Hegemony and Independence: Prolegomena to a Study of the Relations of Rome and the Hellenistic States in the Second Century B.C." In *Actes du VIIᵉ Congrès de la F. I. E. C.*, 397–414. Budapest, 1983.

Balsdon, J. P. V. D. "T. Quinctius Flamininus." *Phoenix* 21 (1967): 177–90.

Bar-Kochva, B. *The Seleucid Army: Organization and Tactics in the Great Campaigns*. Cambridge, 1977.

———. *Judas Maccabaeus*. Cambridge, 1989.

Bauslaugh, R. A. *The Concept of Neutrality in Classical Greece*. Berkeley and Los Angeles, 1991.

Berthold, R. M. *Rhodes in the Hellenistic Age*. Ithaca, 1983.

Bickermann, E. J. "Notes sur Polybe, II: Les négociations entre Aratos et Antigone Doson," *REG* 56 (1943): 287–304.

Briscoe, J. "Q. Marcius Philippus and *Nova Sapientia*." *JRS* 54 (1964): 66–77.

———. "Eastern Policy and Senatorial Politics, 168–164 B.C." *Historia* 18 (1969): 49–70.

———. *A Commentary on Livy, Books XXXI–XXXIII*. Oxford, 1973. [Cited in notes as Briscoe, Commentary I.]

———. *A Commentary on Livy, Books XXXIV–XXXVII*. Oxford, 1981. [Cited in notes as Briscoe, Commentary II.]

Broughton, T. R. S. *The Magistrates of the Roman Republic* I. Cleveland, 1951.

Brown, P. *The Body and Society: Men, Women and Sexual Renunciation in Early Christianity*. New York, 1988.

Brunt, P. A. *Italian Manpower, 225 B.C.–A.D. 14* Oxford, 1971.

Buttner-Wobst, T. *Polybii Historiae IV.* Stuttgart, 1904. [Reprint, 1963.]

Carawan, E. M. "*Graecia Liberata* and the Role of Flamininus in Livy's Fourth Decade." *TAPA* 118 (1988): 209–53.

Catin, L. *En lisant Tite-Live*. Paris, 1944.

Chinard, P. "Polybius and the American Constitution." *Journal of the History of Ideas* 1 (1940): 38–58.

Culham, P. "Chance, Command, and Chaos in Ancient Military Engagements." *World Futures* 27 (1989): 191–205.

Decrey, P. *La traitement des prisonniers de guerre dans la Grèce ancienne*. Paris, 1968.

Deininger, J. *Der politische Widerstand gegen Rom in Griechenland, 217–86 v.Chr.* Berlin, 1971.

Derow, P. S. "Polybios and the Embassy of Kallikrates." In *Essays Presented to C. M. Bowra*, 12–23. Oxford, 1970.

———. "Polybius, Rome, and the East." *JRS* 69 (1979): 1–15.

Dittenberger, W., and Purgold, W. *Olympia*, Textband V, *Die Inschriften*. Berlin, 1896.

Dixon, S. "Polybius on Roman Women and Property." *CPh* 106 (1985): 147–70.

Dominguez-Monedero, A. J. "La campania de Annibal contra los Vaccaeos: Sus objectivos y su relación con el inicio de la segunda guerra punica." *Latomus* 45 (1986): 241–58.

Dorey, T. A. "Livy and the Popular Leaders." *Orpheus* 2 (1955): 55–60.

———. "Massinissa, Syphax and Sophoniba." *PACA* 4 (1961): 1–2.

Doria, L. B. P. "Diodoro e Ariarate V." *PP* 33 (1978): 104–29.

Dryden, J. "The Character of Polybius and His Writings." In *The History of Polybius . . . principally of the Roman People, during the first and second Punick Wars, translated by Sir Henry Sheeres*. London, 1698.

Dubuisson, M. "Sur la mort de Polybe." *REG* 93 (1980): 72–82.

———. "La vision polybienne de Rome." In H. Verdin, G. Schepens, and E. de

Keyser, eds., *Purposes of History: Studies in Greek Historiography from the Fourth to the Second Century B.C.*, 233–43. Louvain, 1990.

Dyson, S. *The Creation of the Roman Frontier.* Princeton, 1985.

Earl, D. C. *The Political Thought of Sallust.* Cambridge, 1961.

Eckstein, A. M. "T. Quinctius Flamininus and the Campaign against Philip in 198 B.C." *Phoenix* 30 (1976): 119–42.

———. "Rome, Saguntum and the Ebro Treaty." *Emerita* 55 (1984): 51–68.

———. "Polybius, Syracuse, and the Politics of Accommodation." *GRBS* 26 (1985): 265–82.

———. "Polybius, Aristaenus, and the Fragment 'On Traitors.'" *CQ* 37 (1987): 140–62.

———. *Senate and General: Individual Decision-Making and Roman Foreign Relations, 264–194 B.C.* Berkeley and Los Angeles, 1987.

———. "Nabis and Flamininus on the Argive Revolutions of 198 and 197 B.C." *GRBS* 28 (1987): 213–33.

———. "Rome, the War with Perseus, and Third Party Mediation." *Historia* 37 (1988): 414–44.

———. "Hannibal at New Carthage: Polybius 3.15 and the Power of Irrationality." *CPh* 84 (1989): 1–15.

———. "Josephus and Polybius: A Reconsideration." *CA* 9 (1990): 175–208.

———. "Polybius, the Achaeans, and the 'Freedom of the Greeks.'" *GRBS* 31 (1990): 45–71.

———. "Notes on the Birth and Death of Polybius." *AJPh* 113 (1992): 387–406.

Edlund, I. "Invisible Bonds: Clients and Patrons through the Eyes of Polybius." *Klio* 59 (1977): 129–36.

Edmunds, L. "Thucydides' Ethics as Reflected in the Description of Status (3.82–83)." *HSCPh* 79 (1975): 73–88.

Edson, C. Review of *Philip V of Macedon,* by F. W. Walbank. *AHR* 47 (1942): 826–27.

Eisen, K. F. *Polybiosinterpretationen: Beobachtungen zu Prinzipien griechischer und römischer Historiographie bei Polybios.* Heidelberg, 1966.

Erbse, H. "Zur Enstehung des polybianischen Geschichtswerkes." *RhM* 94 (1951): 157–79.

———. "Polybios-Interpretationen." *Philol.* 101 (1957): 269–97.

Errington, R. M. *Philopoemen.* Oxford, 1969.

———. "Rome and Spain before the Second Punic War." *Latomus* 29 (1970): 25–37.

———. "The Alleged Syro-Macedonian Pact and the Origins of the Second Macedonian War." *Athenaeum* 49 (1971): 336–54.

———. *The Dawn of Empire: Rome's Rise to World Power.* London, 1971.

Erskine, A. *The Hellenistic Stoa: Political Thought and Action.* Ithaca, 1990.

Ferrary, J.-L. *Philhellénisme et impérialisme: Aspects idéologiques de la conquête romaine du monde hellénistique.* Rome, 1988.

Fornara, C. *The Nature of History in Ancient Greece and Rome.* Berkeley and Los Angeles, 1983.

Freyburger, G. "*Fides* et *potestas*, πίστις ετ ἐπιτροπή." *Ktema* 7 (1982): 177–85.

von Fritz, K. *The Theory of the Mixed Constitution in Antiquity: A Critical Analysis of Polybius's Political Ideas.* New York, 1954.

Fustel de Coulanges, N. *Polybe; ou, La Grèce conquise par les Romains* (1858). In *Questions Historiques,* ed. C. Jullian. Paris, 1893.

Gabba, E. "Studi su Filarco: La biografie plutarchee di Agide e de Cleomene." *Athenaeum* 35 (1957): 3–55.

———. "Storiografia greca e imperialismo romano (III–I sec. a.C.)." *RSI* 86 (1974): 625–42.

———. "Aspetti culturali dell'imperialismo romano." *Athenaeum* 55 (1977): 49–74.

Gelzer, M. "Nasicas Widerspruch gegen die Zerstörung Karthagos." *Philologus* 86 (1931): 261–99.

———. "Römische Politik bei Fabius Pictor." *Hermes* 68 (1933): 129–66.

———. "Die Achaia im Geschichtswerk des Polybios." *AbhBerlin* 1940 (= *Kleine Schriften* III [Wiesbaden, 1964]: 123–54).

Gerber, A., and Greef, A. *Lexicon Taciteum.* Hildesheim, 1962.

Golan, D. "Autumn, 200 B.C.: The Events at Abydus." *Athenaeum* 63 (1985): 389–404.

Goodenough, E. R. *Jewish Symbols in the Graeco-Roman Period* VI. New York, 1956.

de Grazia, S. *Machiavelli in Hell.* Princeton, 1989.

Green, P. *From Alexander to Actium: The Historical Evolution of the Hellenistic Age.* Berkeley and Los Angeles, 1990.

Griffin, J. *Homer on Life and Death.* Oxford, 1980.

Griffith, G. T. *The Mercenaries of the Hellenistic World.* Cambridge, 1935.

Gruen, E. S. "Aratus and the Achaean Alliance with Macedon." *Historia* 21 (1972): 609–25.

———. "The Last Years of Philip V." *GRBS* 15 (1974): 221–46.

———. "Rome and Rhodes in the Second Century B.C.: A Historiographical Inquiry." *CQ* (1975): 58–81.

———. "The Origins of the Achaean War." *JHS* 96 (1976): 46–69.

———. "Macedonia and the Settlement of 167 B.C." In W. L. Adams and E. N. Borza, eds., *Philip II, Alexander the Great, and the Macedonian Heritage,* 257–67. Boston, 1982.

———. "Greek Πίστις and Roman *Fides.*" *Athenaeum* 60 (1982): 50–68.

———. *The Hellenistic World and the Coming of Rome.* 2 vols. Berkeley and Los Angeles, 1984.

Hammond, N. G. L. *Epirus.* Oxford, 1967.

———. "The Campaign and Battle of Cynoscephalae." *JHS* 108 (1988): 60–76.

Hansen, V. D. *The Western Way of War: Infantry Battle in Classical Greece.* New York, 1989.

Harris, W. V. *War and Imperialism in Republican Rome.* Oxford, 1979.

Hauben, H. "A Neglected Detail of Philopator's Policy." *AC* 50 (1981): 389–403.

Havelock, E. A. "War as a Way of Life in Classical Culture, I: Heroism and History." In *Vanier Memorial Lecture,* 1–55. Ottawa, 1972.

Heidemann, M.-L. *Die Frieheitsparole in der griechisch-römischen Auseinandersetzung (200–188 v.Chr.).* Bonn, 1966.

Herman, G. *Ritualised Friendship and the Greek City.* Cambridge, 1987.

Hobsbawm, E. J. *Primitive Rebels.* New York, 1959.

Hoffmann, W. "Der Kampf zwischen Rom und Tarent im Urteil des antiken Überlieferung." *Hermes* 71 (1936): 11–24.

———. "Hannibal und Rom." *Antike und Abendland* 6 (1957), 7–26. [Reprinted in K. Christ, ed., *Hannibal*, Wege der Forschung 371, 40–74. Darmstadt, 1974.]

———. "Die römische Politik des 2. Jahrhunderts und das Ende Karthagos." *Historia* 9 (1960): 309–44.

Holleaux, M. "Les conférences de Lokride et la politique de T. Quinctius Flamininus (198 av. J.-C.)." *REG* 36 (1923): 115–71. [Reprinted in *Études d'épigraphie et d'histoire grecques* V, 25–79. Paris, 1957.]

van Hooff, A. J. L. "Polybios als Machiavellist." *Kleio* 5 (1975): 56–67.

———. *From Autothanasia to Suicide: Self-Killing in Classical Antiquity.* London and New York, 1990.

Hornblower, J. *Hieronymus of Cardia.* Oxford, 1981.

Hoyos, B. D. "The Rise of Hiero II: Chronology and Campaigns." *Antichthon* 19 (1985): 32–56.

Huss, W. *Untersuchungen zur Aussenpolitik Ptolemaios' IV.* Munich, 1976.

———. *Geschichte der Karthager.* Munich, 1985.

Isnardi, M. "Τέχνη e ἦθος nella metodologia storiografia di Polibio." *SCO* 3 (1955): 102–10.

Kallet-Marx, R. "Quintus Fabius Maximus and the Dyme Affair (*Syll.*[3] 684)." Forthcoming in *CQ*.

———. *Hegemony to Empire: The Development of the Roman Imperium in the East, 148–62 B.C.* Berkeley and Los Angeles. [Forthcoming]

Kautsky, J. *The Politics of Aristocratic Empires.* Chapel Hill, 1982.

Keuls, E. C. *The Reign of the Phallus: Sexual Politics in Ancient Athens.* New York, 1985.

Klose, P. *Die völkerrechtliche Ordnung der hellenistischen Staatenwelt in der Zeit von 280 bis 168 v.Chr.* Munich, 1972.

Knox, B. M. W. *Oedipus at Thebes.* New York, 1957.

Ladouceur, D. "Josephus and Masada." In L. H. Feldman and G. Hata, eds., *Josephus, Judaism, and Christianity*, 95–113. Detroit, 1987.

Laqueur, R. *Polybios.* Leipzig, 1913.

Larsen, J. A. O. *Representative Government in Greek and Roman History.* Berkeley and Los Angeles, 1955.

Lateiner, D. "No Laughing Matter: A Literary Tactic of Herodotus." *TAPA* 107 (1977): 173–80.

Lazenby, J. F. *Hannibal's War.* Warminster, 1978.

Lehmann, G. A. *Untersuchungen zur historischen Glaubwürdigkeit des Polybios.* Munster, 1967.

———. "Polybios und die griechische Geschichtsschreibung." In *Polybe*, Entretiens sur l'Antiquité Classique 20, 147–200. Geneva, 1974.

van Looy, H. "Apollonis, reine de Pergame." *AncSoc* 7 (1976): 151–65.

Luce, T. J. *Livy: The Composition of His History.* Princeton, 1977.

Macleod, C. "Thucydides and Tragedy." In *Collected Essays*, 140–58. Oxford, 1983.

MacMullen, R. *Roman Social Relations*. New Haven, 1974.

Marsden, E. W. "Polybius as a Military Historian." In *Polybe*, Entretiens sur l'Antiquité Classique 20, 269–301. Geneva, 1974.

Mauersberger, A. *Polybios-Lexikon*. 4 fascicules. Berlin, 1956–75.

McDonald, A. H. "The Style of Livy." *JRS* 45 (1957): 155–72.

McShane, R. B. *The Foreign Policy of the Attalids*. Urbana, 1964.

Meissner, B. "ΠΡΑΓΜΑΤΙΚΗ ΙΣΤΟΡΙΑ: Polybios über den Zweck pragmatischer Geschichtsschreibung." *Saeculum* 37 (1986): 313–51.

Meister, K. *Historische Kritik bei Polybios*. Wiesbaden, 1975.

Mendels, D. "Polybius, Philip V, and the Socio-Economic Question in Greece." *AncSoc* 8 (1977): 155–74.

———. "Polybius, Nabis and Equality." *Athenaeum* 57 (1979): 311–33.

———. "Messene, 215 B.C.—An Enigmatic Revolution." *Historia* 29 (1980): 246–50.

———. "Polybius and the Socio-Economic Revolution in Greece." *AC* 51 (1982): 86–109.

———. "Did Polybius Have 'Another' View of the Aetolian League?" *AncSoc* 15/17 (1984/1986): 63–73.

Mioni, E. *Polibio*. Padua, 1949.

Mitchell, R. E. "The Historical and Historiographical Prominence of the Pyrrhic War." In J. W. Eadie and J. Ober, eds., *The Craft of the Ancient Historian*, 303–29. London, 1985.

Mix, E. R. *Marcus Atilius Regulus: Exemplum Historicum*. The Hague, 1970.

Mohm, S. *Untersuchungen zu den historischen Anschauungen des Polybios*. Saarbrucken, 1977.

Momigliano, A. "Polibio, Posidonio e l'imperialismo romano." *AAT* 107 (1973): 693–707.

———. "Polybius between the English and the Turks." *Myers Memorial Lecture*. Oxford, 1974.

———. *Alien Wisdom: The Limits of Hellenization*. Cambridge, 1975.

———. "Polybius's Reappearance in Western Europe." In *Essays in Ancient and Modern Historiography*, 79–98. Middletown, 1976.

———. "The Historian's Skin." In *Essays in Ancient and Modern Historiography*, 67–77. Middletown, 1976.

Moore, T. J. *Artistry and Ideology: Livy's Vocabulary of Virtue*. Frankfurt, 1989.

Morgan, M. G. "The Perils of Schematicism: Polybius, Antiochus Epiphanes, and the 'Day of Eleusis.'" *Historia* 39 (1990): 37–76.

Mørkholm, O. *Antiochus IV of Syria*. Gylgendal, 1966.

Musti, D. "Polibio negli studi dell'ultimo ventennio (1950–1970)." *ANRW* I:2 (1972): 1114–81.

———. *Polibio e l'imperialismo romano*. Naples, 1978.

de Navarro, J. M. "The Coming of the Celts." In *The Cambridge Ancient History* VII, 41–74 (= chap. 2). Cambridge, 1928.

Nicolet, C. "Polybe et les institutions romaines." In *Polybe*, Entretiens sur l'Antiquité Classique 20, 209–65. Geneva, 1974.

Nietzsche, F. *On the Advantage and Disadvantage of History for Life*. Indianapolis and Cambridge, 1980. [Originally published in German, 1874.]

Nissen, H. *Kritische Untersuchungen über die Quellen der vierten und funften Dekade des Livius*. Berlin, 1863.

Nörr, D. *Aspekte des römischen Völkerrechts: Die Bronzetafel von Alcántara*. Munich, 1989.

Oost, S. I. *Roman Policy in Epirus and Acarnania in the Age of the Roman Conquest of Greece*. Dallas, 1954.

Otto, W. *Zur Geschichte der Zeit des 6. Ptolemaers*. ABAW 11. Munich, 1934.

Pédech, P. "Polybe et l'éloge de Philopoemen." *REG* 64 (1951): 82–103.

———. "Sur les sources de Polybe: Polybe et Philinus." *REA* 54 (1952): 246–66.

———. "Notes sur la biographie de Polybe." *LEC* 29 (1961): 145–56.

———. *Polybe: Histoires XII: Texte établi, traduit et commenté*. Paris, 1961.

———. *La méthode historique de Polybe*. Paris, 1964.

———. "Les idées religieuses de Polybe: Étude sur la religion de l'élite gréco-romaine au IIe siècle av. J.-C." *RHR* 167 (1966): 35–68.

———. "Polybe hipparque de la confédération achéene (170–69 av. J.-C)." *LEC* 37 (1969): 252–59.

Petzold, K.-E. *Studien zur Methode des Polybios und zu ihrer Auswertung*. Munich, 1969.

Plass, P. *Wit and the Writing of History: The Rhetoric of Historiography in Imperial Rome*. Madison, 1988.

Podes, P. "Handelserklärung bei Polybios." *AncSoc* 21 (1990): 215–40.

Pomeroy, A. J. "Polybius' Death Notices." *Phoenix* 40 (1986): 407–23.

Pomeroy, S. *Goddesses, Whores, Wives, and Slaves: Women in Classical Antiquity*. New York, 1975.

———. *Women in Hellenistic Egypt from Alexander to Cleopatra*. New York, 1984.

Powell, J. E. *A Lexicon of Herodotus*. 2d ed. Hildesheim, 1960.

Préaux, C. "Polybe et Ptolemée Philopator." *CE* 40 (1965): 364–75.

Pritchett, W. K. *The Greek State at War* II. Berkeley and Los Angeles, 1974.

Reiter, W. *Aemilius Paullus: Conqueror of Greece*. London, 1988.

de Romilly, J. "Guerre et paix entre cités." In J.-P. Vernant, ed., *Problèmes de la guerre en Grèce ancienne*, 207–20. Paris, 1968.

———. *The Rise and Fall of States according to Greek Authors*. Ann Arbor, 1977.

Roveri, A. *Studi su Polibio*. Bologna, 1964.

Sacks, K. S. "Polybius' Other View of Aetolia." *JHS* 95 (1975): 92–106.

———. *Polybius on the Writing of History*. Berkeley and Los Angeles, 1980.

———. *Diodorus Siculus and the First Century*. Princeton, 1990.

de Sanctis, G. *Storia dei Romani* III:1. Turin, 1916.

———. *Storia dei Romani* III:2. Turin, 1916.

———. *Storia dei Romani* IV:3. Florence, 1964.

von Scala, R. *Die Studien des Polybios* I. Stuttgart, 1890.

Schepens, G. "Polemic and Methodology in Polybius' Book XII." In H. Verdin, G. Schepens, and F. de Keyser, eds., *Purposes of History: Studies in Greek Historiography from the Fourth to the Second Centuries B.C.*, 39–61. Louvain, 1990.

Schleussner, B. "Zur Frage der geheimen pergamenisch-makedonischen Kontakte im 3. makedonischen Krieg." *Historia* 22 (1973): 119–23.

Schmitt, H. H. *Untersuchungen zur Geschichte Antiochos' des Grossen und seiner Zeit.* Wiesbaden, 1964.

———. *Die Staatsverträge des Altertums* III. Munich, 1969.

———. "Polybios und die Gleichgewicht der Mächte." In *Polybe*, Entretiens sur l'Antiquité Classique 20, 65–102. Geneva, 1974.

Schweighauser, J. *Lexicon Polybianum.* Oxford, 1822.

Schwertfeger, T. *Der achaiische Bund von 146 bis 26 v.Chr.* Munich, 1974.

Scullard, H. H. *Scipio Africanus: Soldier and Politician.* Ithaca, 1970.

———. *Roman Politics, 220–150 B.C.* 2d ed. Oxford, 1973.

Seager, R. *Ammianus Marcellinus: Seven Studies in His Language and Thought.* Columbia, Missouri, 1986.

Sealey, R. *A History of the Greek City-States.* Berkeley and Los Angeles, 1976.

Segre, M. "Duo novi testi storici." *RFIC* 60 (1932): 446–52.

Sherk, R. *Roman Documents from the Greek East: Senatus Consulta and Epistulae to the Age of Augustus.* Baltimore, 1969.

Shimron, B. "Polybius on Rome: A Reexamination of the Evidence." *SCI* 5 (1979/ 1980): 94–117.

Shrimpton, G. "Theopompus' Treatment of Philip in the *Philippica*." *Phoenix* 21 (1977): 123–44.

Siegfried, W. *Studien zur geschichtlichen Anschauungen des Polybios.* Leipzig, 1928.

Slater, P. *The Glory of Hera: Greek Mythology and the Greek Family.* Boston, 1968.

Stahl, H. P. "Learning through Suffering? Croesus' Conversations in the *History* of Herodotus." *YCS* 24 (1975): 1–36.

Strasburger, H. "Posidonius on the Problems of the Roman Empire." *JHS* 55 (1965): 40–53.

Sumner, G. V. "Rome, Spain and the Outbreak of the Second Punic War: Some Clarifications." *Latomus* 31 (1972): 469–80.

Texier, J.-G. *Nabis.* Paris, 1975.

Thommen, R. "Über die Abfassungszeit der Geschichten des Polybius." *Hermes* 20 (1885): 196–236.

Thompson, W. E. "The Battle of the Bagradas." *Hermes* 114 (1986): 111–17.

Touloumakos, J. *Zum Geschichtsbewusstsein der Griechen in der Zeit der römischen Herrschaft.* Gottingen, 1971.

von Ungarn-Sternberg, J. *Capua im zweiten punischen Krieg.* Munich, 1975.

Urban, R. *Wachstum und Krise der Achäischen Bundes: Quellenstudien zur Entwicklung des Bundes von 280 bis 222 v.Chr.* Wiesbaden, 1979.

Usher, S. *The Historians of Greece and Rome.* London, 1969.

Vercruysse, M. "À la recherche du mensonge et de la verité: La fonction des passages méthodologiques chez Polybe." In H. Verdin, G. Schepens, and F. de Keyser, eds., *Purposes of History: Studies in Greek Historiography from the Fourth to the Second Century B.C.,* 17–38. Louvain, 1990.

Veyne, P. "Y a-t-il eu un impérialisme romain?" *MEFR* 82 (1975): 793–855.

Volkmann, H. "Griechische Rhetorik oder römische Politik? Bemerkungen zur römischen 'Imperialismus.'" *Hermes* 82 (1954): 465–76.

Walbank, F. W. *Aratos of Sicyon*. Cambridge, 1933.

———. "Φίλιππος τραγῳδούμενος: A Polybian Experiment." *JHS* 58 (1938): 55–68.

———. *Philip V of Macedon*. Cambridge, 1940.

———. *A Historical Commentary on Polybius* I, *Books 1–6*. Oxford, 1957.

———. "Polybius and Rome's Eastern Policy." *JRS* 53 (1963): 1–13.

———. "Political Morality and the Friends of Scipio," *JRS* 55 (1965): 1–16.

———. "The Scipionic Legend." *PCPS* 13 (1967): 54–69.

———. *A Historical Commentary on Polybius* II, *Books 7–18*. Oxford, 1967.

———. "Polybius and Macedonia." In B. Laourdas and C. Makronas, eds., *Ancient Macedonia* I, 291–307. Thessalonika, 1970.

———. "Livy's Fourth and Fifth Decades." In T. A. Dorey, ed., *Livy*, 74–72. London, 1971.

———. *Polybius*. Berkeley and Los Angeles, 1972.

———. "Polybius between Greece and Rome." In *Polybe*, Entretiens sur l'Antiquité Classique 20, 1–31. Geneva, 1974.

———. "*Symploké:* Its Role in Polybius' *Histories*." *YCS* 24 (1975): 197–212.

———. "Polybius' Last Ten Books." In *Historiographia antiqua: Commentationes Lovanienses in honorem W. Peremens septuagenarii editae*, 139–62. Louvain, 1977.

———. "Introduction." In *Polybius: The Rise of the Roman Empire*, transl. I. Scott-Kilvert, 9–40. Harmondsworth, 1979.

———. *A Historical Commentary on Polybius* III: *Books 19–40*. Oxford, 1979.

———. "Il giudizio di Polibio su Roma." *AIV* 140 (1981): 1–20.

———. "Sea Power and the Antigonids." In W. L. Adams and E. N. Borza, eds., *Philip II, Alexander the Great, and the Macedonian Heritage*, 213–36. Washington, D.C., 1982.

———. "Monarchies and Monarchic Ideas." In *The Cambridge Ancient History*, 2d ed., VII:1, 62–100. Cambridge, 1984.

———. "Profit or Amusement: Some Thoughts on the Motives of Hellenistic Historians." In H. Verdin, G. Schepens, and E. de Keyser, eds., *Purposes of History: Studies in Greek Historiography from the Fourth to the Second Century B.C.*, 253–66. Louvain, 1990.

Walsh, P. G. *Livy: His Historical Aims and Methods*. Cambridge, 1963.

Weidemann, T. E. J. "Thucydides, Women, and the Limits of Rational Analysis." *G&R* 30 (1983): 162–69.

Weil, R. "La composition de l'*Histoire* de Polybe." *JS* 1988: 185–206.

Welwei, K.-H. *Könige und Königtum im Urteil des Polybios*. Cologne, 1963.

———. "Demokratie und Masse bei Polybios." *Historia* 15 (1966): 282–301.

Wood, F. M. "The Tradition of Flamininus' 'Selfish Ambition' in Polybius and Later Historians." *TAPA* 79 (1939): 93–103.

Wunderer, C. *Citate und geflügelte Wörter bei Polybios im Zusammenhang mit der aesthetisch-literarischen Richtung des Historikers untersucht*. Leipzig, 1901.

———. *Die psychologische Anschauungen des Historikers Polybios*. Erlangen, 1905.

———. *Polybios: Lebens- und Weltanschauung aus dem zweiten vorchristlichen Jahrhundert*. Leipzig, 1927.

Ziegler, K. "Polybios (1)." *RE* 21:2 (1952): cols. 1439–1578.

GENERAL INDEX

(Note: P = Polybius)

GENERAL INDEX *305*

Deinon (Rhodian politician), 41, 47
Demetrius I (Seleucid prince, then king):
friend of P, 9, 107; hostage in Rome,
11–12, 105; helped by P to escape, 11–
12, 105–6, 146; drunkenness, deceit criticized by P, 25, 107, 141, 265, 286; as
ruler of Syria, 106, 265; failed attempts
at friendship with Rome, 106–7; overthrown, 107 and n, 113n, 265 and n
Demetrius (son of Philip V), murdered,
215
Demetrius of Phalerum (philosopher and
politician): rule in Athens (317–307
B.C.), 233; Demochares' charges against
(taken seriously by P), 233; on Tyche,
quoted by P, 258, 262
Demetrius of Pharus (Illyrian warlord): as
evil adviser of Philip V, 89, 146–47, 210,
212; character criticized by P, 146–47,
212
Demophanes (Platonist), 148 and n
Diaeus (Achaean politician): from Megalopolis, 3n; character condemned by P,
139, 159, 220, 265–66; generalship condemned by P, 169–70; cowardice condemned by P, 170n, 243n, 265–66; policies condemned by P, 220, 265–66
Diodorus Siculus (historian): use of Polybian material, 76, 106nn, 107n, 111 and
n, 225–229 (on Diod. 32.2 and 4), 231n,
232 and n, 247, 268n; moralism of,
283n
Diogenes of Babylon (Stoic), 138
Diophanes (Achaean politician), 3n, 165
Dorimachus (Aetolian leader), criticized by
P, 139n, 142

Ecdemus (Platonist), 148 and n
Elis (Greek state), 59–60, 62, 167n, 170;
and "peace with honor," 59–60
Epaminondas (Theban general): energy
and bravery praised by P, 20, 36 and n,
276n, 182n; military failure of, 20, 277n
Eperatus (Achaean politician), 170 and n
Epicharmus (poet), and P, 21–22 and n
Epigenes (adviser of Antiochus III), 100
Epirus (Greek state): deceit (220 B.C.) criti-
cized by P, 58, 98; factionalism in (170s
B.C.), 261 and n; relations with Rome,
99; rule of Charops in (160s B.C.),
99–100
Eumenes II (king of Pergamum), 5, 71,

107; greed criticized by P, 73, 113, 261
and n; oppressed by Romans, 131n,
241, cf. 107; benevolent energy praised
by P, 274
Euryleon (Achaean politician), 170

Fabius Maximus, Q. (consul 233), 132n,
185n
Fabius Maximus Aemilianus, Q. (consul
145): brother of Scipio Aemilianus, 8; relations with P, 8; not well off, 81
Fabius Pictor, Q. (historian): source for P,
38, 64, 133n, 154–55; biases clear to P,
64 and n
First Macedonian War (212/11–206 B.C.), origins of, 211–12 and n
Flaminius, C. (consul 223): and origins of
Celtic War, 123n; his land law, 133, criticized by P, 139, 162n; irrational anger
and poor generalship criticized by P,
162n, 192n
Fulvius Nobilior, Ser. (consul 255), 192n

Galatians (Celts of Asia Minor): threat to
the Greeks, 120–21, 273; huge numbers, 120–21; ferocity, indiscipline and
treachery of, according to P, 121–22,
132n
Gaza (Ptolemaic town), bravery and loyalty
praised by P, 22, 23, 68, 111
Gelo (Syracusan tyrant, 480 B.C.), 278
Gelo (Syracusan prince, 230s B.C.), 112
Greeks (in general): greed criticized by P,
71 and n, 157, 167, 260, 266n; deceit
criticized by P, 109–11; indolence criticized by P, 266n

Haliartus (Greek town), 262 and n
Hamilcar Barca (Carthaginian general and
statesman): against Romans in Sicily, 21,
175; against rebel mercenaries (241–
238 B.C.), 174–77; in Spain, 34–35; bravery praised by P, 34–35, 43–44, 55; generalship praised by P, 21, 34, 174–77;
love of hard work praised by P, 176,
179; brave death praised by P, 34–35;
hatred of the Romans ("Wrath of the
Barcids"), 175 and n, 177n, 255, 280;
difficulties he faced, according to P, 255,
256–57; viewed as hero by P, 91 and n,
174–77, 192, 193, 254, 255 and n, 271
Hannibal (Carthaginian general and states-

Lycortas (Achaean statesman): P's father, 3; powerful politician, 3; independent attitude towards Rome, 5 and n, 6, 206 and n. 49, 224; engineers treaty with Egypt, 6; urges Achaean neutrality between Rome and Macedon (170 B.C.), 5n

Lydiadas (Megalopolitan tyrant, 230s B.C.), 2–3, cf. 3n

Macedonians (in P): indiscipline of, 165n; greed, 167n; enormous bravery, 171–72; threat to Greek freedom, 172, 216; self-destructive behavior (150–148 B.C.), 219, 221, 266–67

Machanidas (Spartan tyrant), 31–32, 146n

"Machiavellianism": defined, 1 and n; for other discussions, *see* Polybius

Magnesia (battle, 189 B.C.), 170n, 171

Mago (Carthaginian general), 180, 181

Mago the Bruttian (Carthaginian statesman, 149 B.C.), 217–18

Malleolus, L. (Roman envoy, 149 B.C.), criticized by P, 264n

Mamertines (Italic mercenaries), 25, 91

Mandonius (Ilergete chief), P's praise of his wife, 152, 156

Manilius, M. (consul 149), requests P's military advice, 12 and n

Manlius Vulso, Cn. (consul 189): and town of Perge, 68–69; campaign against the Galatians, 121, 122

Mantineia (Greek city), 152, 163

Marcius Philippus, Q. (consul 186): relations with P, 6–7; deceitful policy toward Perseus criticized by P, 108–9, 230

Marcius Philippus, Q. (Roman envoy, 149 B.C.), 103–4 and nn

Masses (in P): alleged calm of, 130; violence, 131, 136–37, 144; greed, 131n, 133–35; indiscipline, 131–36; anger, 132; lack of foresight, 135; lack of education, 137–38; danger of, 158

Massinissa (Numidian king): source for P, 12; moderation in use of wealth praised by P, 79; aggression in Lesser Syrtis criticized by P, 103; war with Carthage (150 B.C.), 216; benevolent energy and achievements praised by P, 274

Medion (Greek town), Aetolian siege of, 256–57

Megalopolis (Arcadian city): P's birthplace, 1; general description of, 1–2; prosper-

ity, 2; culture, 2; destroyed by Cleomenes III (223 B.C.), and rebuilt, 2; joins Achaean League, 2–3; loyalty and courage praised by P, 66n, 111, 199n; social strife in, 133 and n; indolence criticized by P, 278

Men, young, in P: danger to society, 140–41, 158; uncontrolled, 141–42; shallow, lazy, 142; reckless, impulsive, 142–45; lawless, 145; incompetent, 146 and n; lack of education, 148; hopes for, 150

Menyllus (Ptolemaic envoy to Rome), 103–4

Mercenaries (in P): usefulness in battle, 125; indiscipline, 125–27, 165n, 175, 176; arrogance, 126; anger, 126–27, 175; lawlessness, 126, 175, cf. 247; drunkenness, 126, 286n; treachery, 127; greed, 127, 166; lack of education, 127–28; social origins, 127 and n; cheated by employers, 128; danger of, 129, 158, cf. 175

Mercenary War (241–238 B.C.), 91, 100–1, 126, 129, 147–77, 208; P's reasons for discussing, 129, 174

Messana (Sicilian city), seized by mercenaries, 25, 91, 127

Messene (Greek state): stays neutral in Social War, criticized by P, 28–59, 62; victimized by Nabis, 25; relations with Philip V, 89–90, 246; social revolution in, 136; included in Achaean League (180s B.C.), 204, cf. 247; war with Achaea and role in death of Philopoemen (183 B.C.), 32–34, cf. 61

Metaurus River (battle, 207 B.C.), 43–44

Miltiades (Seleucid envoy to Rome), deceit criticized by P, 25

Minucius Rufus, M. (consul 211), 192n

Molon (Seleucid pretender), 100; defeats Xenoetas, 164–65

Monarchy, Hellenistic ideology of, 273–74

Monomachus (adviser of Hannibal), 240

Mummius, L. (consul 146): victor in Achaean War, 14; destroys Corinth, 14, 15n, 167, 220n; reconstitutes Achaean League, 15n; self-restraint in money matters praised by P, 77, 266n; relative poverty, 77n

Nabis (Spartan tyrant): treachery criticized by P, 25; dependence on mercenaries,

312

GENERAL INDEX

Sparta (*continued*)
League (220s B.C.), 92, 198, 275; loyalty to Cleomenes III, 241, 242n; benefits to, of Antigonus III Doson, 147; disorderly assembly in, 236 n, cf. 165n; corrupt officials in, criticized by P, 71; ephors massacred in, 145; sexual customs of, disconcert P, 157; under Machanidas, defeated by Philopoemen (207 B.C.), 163; under regime of Nabis, 133, 139, 159, 260; revolutionaries in, criticized by P, 139; included in Achaean League (180s B.C.), 204; Philopoemen's policy toward (180s B.C.) praised by P, 84–85; and origins of Achaean War (146 B.C.), 14

Stoicism (Hellenistic philosophy): and P, 18n, 43n, 138; and music, 138 and n

Stymphalia (Greek town): good faith of, praised by P, 111; spirit of independence praised by P, 199n

Sucro Mutiny (of Scipio Africanus' troops), 165–66, 175n

Sulpicius Galus, C. (consul 166), criticized by P, 264n

Syphax (Numidian prince), 86

Syracuse (Sicilian city): threatened by mercenaries, 127; prosperity under Hiero II, 208, cf. 274; catastrophe of, caused by policies of Hieronymus, 143, 211; captured by Romans because of lax and drunken soldiery (211 B.C.), 287; sack by Romans criticized by P, 230, cf. 245

Tacitus (historian): on human psychology, 239n; on drunkenness, 285 and n; moralism of, 283n

Tanaquil (Gaia Caecilia), praised by P, 151 and n

Tarentum (Italiote city): moral failings of, criticized by P, 74, 246; reckless youth of, 146n

Telamon (battle, 225 B.C.), 122

Terentius Varro, C. (consul 216): physical cowardice criticized by P, 37–38; generalship criticized by P, 192n; emotional instability criticized by P, 244; later career, 38 and n; other traditions on his conduct at Cannae, 39

Teuta (Illyrian queen): in P, lawless, greedy, shortsighted, 154; in P, irrational, 152,

210; compared to P on Hieronymus 154n; compared to P on Prusias II, 156

Thasos (Greek state), betrayed by Philip V, 88, 89

Thearidas (P's grandfather?), 3n

Thearidas (P's brother), 3, 4

Thebes (Boeotian city): criticized by P for cowardice in 480 B.C., 58–59; disorderly assembly in, 136n; uneducated populace in, 138; sympathy of Greeks for (335 B.C.), according to P, 241n

Theodotus (Epirote politician): policy of, 40–41 and n, 42; brave death praised by P, 41

Theophiliscus (Rhodian admiral), bravery praised by P, 35

Theopompus (historian), moralism of, 283n, 285 and n, cf. 288

Thermum (Aetolian capital), sacked by Macedonians, 145, 167n, 212n

Third Macedonian War (171–168 B.C.): origins of, 215 and n; deleterious effects of, according to P, 215–16; consequences for Macedon, 219 and n

Third Punic War (149–146 B.C.), causes of, according to P, 216, 218

Thracians (barbarians), in P: threat to Greeks, 119; threat to Byzantium, 121; ferocity, 121; deceit, 122n; as mercenaries, 125n; greed, 127; betray Amphipolis, 127

Thucydides (historian), and P, 56, 60, 151 and n, 182

Timaeus (historian): criticized by P, esp. for laziness, 22, 249, 279; praised by P for diligence with documents, 279; some opinions accepted by P, 234n

Tlepolemus (Alexandrian politician), in P: drunkenness of, 141, 287n; immaturity, 142n; violence of, 287n

Tunis (Punic city), 111, 177n

Tyche (Fortune), in P: definition of, 263 and n; criticized regarding Abydus, 51–54; mutability of, 231n, 235n, 258, 263; capriciousness of, 238, 256, 258, 262, 263, 266, 268–69, 270, 272; power of, 258 and n, 261, 270, 271; punishes evil-doing, 260–61, 262n; influence on history, 255, 258, 260–61; punishes too much success, 231, 263, 269; increasing appearance of "incomprehensible" form, 263–64, 266 and n, 271; and Anti-

INDEX OF POLYBIAN TERMINOLOGY

INDEX LOCORUM

Compositor:	Graphic Comp., Inc
Text:	10/12 Baskerville
Display:	Baskerville
Printer:	Thomson-Shore, Inc.
Binder:	Thomson-Shore, Inc.